ii

Intelligence
The Great Lie

By

Roy J. Andersen

The Moving Quill Publishing House

MQ

Copyright © Roy Andersen 2013

Disclaimer:

ISBN: 9781068529627

A CIP catalogue record for this book is available from the British Library.

I would like to dedicate this book to

Jørn Munk Nielsen and Bent Halbye.

When I lived in England, I once counselled a fortune teller. This very kind old lady told me I would live in Denmark and I would be looked after by two men. One would have the initials J.M and the other B.H, and that one of them would have something wrong with his hand.

This greatly surprised me, for I had no thoughts of leaving my country at that time. However, events moved rapidly in my life, and six months later, I found myself living in Denmark. I wanted to help the society and went to meet a government official. We liked each other immediately and the man sent me to meet a lawyer who would guide me. The names of the first man was Jørn Munk Nielsen and the second was Bent Halbye. Bent had lost half of his left hand during the Second World War.

For the ten years I lived in Denmark, these two gentlemen daily looked after me, prevented me from going into businesses they knew were wrong, and encouraged and protected me in my endeavours to improve education. Without these two earthly angels, I would have been very, very lost. I will always remember them and always keep those memories close to my heart.

Mange Tak Jørn og Bent

Hilsen

Roy

Acknowledgments

There is not enough space here to mention all the many people I have ironed out my thoughts with in the thirty years it took me to complete these books. To those I mention here, and to many others, I am profoundly grateful for their time, generosity, and the great friendship they have shown me.

Prof. / Dean Emeritus. David Martin. Gallaudet University. U.S.A.

Prof. Mads Hermansen. Nordic School of Public Health. Sweden.

Prof. Freddy Bugge Christiansen. Arhus University. Denmark.

Prof. Albert Gjedde. Arhus University Hospital. Denmark.

Prof. Rik Drummond-Brydson. Leeds University. England.

Prof. Jorn Bundgaard Nielsen. Arhus University. Denmark.

Dr. Paul Harris. Southern College of Optometry. U.S.A.

Prof. Cosimo Di Magli. The Anne Frank School. Italy.

Prof. Harry Chugani. Wayne State University. U.S.A.

Prof. Laming. Cambridge University. England.

Prof. Martha Constanine-Paton. MIT. U.S.A.

Prof. Carla Shatz. Stanford University. U.S.A.

Prof. Derek Forest. Dublin University. Ireland.

Ms. Leigh Collinge. Australia.

Prof. Søren Nørby. Denmark.

Ms. Claudia Krenz. U.S.A.

Ms. Sara Lappi. U.S.A.

&

A special thank you to

Prof. Luca Magni. LUISS Business School. Italy

Table of Contents

Foreword

You are about to read a well-researched book that offers to be one of the most important ever written, as it will lead you on a memorable and transformative journey. In this work, Roy Andersen offers a very savvy and constructive account of what intelligence is and the role it has been playing in our global society.

The concept of intelligence has been much debated and much read throughout the centuries; however, Andersen presents a wholly new insight into how this concept came about and how it has been used to bring and maintain order in every social system. Here, you will find how the concept of intelligence we have today arose in times of great anarchy during the 19th century, and how it has been and still is engineered through political, social, and educational systems to underlie all our means of human evaluation.

Although deeply researched, **the book is also very easy to read and enjoy;** the author has spent most of the past 40 years involved in this domain. This is a book that offers to bring profound changes to the ways we educate and teach students, just as it will cause us to understand differently the ways in which students learn. This need has never been more desired than it is now, as our children will grow to face a world dominated by artificial intelligence, with which they must compete for their rights and sense of freedom.

David S. Martin, Ph.D.
Dean Emeritus/Professor, Gallaudet University, Washington, DC.

Introduction from Professor Luca Magni.
Rome Italy.

"The Great Lie" is a groundbreaking work that invites readers to question conventional wisdom and consider the hidden forces shaping our lives and educational systems. I have rarely encountered such a quantity of content in a book that was not intended to be a textbook.

"Intelligence: The Great Lie" is a meticulously researched book, where Roy J. Andersen uncovers a centuries-old social machinations that profoundly impact education and life opportunities. The prevailing belief used to be that intelligence was inherited through bloodlines. Despite the discovery of genes, 150 years ago, and numerous scientific debates about the relative influence of inheritance versus experience, this irrational belief continues to impact our lives. But, what if this premise is flawed?

Andersen delves into a political conspiracy that originated long ago and persists to this day. Through discreet strategies in society and schools, the social construction of intelligence sustains the doors of opportunity, which are either opened or closed based on factors such as social standing, ethnic background, skin colour and religion. These strategies serve to maintain the status quo.

Intelligence: The Great Lie" reveals why this conspiracy was created and why it endures. It is a conspiracy designed to shape our lives and the opportunities available to our children. Neither society nor school were ever meant to be fair, and Andersen sheds light on the hidden mechanisms that perpetuate inequality.

As you will find, as you move through the following pages, this book is extremely well researched. Yet, with the purpose to bring urgent changes into how we may better prepare our youth for the A.I. world that awaits them, it was written in a straight forward and ready language that all will be able to understand, enjoy and dwell upon the implications this book offers.

Professor Luca Magni
Rome Italy.

A Personal Introduction by Roy Andersen

*A new type of thinking is essential, if mankind is
to survive and move toward higher levels.*
Albert Einstein

Education has always faced criticism. This criticism traditionally comes from universities complaining of the low competence of fresh undergraduates, from employers over the poor standard of school leavers to be adaptable to job demands, and from parents worried about the quality of learning their children gain and the effects this may have on their life experiences. However, education is likely to face a far more serious criticism if it does not tailor its design and purpose to the social effects that Artificial Intelligence is expected to create.[1]

To deal with these standing complaints, education has manoeuvred itself through a great number of changes over the years, and yet no noticeable effect has been realised. The same criticisms still remain.

The underlying reason for this failure of education to change is that it has never dealt with the basic problem it has. This lies in the mental competence, or rather the intelligence, of its students in how they are believed to learn. Based on its understanding, the school simply processes its students to learn what is generally assumed to be a combination of their social background, skills, and their "natural" ability, as evidenced through assessment and examination, rather than trying to develop their intelligence.

Although many studies have shown that children tend to demonstrate an ability in school relative to the ways they were raised by their parents, the educational system makes no formal means to address the imbalances in the way its students are raised differently. It is simply that students are accepted as they are, in regard to the abilities they display in reasoning and thinking, and are largely evaluated on these abilities, with no real intervention taking place. There is, for example, no formal subject in the curriculum dedicated to the education of **reasoning** and **thinking**.

Yet, sense would have it that if children were taught how to reason and how to think, they would better understand what they are taught and would learn better, which in turn would do much to negate the criticisms levelled at education. We are prompted by this to ask the question, Why have schools persistently avoided the education of reason?

The simplest answer, although this is not openly discussed today, is that school sees the intelligence of the child as being more or less limited by the genes they inherited. From this understanding, any attempt to develop their intelligence would be largely a waste of time, effort, and expense in trying to undo what "nature" has already done. Yet, what most do not realise is that this impression of an inherited intelligence is one that evolved only out of a desperate political struggle in the 19th century. It is not rooted in scientific fact, as psychologists have long sought to give this impression.

Education clings to the reasoning that intelligence is largely inherited, because by doing so, it can most economically fulfil its purpose. The basic purpose of school, we may be surprised to know, is not to teach children how to learn. It is to sort them into categories and process them based on what is assumed to be their intelligence (although ability in school is actually based on: linguistic skills, the ability to avoid distraction, and the effort to keep up with the steady progression of learning), so as to produce a citizen who will take either a manager or a managed role in work and in society.

While this design fitted the operational needs of the 19th and for most of the 20th century, it will likely bring serious trouble to us as this century advances, because it limits the true potential of the individual in the part they must play in a world that is rapidly becoming dominated by artificial intelligence. As we discuss in other books, artificial intelligence is already clearly demonstrating the ability to manage, if not control, how we work and how we may live. Such a world of A.I. will demand a higher-minded and more responsible citizen than school is designed to produce.

While the purpose of school is to prepare its students to take on different qualities of job responsibility, it must be realised that A.I. is expected to evolve to create a high level of unemployment permanently. From this state of affairs, the purpose of school must change to focus on developing the reasoning ability of its students (in both an intellectual and a behavioural sense), so they will later be better able to maintain a high level of harmony in their society.

If our future citizens do not achieve an acceptable level of harmony, through their own sense of reason, in the face of high unemployment with all the ills this may bring, and we may think in this of high levels of depression, domestic violence, alcoholism, drug abuse and a crime level difficult to control, then it will be imposed upon them through the capabilities of A.I. A scenario such as this will deteriorate the freedom of the individual and the concept of a free government under a democratic concept.

What will prevent or hinder the transition of the school to centre its operations about the formal education of reason, and so achieve this new purpose, is the belief that intelligence is largely inherited through family lines, which in being so is stable, relatively unalterable and therefore predictable throughout the lifetime of the individual.

What is little realised here is that this understanding we have of intelligence came about in a time when the workings of the brain were unknown. In the second half of the 19th century, the brain was understood to be little more than an organ and taken to work much the same as any other organ of the body. As the heart and lungs were naturally created in the body and worked to their own efficiency, so was the brain reasoned to do so.

At that time, nothing was known of brain cells or neurons. In fact, nothing was known of genetics, and therefore, the vital role of the environment in affecting the design of gene coding. The knowledge we have today of brain plasticity, how neurons link to create networks through emotional interest, and even how new brain cells are created, was totally unknown at that time.

Yet, once this theory of an inherited intelligence took hold, as it did in the desperation of those political times, a tradition very quickly built up to support it. Tradition, of course, is the enemy to free reason, as it seeks to close minds in self-preservation. All of which we will come to understand.

So extensively was this view of an inherited intelligence propagated since that time, that it infected the minds of everyone, including those of geneticists. Few, we shall see, rose to challenge what inheritance could actually mean in regard to intelligence, and so the real effect of how the environment is able to direct its development.

However, by the end of the 20th century, our level of technology had so advanced that we were able to gain a greater understanding of how the brain works and so how the environment affects its development and even its basic construction. Through such advancements in neurology, statements began to increasingly appear in public forums and the media relating to the effects of the environment on the IQ of people and even how IQ can be affected by certain foods.

Yet, it is to be realised that it is a great mistake to refer to IQ as meaning intelligence. IQ is not intelligence, and this term gives no understanding of what intelligence is or how it comes to be. The Intelligence Quotient, or IQ as it is more commonly known, is simply a score based on one or more tests and nothing more. However, the requirement for these tests to exist lies in the belief that intelligence is essentially inherited and so is largely stable throughout the lifetime and therefore predictable enough to be measured.

We will have much to discuss about a graph called the Bell Curve, but it may be simply understood to display the range of intelligence in a population, based on the quality of the genes individuals inherited, plus or minus the effects of the environment. However, as we shall see, it is totally impossible to ever know the quality of genes for intelligence that an individual has inherited. There is no measurement of DNA here, and we do not know which genes are actually responsible for intelligence, because their functions overlap in a multitude of ways. It may be, as with many features that have to develop through shifting environments, such as language, that the gene code is only responsible for allowing this feature to develop, and in normal circumstances carries no or very little differential quality.

All that psychologists have done is to identify with human beings who have incurred such conditions as Down Syndrome, through the mutation of chromosomes, and used this to explain that their low intelligence is caused by the quality of genes they inherited. They, then, use this example to explain how the qualities of all children, born normally, vary in gene quality to the extreme level of genius.

Yet, as we shall see, no said genius ever came from a line of geniuses and never parented a line of geniuses. The ancestors and descendants of geniuses were people of very normal ability. What caused the difference is the environment, as we shall come to see. However, it may be realised here that there is no evidence that the positioning of any normally born child on this bell curve has anything to do with the qualities of the genes they inherited. The reasoning that they do hides many rabbit holes of prejudice and inequality, which serve political agendas.

The lifelong stability so said of an individual's intelligence is not limited by the quality of genes they inherited. It is simply the cause of a natural process. By design, we customise our manner of thinking and our social identity to the environment, as we perceive it. This gives us a stability by which we know ourselves, and so how better to adapt to changes within this environment.

However, if our perspective of the environment radically changes, we all have the potential to radically alter our means of interaction with it. This is why psychologists have to ignore the role of emotion in the intelligence studies they make, because it gives no predictability to their statistics. In fact, over a thousand case studies have proven that if an individual's perspective of their environment can gain a deep enough change, then so will their level of intelligence.[2]

Such evidence clearly undermines the stability that is associated to intelligence, which questions the whole concept of it being predictable.

As it does so, it brings into question what we think the environment of intelligence is and what the purpose of the gene actually is. To which we may add that geneticists are still trying to understand the complexity of genes. They are not as simple as they were thought to be 100 years ago.

It is very important that we understand, at this introductory stage, **not** that the gene simply has a design which the environment builds to create the purpose of this design, but that any gene has evolved, through natural selection, to serve the better survival of its organism through its interaction with the environment. Being aware of this causes us to realise that not all genes have the same purpose and that they can work with the environment in different ways.

If we look at two extreme examples, we would find one gene coding is responsible for the creation and development of our skeletal structure, while another would enable us to dream. After all, without a gene coding for this, we would not be able to dream.

Our ability to dream evolves through a very complex environment of the experiences we have built up through our desires and fears. The environment that works in conjunction with the development of our bone structure is far simpler to evaluate. Yet, it is nevertheless not as straightforward as we may think. We understand that diet and the chemical effects of exercise feed this design, but it has recently been realised that psychological states, such as depression and anxiety, those features that play within our dreams, also play a role in developing bone density.3

We are led by this to realise that the transition from a gene code to the feature we witness (called the phenotype in genetics) involves some form of mental attitude in the development and functioning of all of our features. This immediately causes us to realise that the rules of genetics are far more complicated to understand with human beings than, for example, with plants.

It follows from this that intelligence is not simply a matter of a gene design developing through an environment of mental exercises and social experiences, but of genes evolving their designs through an environment that is extremely complex and far more determining in the construction and development of the sensory system, brain matter, neurons and neurotransmitters than is thought to be.

By their experiences, a bullied or abused child may alter their hormone level, which can alter the number of spines on the dendrites of their neurons, to affect the speed at which they process information. Indeed, it is well recognised that stress can reduce dendrite branching and the loss of spines, which impairs the function of neurons for plasticity and biochemical compartmentalisation.[4] All of which affects what is thought of their intelligence, without any relevance to the quality of genes that are used to explain their poor performance in IQ tests.

Indeed, there is no consideration by psychologists in their psychometric testing of the effect of the psychological state, which much controls the activity of the sensory system, which feeds the developing brain from infancy and throughout life. Thus, if the mind is calm, it directs its sensors to rationally evaluate what information there is. If it is stressed, it irrationally directs its senses seeking means of calmness and so security. By this difference, information is defined in detail or with vagueness, which determines all the neural processes that follow.

A far more extreme example would be in how curiosity and the drive of the human spirit constitute elements of the environment that are not considered in the evaluation of intelligence. Yet, they exist and they do play determining roles, as we shall come to see.

May we understand from this simple introduction that the environment of intelligence is far, far more complex than psychologists consider it to be, as they try to categorise it into elements that may be compared and so measured to evaluate the differences in the intelligences of any two human beings.

It further follows that if the environment of intelligence is far more complex than it is understood to be, as we shall find it so, then our understanding of what intelligence is must come into question. In fact, despite 150 years of discussing what intelligence is, there is no agreed-upon definition among all concerned as to what intelligence actually is.5 Different people still have different ideas.

This is important to realise, because it is upon what intelligence is reasoned to be that education operates in the ways teachers teach and students are taught and evaluated, and in fact, how the whole educational system operates.

What we need to grasp from this is that the planned use of the citizen in society is based on their performance within the current system of education, and that this performance is greatly determined by political and social planning based on an understanding of what intelligence is. We have yet to examine the various guises under which the politics behind this have operated.

Through the many books we have written, which are said by experts in education around the world to be some of the best written about school, society and learning, we try to offer thoughts on how we can all help the global child be better prepared for the A.I. world that awaits them.

These books discuss no minor thing, for the quality of the education our children receive and the level of reasoning they are educated to, may well determine their ability to maintain a democratic world, as we have just indicated. These books are:

Brain Plasticity,

The Illusion of School,

Ben Learns to Get Smart,

The Illusion of Education,

Teach Better, Learn Better,

Intelligence: The Great Lie,

Five Ways for Better Grades,

Memoirs of a Happy Teacher,

Is AI Making Our Kids Stupid?

Reimagining Education for the AI Era,

Mediation: Crafting the Ability of the Child,

What Every Parent and Teacher Should Know,

All That is Wrong with School: How Teachers and Parents Can Fix It,

&

The Real Dangers of A.I: The Struggle of Man to Survive by Natural or Artificial Intelligence - A New Role for the School.

Through the aforementioned books, we have sought to raise our understanding of how we can better prepare our children for the world that awaits them. All of the knowledge and reasoning they contain rests upon a new perspective of how the mind and the brain work together to enable the student's ability to learn. In short, we seek to discuss why our understanding of the effects of the environment has never been truly understood in the construction of intelligence.

The answer we shall now move to discover, lies in the manner by which our understanding of intelligence has been politically cloaked for over 150 years to obscure the real effect of the environment on intelligence.

The philosophy that grew out of this management of our understanding of intelligence, has been the sole means by which children and then adults were to be selected for roles in work and society — according to their social level, ethnic background (which is most easily associated with skin colour), culture, and even religion, as all were to be set to the maintenance of the societal status quo.

Our account, then, must be a long one if we are to understand all we have mentioned here in greater detail, for we have nearly two centuries of conspiracy against the common man to reveal. Yet, I do assure you, it will be a very, very interesting one.

Roy Andersen

What the Experts say

"The books of Roy Andersen are important books that should be read by every parent and educator in the world. They represent a real breakthrough in our understanding of what intelligence is and how it develops, and the importance of changing the ways students are both parented and educated. Roy is doing for learning the work that is as significant as was that done in the past by such figures as John Dewey. These are must-reads for both parents and educators alike."

Dean Emeritus/Professor David Martin Ph.D,
Gallaudet University, Washington, DC.

It will probably take a few years, possibly even a decade before the public at large will get how revolutionary the ideas of Roy Andersen are. His ideas resonate perfectly with the Learnable Theory and are destined to impact not only teaching in schools, but also the way human resources are selected and developed in organisations. Indeed, Roy's deconstruction of intelligence goes well beyond Daniel Coleman, Howard Gardner and what others have done so far. Roy goes at the root of learning, he links it to the creation and leveraging of meanings and how the symbolic process of language plays a key role in what we generally identify and name intelligence.

Professor Luca Magni. LUISS Business School. Rome. Italy

"Roy's series of books clearly and methodically maps out exactly how students learn. He isn't afraid to address head-on the many misconceptions that are plaguing our society and thus having a negative impact on our students' learning. Parents and educators who read these books will not only have a better understanding, but will also be inspired to change in their attitudes and preconceived notions on how students can excel in their learning. If you've ever wanted to unravel how students learn, then these books are the answer you have been looking for! They should be mandatory reading for every parent and educator."

Erin Calhoun. National Institute of Learning Development. USA

"The most important books I have ever read about a child's intelligence."

Prof. Tatyana Oleinik. Pedagogical University. Ukraine.

"Roy, I would like to thank you for sharing your passion, heart, brilliance, and intellectual journey with me. I am very much enjoying your knowledgeable perspective on some very important challenges."

Dr. Christopher John. Psychologist. USA.

"Roy Andersen's deep understanding of children's behaviour gives a new perspective to parents and educators in directing and re-directing student potential -- where their unique individualities can be given proper attention to shape their creative ideas into reality. Andersen's books are really a heart-touching narration of his experiences in dealing with children who need empathy and understanding. Educators and parents alike may use these books as the basis for learning -- to create a genuine culture of assisting children in the optimum development of their full potential."

Prof. Marinel Dayawon Ph.D. Assoc.Dean of Education.
Isabela State Univ. Philippines.

"These books should be in the library of each school in every corner of the world. They should also be part of the syllabus in the institutions who are offer child psychology programmes, and teacher training diplomas and degree programs, or at least they should be the part of a refresher course."

M.Imran Khan. CEO AIMMS Universities. Middle East.

"Roy Andersen's research and writings provide deep insights into the minds of children. His works are always easy to read and understand. His books are assets that are good material for professional development on every teacher's table."

Daniel Tay Xiong Sheng. Educator. Singapore

"Your observations on the way 'education' is delivered, and all the things that are wrong with the current model of public education, are an eye-opener. It's plain to me that many of your proposals are not only well-reasoned, but absolutely necessary if we are to achieve any semblance of an egalitarian society in which every child can develop to his or her full potential."

Dr. Sara Lappi Educator USA

Roy Andersen is an enlightening human resource, whose brilliant potential is enriched with amazing vision and pertinacious endeavour. He is a treasure trove of knowledge who puts his soul into every aspect of education. His contribution to inculcate knowledge is beyond the borders of racial discrimination as he believes in dispensing the light of education to the ones who are deprived of seeking knowledge. His methodologies are not conventional, rather they are contemporary driven to be group focused and inquiry driven. Roy Andersen is like a beacon who may inspire, make his students to pinnacle aspire, kindle their imagination and foster their love of learning.

Huma Kirmani
UN Representative for Pakistan

A Guide to Assist You in Your Journey.

The path that we must unravel in our account will begin by understanding how society works and how people are so governed to maintain a sense of working and social harmony. With a rudimentary understanding of this, we move back 200 years to the beginning of the Industrial Revolution, where we discover the very serious but little-known social problems of that time.

As this new industry demanded workers, families from rural districts were enticed to relocate to cities and their factories by thoughts of running water, private lavatories and a reliable wage. Crowded together, they soon realised the power of strike action and saw through this how they could create a better life for themselves.

While new political ideas of equality were simmering, harvests failed badly, the cost of living rose dramatically and with most of Europe hungry and dissatisfied, the people broke out in a revolutionary anger, far greater and far more serious than our history books have desired to reveal.

Desperate to restore order, the establishment reacted swiftly with military force and widespread executions, which is little discussed in our history books. Yet, some means other than oppression was needed to temper the minds and hearts of the people, if order was to be restored in the long term. The solution most desperately needed was offered by a cousin of Charles Darwin.

The idea was simple and fitted the needs of the times exactly. The social worth of a family was to be judged by the work of its ancestors, with the capability for this work transferred through bloodlines and witnessed by the similarity of nose or chin.

Most simply, if the father was a king, then his son was said to have the capability to be a king, because he would have inherited some facial feature that proved this link of competence. The basic idea was that all features, skills and capabilities were to be completely inherent by nature. As this principle was to be applied throughout the population, from lawyers to merchants to labourers, it created a belief that each was born with the skills and limitations of their fathers.

From this reasoning, a mindset was propagated through pulpit and media that every man should know his place and respect his betters, with each being born to serve society as his forefathers. The idea was an ingenious means that negated the desire of people to rise above their station and so gave reassurance that a hierarchical social system was for the greater good of all.

As industry rapidly expanded and greater efficiency was desired, a need soon arose for each man to have a known value of capability. From such demand, this idea of inherited capability was forged to create the new science of psychology, where it was desired to classify each worker according to their worth. Yet, this was a century of science, and any sentiment was to be proved by mathematics if it was to survive.

In desperation for a means to do so, psychologists from America corrupted the idea of a French scientist to devise a system that would promote the type of citizens most required for their nation and exclude those not so, on account of their ethnic background or social heritage. This brought about the birth of IQ testing, which was used to open doors of opportunity for those from a white protestant background and proportionally less so for those of other backgrounds.

As the belief that intelligence could be measured spread globally, it became part of the foundations of every educational system in the world, and by which children were steered to roles in society according to the policies of their land.

Selected by different criteria, children were either schooled with no education in their reason, causing them to be more compliant workers after school, or they were so educated for the more responsible roles they would take in society and industry. To the error of our youth today, education still operates about this 19th-century design, despite the very different level of technology we now operate in a very different social atmosphere.

However, as this idea sought to contain the political turmoil of the 19th century, it was forever steeped in politics itself. As two sides of interest evolved, one seeking an egalitarian society and the other an authoritative one, so great scheming took place, often involving falsification of information, the fabrication of accounts and the manufacture of lies — as each side sought to exert more influence on the political design of their society.

Forty-five years ago, and with far too much innocence, I entered into the purpose of understanding why an individual is said to be limited by some genetic factor in developing their intelligence, when I had found it not so. Since that time, I have gone far beyond what appeared obvious to discover the intricate weaving of facts that led one to another to make everything appear naturally correct and so acceptable to all.

To understand why this is not so, we shall delve into the origins of many aspects of different sciences to discover how alternative ideas could have come to the forefront in our understanding, but failed to do so because they lacked the political strength to fit into the jigsaw that was being constructed. As we unravel our account of such great deception, our journey will move through many facets of psychology, social planning, political design and into avenues of human development, neurology and from this into the means of "inheritance". This is a word that the man who discovered the importance of how the environment affects gene coding said should never be used in genetics!

Once past the historical and social arguments, which sought to uphold this simple idea of inheritance, we move into understanding what genetic inheritance was meant to be and what we now know it means. Eventually, we move to explain how factors of intelligence are conveyed to siblings by different means, not just simply by the stability of DNA but more by the shifting impressions that drive epigenetics and imprinting. As we do this, we dissolve this political idea that was so eagerly germinated by the 19th-century establishment, as it struggled to retain power, wealth and influence over the masses.

With new insight, we come to understand the real meaning of genetic design and so the true complexity and influence of the environment, as we are brought to understand how any normally born child, regardless of their ethnic or social background, has the potential to develop their intelligence to equal that of any other human being.

As our journey takes us from understanding the political manipulation of people in the past and so in the present, we move to consider an unpredictable future. Today, our youth face a world that is dominated by, if not controlled by, artificial intelligence, which must alter the fabric of their societies. They will be sorely unprepared for the challenges of this new world, unless education changes from the way it currently operates to educate them in the skills of reason and critical thinking.

That education has never truly done this is because the power of this idea of an inherited ability so influenced educationalists to believe these skills were inborn, and by this largely unteachable, that they never realised how, by failing to teach them, they were creating the same mindset in each working generation to comply with the design laid out for their lives. So, shall we find why and how education creates the manager/managed citizen and dumbs down our children to make them more compliant citizen workers easier to be managed by the media consortium.

For this change in education to occur, those behind and within its hallowed halls must understand that intelligence is not what they have been raised to think it is.

Once this understanding is realised, then, and only then, may the fabric of school be changed, as will the whole curriculum need to be, if we are to prepare future generations to live with a self-imposed harmony by the education of their intelligence, ever wary of the consequences of an A.I. surveillance and policing authority if they fail to do so.

As you may now understand, this book is not just about intelligence; it is mostly about how we may better prepare humanity to survive artificial intelligence.

"Every man can, if he so desires,
become the sculptor of his own brain"

Ramon y Cajal 1852-1934

Intelligence:

The Great Lie

This book is about you and your child.

*

This book builds upon the explanations of intelligence and learning as previously discussed in:

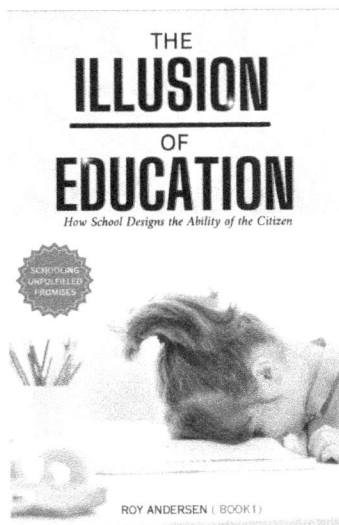

THE
ILLUSION
OF
SCHOOL
The Real Reason why Children Fail!

ROY. J. ANDERSEN

THE
ILLUSION
OF
EDUCATION
How School Designs the Ability of the Citizen

SCHOOLING UNFULFILLED PROMISES

ROY ANDERSEN (BOOK 1)

In this book, we will consider three main questions:

a)   How does human intelligence come to be?

b)   Is it possible to measure human intelligence?

c)   How may we better improve the intelligence of our children, so they may better survive in a world dominated by artificial intelligence?

The quest we now embark upon is neither straightforward nor simple, for we have over 150 years of lies, fraud and deliberate falsification of data that have come to design how children should be taught and evaluated in school, and so how adults are to be judged in their society according to their social class, race and ethnic background.

As we shall now begin to discover, intelligence is not what you may think it is. .....

Chapter One

Management of a People

The foundation of a society, believe it or not, is its education, the means by which the future working generation is prepared to conform to its social rules and have the capability to work the technology that enables the society to function. It is, therefore, of no small relevance that we begin our odyssey into intelligence by understanding how education works, since this is the preparatory stage for all that follows within the society.

Consider, then, the situation of a teacher confronted with two students, one of whom may have been you in the past or your child today. One student will instantly understand this teacher and respond with clear intelligence, while the other may seem mystified by the same question and be quite unable to construct a good response. The teacher, we would suggest, is apt to reason that both were taught equally and so believe that the differences in their responses are explainable in some part by genetic differences.

In believing this to be so, they will generally accept the response of the less able student with a few vague suggestions on how they may do better, instead of deeply reflecting on how they could reconstruct this student's understanding and belief in themselves, so they may more closely equal the better student. The teacher is not to be blamed in this, least because they have little time to do otherwise with many in the class, but mostly because we widely reason that intelligence is in some part inherited and some part developed. Indeed, it is a common belief created by psychology that human beings are born with natural differences in their intelligence, which, when inherited, may be little improved upon.

Yet, despite a century of arguing between themselves, psychologists still do not know how these portions correctly lie, so that the inherited part of intelligence remains a mysterious enigma. It may, then, come as a surprise to many that we don't actually know, or at least all agree upon, what intelligence really is.[6]

Simply said, intelligence can be seen as an act of thinking defined by others according to their values, which is why intelligence has different values in different cultures. All we may say of intelligence is that it is a term vaguely and far too easily used to explain some limitation that appears in one when we compare them to another. Indeed, we may think of one individual being compared to another, but the real meaning has far deeper connotations and a purpose of its own.

After all, the concept of inheritance implies that a child will inherit some factor of intelligence from their parents, which will limit them, more or less, to the intelligence of their parents, and so the work and social responsibility that can be said of them.

Very simply, and although it has become clouded today by social issues, the concept of intelligence is used to categorise families to limit the roles they may take in their society.[7] Intelligence, in this sense, has been used since it first became a political tool to open opportunities in society for some families and close those to others.

We may see in this that any comparison of intelligence is seldom innocent, because it underlies political strategies that seek to ensure a social or ethnic and even a religious continuity in a society. So we find, for example, that Catholic children are purposely deprived of the higher quality of education available to Protestant children in Northern Ireland, to limit the jobs available to them after their education, and so the extent of the social and political influences they may bring into their country.[8]

We can find the same principle in most countries of the world, with strategies more open or more concealed according to the strength of their politics.[9] We would do well, by understanding this, to be wary of data relating to intelligence and always consider how it was actually created and for what actual purpose.

Indeed, it is to be realised that psychologists do not determine their statistics of the inherited aspect of intelligence through measuring DNA. This is not possible. There is no feature within our brain or in our DNA that is solely attributed to intelligence. The thought that there is comes from a paper Spearman wrote in 1904, which has never been substantiated.[10]

In trying to evaluate intelligence, all psychologists may do is tick boxes to gauge responses. Yet, all human responses are laid upon an emotional base, which psychologists ignore in their statistics because emotion is not a stable enough feature to be measured with any prediction. Thus, as they ignore human emotion in their statistics, so they have to ignore the role of the human spirit, because it cannot be classified into their concept of the environment. Yet, this is the most important factor in the purpose they have to measure intelligence, because it is this that is really the only factor that drives all levels of accomplishment.

One of the many issues we will come to examine in this book is the actual purpose of gene codes, because they do have different purposes and do relate to the environment in different ways. As we shall see, in some instances and especially those relating to how the mind interacts with the outside world, the environment can completely obscure whatever impression we may have of a gene.

In the opening pages of this book, we should explain that every feature we have as human beings comes from genes we have inherited. It is very important for us to understand that the gene is only the instruction for a feature to exist. It is not the feature. For that feature to come into existence, it must evolve through its environment. There is a common understanding that genes naturally vary in their quality of coding and that this naturally creates differences in the feature as it develops through the environment.

It is very important that we now understand that with certain features, the environment can be the deciding factor against any quality a gene coding may be suspected to have. It is not, then, a black and white situation where a feature always exists through a combination of gene quality and environmental influences. This is certainly the case with plants, but, as we shall see, it cannot always be so with the features of the human being.

Having stated this, I would like to demonstrate a situation where the environment completely took over the genetic design of a feature. We will consider some examples of this occurring in our following book, *Brain Plasticity*, and it is from this book that I borrow a section relating to the development of the visual system.

"In our species and with other mammals, the signals from each eye are compared in the Ocular Dominance Columns (at the back of the brain). This comparison of the signals from both eyes provides the feature of binocular vision.

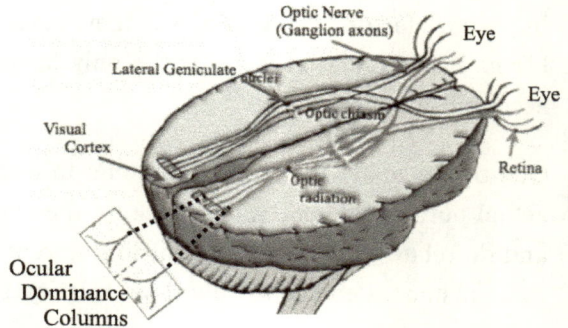

However, this is not so with lower vertebrates such as the frog, because the signals from each of their eyes are not compared. In their case, the entire visual information from one eye is transferred to an optic tectum

on the opposite side of the head, and kept isolated from the visual information received by the other eye. Frogs have monocular vision.
Fig.6

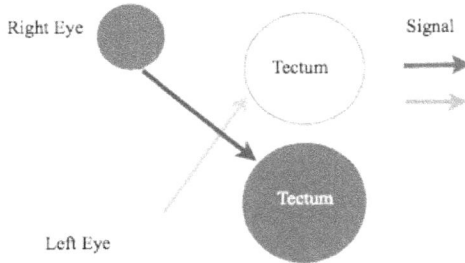

As we know, the brain of the frog has a genetic design to accommodate signals from two eyes, with systems that are not related to each other.

To investigate how environmental signals could override the genetic design, a number of experiments were conducted early in the 1980s on frog embryos. These experiments are no longer fashionable, but at the time, a third eye was grafted onto the head of an embryo. The researchers discovered that an axon developed from this third eye and grew within the brain to connect with one of the tectums that a normal eye had connected to.

Fig.7

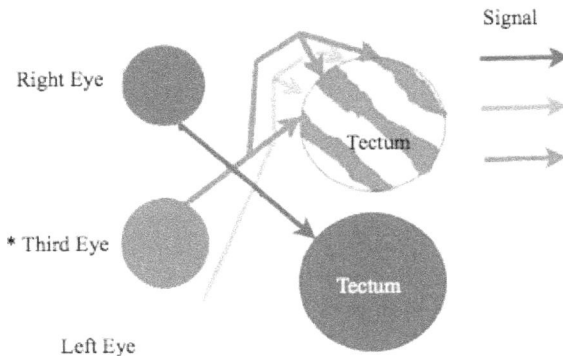

We are shown here a demonstration that without a genetic coding to know of a third eye, the brain of the frog accepted this extra eye, and developed it as normally as the two eyes it was genetically designed to handle. However, something else happened here that was even more astonishing.

As we can see from the illustration in Fig.6, the frog does not have the genetic design for ocular dominance columns. There is simply no DNA coding to allow the higher level of visual detection that we have.

Yet, as we can see in Fig.7, when the third eye was connected with one of the tectums of the frog, it did create ocular dominance columns. The presence of these columns enabled the signal strength received from the two eyes to compete for allocation. When they did this, they created the ability for binocular vision in a species that has no genetic design for this.[11]

The example of how environmental information can drive a foreign eye to adapt as well as any of the normal eyes beyond a genetic plan is remarkable enough, but by the realisation that this environmental information also changed the genetic design, we are woken to how the brain gains its adaptability in functioning through the environment at a very primitive level."

This example of how the environment can overtake a genetic design is an extreme one, but it does help us to understand that the environment can have far more influence upon a gene design than we would normally think. To our interest, this knowledge begins to question the standing belief that different individuals inherit different qualities of gene codes that directly determine their level of intelligence, because the role of the environment is generally ignored when people think of the intelligence of others. So we hear the comment "She's intelligent", which implies she was born this way, with no consideration to how she may have been conditioned to be intelligent through her experiences.

Once we can begin to understand that the environment may be far more influential than we may imagine, we may begin to wonder not only how gene design develops through the environment to create intelligence, but also what the purpose of this gene coding may actually be.

We are still at the introductory stage of our account, but let us begin to realise that intelligence is not a singular feature, which it too often is taken to be. Rather, it is a combination of many components. Let us consider for a moment two of these that are fundamental in an act of intelligence.

One of these would certainly be language, because it is only by language that we may know of our world and how factors within it interact. Language, then, is the main means by which information is given, designed, recognised, processed and presented by one to others in all acts of intelligence and from which evaluation is made of their competence.

Accordingly, we may know that our inherited ability for language has no predetermined level of competence created through genetic variation. After all, genetic variations primarily affect an individual's biological traits, physical characteristics, and susceptibility to certain medical conditions. They do not directly influence forms of language, such as grammar, syntax, or vocabulary. Language development and usage are predominantly shaped by environmental factors, including cultural, social, and linguistic influences.

Language is a complex and dynamic system influenced by a wide range of factors, including exposure, education and social interaction. Naturally, all humans inherit the genetic ability for language; we must do so or we could not have it, but genetic variations do not affect how an individual develops their ability in this regard. Thus, we are introduced to a very important component of intelligence, where the individual gains their competence only through environmental experience — with no regard to genetic variations.

To expand upon this, we should know that the most noticeable characteristic of intelligence lies in the ability to relate to detail and therefore to clearly distinguish differences. The ability for this lies in emotional interest that generates levels of sensitivity. The relevant gene codes for emotion, so allows the environment to decide the emotional base of each individual, as each learns to adapt to the behaviours of those who raise them and of those good and bad whom they share time with in their life.

Thus, language and emotion, two of the main components of intelligence, are regulated in the individual through their social experiences. These components are not stable or rather "fixed" and can be completely altered at any time of the life cycle, according to the experiences the individual engages.

We are led by this to wonder and so question if the inheritance factor of intelligence in schoolchildren really does create some part of the differences in their efforts that are marked and graded.

To explain why it is not, we should know that knowledge in school evolves through the steady buildup of rules, by which facts may be related and explained through language. Although it is too often believed that differences in student ability do lie in some part by genetic differences, we can explain that this is not so with fully functioning children. Competence, or rather ability in learning, can be explained purely through language experiences and emotional interests, by which rules are easily learned and practised — when there is an inner desire for this.[12]

As we shall come to see, the problem with any discussion of genetics lies in understanding the effect of the environment, which is very seldom understood because of its complexity. Our recent knowledge of epigenetics has confounded what was once an extremely difficult task, at least within human beings.

Therefore, if competence in learning comes through language and emotion, by which strategies are devised to understand and practice to proficiency the rules by which knowledge is defined (as we shall show it to be in later chapters) and not so differences in intelligence, we must rethink how our entire operation of education works. This must be so in how information is presented to the student and how we think the student is able to relate to and display their understanding of this.

After all, despite 100 years of theories on how students could be better taught, we still educate and evaluate them on the 19th-century principle of the brain being a simple organ that functions as well as it was inherited to do. So we find that all theories of how children learn, such as those of Piaget and Gardner's multiple intelligences and even Kolb's learning styles, are rooted in the concept of an inherited intelligence and, by this, do not achieve the greater learning hoped for by them.

Still today, children in every class in every country of the world are largely confused with what they are to learn and how they are to learn this. In consequence to this, the same variation of student ability still appears as it always has done, with one or two appearing to be most intelligent, the general mass either less motivated or less able and a few of lesser ability who seem only intent on disrupting the lesson for the rest of the class.

The purpose of school, we need to realise, is not to teach children how to learn, for it does not teach them how to think nor how to reason in order that they would learn better and more so by themselves. It is instead that school gives information and evaluates how the student more or less handles this from their own background influences.

Teachers try to help their students to understand what they are learning, of course, but by a combination of factors, too few students really manage to keep up with each lesson as it moves to the next.

From day one of school life, a variation in ability soon appears as each child struggles to understand what the teacher wants from them, as each struggles to identify with who they are amid the confusing and distracting personalities they must learn with. As the many years of school pass, about 20% of their lives, children are marked and graded without really understanding why.

The actual purpose of education, we should know, is to create two qualities in a future citizen worker who will manage the operation of the society. These are the managers and the managed.[13] The American president Woodrow Wilson gave insight into this when he explained:

"We want one class of persons to have a liberal education, and we want another class of persons, a very much larger class of necessity in every society, to forgo the privilege of a liberal education and fit themselves to perform specific, difficult manual tasks."[14]

In a very basic sense, education traditionally achieves this social purpose by dividing itself between the school and the university.

At the school level, students are not taught to question information in any real sense and nor are they taught how to think. They are simply processed based on the abilities they have acquired in this, which is essentially through domestic and so social and cultural influences.

School, then, achieves its purpose by processing students based on what is assumed to be their intelligence, but is instead only a combination of language ability, presence of mind to avoid distractions, of which there are many, and a drive to want to learn for a purpose the individual has.

It is by these three factors, which tend to be socially constructed, that the student is able to keep up with the increasing complexity of rules by which information may be known and understood, and upon which their grades and so purpose in society will ultimately lie.

It is important to understand that routing to university is not coincidental of students simply displaying better grades in school, because here lies the mechanism that divides the manager from the managed citizen.

While school students are purposely not taught how to think in school, those who achieve the necessary recognition of ability go to university, where they are taught how to think. Indeed, the prime purpose of the university is to teach them how to think. So, undergraduates are schooled in, for example, Aristotle's Rhetoric, to learn to make fine differentiation with Ethos (the ability to trust information based on how credible its owner appears), Pathos (how the perspectives of information change with its emotional appeal), and Logos (how focus is given to the way reason is defined) —through numerous interactions of different and complex forms.

When these men and women become parents, they transfer the skills of thinking (we may say those of intelligence) they have been educated in to their children, who in turn perform highly in school because of the mental skills and sense of self-discipline they have been raised in.

In simple terms, we may identify these skills as high levels of attention to detail, mental stamina to keep up with the movement of information, sensitivity to differences by which information is recognised and stored and a high language skill to interpret the meaning of information and, most importantly, to explain their understanding to another by which all evaluation is made.

We may see by this how divisions are easily created and maintained within society. Risley and Hart gave testimony to this when their extensive research showed that children raised by academically minded parents have some 30 million more words in their vocabulary by the age of three than children raised by less educated parents.[15]

Accordingly, those who leave university to take managerial roles in society and industry have been prepared with higher reasoning skills for the greater responsibility they will have. Those who left school and did not go to university will take managed roles in their society and will have been deprived of this education in reason. This causes them to be generally reliant upon the guidance and direction of their managers and also be less able to contradict or be rebellious.

It also means, of course, that since they were educated to less question information that they are the more easily influenced by media information to accept decisions made by their political authority. We will come back to all this much later, but we may see from this 19th-century design how education is designed to manufacture the government of a people through the manipulation of their intelligence.

This is the design of education as it came about in the 19th century and was strictly maintained until our technology developed after the 1960s. From this time on, more schoolchildren were required to go into higher education, to be able to make better use of newer levels of technology. In turn, this opened up various social movements that began to erode this distinction in how children were raised and so how school worked, which offered more children a better chance in education.

These movements in society and school gave children of working-class backgrounds a greater chance of a higher education, enabling them to more easily obtain jobs in the professional class, provided that they acquired an understanding of how the school really works. For those who didn't and struggled uncomprehendingly through their schooling, education had the problem of how to push the necessary number of these schoolchildren up into college and university to meet the demands of the working world.

In *The Illusion of Education,* we discuss how this greater movement of school students up into higher education is made possible today, while education is still able to adhere to its basic purpose of providing the future generation with a governing ability.

In the simplest sense, education achieved this in two ways. In the first sense, schools now "teach to the test". This means that students focus more on how to answer questions than on learning to understand what they are learning. This, of course, has a social connotation, because while children from higher socio-economic backgrounds will have been better prepared in their reasoning for school, children from lower socio-economic backgrounds are unlikely to have had this experience, and will now be deprived of the opportunity for it. In turn, this satisfies the criteria of the school to prepare those who do not get the necessary grades to continue into higher education, to be the managed citizens of lesser educated reasoning.

Secondly, colleges, but mostly and especially universities, lowered their entrance standards to enable more students to take advantage of this opportunity. However, to maintain a degree of selectivity, the university placed a high cost on its service to more control who gains access to the education in reason it is designed to provide. After all, putting a price on the right to education has always been and still is one way to restrict the opportunity of children from poorer or undesired backgrounds to eventually rise to challenge the designs of the status quo. As we shall come to see, the word intelligence is really about the government of people through the guise of individual attainment. This brings us to how the intelligence of a student is regarded in school.

The general belief in education is that children inherit the intelligence of their parents, to some "mysterious" extent. A reasoning developed through this that since social standing is much related to income, and income to job worth, which is related to ability (which is mistakenly taken to mean intelligence), that the job worth of the parents reflects their natural intelligence which they passed on to their child genetically, which in turn is demonstrated by the grades their child "naturally" earns.

When teachers fall into the trap of believing this, which they too often did in the past and still do, but to a lesser extent, they readily accept that different children have different "natural" abilities. We will later discuss a senior student who was believed to be dyslexic. His teachers followed the advice of the school psychologist not to push him to learn beyond his "inherited" ability. In consequence of this, he was left in the class to manage as best as he could. In effect, a self-limiting environment was created for him. When I met this 16-year-old, I discovered he was not dyslexic but only appeared to be so through the long history of his father's bullying, which caused him to be insensitive in his early learning. Once this was understood, and appropriate action was taken, he was performing equally well as the rest of his class by the end of the year.

Trained in this belief of genetic differences and forced to work in environments that do not give them time or energy to explore and make use of better teaching techniques, teachers invariably accept the differences presented by different students. The teacher will make some effort to improve the understanding of their students, but under the pressure of time and workload, they will invariably come to mark, stamp and record, which is what is expected of them as part of a processing society. This is the processing reality of school.

In other words, when this happens, it means that the thinking abilities of families are little disturbed by education. So, families who have developed better strategies for thinking produce children who think better, gain better marks and move into the university to become managers in society and industry, as their parents before them.

By the same means, families who are less aware of such higher thinking strategies produce children who think less and do not gain the marks to go to university. These children, the vast majority, move from school into employment and remain lower in their thinking, which renders them more reliant upon the guidance and direction of their managers.

The school achieves its aim of classifying student ability through a weeding-out process. It is actually a system designed to ensure the survival of the fittest, while ignoring the different advantages and disadvantages children find themselves in. Accordingly, it was long intended, and much remains, a system for those to survive better in who are better prepared for this by their parents, which has a strong socioeconomic factor.

Indeed, the system was always designed this way to maintain the status quo through generations, as we have just indicated. The educational system was never intended to be fair, and those proclaiming recently "No child left behind" clearly do not understand how it operates.

Once we begin to see this picture of school and society, we begin to see what is really happening, especially if we replace the words thinking abilities which are socially inherited with the word intelligence which is reasoned to be genetically inherited, with all the political connotations we have yet to discover.

It is to specifically dispel this belief of an inherited intelligence constructing the ability of the normally born individual, and so to ensure all children do actually obtain equality in learning, for which this book was originally written.

However, as we are to see, other factors have since come on the horizon. We must now understand the need for the general citizen to have a far higher level of general reasoning if they are to control the politics that seek to control their life, and also to prepare them better to face a world dominated, if not controlled, by artificial intelligence.

As artificial intelligence rapidly challenges the role of the human being in society, it is imperative that we better prepare our youth for the challenges that will await them in the times they will live.

To do this, we need to understand why their ability to reason has always been desired to be controlled, and so why we have never really understood what the word *intelligence* actually means and what role it really plays in our lives.

———————————

Chapter Two

The Ordering of a People

"Rationality belongs to the cool observers, but because of the stupidity of the average man he follows not by reason but by faith. And the naive faith of the proletariat requires necessary illusion and over-important oversimplification, which has to be provided by myth makers, to keep the ordinary person on the right course."

Noam Chomsky.

From our most primitive times, we have lived in fear of each other. The drive that enables us to survive is also the drive of our insecurities. As the insecurities of one caused them to seek to control others to gain a higher sense of self-security, so a system of community control became established. As the size of the community expanded, it became a nation and from nations a civilisation was brought into being.

The ability to talk freely and to share feelings openly was and, of course, still is the way to overcome the insecurities that play in the minds of people. On the political level, this ability to talk freely is the means to find a common path by which all may live in a state of relative harmony. It was to promote this ability to talk and to compel another to listen that the concept of democracy arose.

The idea of democracy is to provide a means of government, where people can live in relative peace with each other. Democracy is the concept of freedom through mutual respect within a community, maintained through the free expression and action of thought. This is in contrast to unjust political systems, which use means of intimidation and force to control their people.

Yet, democracy can be less than it is thought of, when a controlling minority acts without the intelligence of the majority in the decisions that affect the lives of all.

Both world wars and all those before and since occurred because democracy failed. When wars occur, the majority become conditioned by the controlling minority to murder and do horrendous things to other human beings they know nothing about, save that they wear a different uniform and follow a different flag, who are themselves a majority controlled by a minority. When in peace, the majority can be conditioned by the control of their intelligence and raised through insecurity to conform to the designs of the minority. When this occurs the citizen is not to dwell too much upon this control.

So, as the child in school is prepared to be a citizen, they are raised on patriotic themes. They are inspired to follow the design created for them by learning of great rulers and glorious battles, of empires created, and of great deeds done. They are not to know of the innocent men and women in the past who were beaten, imprisoned, tortured and exiled to prevent them from infecting the minds of those more ready to conform, just as they are not to dwell upon neighbour spying upon neighbour and secret organisations of informers which their own democracy evolved out of. It is not difficult in discussing this to understand why the history of man lies in the control of information. Civilisation is the control of information, and by this it is the hidden history of the control of intelligence.

This is the real history of man we know too little about, and little dwell upon in our cosmopolitan life. Unless, that is, we hear some fleeting incident of slave labour or torture in a third world country while we are eating our breakfast cereals, and momentarily wonder how this could happen before we rush to our first appointment, realising the stress we will be in to find the money to pay the debits we hide ourselves from that hold us within a web of insecurity. To make our lives easier and safer, we seek politicians to act for us, and choose them based on the efforts they promise.

Democracy, we believe, is the right to vote, and by this, the means to control the society we live in. The greater truth, which is not so obvious, is that democracy means to have unrestricted access to, and to be provided with all the information relating to that vote in an unbiased manner, **to be educated to understand how to evaluate that information,** and then to have the right to vote freely upon it.

When we think of a democratic society today, we think of different political parties and how they represent the needs and desires of those who support them. Indeed, this appears so, when prior to an election each party will present their manifesto, as it plays to the concerns and interests of the electorate. However, once a party obtains office, that manifesto may change, as the political leader is influenced by the financiers of their country, whose money controls the movement of people, food, production, and communication. Therefore, behind every political leader, there will be a controlling faction that, by controlling the lives of the people, can influence the actions of their government.

This body of private interest can devise a plan to serve their sole concerns and use "their" politicians to present their plan to the people. This is done in such a way that it appears to emanate from the people. So, the media and newspapers tell the people what they are to know, and guide them in how they are to think upon this. Once the people believe in the need for this plan, the politicians appear to take it over as if they are representing the people's interests. As the politicians control the development of this solution, they convince the people of their satisfaction with the progress and outcome of it. They achieve this through their control of the information they release and by how they seek to persuade the people to trust them through their control of the media.

Bluntly stated, one purpose of the school is to cause the general citizen to be so easily governed. As we saw in *The Illusion of Education* and hinted at in the previous chapter, the child in school is raised to be a dualistic thinker and so largely remains one as an adult in their society. In other words, when information is very clearly presented and the individual can understand the pros and cons of an argument (in the ways they are presented), they can feel able to make a sound "Yes" or "No" decision. However, when they are provided with confusing half-truths, the citizen moves into a state of uncertainty from which they either become apathetic and lose interest or desire to trust a more knowledgeable person to make the decision for them - this, of course, will be the politician they feel they can most trust.

So, we find that, in general terms, and as we have just discussed, when the school child is not taught how to think, then their later reasoning ability as a working member of their society tends to cause them to comply with the decisions made for them. We can recognise this in many of the major policies that governments make, which, while directly affecting the lives of the people, such as trading options, environmental policies and going to war, are based on decisions not made by the people.

Of course, we cannot all make the decisions, and so we elect those whom we trust will work to our benefit. In doing this, they rely upon experts to advise them. Human nature inevitably plays its part when aspects of power are involved, and so personal interests distort the process of what should be of equal benefit to all. Such is the reality of democracy as it has evolved, with the electorate being largely inconsequential and raised to be trusting to the greater movement of their governing body.

One of the reasons these now fourteen books were written is to enhance the transformation of democracy, from one that less represents the individual to one that more represents the truer concept of democracy. This may only come about through the greater education of the individual's intelligence. As we now realise, we must educate the individual in how they think, and not simply assess the way they do this.

Such an action will require our awareness of how intelligence has long been cultivated to allow the ease of man's government. By the nature of a lesser means of communication than we have today, and by receiving a general education where they were not taught how to evaluate information, the general citizen of earlier times was guided to play an illusory role in the democratic process. We have not yet evolved out of this framework and do not envisage the danger of this when our children will live in a world dominated, if not controlled, by artificial intelligence.

However, the dramatic developments in the movement of information this century, as we have witnessed through the Internet and social media, must to some extent change how a government works. As we shall discuss in a later book, our technology today suggests fundamental changes in the democratic process. Iceland has already opened up the way for this to occur through the technology of social media. By the establishment of a crowd-sourced constitution, Iceland enables its citizens greater control in the many different processes of their lives.

Since the development of democracy hinges upon the extent by which people can share their feelings and views, and so how information is evaluated without bias, it is a concern to us to understand why there never was a desire for children to be taught how to learn to reason or how to think better in school — ignore for the moment the ineffective designs to induce critical thinking in lessons.

To understand why the child in school was never designed to think beyond the cultivated intelligence of their parents through the jobs they do and the social opportunities they gained from this, we first need to understand that even though our times are different from those of the 19th-century, the processes by which we govern and educate have their foundations in that time. Those foundations were not wholly overturned by the social developments of the 1960s and afterwards. It is rather that they evolved from what they were, to what appears to be more acceptable in a different social atmosphere.

Chapter Three

The Conspiracy of Civilisation

Until the Industrial Revolution, the economic base of virtually all civilisations lay rooted in agriculture, where ownership of land determined both social rank and governing responsibility. Historically, a country was normally acquired in the very beginning by military operations, led by a strong leader. Once the occupation had come into order and people no longer posed a threat, the military style of government imposed to keep order changed as quickly and as smoothly as possible to a form of civil administration. This administration appeared to represent the interests of the ruler, while being considerate of the needs of the people.

In practice, this saw how a country was owned and governed by the ruler who rented their lands to a circle of nobility, who supported their right to power. In their turn, the nobles rented their land to farmers who employed labourers to work the fields. The administration, the supplies, and recreation that kept these forces together were provided by a small number of enterprising middle-class members.

This system of people organisation was laid upon a hierarchical structure of social ranking, where imbalanced possessions and privileges induced into the members of the society a sense of insecurity. This insecurity tied the people to the concept of work, suppressing their tendency towards lethargy and fuelling their inventiveness. By each labouring for the other, compliance to the hierarchical system ensured that the general requirement of each was met and their society maintained its ability to function.

Central to this manufactured stability was the means for work, which brought a measure of respect for the society. It was this that kept people living together in an acceptable state of harmony. We will return to this point when we eventually come to discuss the effects AI could bring to our future societies through the creation of mass unemployment.

However, whatever injustices arose from a social system designed to support a ruler, and there were many, a working order for a large collection of people was established and maintained. In an idealistic state, the more competent were to care for the less competent, but the nobility of this seldom became practised. In the face of ill government or selfish administration, techniques of intimidation and violent oppression held the support of the people. Yet, suppressive techniques invariably fuelled the insurrection they were designed to prevent, and the machinery of government desired some means of educating the people to accept the social role of their family for the greater good.

When Glaucon asked Socrates how they could maintain social stability in the face of social injustice, Socrates replied, "We will create a myth. This myth will state that although all are brothers, the gods created the people out of different metals: gold, silver and brass or iron. We will, then, invent an oracle foretelling how the State will come to ruin, should it be ruled by a man of brass or iron".

Such a myth, and all civilisations have created their own version of this, as in Europe, we have the old belief that royalty has blue blood, required a mechanism to uphold it.

Religion, as it arose through man's political manipulation of divine inspiration, came to satisfy this need. It was solely through the organisation of religion that a solidarity within people could be manufactured, as each was caused to focus upon a force greater than that which separated their interests.

This relative harmonisation of a collective people was the greatest achievement of religion. It accomplished this by impressing upon its members a complete dependency in the spiritual force it identified with, and by causing them to recognise the civil authority that guided them. By welding both together in the minds of the people, religion was able to guide them in their acceptance of their governing power when its behaviour was neither unjust nor cruel. When it was, religion distracted the people's objection by bringing focus upon spiritual salvation. This was only possible through the engineering of an unquestioning blind faith.

The genius of religion to acquire this blind faith lay in its invention of the art of tradition, where, through rituals and ceremonies, it removed from man the search for explanation. To do what has always been done is to preserve a habit. A habit is a function that negates the necessity of reason. As Koestler described it, "Habit deprives man of originality, causing him to do what he does without reasoning why".[16]

So it is that from the moment civilisation began, the common man was taught to convey his sense of responsibility to a higher force, where in doing so, he was induced to surrender his sense of reason. (We may reflect here, how and why school today does not teach its students how to think or reason.) However, the test of man's faith and the value of his social existence lay in how he could release himself from the insecurity by which he judged others, in the belief that a higher force was judging him.

So complete was this process of tradition that once a person entered into it, it took over the order of their life, and was thereafter able to control the lives of their children and the generations that followed. Each individual, in their turn, being indoctrinated from birth and raised within an unyielding order.

To bring into effect its purpose, religion enticed its ways into the life of man, where it required of each complete dedication. Yet, man could be distracted, and to impress upon him the power of its existence, inspiring temples and grand buildings were erected by religion under its partnership with government. The power that was sought and gained, acquired its stability through the endorsement of legal laws and religious codes, which supported this dual authority

Through its power to bind people to a common goal, religion provided the essential ingredient to the creation and maintenance of a civilisation. It was in recognition of this that when Communism, and later Fascism, came about in the 20ª century, each in its own way sought to substitute the role it played.

Russia, for instance, after the revolution, replaced the purpose projected by religion with that of the state. Aware that workers were as productive as their reward, it replaced the concept of individual gain with that of a collective ideal. The difficulty in maintaining this was to produce an accepted philosophy of endurance, which would overcome disillusionment brought out by hard work with little gain. This was a situation religion never had to contend with, because its followers had been raised to expect hardship and failure in this lifetime as a test for the next. However, it was in struggling to maintain the conviction of its philosophy that Communism became increasingly oppressive, where, in the hands of Stalin, it became the opposite to the ideal of freedom of reason and expression that Marx had designed it to provide.

By contrast, Fascism, under Hitler, replaced the idolisation of the state community with the personification of its dictator. Hitler had realised in his youth, by the long and detailed studies he had made of the works of Schopenhauer, how the collective consciousness of a people could be directed through a ritualistic order.[17]

Such control over a collective people, as woven by Communism and Fascism, was visible and, in being so, invariably sought to preserve itself through intimidation and force. Religion, by claiming to be directed by a force far beyond human comprehension, less visibly sowed its censorship of reason. Yet, its greatest threat was always in heresy.

From the Greek word hairesis, heresy demanded freedom of choice. It was because Socrates had taught, encouraged, and demanded independent thinking, and had so interfered with the teachings and identity of the religion in his time that he was brought to execution. Therefore, the rack of the Inquisition, the burning of heretics, and the suspicion of witchcraft were nothing more than tactics of religion to maintain its influence over people by opposing this right to heresy.

The age-old conflict, therefore, between civil authority and intellectual leadership was nothing more than a guise for the struggle of religion to control technological advances, which would encourage open thinking. So, while we may look upon the inventions of the past as the accumulation of knowledge, it would be more true to see how centuries of wisdom have been censored to administer the social government of man.

Ptolemy's mathematical support of Aristotle's idea that the Earth is the centre of the Universe remained unchallenged for 1,500 years, because it gained the sanction of religion. Through belief in this reasoning, religion could explain how Earth and Man were created by God for God's special purpose. Yet, Ptolemy's mathematics only held if the Moon swung closer at times to the Earth, making it appear twice as large on these occasions. All astronomers knew this was never so, and yet to question this knowledge was unthinkable. When Galileo finally did, it was not before he faltered twice, having been shown the instruments of torture.

The reasoning of man was always to be kept under control, because religion well knew that as the intelligence of man developed, so would he come to question its wisdom, and after this, its authority. It was for this greater reason that William Tyndale, who made the first translation of the Bible from Latin to English so that all could read and understand it, was dispatched from this life by the fire of the Holy Inquisition. The problem was not so much in the wording of the Bible as conveyed from God, but in the Canon Laws that had been secretly laid between its pages. These were the personal directives of popes, as seen in the worship of saints, who sought to achieve their human aim under the guise of God's authority. The existence of these laws were to be kept hidden from people who were not allowed to learn Latin.

As we may see, the history of civilisations is founded in the censorship of reason or what we today may more commonly see as intelligence. As religion and government vied for control of the people, both knew that real stability lay in how they could control the minds of the people. Their tool for this control lay in how education was to be administered.

Accordingly, when the technology of a society did not demand it, education was to be deprived to all, save those required to maintain its administrative functioning. When we read of James Mill, who wrote in the beginning of the 19th century that "The purpose of education .. is to render the mind, as far as possible, an operative cause of happiness,"[18] we may be inspired to conjure up a vision of an idyllic Byron romanticising his way through the Grand tour. If we do, then that is all we may do, for although education to the poor had been introduced since the Middle Ages, its purpose was more to breed within their ranks discipline and obedience than to give them access to knowledge. Such education as they were provided with was elementary and designed to give no more than a basic proficiency in the tasks expected of their rank.

However, as the technology of man inevitably rose in the 19th century through industrialisation, so a more general application of education became necessary, and with this came a greater awareness of how to change the order of things.

The enigma that has always faced the partnership of civil authority and religion, and indeed it is the one most addressed by the writing of these books, is how society may advance its technology and yet balance the reasoning of its masses so that they will maintain an ordered state of living.

As we saw in our books *The Illusion of Education* and *The Illusion of School,* the education of reason was to be reserved for those who gained access to university (usually through influence), for the more responsible work roles expected of them. May we see that the concept of civilisation, by its very nature, relies upon the conditioning, if not censorship, of intelligence.

Poor schools, industrial schools, church schools and private schools, not to mention the public and later state schools, were all built upon a religious framework. Therefore, until the expansion of the school system in the 19th century, when more teachers were needed than religion could provide, teachers in school were traditionally ordained.

In point of fact, the opportunity of education was so restrictive that one of the very few ways a child of poor origin could gain an education was to join a branch of religion, and so become a servant to it. This was much the case with Johann Mendel, who, as the son of a farmer and plagued by debt, joined a religious teaching order to continue the education he could no longer afford. The consequences of this enabled him to discover the mechanics of genetic inheritance, as we shall later come to discuss.

However, the old idea of The Grand Ascending Chain of Perfection saw that God created life on different levels, with man being on the top level. It was a natural consideration of this thinking by the church that God also created men of different abilities, since this allowed it to endorse the ancient belief that a ruler was divinely chosen. In turn, this spiritual support for the ruler's right for absolute control maintained the power link between the government and the religion of the people.

Because education was to be an arm of religion, and as religion was based upon conditioning the reasoning of the citizen, it was a natural condition of their education that the intelligence of the child was to be more conditioned than developed by school. This is the root of why we do not teach children how to think in school today.

We have long forgotten this in the world in which we live, but it was well known by our forefathers. Yet, the way we teach children today is still based on this expectation of control of intelligence, even though most educationalists are totally unaware of it.

The secret of civilisation, then, is religion, because it manufactures stabilisation. In the long history of civilisation, the role of religion has been imperative in causing people to comply with the inequality of their social systems. The common man struggled against this inequality, as he strove to gain his own identity.

The way for this, he was coached to realise that commerce (the lifeblood of civilisation) was to be found in wealth. Wealth, he realised, gave him the means to control his own destiny. But as wealth was the bait that drove him, it was at the same time the means that trapped him into maintaining the operations of his society. The opportunity to change social position depended upon wealth. This was carefully controlled in the agricultural era because it was the key to stability. However, when the Industrial Revolution occurred, it changed once and for all the means by which this stability was to be governed.

The importance of the Industrial Revolution lay in the means it gave for the middle class to disturb the political control of the ruling class, and for the poor to find a way out of the ignorance and poverty they had long been trapped within. The contained pressure of this social disunity finally blew through the French Revolution. When it did, it heralded a warning to all nations of a deeply threatening political turmoil that could not be ignored.

Chapter Four

The Industrial Era unleashed a Frightening Chaos

The history of each country is written with revolts, and in most cases civil wars that sought to correct the injustices that arose within the agricultural civilisation. Yet, so fearful and so radical were the objections witnessed in the French Revolution that its reign of terror inspired a change in the form of government of all people. Before the revolution, there was so little of the happiness and shared well-being that is necessary to maintain a strong society. Without the strength to suppress objections or hold support for its religion, the system crumbled due to the dissatisfaction it had created.

In France, and in the world of its European influence, Napoleon brought wonderful order to the chaos that spewed out of the legacy of Louis 16th. However, he belonged to a new order and was unwelcome by the older power structures that struggled to overthrow him. When eventually they did, all European policy was dominated by the personality of the Austrian Prince Metternich.

Metternich saw revolution as a disease, and warned that any indication of revolt anywhere, in any country, must be ruthlessly suppressed if it were not to infect another country. This "Coachman of Europe" bullied and cajoled every European power, except that of England, to crack down on civil liberties as he sought to reinstate the political stability that Napoleon had so effectively taken from them.

Yet, Napoleon had only become the figurehead of a change that was far deeper than his order of power. The roots of this change lay not in the metal of the French cannon, but in that of the English Industrial Revolution. As machines had taken over the place of men, the structure of civilisation had shifted from an agricultural to an industrial economic base. It was the social changes that came through this that were to give birth to the transformation of the state, from one ruled by aristocratic and administrative rule to one defined by The Rights of Man.

The birth of the professions, which served the mechanics of this new state, widened the influence of the middle classes and gave fuel to the philosophical ideas of individual freedom, which this decree personified. That it did not explode in England, but in France, was only a consequence of the earlier social changes by which the British had gained a sense of freedom that had been too long denied to the French. Thus, it was through the blood-stained scythe of the French Revolution that this sapling of civil liberty sprang.

Yet, while it was this very civil liberty that pushed Napoleon to prominence, so was it this that became the very threat to the stability he was seeking to establish in his new empire. As Napoleon struggled to impose his order, he did so by imposing curfews that controlled this liberty, but it could not now be smothered. During his reign, this dream of civil liberty moved from the desperation of the lower class to the newly educated sons of the middle class, who now held greater influence over the economy.

While many focused upon Waterloo as removing a tyrant, too few were aware of this liberty seeking to rise again. When it burst out once more, it did not do so with the frustration to mindlessly destroy as it had earlier. Now it had direction from the minds of the young intelligentsia who sought to give birth to new ideas and new designs for society, all with the vigour of youth. While Metternich sought to outmanoeuvre this "disease" by outlawing political associations through the spying and marking of radical professors and students in universities, he could not contain the breadth of this movement.

Even in England, conspirators were caught hatching a plot to blow up the whole British cabinet in 1820. Like whispers in the dark, discontent spread through the ranks of an undisciplined corps of intellectual idealists, patriots, and liberals who dreamed in the splendid romance of a free people to live under the right of a free government. With their sense of nationalism and liberalism, they gave fire to all that could be different. "In the two thousand years of recorded world history" wrote Stendhal in 1824 "...so sharp a revolution in customs, ideals and beliefs has perhaps never occurred before."[19]

At this most inconvenient of times to civil authorities, a series of agricultural failures led to serious depressions in industry and commerce that gave birth to a dangerous economic crisis. The cost of living went beyond most people's means, agitating the long-term frustration held towards political suppression, and brought threat to the breakdown of society. The 7th edition of the Encyclopedia Britannica, written in 1830, explains how "The frame of society seemed breaking up, and a wild deluge of human passion, untamed by moral feeling, unchecked by law, threatened to overwhelm all .... with a nation apparently resolving into anarchy .... there was no hope."[20]

England reacted swiftly to her problem by bringing in reforms and easing upon the infantile surges of union activity, where, by so doing, she escaped the powder keg that was building up in Europe as she had long done. Equally, American society was not immune to the agitation boiling across the Atlantic and had to introduce its own political concessions to appease its population. As America struggled through its own economic depression in the 1830s, President Jackson was prompted to give more citizens the right to vote, and so bring about his great transformation of the American government, making it more than ever before "a government of the people, by the people". Before this, such representation of right had been restricted to landowners in the tradition of European aristocracy.

On the European continent, however, agricultural failures followed one after the other, until they triggered off a domino effect in the mid-1840s, bringing widespread industrial and economic collapse. Unemployment soared more than it had done previously, and demonstrations became ever more violent. Machines were smashed, property destroyed, and innocent protestors hanged. The smell of anarchy drifted up from the discontent in which the mass of the people lived.

In the two decades that followed 1830, over three million people (a great number in those days) left Great Britain and hordes more from Europe and Scandinavia to find a better life in the New World. Inspired by the genius of Jefferson's words that "All men are created equal…life, liberty and the pursuit of happiness," and that land was to be freely gained, the poor left their countries in droves, all believing they could find a way to control their own destinies. Those trapped in the Old World became increasingly frustrated. All that governments could do was to invent worthless polices to bide time, and use militia to maintain order.

Finally, in February 1848, a violent turmoil broke out in Paris over job losses and price increases, setting loose a chain reaction that spread rapidly to other capitals of Europe. Sentiments spread faster than the words that carried them, and suddenly, all countries of Europe were witnessing a massive reaction to authority. Panic struck their establishments, and leaders lost their nerve.

King Louis Philippe of France, cousin to the beheaded Louis 16th, fled to England to keep his. The Emperor Ferdinand of Austria (then the most powerful country in Europe) declared he would agree to anything to regain peace. After which, he and his chief minister Metternich, who once had boasted that the troubles of the preceding twenty years had been a loudness about nothing, found themselves following the French king to England. The only country that appeared stable, and only so because its middle class had gained what they wanted by earlier reforms, and had contented their workers.

Yet, the British establishment watched nervously the events on the Continent and kept a very tight rein on political opinion in their own backyard. Ernest Jones, a prominent leader of the Chartist Movement, was sent to prison for two years (solitary confinement without the right to speak to anyone) for making inflammatory speeches. Many other such insurgents were transported to a sunnier climate.

Meanwhile, Metternich's reactionary period of Europe viewed its own end, as people violently demanded constitutional rule, expansion of the suffrage, freedom of the press, the right to join a trade union, and the right to take strike action. All these are the intentions of the people to govern themselves. So real was the danger behind these claims that they were readily agreed to by governments.

Almost instantly, thousands of uncensored newspapers sprang up, giving further fuel to feelings. Now, free to meet in political discussion, tens of thousands attended mass rallies. The like of which had never been seen before. By mid-April, scarcely two months since this pregnancy had burst, the whole of Europe was in a wild frenzy. Drunk with too much freedom too soon, the people believed nothing could stop them.

Yet, all this was an ill-borne illusion. Desperate to bring order to their collapsing world, rulers now brought their armies into the cities. Military suppression was fast and ruthless. In Paris, in June of this year,

3,000 people suspected of being involved in a worker's dispute were dragged from their homes and slaughtered in cold blood. The carnival of gaiety had turned into one of terror as widespread executions took place in every capital, and most cities and towns across Europe.

Socialist organisations and free newspapers were closed down. Paranoia became widespread, and extensive secret police networks infiltrated any aspect of political interest. Freedom of expression was harshly suppressed, and newspapers were heavily censored.

By the winter of 1848, it was all over. Much had been gained by the people, and almost just as much lost. Although in other ways, civil liberties had gained a certain recognition, even if they were heavily controlled. Military suppression was quickly replaced by the passivity of a new policing order, and an army of bureaucracy was trained to construct a machinery of modern state that gave more power to a centralised government than it had ever had before.

To the colossal disappointment of many, 1848 appeared to be a fruitless exercise of revolution against order. Yet, this was not so, for a political revolution was beginning to unfold piece by piece. This year had merely been the preparation for a gentler, though far deeper disturbance of what was to come.

While riots in Berlin were dwindling, and Viennese students were beginning to pick up their books again, two German political refugees in England were conspiring to change the structure of civilisation. To this aim, Karl Marx and Frederick Engels had recently published their Communist Manifesto in England, and were eagerly engineering branches of underground movements throughout Europe. These people were not a union of cloth cap grumblers. They represented a fanatical movement, dedicated to promoting the joint political action of working-class people in all countries of the world to end social inequality.

As Engels warned the new middle-class in 1848, "Fight on bravely, then, gentlemen of Capital! We need your help, we even need your rule on occasions. You must clear from our path the relics of the Middle Ages and absolute monarchy. ... You must centralise, you must change

all the more or less destitute classes into real proletarian recruits for us.
... Your reward shall be a brief time of rule. You shall dictate laws, you
shall bask in the sun of your own majesty, you shall banquet in the royal
halls and woo the king's daughter, but remember, the hangman stands
at the door." [21]

Marx 1848

It is worthwhile pausing for a moment here to reflect upon what this
really meant, because to discuss the ideology of Marx is to only give the
discussion relevance when the conditions and times in which he
appeared can be found. This was a time when social deprivation and
illiteracy were the normal conditions under which the masses of people
lived 150 years ago. To say that Marx, and the like-minded people who
followed him, desired the collapse of a governing system that provided
advantages for a relative few at the cost of unimaginable poverty and
suffering for the many, is to dilute the fears of poverty, hunger, dirt,
illness and ignorance in which most of civilisation struggled. What is
little realised is that a key article of Marx's manifesto demanded:

"Free education for all children in public schools, and
abolition of child factory labour." [22]

The education of reason, the means to achieve this, and the reason for so doing, is, we are to find, the issue upon which much of these books revolve. However, when Marx died in 1883, Engels said at his funeral: "Just as Darwin had discovered the law of evolution in human organic nature, so Karl had discovered the law of evolution in human history."[23] For the reasons we may now understand, while the establishment applauded Darwin, it was less generous to Marx, as capitalistic systems remain so to this day, where they promote the image of a Marxist as one intent on the destruction of moral virtues and a respectable society.

In truth, and its testimony can be found in any history book, it was only through such radical characters as Marx that a more balanced society was forced into existence, so that today most people live above the poverty line, all children have a right to an education, and as I was able to publish this book so you are free to read it.

Chapter Five

The Struggle for Order

The greatest problem that had faced earlier social movements had lain in their difficulty to unite a people who would be committed enough not to fail under intimidation. As we have seen, the masses of people who lived under an agricultural system were kept in a state of ignorance and simple reason by the low level of their schooling. Tied to rural farms, they were widely scattered and too vulnerable to landowners to take stance with their objections. Fear of eviction from their home and community was a ready answer to any complaint they may make.

The Industrial Revolution brought irreversible change to this. Its greatest contribution to mankind was not to be measured in steam and steel, but in the organisational possibilities it gave to the lower structures of society to improve their living conditions.

Large-scale manufacturing demanded factories, and these required labour. To accommodate this need, massive relocation programs were instituted, which brought fragmented rural populations to form dense communities of workers. To house and supply the needs of these people, new industrial cities sprang up, and quiet market towns were transformed into gigantic metropolises, which bulged at their seams. Within the space of 30 years, from 1861 to 1891, Birmingham swelled from 296,000 to 523,000, Liverpool from 444,000 to 704,000 and Manchester from 339,000 to 645,000 inhabitants.[24]

Attracted to these urban slums, which replaced their rural slums with the utopia of running water and lavatories, people were compacted in a manner that gave them strength in a solidarity they had seldom had before. Yet, it was not until the 1848 revolutions, inspired by the middle classes struggling over idealist and national causes, that the lower classes gained confidence in the belief of what may be possible.

By this inspiration, by the security they received from each other, and by the direction provided by philosophers such as Marx, differing factions of a socialist movement began to sprout everywhere. In the early stages, divided by strong differences of opinion, they kept themselves weak in negotiations. It was to be many decades before a single well organised movement was to come into being. Delayed as it was with the threat of imprisonment or transportation, the right to belong to a union did not come until 1871. In our day and age, it seems innocent enough to want to belong to a union, but just 150 years ago, such thoughts could have placed you in jail, or seen you ripped from your family and sent to the other side of the world in a prison ship, never to see your wife and children again!

Despite the mishmash beginnings of these various social factions, which were disorganised and undirected, the establishment took them extremely seriously. It had no choice, for it realised that once these teething problems had been resolved and the socialist movement could operate in unity, it would have the ability to completely disrupt the whole economic framework of this "new" industrialised civilisation.

So rapid was the impact of this movement that by the 1880s, those countries whose government was chosen by the electorate found a new political force in their midst. Countries that tried to suppress this open movement found they only caused it to go underground and turn to terrorism. The assassination of the Russian Tsar Alexander 2nd in 1881 sent a shockwave through the establishment of every country in Europe.

From 1848, Europe had more than ever been beset with secret societies. The whole structure of European civilisation was infiltrated with secret organisations containing spies and informers. Some of these organisations aimed to spread the growth of socialist ideas, while those from the establishment sought to contain them.

The problem for those in the design of the social and economic structuring of society was how to control this rising socialism.

As civil authority and religion had always known, the key to controlling the people **lay in the control of their reason,** and in this, their sentiments. Providing the people were not starving or terrorised, they were congenial, even if they grumbled along the way to follow the banner of God, King and Country and in so doing conformed to the order and stratification of their society. There were two essential requirements to maintain control of this reason:

First. It was important to keep the people in small and relatively isolated communities. This kept them weak and subservient to the organisation of their higher authority.

Second. They were to be kept in a general state of ignorance, not just to prevent them from questioning their authority but also to keep their knowledge of the world in which they lived minimal and unrelated. The people were to think of their wives, their husbands, and their children, their health and happiness. They were to dwell upon the changes of the weather and the personalities of those about them as they struggled through life from youth to old age. They were to live within an economic climate that was never to satisfy their needs, and always to be caused, with a careful balance, to struggle for them. They were to dream, but not to know the dreams of others, or the challenges that others had faced and overcome. They were to face life with their limited experiences and not to know of what others had once achieved, unless those achievements honoured their system.

However, as the Agricultural Age moved into the Industrial Age, both of these factors of population control were tested. The first had worked admirably when the economic base lay in agriculture. It never would again with, the occurrence of the Industrial Revolution.

Of the second, the standing ignorance of the people had to be reduced as their technology rose, and so demanded of them greater working competence.

When a general education was introduced to satisfy this need, it brought with it access to the experiences of other people and other times. This knowledge built within the student a reservoir, or arsenal, of solutions to the problems of their life. This knowledge strengthened their desire to question the forces that played with that life, and so they sought to seek and suggest alternatives that could change it for the better. Education, for this reason, was the greater factor that threatened to wither the establishment's control of its people.

So, we find that in the time when the managers of civilisation were greedily exploiting every asset they could, and found themselves held back by a general illiteracy, the greatest problem they faced was how to control the education they were being caused to release, while preventing the social turmoil they knew it would bring with it. The problem in short, as it may be imagined, was how could:

a) The social position of families in a society, be linked with

b) the educational needs of the new industrialised society. In such a way that,

c) it would be acceptable to all political elements in these most turbulent of times.

Graphically, the problem was seen in the following way:

First: The relationship between the members of a population, and the wealth that was distributed between them at that time, and their political affiliations, could be identified through three groups.

Group a) of the population was the wealthiest. Group b) the middle class, and group c) contained the poorer and illiterate members.

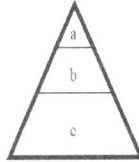

The boundaries of these and the proportion of each changed, of course, as the lower class gained greater opportunity and the middle class expanded.

Second: The organisation of every governing, commercial, industrial, and social structure that rose out of the Industrial Revolution was also based upon a pyramidal system of operation.

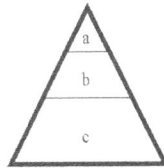

Group a) represented the owners and administrators. Group b) the skilled workers or clerical staff, and group c) the unskilled or manual workers. The problem was, how could the traditional loop of .....

Family - Education - Employment - Family

.... be given any stability, when employers were screaming for better educated workers, while at the same time the higher tiers of the social order were staunchly resisting such a demand?

As we are to see, this problem would be solved if mental worth could be explained as a consequence of inherited worth, because this would justify the arguments for social inequality, with each educated to know their place. This argument would require some type of scientific reasoning that would need to be understandable to the less educated, if their compliance to it were to be gained.

Conviction of this reasoning was gained through the creation of a graph. Since this graph plays a central role in much of our discussion, let us present it in a pictorial description of the use it plays, with the help of political colouring to emphasise what is happening here. Accordingly, we can see how the middle class merges from red into blue as their politics change, as their opportunities do.

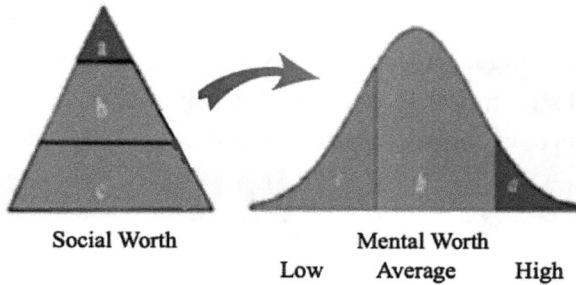

Social Worth　　　　Mental Worth

Low　　Average　　High

By this means, the stratified order of the social world could be retained through the acceptance of ability being genetically stratified.

In other words, each child can be said to be born with a different ability, but with the value of that ability said to be witnessed in the social success of their family line. To understand this is to begin to understand why this book was given the title of

"Intelligence: The Great Lie."

————————

Chapter Six

The Problem

The Peterloo Massacre

Man's primary urge within a group order, which we may conclude from all the points we have so far raised, is to preserve his identity and his values. He achieves this by the strength of the influence he can gain. Indeed, the history of civilisations is written, page-by-page, with accounts of individuals and orders of people who, for personal gain or some higher ideal, strove to maintain the continuity of the social order that most benefited their interests.

One does not have to read or even know of Machiavelli's book *The Prince* to comprehend the desperate measures by which one people will resort to, to maintain their influence over another people. In the range of ruthless tactics to subtle scheming that could be engineered, we may dwell upon how the ruling classes of the 19th century devised all manner of plans to control the rising influence of the middle and lower classes. With each gain these classes achieved came a loss to the establishment in its influence of control and the character of its identity.

In earlier times, military force had been an easy answer to social dissatisfaction and civil disorder, but the reverberations that followed the Peterloo massacre that occurred in England of 1819, which saw sabre welding cavalry attacking a peaceful demonstration of 80,000 people, still served as a warning in the political folly of any brutal attempt to suppress a cause of the people in these new times.

The solution, it may be imagined, was not simple. Those in the controlling structures of society were too well aware of how a growing socialism could take from them the world they knew, unless they could stop it. They also knew that if they employed force to control this movement, such action could well bring about the result they most feared. Indeed, some persuasive tactic was required, some means that would desire those in the lower structures to accept the situation and realise how better everyone would be if they remained in their place.

An idea was sought that was as subtle and as ingenious as the ruler/religion pact, which until now had ensured this order of civilisation. Some notion was urgently desired that would demonstrate the natural order of things, where this order should be the continuation of the system, albeit with better living conditions for all.

Following the 1848 revolutions, voices of philosophers rose for and against this tune. Those against the establishment, however, were suppressed by one means or another, so that their circulation was limited to underground information systems. The views for the establishment were, by comparison, freely and openly circulated, where they ranged from mild humanistic concern for the lower classes to entice their support to harsh warnings of the end of civilisation to inspire all to take these times seriously.

By the 1850s, the circulation of right-wing newspapers had increased dramatically, opening the way for a vast propaganda machine to come into function. This willingly depicted evil little men seeking to destroy the livelihood of the middle classes, and to violate the innocence of the ruler that God had provided for them.

Indeed, literature and entertainment have always been an invaluable source of manipulating the sentiments of a people. See in this Shakespeare's heroic portrayal of Henry V, which catered more to the political designs of his patron Elizabeth I, who sought to exemplify the glory of her lineage, than to an honest portrayal of the tyrannical butcher Henry really was. That human reason can be so easily swayed by compassion is as much a fortune as a misfortune to the defence of man's identity.

As the virtual whole of society was obliged to attend church service every Sunday, so the pulpit was the ideal platform to espouse the natural right of social inequality. In the same year that Marx published his Communist Manifesto, the hymn "All Things Bright and Beautiful" first appeared. For well over a century, this hymn indoctrinated and moulded the minds of churchgoers in Sunday service and small children in school assembly every morning of the week to believe that it was always correct to think:

> "The rich man in his castle, The poor man at his gate,
> God made them high and lowly...."

Beyond this, fictional stories and novels carry within their texts underlying themes that prompt sentiment and direction of values in the real world. Dickens' *A Tale of Two Cities* published in 1859, leaves no question as to the political direction its hero was drawing the reader. Later in the century, when Thomas Hardy so charmingly portrayed the life of simple people, he nevertheless weaved into these an admiration for inherited authority. The avidly read stories of Conan Doyle, equally centred upon characters who were pinned to a social structure that appeared to exist by its natural right.

Perhaps such authors merely reflected the flavour of their times, but by appealing to this, they gave witness to the contention that society ran smoothly when everyone knew their place and respected their betters. This was a tenet that would best be served by the categorisation of ability through social classification. A particularly extreme advocate of social classification was the French aristocrat, turned diplomat and novelist, the Comte de Gobineau.

In 1855, de Gobineau wrote, with sentiment and not scientific reasoning, *The Inequality of Human Races*. This was an anti-socialist work that stressed how the success of a society was dependent upon the quality carried through its bloodlines. Although the belief of race superiority was not a new one, and had at this time been much fuelled by colonialism, de Gobineau gave it substance and social application. "People...." he wrote "...no longer have the same blood, the worth of which has been gradually modified by successive mixture".[25]

De Gobineau's anti-democratic writings and excessively racist theories, expressed through the popularity of his novels, left great stains on the political designs of Europe. This was especially so when their flavour permeated through the influence he made upon Richard Wagner and more notably Friedrich Nietzsche.

The difficulty of qualifying such ideals of inborn elitism became more difficult as opportunities for people increased through technological advances. As different opportunities arose across the board, so it enabled people to erode the social barriers that had contained their parents. The problem that became more addressable was how could people be told without objection that their social standing was a consequence of their natural inheritance, and that it would be in their interests to comply with the existing stratification. This was a sentiment that ebbed social status with work responsibility.

Religion had always argued for the stability this gave, but people were becoming more informed of its intention and increasingly wary of it. That this was the age of science made it appropriate that the solution desperately sought after, which would maintain the socio-economic structure that fed this civilisation, would lie in "scientific" evidence. The man who was already underway with providing this solution was Sir Francis Galton, second cousin to Charles Darwin and the man who, more than anyone else, was to give de Gobineau's sentiments motorisation.

In fact, all our understanding today that intelligence is to some greater or lesser extent determined by inheritance, which is linked to the social achievements of a family line, and that it can be measured, can be traced back to Sir Francis Galton.

———————————————

"There are three kinds of lies.

Lies,

Dammed Lies, and

Statistics."

Benjamin Disraeli British Prime Minister
1868-1868 and 1874-1880.

Chapter Seven

The Solution

In 1869, Galton's first book, aptly named *Hereditary Genius,* came into print. In its introduction he gave approval, with the general concern of his class, that social turmoil would endanger the potential achievements if not survival of their civilisation.

"I propose to show in this book....." he wrote, "... that a man's natural abilities are derived by inheritance, under exactly the same limitations as are the form and physical features of the whole organic world."

He further wrote, and in these words lie much of a key to understand all that will follow: ..

"I shall show that social agencies of an ordinary character, whose influences are little suspected, are at this moment working towards the degradation of human nature."

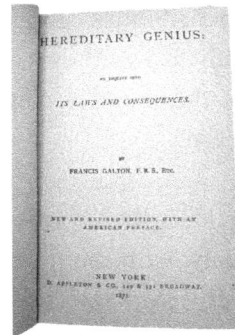

To make sure there was no misunderstanding about this, he drew on the French example where ....

"The Revolution and the guillotine made sad havoc among the progeny of her abler races."[26]

This was as much a theme to the introduction of his book as it was to his life's work. Galton was driven by an intense desire to show that ability was, to all intents and purposes, inherited. He was driven by a compulsive nature to convince everyone that civilisation would only do harm to itself if it failed to recognise that the best potential for the sons of a family were to be witnessed in the work held by their ancestors. Such merit, he insisted, reflected their calibre for work responsibility and social competence.

It may not be known precisely how Galton came to link social rank with work capability and this to reflect social responsibility, all tied to a neat inherited base, but it was certainly not a new idea. Five years before *Hereditary Genius* came into print, Fustel de Coulanges had finished his classic work *The Ancient City*. This book gave a detailed explanation of how the social structures of ancient civilisations came to be and how they worked. In this, de Coulanges related how social harmony was dependent upon a belief in the people that administrative and work responsibilities were passed through the mind and body skills of a family. It was thus a common if not traditional concept of Pagan orders that the life of a community depended upon the survival of discrete lineages.

The idea, then, that different families need to play different roles in a society, with the necessity that they be educated in the belief that this order is heritable, was not new. We may consider that it lies deep in the craft of kingship, along with the idea of blue blood, and is assuredly older than the recorded writing we have. We may add to this account a recent discovery in South America, which found that the Chimu people of ancient Peru (a vast civilisation before the time of the Incas), were impressed to believe that royal males came from a golden egg, royal females from a silver egg, and everyone else from a copper egg.[27]

Needless to say, it would not have been a big step for Galton, who was never a fan of religion, to take this pre-Christian idea, and in resurrecting it, fashion it to serve the needs of his time. Yet, wherever the idea came from, his book *Hereditary Genius* did appear in the most needed of times, and its author was swirled, as if by invisible forces, into public prominence.

Galton's book, however, was not projected to represent a nervous establishment warning the lower structures of unbalancing the system. It was to be the presentation of an honest scientist that the most reliable social design was created by inherited ability, and not by social injustices. This was the line adopted more recently by the authors of a book entitled *The Bell Curve*, as we shall later examine.

Embedded in a scientific presentation, Galton's book directly avoided the heated political arguments of that time, and yet its theme directly sought to solve them. Since the root of Galton's case always lay in his claim that social success was a testimony of inherited ability and not social influences, it is worth examining the connections upon which his own life was built. By inheritance, Galton was of immense personal wealth, and never slow to relate his exploits to those of the line of his world-famous half-cousin Charles Darwin.

The relationship between the Galtons and the Darwins was seeded when Darwin's grandfather, Erasmus, a prolific scientist and naturalist in his own right, published *The Laws of Organic Life* in 1794 and founded with other idealists the Lunar Society in Birmingham. This was a scientific group much in faith with the innovative thinking of Benjamin Franklin, which acquired its title through the nature of the society's meetings. As its members were busy people and could only meet in the late evenings, they chose to do so only when the moon was full, for the roads along which they travelled were often frequented by robbers. The title "The Lunar Society" was taken from their late-night activity.

The intentions of this so-named "The Lunar Society" attracted such forward thinkers as the innovative Josiah Wedgwood, and amongst others James Watt, who, by inventing the steam engine, had set forth the Industrial Revolution. As a friendship began to develop between Erasmus and Josiah, so the latter was elected by Erasmus to become a Fellow of the Royal Society in 1783. This was an influential scientific body with very strong political affiliations.

Thirteen years later, Josiah Wedgewood's daughter Susannah married Erasmus Darwin's son Robert, from his first wife. From this union came the infant Charles Darwin in 1809. Two years after Josiah had joined the Royal Society, Samuel Galton was elected to its ranks. In turn, his son, Samuel Tertius, then married Erasmus's daughter Frances, from his second marriage. From this union came Francis Galton in 1822.

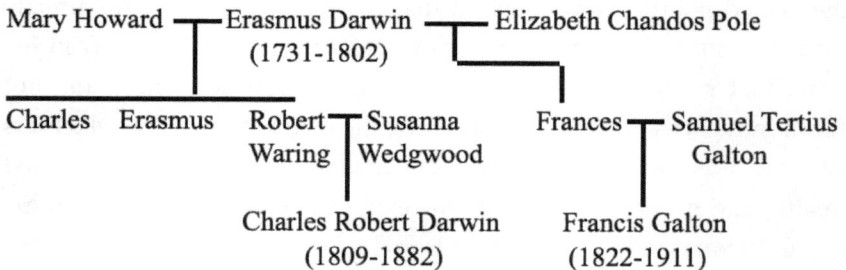

```
Mary Howard ──┬── Erasmus Darwin ──┬── Elizabeth Chandos Pole
              │    (1731-1802)      │
              │                     └──────────────┐
   ┌──────────┼──────────┐                         │
Charles   Erasmus   Robert ─┬─ Susanna     Frances ─┬─ Samuel Tertius
                    Waring  │  Wedgwood              │     Galton
                            │                        │
                   Charles Robert Darwin      Francis Galton
                        (1809-1882)           (1822-1911)
```

The environment, as it may be imagined, in which Galton was raised was both wealthy and energetically involved in innovative thinking. When we understand the type of childhood Galton was raised in and the people who were likely to have influenced him, it is understandable why he became so intrigued with the concept of science. In fact, Galton was struck with a fever to measure and classify any imaginable phenomena. However, before he was to make his name in science, Galton was to gain a reputation as an adventurer.

At the age of twenty-two, his father died. With the vast amount of wealth he inherited, Galton was able to leave his studies, which alternated between medicine and mathematics, to embark upon a number of adventures into the unknown wilds of Africa. It was through his writings of these adventures that Galton gained notable credibility as an explorer, and with this a reputation that brought him an appointment with the Royal Geographical Society. From this, he followed his paternal grandfather (Samuel Galton), and his maternal grandfather (Erasmus Darwin) into the Royal Society. It was while he was connected with this illustrious body that Darwin's *Origin of Species* was published in 1859.

The reasoning that God had created life on different levels, which was known as the "Grand Ascending Chain of Perfection," had already been whittled away by scientific theories at this time. Much of this was due to Lyell's theory, which described how life had been wiped out a number of times before by natural disasters, and by Lamarck's inheritance of acquired characteristics.

Lamarck was aware of an older species of giraffe with a short neck. He reasoned from this that subsequent generations tried to reach leaves beyond their height, and in doing so had stretched the neck. This theory reasoned that desire could change physical form, and so gave one of the first suggestions of how evolution could occur. Actually, Lamarck's theory was a serious contender to Darwin's for over half a century, even though it had been seriously undermined by Weismann in the 1880s. Therefore, before Darwin, there was a general acceptance that life was in some way linked together. That is, of course, with exception to the origin of that most noble species, religion had a vested interest in.

In an attempt to identify and classify life forms, religious concerns had hoped to find substance in the old idea of the Grand Ascending Chain of Perfection. It was to this aim that the ship "The Beagle" was acquired, and a young naturalist by the name of Charles Darwin set off on his voyage of discovery.

Darwin's findings were to prove otherwise, and for 20 years, he struggled with how he should reveal them. When he finally did, they were expounded with such clear logic that they immediately took hold of people's imagination. Infected by the aura surrounding the reasoning of his half-cousin, and how organisms could thereafter be classified, Galton found his niche by recognising the demand and supplying it.

However, the classification Galton was interested in, lay not with biological taxonomy but social taxonomy. In short, how each family may be ascribed their place in the structure of things, according to their natural ability.

So great was the zeal with which Galton pursued this interest that it devoured his energies for the remaining fifty years of his life. At heart, he was a true scientist, and consumed with a relentless urge to measure anything and everything. Prof. Forest (in discussion with me) raised the point that this restless need to measure may have developed from a long-term obsessional disorder that stemmed from his university studies. Yet, nothing consumed Galton more than his efforts to establish the rank of eminence as a proven inherited trait.

The lingering question that faces us is what drove Galton with such vigour for so many years of his life. Was he driven to such an endeavour merely to satisfy a scientific accomplishment, and was he and his work then taken over and given a boost by political factors?

Or, was it that as a man of great personal wealth and high social standing, he was driven to embark upon a political crusade for which he may have ultimately received his knighthood, when Darwin, who achieved immeasurably more, did not? We may not know, but it is true that Galton detested the lower classes and believed the highest breed of dog to be of higher intelligence than the lowest breed of man. After all, he had everything to lose by them.

Whatever conclusion we may come to, we must hold in mind the fever of those times — a mere 20 years after the 1848 revolutions by the common man that very nearly wiped out the civilisation Galton knew and cherished. Yet, this was now a time when socialism had burst out from its shell, demanding equality, and was prepared to fight tooth and nail for it. It would, then, have served the purpose of the establishment to have remained unseen while orchestrating such politically dangerous definitions of the rights, purposes, and opportunities of the masses.

In conclusion, all we may say is that some of Galton's personal papers show definite objection to democracy. He was noted for his distaste of people with average ability. In fact, he was contentious of equality in all manner. "Women," he saw, "were to function as a medium for the transmission of genius from father to son." In his unpublished utopian novel *Kantsaywhere*, Galton advocated an authoritarian rather than a democratic government as being the most ideal. As Sweet put it:

"So the land of Kantsaywhere is, despite the coyness of the title, a country that may not be quite so alien as it first appears. Some version of its structures and processes is legible in the OFSTED report of 2013 (See p.60), in the psychometric test at the job interview, and on the Internet dating site. (OFSTED is the educational arm of the UK government.) You might also hear their echo in government statements on the wisdom of early intervention in the lives of children who have been judged statistically likely to develop into underachieving or socially disruptive adults."[28]

To the end, Galton was well noted for his strong objections towards socialism. This was well illustrated in the scientific authority he created, which restlessly sought to prove the importance of a minority controlling the activities of the majority, directly determined by their natural abilities.

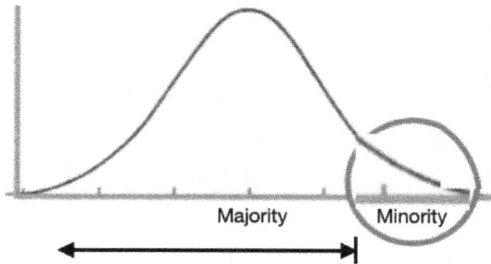

The guise through which Galton placed his intentions of population control lay in the philosophy that the ability of each man arose from the seeds of his father's. We may recall mentioning this in Chapter One, with the wording: "The word intelligence is really about the government of people through the guise of individual attainment".

In the materialistic world he believed in, Galton saw that the course each man took could be little affected by divine intervention or free will. In attempting to prove this, he actually sought instances where prayer had failed to provide the sought-after gain. Natural selection in natural science, he believed, was conclusive of natural selection in social science. It was a view that saw social stratification as a consequence of biological ordering that asserted the need for elitism, and for this elitism to be recognized for the benefit of all.

However, the social imbalances that prospered under these ideals were less welcomed by those at the bottom of the ladder than by those at the top, where Galton resided. While Marx declared, "It is not the consciousness of man that determines his existence, but his social existence that determines his consciousness...." Galton wrote a vast number of scientific papers and a number of books to convince the population otherwise.

Within five years of the formation of Marx's "The International Working Men's Association," Galton had published his first book *Hereditary Genius*. We must be in no doubt that the sole purpose of Galton's book was to present a pseudo scientific argument that directly countered Marx's contention that all men are born equal, for Galton saw to prove that all men are not. *Hereditary Genius* was simply written to prove that within every population there will be a very few men who are born with the inherited ability to rule the rest.

Galton, outlined in this book, an understanding that all aspects of the individual were inherited through their family line. This is to say that as the child inherited the family nose or family chin, so did they inherit the family brain and so the mental capability of the family. This capability, he reasoned, could be measured by the social success of the family line.

Accordingly, a blacksmith would have a particular nose which he would pass to his son with the same mental capability to be a blacksmith, but not that to be a lawyer. Equally, the lawyer would have a certain chin, which he would pass to his son with the capability to be a lawyer, and serve society no good if he became a blacksmith. This evoked a saying, which in my experience was to last right up to the 1960s, where children were told...:

> *"Not to think they are better than they are, and*
> *to respect their elders in age and in society."*

Galton argued from this idea of inheritance (which we now know is not valid) that in every population there will always be a small number who have the natural and proven ability to lead the rest. Here was the 'evidence' for royalty and the establishment behind them, that they were to be needed by the common people. So, it was argued that civilisation would be seen to suffer and likely collapse if people of lesser pedigree came to rule. Galton had taken a leaf out of Socrates' book.

The great error that too many make in discussing Galton is that they see him as the father of intelligence testing. In one sense, this is nearly true, for although he never actually found a way to measure intelligence, he did devise a sort of vague system by which the intelligence of family members could be said to be recognised through the work they did over generations. Although we may know that he only managed this by deliberately ignoring all aspects of influence and opportunity!

Thus, family members who were lawyers were classed to be more intelligent than family members who were merchants. In turn, these were classed as being more intelligent than families of labourers. Although today we see intelligence testing to be about individuals, Galton was more interested in the intelligence of the family and so their role in the structure of society.

The purpose of Galton's work was least to measure individual intelligence and far, far more to show how members of a family could be recognised to have a social level in the scheme of things.

He used a particular graph, actually designed by an astronomer, to show how families of higher intelligence, decided by their social role in society, should govern other families.

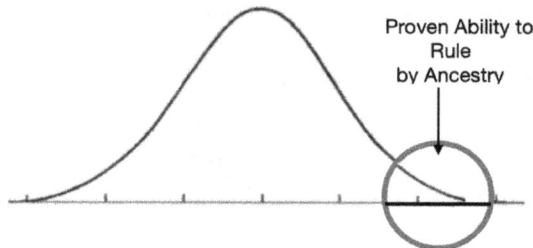

This graph, which we today call the Bell Curve, will play an important part in much of our discussion.

Today, we may think this idea of categorising family intelligence through the work they do to be ludicrous, but this is because we have freedom of education and freedom of opportunity. Victorian England was markedly different and operated under a very strict class system.

(I may add a personal note here. I once attended an interview with a department of the British government in 1980. The very first question I was asked was: "Which school did you go to?" In other words, I was being preselected on the quality of the education my parents had afforded, with clear social and political meanings behind this. Despite having attended a not very good government school, my interview lasted two hours, but I witnessed at this time how there was still some desire to maintain a stratified society.)

Galton's aim was very simply to provide evidence that everyone should know their place in the workings of society and respect those above them to maintain order. His purpose was to quash the ideas of Marx and dissolve the growing support for socialism that had come so close to destroying his civilisation in 1848.

In time, Galton's real purpose became overshadowed by the rise in intelligence testing, which more subtly and more discreetly sought to obtain the same objective. This is the maintenance of the status quo, by 'proving' through tests that people of a lower social level or of an undesired ethnic or cultural background have such a low intelligence that they should be denied the opportunity to gain better jobs and by this, rise within and so disturb the social operation of the society. The book called *The Bell Curve,* which was published in 1994, had exactly this intention.

This idea of creating a mindset to convince everyone to support the order of things was not actually Galton's, as we have seen; it can first be attributed to Socrates thousands of years earlier. However, as Galton based his reasoning upon this, so, as we will come to see, the establishment built the Science of Cognitive Psychology upon his reasoning. This new science spread rapidly throughout the world, seeking to devise methods of measuring human intelligence, so that all people could be kept in their place. However, the problem was that no one at that time knew what intelligence actually was. In fact, we still do not know what it is today. As we mentioned earlier, there is no common agreement to what intelligence is, as people differ in their assumptions of this.[29] All this, we shall come to in time.

Hereditary Genius was followed in 1874 by *English Men of Science,* and in 1883 by *Inquiries into Human Faculty and its Development. Natural Inheritance* was published in 1889, and then came *Worthy Families* in 1906. His autobiography, Memories of My Life, was published in 1908.

Once Galton had acquired a strong following from the ideas he brought forth in *Hereditary Genius,* his next step was to follow de Gobineau and build up public concern about the dangers of marrying into inferior stock. In the publication of *Inquiries into Human Faculty and its Development,* Galton devised the science of eugenics. This is a study dedicated to the preservation of the higher stock in human societies, and accordingly to the removal of inferior stock. "Eugenics ..." he explained, "... co-operates with the workings of Nature. What Nature does blindly, slowly and ruthlessly, man may do providently, quickly and kindly."

Galton was the founder member of the Eugenics Society when it was finally established in 1907. In 1911, the year of his death, he promoted a eugenic laboratory designed to further this research. However, eugenics is a most regrettable science. It has brought compulsory sterilisation to hundreds of thousands of human beings who were of low "calculated" ability, and to which we still bear the consequences today. Equally, apartheid is rooted in eugenics, just as was the Aryan cleansing campaign that took place in Germany between 1933 to 1945.

Unfortunately, the ostracism of a minority group, as fuelled by fears of racial-mixing or miscegenation, tends to be a fruitful political strategy.

Yet, all Galton's publications were only the tip of the iceberg, for through the positions he had once held in the British Association for the Advancement of Science, the Royal Society, the Royal Institution and the Royal Geographical Society, he was able to muster a vast amount of influence to extend his views into every journal, magazine, and newspaper. Nor was his influence contained just within Great Britain, for the circles in which his work moved influenced the founders of social science in most countries of the world. The contention that he manufactured emanated into every aspect of human evaluation. Today, any system, anywhere in the world that compares one individual to another, be it child or adult, has the roots of its philosophy and the principles of its mechanics in the work of Sir Francis Galton!

It is insufficient to say that Galton was more responsible than anyone else for the introduction and the overwhelming acceptance that intelligence is inherited and that it is measurable. Very simply, without Galton, we may not have social science. We may not have the supposed "scientific" means to view the intelligence of one against the intelligence of another. Predictions of human capability that are devised by psychologists, and the political frameworks they serve, would be reduced to unqualified guesswork.

Equally, education would be unable to operate as it does with such hidden biasing, and it would demand far, far more finance and resources if an egalitarian population were to have an egalitarian education. The assessment of the child would then demand an assessment of all those individuals and factors incorporated into their development, and the conveyor belt system of education, with the final stage of its delta effect, directing different students to different work options, would be exposed for the political design it serves.

The science of a mental measurement that classifies an individual's potential for work responsibility and directly connects this to their social rank was, and is, the most ingenious formulation. It negates the desires of people to raise themselves above the standing of their forefathers, and it all began with the publication of *Hereditary Genius*. The author of which was the first to put into print that .. "Not all men are created equal", and who then set out to prove it.

On the face of it, Galton's reasoning was simple, as was the solution that came with it. It is important for us to review his reasoning again. So, to begin, he noted that family lines could be recognised by familiar features, such as the shape of the nose, chin, etc. Equally, he observed that spheres of employment, certainly in agricultural societies with their limited job tasks, tended to be family related, such that the son of a butcher invariably became a butcher, just as the son of a doctor was likely to become a doctor.

It is important to understand that the whole reasoning we have today that the intelligence of the individual lies in the quality of the genes they inherited, comes from Galton's explanation in 1869 that ....

"Whatever causes the similarity in the features of a family line (nose, chin, etc.) also gives explanation for the work capabilities of that line (since their brain was inherited in the same way), and through this comes evidence of their aptitude for social responsibility."

In other words, the son, father and grandfather may have a similar-looking nose. Galton used this feature to say that the son inherited the same physical attributes of his father. This would be the nose and the rest of the body, including the brain and its efficiency to work. In turn, the father had inherited the same attributes from his father (the grandfather), who rightfully inherited the same attributes through his family line. Galton knew nothing of genetics at this time. However, with the inheritance of the brain and its working capability came evidence of the family's success in employment and from this the social responsibility they held.

When Galton wrote this, he thought of the brain operating as an organ in the body, such as the heart or the liver. The structure of the brain, composed of living neurons that learn to connect, was not discovered until many years after Galton's book had been published; by which time a movement had rapidly grown to protect the philosophy that sought to preserve the order of things. From that moment onwards, psychologists would forever fashion the developing knowledge of geneticists and neurologists into their understanding of intelligence with the same purpose.

Accordingly, the identity between inherited worth and job worth that linked both to social worth, however vague or questionable, fitted exactly the need of the establishment. It offered both explanation and justification for their rank and privileges. More importantly, it offered a route that would overcome the increasing need to educate the lower classes, while restraining their opportunities in education to maintain some stabilisation of the social work order problem.

Galton's idea was to engineer a system where each child could be allocated a degree of opportunity, or education, on the basis of the social responsibilities of their parents. License for this was given on the merit, as he so eloquently expressed, that: "The life histories of our relatives are prophetic of our own futures, ..."[30]

However, the neat order of this social/work responsibility, which he hoped to hold on to, was becoming increasingly less tenable as mechanised industry ever took over the economic design of civilisation. As radical changes emerged in the types of jobs required and the skills needed for those jobs, so a shuffling of people began to take place. All of this threatened to overturn the order of the civilisation he knew and had a deeply vested interest in.

Chapter Eight

The Difficulty of Labour Reorganisation

We can see that at the time of Galton's rise, the world was a very different place than we know today. To understand this, would be to comprehend the interaction of a largely simple minded and illiterate population with the clash of steel and the hiss of escaping steam. It is to envisage a superstitious people trapped in ignorance, some of whom were still terrified of being consumed by the monstrous mechanical ploughs and threshing machines that began to replace horse and muscle. While the economical savings gained in the use of such machinery was obvious, so may we see that it was also evident that people needed to be more proficient to handle the changes and demands brought about by this mechanisation. This was not a happy confusion.

In the early part of the 19th century, England was in a sorry financial state with political turmoil rife. People were hungry, angry, and determined to bring control to their unjust plight. This was a time when "The Bloody Code" was still fresh in the minds of people, as it had been devised to be a form of class suppression by the rich upon the poor. This unofficial name was given to the eventual 220 offences that carried the death penalty in defence of property. "A man would be hanged not for stealing a horse," said the Marquess of Halifax, "but, because a horse may not be stolen.[31]" A clear statement that the life of a person was worth less than anything a richer person could afford to own.

Such was the incredibly high level of tension in the decade before Galton was born that the British Prime Minister Spencer Perceval was assassinated. While it was said that his assassin claimed he had acted on personal reasons, he was hailed as a social hero by the general public, and a large and angry crowd tried to free him before he was very hastily tried and executed. All of which left behind rumours of a deeper plot.

Not too long after this, a new political group appeared, calling themselves the Spenceans. Assuming the role of early communists, they demanded equal land and equal rights for all. Determined to save England, they plotted the assassination of members of the British Cabinet, believing this would spark armed riots that would lead to the overthrow of the government. Caught before they could act, their ringleaders were hanged and the rest transported to Australia. The whole of Great Britain was a seething pot of anger and resentment. As the English Lord Shaftesbury was to witness: "The mass of mankind whom nothing retains but force or habit... are so in a state of revolution that nothing but ..... a standing miracle ..... saves us. "[32]

This miracle faltered briefly in 1848, and we would do well to consider that miracles are not left to chance. Certainly, force was used, but the wisdom of a created habit (this continuity of religion) was the solution that saved the day, and as religion had always known, indoctrination needed to be applied in youth. So, as a general education was wheeled together, its purpose was more to instil within the young a respect for authority than to prepare them for the job skills to be later required of them.

Yet, still in stable times, neither religion nor the establishment were prepared to trade the general release of education, with the possible gains of a more enlightened civilisation, for the privileges of their position. As the Bishop of London had earlier stated: "It is safest for both the government and religion of the country, to let the lower classes remain in that state of ignorance in which nature has originally placed them."[33] Despite objections from industrialists for a more educated workforce, the British, as all other governments, were too wary in the early 19th century to implement it. As one member of the government put it: "To give education to the labouring classes of the poor would be prejudicial to their morals and happiness ... It would render them fractious and refractory."[34]

As people did become more fractious, as the 19th century became more decidedly shaped by industrial progress and unions began to appear, so education became the necessary evil it was always feared it would be; as it opened up a scope of possibilities to people that had seldom been available to them before. As the more enterprising of the lower ranks elevated their position to the middle-class, so the influence of this body grew and became more decisive in the running of the country. By the last quarter of that century, political demand for a general education could no longer be deferred, and governmental spending was altered (in some small way) to begin this provision.

We may realise from the violent suppressions that followed the 1848 revolutions, the secret societies that bloomed from this time, and the increasing ability of the lower structures to organise themselves to disrupt the operation of society, that the time of Francis Galton was one of extreme political sensitivity. In fact, this century became known as the Age of Assassination, in view of the large number of attempts to assassinate prominent members of the establishment throughout Europe. Indeed, Queen Victoria survived eight assassination attempts.[35] When we really understand all this, it is so clearly obvious why the solution Galton offered was as eagerly accepted by society before the First World War as was his legacy after it.

There have been many suggestions as to why this human calamity occurred, but in the "short" war it was expected to be, it did offer a means for the ruling systems to pull together the fragmenting world they were facing. Accordingly, the event that took place on that warm summer's day in 1914, when a small group of youths calling themselves the Black Hand assassinated the nephew of the Austrian Emperor, could simply have been smoothed over. Yet, it was used to bring order to the escalating industrial and social pressures building up within the European powers - that this was delayed until 1914 was a surprise to many.

17 years before the First World War began, a Polish economist by the name of I.S. Block wrote *The War of the Future*. In his book, Block predicted: "A civilisation which has advanced from an agricultural base to an industrial one, must not expect a simple war of bright uniforms and splendid cavalry attacks, but of famine at home and of bankrupt nations drowning in the disintegration of their whole social organisation. For an industrialised civilisation is not one where its members may isolate themselves from each other, for they are bound together by each other's needs."[36] Block, as the world was to find, was incredibly accurate. The economic aftermath of that war so exhausted the resources of governments that, with nearly one million civilians dead through famine or diseases related to undernourishment, each had great difficulty controlling their internal political forces.

While the history books of the victors tell that it was the defeated countries who turned themselves inside out, they relate too little to the shades of socialism and communism that spread into their own backyards. Such was the menace of these movements that civil authorities were forced to introduce improved living standards, better education, and easing of prejudicial restraints in work and society, they had so effectively manoeuvred around throughout the 19th century. Although it was to take another world war that grew out of this and the technology and social changes it sparked, before Western Civilisation would be forced to redesign the arrangement of its education and bring with it one of the highest attainments of a seemingly egalitarian society.

Chapter Nine

Setting the Guidelines for 19th Century Education

The issue with education, we may be reminded, was not in the acquisition of reading and writing skills, but with the further inquisitiveness and development of reason that comes through these. More simply put, the fear was that education would inspire too much confidence in too many, to question too much in the affairs of their life.

Galton's philosophy of inherited ability, which went against the accepted philosophies of John Locke's human understanding, and Rousseau's writing of *Emilie* (both of which saw ability as an after-birth occasion), promised to bring control to the necessary development of education and maintain social stability in the society by doing so.

If Galton's argument could be largely accepted by the population, then it would provide the base upon which all educational programs and all the selectional procedures involving society's use of human resources could be set. The potential this offered was unlimited, for it would enable all training and assessment techniques to be rigidly controlled and fine-tunable in their application to the needs of their time, all appearing to be politically unbiased, but all precisely the opposite.

The concept that intelligence was definable had profound meanings to the worth of a society and the individuals it contained. It allowed opinions to be presented as "scientific," by which arguments were seen to offer "proof" that intelligence, as a quality of thinking, was strictly hereditary and thereby classifiable. The difficulty facing Galton's assumption, and all the generations of those who have bathed in this dogma ever since, is to actually provide proof of it.

They never have!

However, let us now see the path they took and come to understand why and how education became so designed that it actually prevents children from learning fairly and equally. After all, when we think of our children going to school today, we do not realise how their education is still centred upon a 19th-century political design. The purpose of this design, as we have discussed, is simply to channel children into either a manager or a managed role in their society. Since each role requires a different level of reasoning ability, it is a basic purpose of education to guide the development of how its students reason for the citizens they are prepared to be.

May we be reminded that those who attend only the general, and even the avenues of the higher general education, are taught to accept and to trust information in school and so in society. However, those who continue to a university education are taught to understand that information has different perspectives, as they become skilled in the management of reason. The social and educational policies that both create and feed this design today differ in different societies, but they commonly serve the dictates of an industrialised base. This is a design that will badly serve the highly computer-driven societies we will increasingly evolve into as this century progresses.

In order that we can create a better design for the model of the future citizen, it is essential that we understand how the model of today's citizen came about. In *The Illusion of Education,* we saw why this model of a citizen was needed in the past. In this book, we shall examine how the design for this model came about. In order to do this, we shall examine how the belief of a measurable intelligence arose and how this played a pivotal role in maintaining a sense of order through the politically turbulent times of the 19th century, and so the later ordering of the 20th. The key to understanding how this was achieved lies in realising how people were cultivated to accept the discrimination brought out by the idea of a natural hierarchy of intelligence.

As we saw how Sir Francis Galton stimulated the idea of inherited ability as a political weapon to counter the rise of early socialism in the 19th century, so we shall see how he inspired Spearman to create the idea that intelligence is a singular feature of the inherited brain, which by doing so opened it up to a way of being theoretically measured. From this, we shall see how Pearson devised Correlation Coefficients that claim to show, but do not, the relationship of the genes to the environment in intelligence. We follow this by discussing how Burt, as a disciple of Galton, was exposed for fraud after purposely falsifying test data for three quarters of a century, as he purposely directed British and Commonwealth education to serve his personal political interests.

In conjunction with this, we shall see how the French scientist Binét, who fervently believed intelligence could never be measured, did not live long enough to see how the simple test he created to differentiate normal children from those who may be retarded was corrupted by the German Stern into the first IQ formula. We examine from this how Goddard and Terman in America further falsified Binét's one-to-one verbal assessment into a written "Yes or No" questionnaire, so enabling them to index human intelligence on a massive scale in their attempts to purify and politically structure American society. This will lead us to understand how Brigham moulded the IQ test into the SAT, as a means to preselect white children from wealthy Protestant backgrounds towards leadership positions in American society. Intelligence, we shall find, is not what we think it is.

It may be seen from this that the prime purpose of this book is to demonstrate why the intelligence of an individual cannot be said to be determined by a factor of inheritance. If this is so, as we shall prove it to be, it means that in the ignorance of this, children in school today are not taught as effectively as they could be.

The belief that a student reveals their natural ability in the responses they make, however vaguely this may be taken, enables education to largely ignore how they could be developed better, as it processes them towards a work function in their society as cheaply as possible -- after all, and for all the reasons we examined in *The Illusion of Education,* education is a very cost-conscious machine. Such a belief is enforced within the minds of teachers through the conditions they are caused to work under, as they have too little time or energy to acknowledge that it is the quality of effort, which they themselves gave in the first place, that enabled their students to respond in the ways they do. Without accepting this, teachers too readily see the responses of their students as an indication of their inherited worth, if not some social factor beyond their control -- although the cause of this is too often also tied to a genetic base.

Very simply, then, rather than education accepting its responsibility to significantly improve the ability of its students by changing the way it operates, which it could do as we explain in other books, the reasoning that intelligence is inherited gives it license to process its students on the ability they demonstrate, without being said to be too much responsible itself for that ability. In the simplest sense, the concept of inherited intelligence shifts the responsibility for the child's education from the body of education to some mysterious factor that cannot be blamed.

If we are to change this operational mind of education, if we are to give all children a fairer chance in school, and if we are to educate them in reason so they will be more responsible citizens and be more adaptable in their intelligence to the very different challenges they will face, then, we need to understand what intelligence really is -- and why we confuse its meaning with the performance a child makes in their lessons or a worker in their job.

After all, as artificial intelligence is rapidly taking dominance over all spheres of society and work, as our children are likely to face greater social troubles than we do, brought about by climatic based disasters (because global warming is a reality), we are caused to realise that never before in the history of civilisations have we needed to produce an upcoming generation more able to think and reason about their role in society, than we will be caused to do, as we progress further into this 21st century.

Let us continue with our account to understand why intelligence is not what we have been led to believe it is; although, as we do this, we should bear in mind that this account offers no villains or heroes. It only describes how various individuals strove to follow their beliefs, as each in their turn gave shape to what we today believe.

Chapter Ten

Galton's Legacy

Each born to their line

Sir Francis Galton wrote, from 1869 until his death in 1911, upon the social use of inheritance through bloodlines. Ever since that time, his theories have set the stage by which human resource has been gauged, and individuals measured for the part each may play.

Today, we know too much about the effects of childhood influences to relate the potential of a child to the lesser achievements of their parents, let alone their grandparents. So, we think it is very normal to witness how the children of yesterday's plumbers, painters and truck drivers now leave university to pursue roles in their society as lawyers, accountants, and computer programmers.

Yet, even though we see all this as normal, we still cannot move away from the shadow of inherited intelligence that lives within our minds. When we witness the difficulties children have in their learning and the variations of competence they produce, or when we meet others who seem very clever or the corresponding opposite, we somehow link their intelligence to some mysterious factor we imagine they were born with. The root of this reasoning lies in the philosophy Galton set forth in 1869, when he published *Hereditary Genius*.

Galton set forth a philosophy that essentially ignored the role of development in intelligence, and followed an ancient belief that the characteristic (and so ability for intelligence) witnessed in the child came directly from those of their parents. It is a philosophy that has survived to this day because it became one of the founding blocks of psychology, and its proponents managed to adapt Galton's idea to our developing knowledge in genetics of how the environment influences the design of the gene.

Because of the political influences that drove and still continue to drive psychology, we became impressed to believe that intelligence is largely inherited but can be improved to "an extent" by development. This belief is endorsed by seeing intelligence as "a one thing" that works differently in different individuals.

This is not a philosophy that recognises intelligence purely as a series of acts, with one building upon another as the individual develops their understanding of how to interact with the world about them. Nor is it a philosophy that recognises each act of intelligence as the projection of a number of components that came together to create what is witnessed.

Such thinking, as this, does not understand that many of these components that create intelligence are inherited for different purposes, and so bring different designs for the environment to work with, which we more autonomically than consciously bring into a unified order as we engage a task.

We may think here of language and the ability to understand syntax, or how words are arranged in a sentence. This ability comes from a gene design that allows the environment to totally construct and reconstruct this ability, should any failings have occurred through the environment. We may think of a low factor of environment in this regard to be a child raised with a poor knowledge of syntax. Further in our account, we will discuss the case of Genie, a girl who was locked in a room for most of her childhood and deprived of normal language exposure, but was later able to entirely reconstruct her ability in language.

Without understanding that different aspects of intelligence are served by genes having different purposes, and affected by the environment in different ways, the inheritance of genes is regarded en masse to create a different quality of intelligence within each individual. By this reasoning, different individuals are regarded as having different levels of innate capability.

If we may understand, however, that intelligence is composed of many different components, and not so the single feature we too often take it to be, we may better understand how it is constructed and therefore how it operates as a whole.

This returns us to the awareness that some gene designs allow the environment to totally construct the capability of the part they play. This is to say that any normal variation in their coding would not necessarily inhibit the constructing factors of their environment.

Fodor saw to emphasise this, when he explained that while there are certain features of intelligence that operate upon an architectural design and so can be expected to be affected by genetic diversity, for example, the ability to see colour and to perceive movement, that there are other designs that may not be affected by genetic diversity in their ability to function. These designs provide a feature that obtains parity with that of other individuals purely through environmental experience.[37]

We have just seen this with the example of syntax, but there are many other examples. For instance, the different ways in which beliefs can form, the ability to adopt new thinking strategies throughout the lifetime, the ability to know language, the ability to freely reason and most importantly to relate to information with competence in accuracy and speed being purely developmental.[38] All these and many more components of intelligence are not normally affected by genetic diversity. However, let us backtrack for a moment, because there is something very important we need to discuss.

In seeking to explain that some features relating to intelligence are free of genetic diversity, Fodor gave contrast with those serving architectural designs that are prone to genetic diversity. It is upon this wording of genetic diversity that we need to bring clarification. This will be very important for us to discuss in this earlier stage of our account and to hold in our thoughts as we progress right through the book to the very last page.

The meaning of genetic diversity is that, hypothetically, there was once an original gene design for each of our features. Due to the process of meiosis, where gametes are shuffled for reproduction, this gene design altered and continues to alter through each generation. Thus, every genetic line will have its own version of this original design, which will also vary with individuals of the line. We may imagine from this untold variations of the original design for this feature. However, genetic variations take different forms, which can bring different consequences to the operation of their feature.

Fodor gave the example of being able to see colour. According to the principles of genetic diversity, this would be to say that there would be untold variations of being able to see colour, but this is not so. All human beings see the same colour of blue, red, green etc, unless they are colour blind. Those who are colour blind, are so because they have inherited a genetic trait or a mutation from the norm. So, we have a case where the ability to see colour may incur genetic diversity, but this does not affect an individual's ability to see the same colours as everyone else, unless they have a mutation.

Therefore, there is an important difference for us to be aware of between how a normal variation and a mutation may affect the design of the gene.

Fodor's example of our ability to perceive movement as having genetic variations also needs to be qualified, because whatever variations may exist, outside of a mutation, they will not affect an individual's ability to perceive movement. Let me try to explain how we relate to perceiving movement with an analogy.

According to Gestalt Psychology, "The Law of Organisation" and "The Law of Good Continuation" operate within the individual according to genetic variation. The former deals with how we define the breakdown or build-up of stimuli, to explain why we understand information in terms of figures to backgrounds. The latter, based on the "Principles of Closure and Good Form," reasons that we naturally connect incomplete information to make sense of what it represents.

Accordingly, any individual would be able to look upon a circle or a square that is almost complete but not so, and naturally see them to be complete. In other words, their internal mechanisms join the small break so that they visually recognise a complete form.

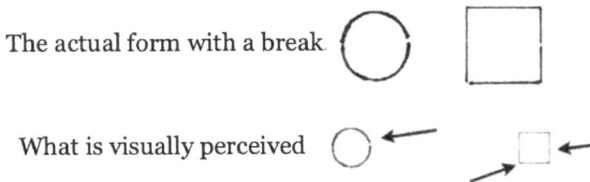

The actual form with a break

What is visually perceived

However, there are some individuals who do not do this. They look upon the broken form and see it as broken. This inability is attributed to a mutation, which causes their ability to differ from the norm.

Building upon the work of Rev, Feuerstein found this inability to have a psychological cause, which could be overcome by settling the disturbance the individual has mentally incurred. As he pointed out, "The projection of a virtual relationship ... does not occur as a spontaneous response to the pressure of stimuli."[39]

According to Hochberg, "We perceive whatever most probably produces the stimulation we receive. In other words, a 'learning' psychological structure generally reflects the physiological arrangement of how we perceive.[40]

This is to say that the correction to this inability came from within the individual to desire this change and to then know how to achieve it. In other words, what is believed to be caused by a genetic mutation was actually caused by an environmental factor, which in this case was stress and rectified by psychological therapy. Therefore, there was no genetic diversity in this feature that caused individuals to vary in their ability of it. We may apply this principle to how we perceive movement.

We have a great deal to discuss about the meaning of the environment in genetics, but at this moment, we may understand that genetic diversity does not necessarily suggest a difference in the quality of the feature to function, while a mutation may do.

If we apply this to intelligence, we may know that a chromosomal mutation creating, for example, Down Syndrome, produces an individual with some difference in their general morphology to that of those born through normal genetic diversity. Such human beings, just as those who incurred oxygen starvation in the birth process, do not interact with the environment with the same capability as a human being deriving from normal genetic diversity. For the purposes of our discussion, we regard these human beings as non-functioning human beings compared to fully functioning human beings.

When this difference in their inability to function normally is ignored, all are said to be of normal functioning, but having different capabilities for intelligence. From this stance, all are tested by the same means, with the lower intelligence of none fully functioning human beings used as evidence of the varying innate capabilities of all. There is no evidence for this, as we shall shortly come to see.

It is a little too early in our account to discuss genetics, but we should know that Galton's explanation that the child inherits the intelligence of their parents, who inherited this from their parents, is not so simple. Certainly, this direct continuity was important for his argument in defending social responsibility in a family line, but genetic inheritance does not work in this direct way.

We have gained an understanding that genes are shuffled in meiosis, but these genes are not only those of one parent and may contain genes from a number of generations earlier. It is not only that the genes of each parent are shuffled before the egg is fertilised, but as it is, the genes from only one parent are selected for each feature. Thus, a gene coding from one parent may be active or inactive in their child's genome (or their DNA). If it is inactive, then, the corresponding gene from the other parent will take its place.

As we can see, genetic inheritance is not as predictable as Galton believed it to be, as he relied upon the theory of pangenesis and its associated blending theory, which was eventually discarded once Mendel's work was discovered very many years later.

From what we have discussed, it is important that we understand that intelligence is not simply a singular feature, inherited in different degrees by different individuals, for this is a view that gives little recognition to the true influence of the environment. However, if we realise that the word intelligence is merely a label given to numerous components, which interact through their environment in different ways to produce the overall effect that is witnessed, we may better see how we can alter our impression of intelligence by improving the parts that make it up. This was the secret to Feuerstein's success.

In time, we will unravel the causes of this effect. As we do this, we may come to better appreciate how the environment can play a greater role in the development of intelligence than was previously implied by the term genetic diversity.

However, let us now return to our discussion, where Galton argued the case that the intelligence of the child is limited to the social background of their parents or their particular ethnic identity by the blood of their ancestors.

In his attempts to prove this, he always sought to limit the role of the environment so that it could never be seen for what it really is -- an entangled mayhem of information through which the personality struggles with and against those of others to define its identity, as the individual seeks to secure a purpose for what each engagement may mean to them.

By ignoring factors of development and in line with de Gobineau's book *The Inequality of Human Races,* Galton focused purely on the idea of bloodlines to explain how intelligence (just as any other social attribute, such as good morality, criminality and sexual deprivation) is inherited.[41]

However, as we mentioned earlier, Galton presented all his claims on inheritance a third of a century before genes were discovered, and as he sought to define intelligence through the ability of the brain, he did so in a time when its workings were virtually unknown. Thus, he saw to give proof of intelligence being inherited by defining mental ability through the inheritance of the "..weight of grey matter, number of brain fibres...."[42]

Yet, we know today that the weight of the grey matter to which intelligence relates is decided by diet and environmental experience, and so can be as different between father and son as it can be similar to a non-relative from a distant land. Equally, while Galton wrote in 1869 about the number of brain fibres, we may know that even with our technology today, we cannot count the specific number of cells in the human brain. That Galton described them as fibres is testimony that he did not know what he was talking about. In fact, brain cells in the very simplest sense were not discovered until four years after Galton had published *Hereditary Genius*.

It was only when Camillo Golgi accidentally knocked a sample of brain tissue into a solution of chromate of silver and was able to visibly see brain cells under a microscope for the first time, that we came to know of their existence. Before this, the brain was seen as an organ not dissimilar to any other organ in the body, and thought to work along the same lines as the heart, the liver and so on. In other words, when Galton first laid his claim about the inheritance of intelligence, it was in a time when the brain was seen to be simply inherited and to work in the same way as any other organ of the body, such as the heart, spleen or kidneys. Such is the base from which we today still judge a child's ability to solve a problem, learn a task and pass a test.

Galton is described as a scientist, and he was in the sense of the research he tirelessly employed himself in. However, this was a time of infantile sciences and many of them, including very many of those he was associated with, did not stand the test of time. The claims he made and the arguments he supported them with were more pseudo-scientific than scientific. With great endeavour, Galton wrote upon the inheritance of lack of stamina, of idleness, of perversion, and of criminality. All these, of course, are facets that hallmark the decay of a society.

So it was that in his efforts to preserve the social world and so his civilisation as he saw it, Galton explained how "The ideal criminal has marked peculiarities of character: his conscience is almost deficient, his instincts are vicious, his power of self-control is very weak, and he usually detests continuous labour. The absence of self-control is due to ungovernable temper, to passion, or to mere imbecility...."[43] In explaining that this type of humanity is "...exceedingly ill-suited to play a respectable part in our modern civilisation... ," Galton stated that it is heritable, by evidence of the singular example he gave of the Juke family in America. The Juke family, he described, was well known to the police for their criminal activities over a number of generations. We will shortly review the inaccuracy, misunderstanding, and deliberate elements of fraud involved with the presentation of this case.

Today, there can be few people who do not understand how the environment cultures criminality. A criminal can be taught by reason not to be so, while a citizen of excellent standing can be just as easily coached into crime. In all the human attributes that Galton laboured to describe, all except intelligence have been proven to be of other origin than he determined. Epilepsy is not the madness he described it to be. Nor are people with slavish dispositions inferior to those of other races, and neither are perverseness nor idleness attributes of inheritance. When all these are now accepted to be purely constructed through the environment, or rather factors of development, why should intelligence alone remain as Galton described it?

To prove that intelligence is inherited and make use of it as a social tool, Galton needed to pull together a number of quite unrelated factors. First, he needed to show that achievement ran in family lines. He did this by drawing upon examples of a number of professions where the son had followed the father who, in turn, had followed his father.

While it was traditional to transfer work skills through a family line in the Agricultural Age, where he drew his references from (even though his time was of the Industrial Age), Galton had to present this continuity of profession in some way as a cause of inherited ability.

His major task in doing this was to devalue the weight of family and social influences. The problem, as it is obvious, is that he needed some way to prove that it was only because of the value of the bloodline that the son followed the capability of his father, and not because of the influences and opportunities the father could provide.

As a means to prove this very vital point and so explain that opportunity was of lesser importance than inheritance, Galton argued that if social influences were more important than ability, then the nephews of popes would be expected to have as much eminence as the sons of eminent fathers. To defend himself from accounts that could prove this not to be so, and Galton well knew how to present an argument, he suggested that while a few offshoots of the Medici line may prove him wrong, he knew that they would be the exception. He saw to dismiss such a counterargument entirely with the wording, "I do not profess to have worked up the kinships of the Italians with any especial care, but I have seen amply enough of them, to justify..."44

Upon such as this did Galton rest his "scientific argument" for the insignificance of family influences against the quality of ability inherited. It seems hard to see why he played down the significance of family influences so much, when we remember the incredible extent of his own and how these raised him to public prominence.

However, having so explained that eminence was a quality of ability and not circumstances, Galton needed to demonstrate how ability could be linked with family lines. As we have seen, he did this by declaring that brain design, and so brain performance, could be recognised within families. Simply put, and as we by now well understand, Galton was saying that because the nose has a family resemblance, then so also must the brain, and with this, how well it works. This, as we shall come to see, is quite wrong!

Once Galton had argued that people followed the work line of their ancestors because of their inherited ability, and had linked this inherited ability with distinctive features in family lines, he then needed to show that these relationships were continually recognisable in any group of people.

This distribution of ability was a central issue in his claim. It not only demonstrated how authority in any location was a consequence of natural ability, but by its regularity, it exemplified the sense of permanence Galton was really seeking to prove. We must hold on to the fact that while Galton was talking about inherited ability, his purpose in doing so was to maintain the social order of his world, from the monarch at the top to the lowest person at the bottom.

Galton's world, we may remember, was not that of ours. It was a time of profound and deeply disturbing social changes, with revolution lying ever below the illusion of a contented society. As Galton strove to keep this illusion in order, he tirelessly worked to pull together any fact that would give his idea more scientific credibility. After all, this was the age of new science and anything worthy had to be shown to be so.

While Darwin had gained his direction through Malthus' principles of population control (which had guided European politics through the first half of the 19th century), Galton took his from the work of a Belgian statistician named Lambert Quetelet.

Galton first became aware of Quetelet's work after reading John Herschel's review of his exposition on the theory of probability.[45] This theory was essential for Galton because it gave him the license he needed to explain how a minority of people, having a higher quality than the rest, could always be said to exist in any group.

Of great significance to the work that Galton was building up was that Quetelet had also provided theories on how moral and political interests could be analysed, predicted, and so given direction by a form of scientific reasoning.

This scientific reasoning was to be essential to Galton, for while it gave his theory a degree of respect that went far beyond the actual worth of the mathematics, his later colleagues managed to create, it more importantly gave him the means to index the social achievement of a family line with its mental worth. This was the means by which he could argue that a stratification of natural ability, albeit intelligence, exists in any society.

While Galton himself was never to devise a means to actually calculate intelligence, he sidestepped the need for this by assuming that since all the points he raised were true to him, all he had to do was devise some means of classifying the differences he believed existed.

In other words and **may we be very clear upon this**, Galton could not prove that intelligence was inherited, but he used the argument that since physical features could be proven to be so in a family line and by assuming that a quality for intelligence is inherited in the same manner as the shape of a nose, he set about classifying the use of a family in their society to the work responsibility of their ancestors. All this, he argued, was determined by what we today call genetics.

Let us now examine the means by which Galton attempted to explain this, and so why we today think that intelligence can be determinable, can be measurable, and can be predictable. After all, our belief in the philosophy he created that the physical features of a family explain the efficiency of their mind to reason, is as true to us today as was the belief to people 500 years ago that the world was flat— even though every night they could see the Moon and nearby planets to be round.

———————————

Chapter Eleven

To Measure What Cannot be Defined

The Ancient Greeks and those before them had long been trying to deal with calculations that could explain an effect caused by factors it could not be separated from, and which were in themselves unknown. It was not, however, until Newton devised his system of calculus in 1665, that a reliable mathematical process was put forward that could deal with infinite data in the sense that it was unlimited and hence unknown.

Following his realisation of the effect of gravity, Newton began to consider why stars in the night sky were not pulled towards a central point. After all, if one star pulled another towards it, then surely the combination of their force would attract other stars and a central force of attraction would form. As this central force increased, so it would pull more and more stars into it, with the final result being a dense cloud of stars in the universe and none spread about. Newton reasoned that this did not happen because space was infinite and contained an infinite number of stars. All of which negated the effect of each other, and prevented this central force from developing.

It was in trying to qualify this reasoning through mathematics that Newton followed up on the earlier work of John Wallis. Wallis had devised a process that could deal with infinite numbers from formulas, which had been devised to deal with finite numbers. In continuing Wallis's work, although he never liked to admit it, Newton devised the system of calculus. This is a mathematical process that enables the calculation of infinite factors. Through calculus, Newton was able to prove his theory of a static universe. While this theory has now given way to one of an expanding universe, explained by the momentum of each star to negate the gravitational attraction of another and so move apart, the principles behind calculus were extremely important at that time.

The importance of calculus was that it opened up mathematics from a system that dealt with formal deductions to one that could be used with application in verifying scientific predictions by measurement. An important by-product of this was the belief that events could be predicted through the occurrence of factors relating to them.

Since the 17th century, interest in gambling as well as that with economics had sought to devise a method for predicting the outcome of probable events. To satisfy this need, the law of probability had come about. The law of probability reasoned that the likelihood of an event occurring could be estimated by dividing that event by the total number of events that were related to it. Thus, on the role of a dice, the probability of landing a number one could be calculated by dividing one by six. One is the number desired in this case, and six represents the six sides of a cube.

In 1778, the French scientist, the Marquis de Laplace, combined the principles of probability theory with those of Newton's calculus to create a non-finite calculus of probability. This became more simply known as the normal law of error. Its basic theory lay in the belief that the greater the number of samples measured, the smaller the error gained through their comparison. Thus, while measurements of 4, 6 and 9 would give an average of 6.3, the measurements of 3, 4, 4, 6, 9 and 10 would give an average of 6, which would be the more accurate. Laplace's law of error brought reasoning that a "true" value could be estimated from the examination of events that varied with instability.

From the beginning of the 19th-century, the Industrial Revolution began to bring great changes to the structure and organisation of societies. As a means to keep pace with what was happening and what could happen, governments began to make surveys of population movement and the changes that were beginning to take place in their societies. As this developed in Belgium, a number of statisticians were employed to deal with this task, one of whom was a man by the name of Lambert Quetelet.[46]

The problem for statisticians at that time was that there was no means to understand how events might stand in the future. Events could be recorded, but with the speed at which progress was moving, what was recorded one day was out of date the next. Building upon the concept of averages, as this underlay Laplace's law of error, Quetelet began to reason that if a group of people fired arrows at a target that most of these would land in an average area. He further reasoned that, as some would fall closer to the archer, others would land beyond the average place of the arrows. The more Quetelet thought about the density of the average, so the more he reasoned that the arrows which fell short and those more distant would do so in a strict relationship. This is to say that of 22 arrows fired, 10 would land together, 3 would land either side of these, 2 would land an equal distance away from these, and one a further distance away.

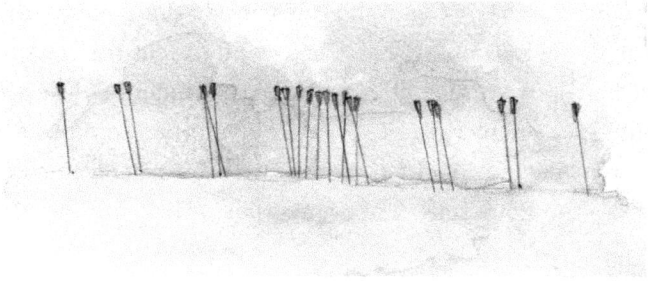

It was this theory of how events moved in equal steps, either side of the average position, that was to be the founding idea upon which the law of deviation from an average would become based. This is the very basis upon which we today believe that human intelligence varies proportionally about the average, and in being so can be calculated.

In the purest sense, Galton took Quetelet's idea of how arrows would land to explain how intelligence is inherited in different degrees by different children. This is the base upon which the whole edifice of human categorisation lies, as it stretches from the results recognised in school grades to those obtained in IQ tests.

Once Quetelet had convinced himself that variation about the average was regular and equally balanced, he realised he had found the way to explain how any varying factor may be defined and given prediction. Thus, if in a measurement of height, it was found that only one man per hundred was taller than 78 inches, then it could be said that in any future sample taken one man in every hundred should fall within this category.

This was Quetelet's refinement of Laplace's law of error, and he became most ingenious in the applications he derived and to which he applied this. He once, for example, recorded the drinking habits of a number of people, and suggested from this the inclination towards drunkenness in his society. Quetelet was obsessed with averages, and it was he who coined the term "l"homme moyen" (the average man).[47]

However, while Quetelet was fascinated with statistics, he was also very interested in astronomy. It was through this interest that he built up a relationship with an astronomer who would bring him an incontestable way to demonstrate this principle of equal movement about the average.

In 1809, Karl Gauss, the then Professor of Astronomy at Gottingen University, had published a paper discussing errors in astronomical observations. Gauss had been increasingly troubled by the tendency of his students to adopt Laplace's generalisation of an average in their calculations of a star's position.

To overcome this, Gauss reasoned that it was not correct to promote a singular position for a star as a representation of a number of positions gained. Sooner or later, he suggested, this would lead to the impression that only one position was obtained, when this might not be the accurate one. To overcome this, Gauss suggested it would be far wiser to explain a star's position through the variations taken in its measurement. Thus, and to simplify the example, if an average of 5 were obtained from the numbers 2, 4, 6 and 8, the star's position would be better said to vary between 2 to 8, than to simply state 5.

The True Position

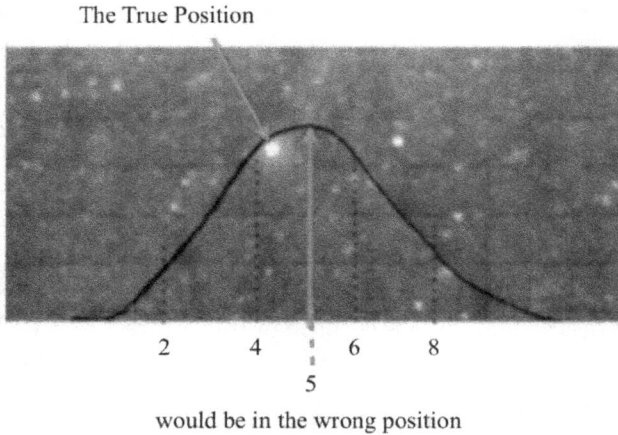

2   4   5   6   8

would be in the wrong position

To give demonstration to this, Gauss designed a graph that emphasised that it was not the position of the average that is important, but the area of uncertainty that suggests it. This eventually became known as the Gauss Curve. This graph will play a fundamental role in all that now follows.

According to Bracke, Quetelet visited Gauss in 1829.[48] So it is reasonable to assume that from this time, if not before, Quetelet was aware of this graph and the invaluable means it would give him to present the concept of the average he was discussing. Therefore, it was through Quetelet that Galton acquired the means to explain how a minority group of superiority could always be said to exist as if by a law of nature, and with Gauss's graph, he had the means to visually demonstrate what he meant.

Galton's gaining of this knowledge may be said to be beyond his wildest expectations, as he avidly expressed his delight: "I know of scarcely anything," he wrote "so apt to impress the imagination ... "The Law of Frequency of Error". .... It reigns with serenity and in complete self-effacement amidst the wildest confusion. The huger the mob, and the greater the apparent anarchy, the more perfect is its sway.... (*note here the emphasis on social instability)*

...... It is the supreme law of Unreason. Whenever a large sample of chaotic elements is taken in hand and marshalled in the order of their magnitude, an unsuspected and most beautiful form of regularity proves to have been latent all along. .... If the measurement at any two specified grades in the row are known, those that will be found at every other grade, except towards the extreme, ends, can be predicted in the way already explained, and with much precision."[49]

Such an instrument gave Galton the statistical means to declare: "This is what I am driving at, that analogy clearly shows there must be a fairly constant average mental capacity in the inhabitants of the British Isles, and that the deviations from that average upwards towards genius, and downwards towards stupidity must follow the law that governs deviations from all true averages."[50]

It was in this very publication of *Hereditary Genius* that Galton officially changed Laplace's "law of error of observations," which Quetelet had termed the "law of accidental causes," into a more recognisable identity for the purpose with which he would use it. After all, Galton could have no suggestion of "accidental causes" in the theory he would develop, and so termed it "the law of deviation from an average."

As he wrote: "It remains that I should say a very few words on the principle of the law of deviation from an average, or, as it is commonly called, the law of errors of observations, due to Laplace. Every variable event depends on a number of variable causes, and each of these, owing to the very fact of its variability depends upon other variables, and so on."[51]

Much quoting and relying upon the prestige of Professor Quetelet, whom he referred to as "... the greatest authority on vital and social statistics,"[52] and armed now with a much more appropriately named law to give his political vehicle scientific creditability as he was with a graph of unimaginable importance, Galton embarked upon his crusade to stabilise the civilisation, he saw, to be under constant threat.

The graph that Gauss designed to explain the approximation of a star to his students, coincidentally, matches the phenomenon of a population average. It was by this coincidence that Galton was able to adapt Gauss's graph to visually demonstrate his theory of deviation from the average. Since this graph will play a fundamental role in our account, we should understand how it is constructed to show variations in intelligence.

The Bell Curve:
On the x-axis (the bottom line), we have a range of intelligence represented by scores varying from zero to 200. This sets the average score at 100. On the y-axis (the vertical line), we have the population, or the number of people who were tested.

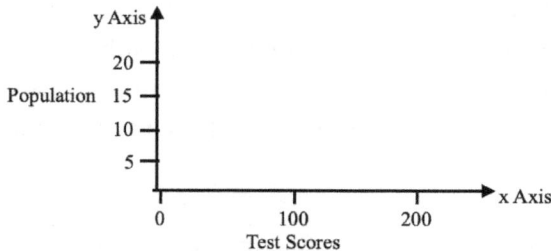

The height of each column represents the score obtained by a number of people. The score an individual obtains is said to represent the worth of their inherited genes and how much their worth can be developed by environmental factors. By Example, we can see that 15 people scored 70 points, 20 scored 100 points, and 10 people scored 160 points.

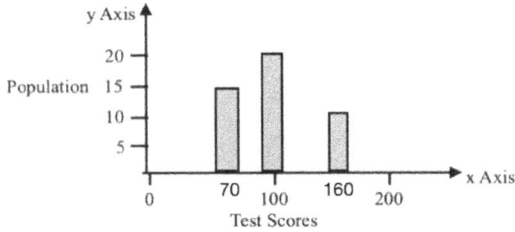

According to Galton's theory, all scores will move away from the average, as Quetelet believed his arrows would have landed. It is, therefore, assumed that the number of people taking the test will vary continuously in their intelligence, as will their test scores.

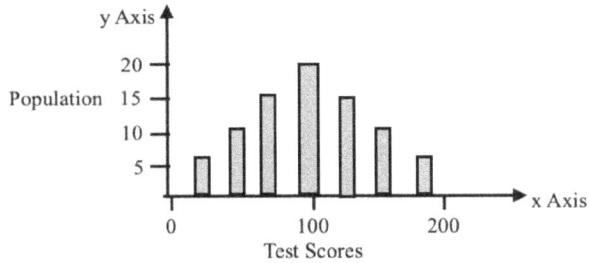

The heights of all the scores are joined by a line to represent the overall variation.

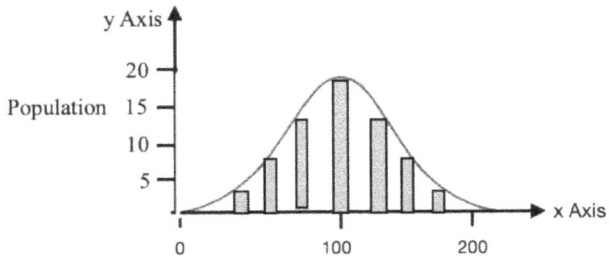

This is the Bell Curve.

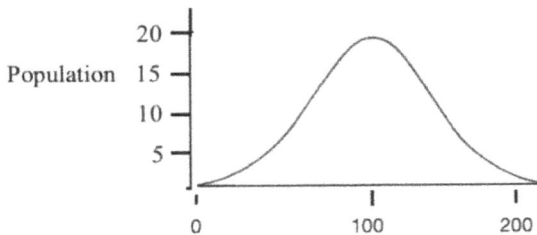

We are impressed to understand that the score an individual gains in an IQ test, and so their placement on the Bell Curve, is based on questions that are fair and impartial to all tested. We shall come to see how they can very easily be otherwise.

Yet, the importance of this graph cannot be underestimated. Should people doubt Galton's argument, or not understand the later mathematical formulas that purported to prove how human beings were born ranging from stupid to brilliant, they could imagine this to be so through the picture they were directed to understand.

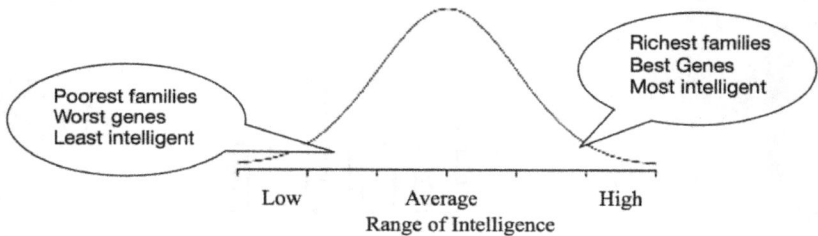

Poorest families
Worst genes
Least intelligent

Richest families
Best Genes
Most intelligent

Low   Average   High
Range of Intelligence

This point is equally valid today. People will look upon a graph or an illustration and, in being able to easily recognise an effect, will too easily fail to see the necessity to question the factors said to produce that effect. Essentially, the picture sells the story. Thus, everyone sees the same picture and everyone is happy with it, but nobody knows why! People, it is to be said, are more inclined to follow an idea they may know nothing at all about if they can visually picture how events interact, and so believe that they understand why they do.

In fact, it is difficult today to wonder how Galton's theory would have been maintained in the manner that it was throughout the 20th century, if it were not for the tremendously influential use of this graph. This is made very clear when we learn that an associate of Galton named Karl Pearson subsequently renamed Gauss's curve as "The Normal Distribution Curve," and in doing so gave it a more scientifically appealing nature.

In order to give mental capacity (as Galton termed intelligence to ally it to social capacity) a definable quality, he took examples of eminent men (said to be so because they were named in the Times obituary) and compared these to the population of the British Isles. This, he reasoned, gave evidence that 250 of every 1 million men would be of eminent character. This, of course, completely ignores the fee that would have had to be paid for mention in this distinguished newspaper, let alone the fact that too many of the population at that time would not have been able to read it.

By applying the logic of Quetelet to this proportion, Galton devised a scale of 14 points to represent the degrees of human intelligence, and so how any population could be graded on the basis of their "intellectual gifts." He concluded this chapter, the most vital in his whole argument, with the conviction that: "Certainly the class G (just above average) of such animals (referring to dogs) is far superior to the g (the lowest category) of the humankind."[53]

The failure of Galton's system of classification is not so much that he gave dogs a higher status than the lowest form of human beings (whom he detested), but that **Quetelet's idea of variation is only coincidental of a phenomenon. It is not a scientific law!**

First, Quetelet's reasoning that arrows fired at a target would fall in equal proportions on either side of the average is only an assumption. Most may land in a similar area, but it is also true that they may be unevenly distributed when they land. It cannot be stated (as we have just illustrated) that there is a law that proves that if 22 arrows were fired, 10 of those would land in a cluster and 6 would fall either side of this as 3, 2, and 1 separated by equal distances. Yet, this is precisely what Galton's law of deviation from an average is said to prove!

After all, it may be that 2 would be closer to the target, 7 further away, and the remaining divided into 2 groups of averages. This is extremely important to realise, and one to hold in memory for when we discuss how social scientists state that the law of deviation from the average is unchangingly precise. It is only by this conviction that they are able to define human intelligence into very specific and predictable categories.

Accordingly, it is of equal significance to understand that the logic Quetelet applied to the way arrows would land is not evidence of the way genes code vary and so how intelligence can be defined. Yet, Galton believed it was, and he used Gauss' curve to assure his audiences that the value of what can be seen corresponds directly to the value of the genes that cannot. This is a complete fallacy.

While the use of Gauss's curve supports Galton's explanation of deviation from an average, the real curve for any feature of the environment can vary tremendously. We have just suggested this in the landing of 2, 7, and two averages of arrows. We have much to discuss about this, but in principle, the way gene codes vary cannot be directly related to the way the products they are partly responsible for vary. This is because the environment can change this relationship beyond expectation, as we indicated in the previous chapter.

May we begin to understand, then, that any variations we notice between the intelligence of individuals cannot be proven to be caused by variations in their gene codes. Consider that the gene coding for the human red cell acid phosphatase produces not one, but five very different variations once it develops through different environments.[54]

Fig.1

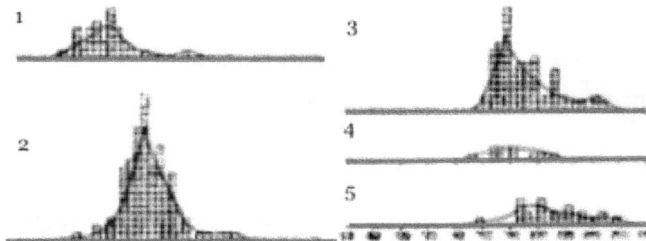

These five variations show how the environment can create very different graphs from the exact same gene code. As we can see by these variations, the graph that is produced from one is not similar enough to any other to be divided into categories and then related to any of the other graphs. Each graph is unique to itself, and none of them show any similarity to Gauss's curve. The truth of the matter is that Gauss's curve can be applied to Quetelet's reasoning only because one is coincidental with the other. We shall return to this issue towards the end of this book, where we explain how the Paretian distribution curve completely makes the whole existence of the Gauss Curve invalid when it is used in regard to human ability.

However, such different variations as above would not have been acceptable to either Galton or those who followed in his steps. The survival of their whole argument lay in the complete acceptance that Gauss's curve would always be said to demonstrate how an average would form in any aspect of an assembled people, with lesser and higher qualities moving away from the average in equal steps.

Belief in this was fundamental to Galton's theory that there would always be found a select few, in any group, who were superior to the rest. The application of Gauss's graph could not be seen as coincidental. It had to be believed to comply with a natural and so an incontestable law.

In an attempt to show how the law of deviation from an average is always present in any population, Galton referred to test results at a military training school. In the example to which he referred on page 33 of *Hereditary Genius*,[55] he pointed out that 73 candidates had varied in their scores from 6,500 down to 1,600. He tabulated these candidates into 8 divisions, and explained how the greatest cluster of candidates was found to lie about the score of 3,000.

Actual divisions: 8, 22, 22, 11, 6, 3, 1, 0

Fig.2a

No. of
Candidates

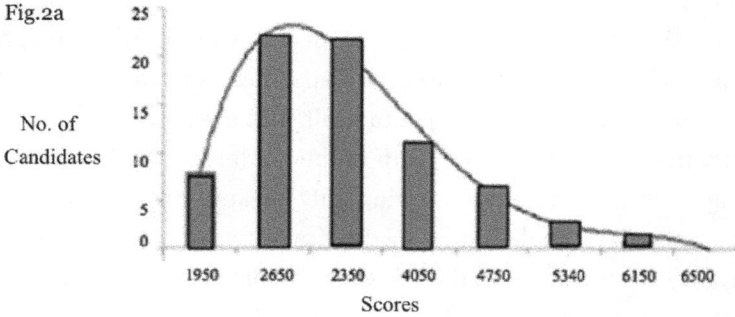

Scores

Galton did not display this as a graph in his book because it better served the illusion he was creating, not to do so. However, we can see in our graph here how these candidates and their real scores are in line with the factual graphs in our previous illustration. Fig.2a does not conform to the law of deviation from an average, because the numbers extending either side of this show no progressive balance.

Making this the example to prove his point, Galton then explained how this score of 3,000 could be taken to be the average, if the scores of more candidates were taken into consideration. To demonstrate how this would happen, he added 13 imaginary candidates and manufactured scores for them to create a further 3 divisions. Having done this, he made a second tabulation.

Galton's divisions: 0, 1, 5, 8, 13, 16, 16, 13, 8, 5, 1, 0

Fig.2b

No. of
Candidates

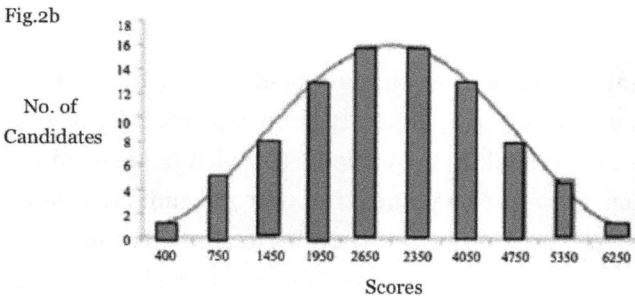

Scores

We can see that Galton took a factual example of scores that did not conform to what he wanted, and changed enough of the information to make the scores create what he did. He justified this by saying that this would have happened anyway if more information had been available, because (in his own words) the natural law of deviation from an average is unavoidable.

It is extremely important to realise here, that this practice of arranging test data to prove the validity of this graph became a common feature in intelligence testing. In other words, questions were selected that will give the responses that support the impression of the curve. Thus, a question that can be answered by only half of those tested will place their score in the mid-point of the range. We shall return to this in a later chapter with much significance.

However, as we can see from the five graphs in Fig.1, populations do not necessarily conform to Quetelet's arrangement. This is only a natural phenomenon that can appear. It does not appear as a natural law. Sometimes it appears in a population, other times it does not, and even when it does, it may only be similar in appearance without providing the precise balance Galton said of it. This will be more understandable when we later come to examine the Paretian Distribution Curve.

Yet, Galton used the example of these test scores as evidence that his law of deviation from an average was a fact. However, despite this example being one of the foundations of why we today believe intelligence is genetically inherited, we can see there is no evidence here for what he states. In fact, when we examine the credibility of the law of deviation from an average, we inadvertently open up a whole can of worms. Let us now begin to do so.

When people look upon the Bell Curve graph, they are caused to think of a general population affected by a general condition. Galton said this general condition is the value of intelligence inherited. However, it could be equally true to state that the intelligence of the vast majority of people is not proven to be affected by differences in their genes, and that what we are really witnessing may only be the effect of a very complex environment.

Indeed, although we know that gene designs naturally vary, it is important to realise that we cannot always know if a normal gene variation is responsible for a difference we witness between normally functioning human beings. Such a difference may have been caused by factors in the environment. As we shall come to see, it is this confusion as to how much the environment can influence a gene design that led to the creation of the nature/nurture study.

This study has been rigorously examined for over 120 years of continual effort, and yet has not been solved. We hope that you may find the solution to this enigma in the final pages of this book.

The basic problem is that with normal genetic diversity, we cannot know how the gene design has varied in functional quality, because of the complex environment it must appear through.

This raises an extremely important point that is not recognised in understanding how the genes that code for intelligence are believed to vary, because they may not or at least not as Galton believed.

If you consider that IQ scores range from zero to 200, it is important to know that those who score very low, say those who gain 30 to 50 points, tend not to be the same cognitively as those who score higher. These human beings usually have some differences from the norm in their physiology. They may have Down Syndrome and have evolved from a chromosomal disorder, or they may have inherited normal genes but incurred oxygen starvation in the birth process.

Yet, because of their condition, it will not only be their ability for intelligence that will be restricted, but also their overall ability to interface with the environment. We may witness this in their neurological and motor abilities and so in their general morphology. Thus, none cognitively fully functioning human beings tend to operate outside the normal framework by which we compare the intelligence of those normally born.

This is absolutely not to suggest that we should classify such human beings differently in our societies, for each brings their own human and very essential values and meanings. The point here is only how they are used to explain statistics in intelligence — that cannot be otherwise explained, and not so for their use in a social community. In my experience, individuals with Down Syndrome have a far greater capacity to share love and inspire compassion, which is so much missing in our debt-ridden, stressful societies.

The only important point we stress here is that such human beings are not cognitively fully functional. Yet, their restriction in functioning cognitively is used to explain how the value of all gene codes vary in quality through continuous steps — even though the cause of their restriction may not be genetic. Consider here those who incur oxygen starvation in the birth process.

Yet, this is the root of why we think those who inherit poor gene qualities will have low intelligence, those who inherit higher qualities will gain higher scores, and those who gain the highest quality through inheritance will gain the maximum score in an IQ test. Such reasoning underlies the whole of Galton's philosophy and work. Yet, there is no evidence for it.

In fact, as we shall examine in great detail later, those who do score the highest, said to be geniuses, do not come from a genetic line of geniuses

114

and nor do they produce a genetic line of geniuses. A genius is a one-off, which can only be explained by environmental factors, as we shall see.

Accordingly, it is wrong to place all human beings on a scale of zero to 200 and use those who were born with some cognitive difficulty as evidence of genetic differences in those normally born.

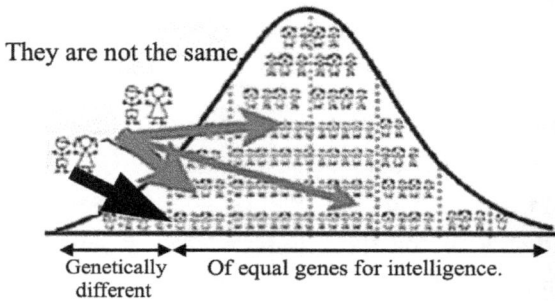

They are not the same.

Genetically different   Of equal genes for intelligence.

After all, if we do not include those who are none cognitively fully functional in IQ tests, we have no reason to assume that those who score higher do so because of some different quality in their gene order. This must be especially so, when we realise that geniuses do not have different qualities of gene competence from the norm.

This is a very serious point that is not understood when it is claimed all human beings vary in their intelligence because of genetic differences. In the case of human beings normally born, there is only the assumption, based on comparison to none cognitively fully functioning individuals, that they do inherit gene designs of different functional qualities, which give reason to Galton's deviation from the average.

Accordingly, if none cognitively fully functionals were withdrawn from test scores, there could be no assumption and certainly no evidence that those who are fully functional demonstrate differences in their abilities because of genetic differences. With this being understood, all differences witnessed in those who function cognitively normally could be explained by factors of environmental development. We are led from this to ponder if variation in a group is actually ....

a) created in one part by a singular class of gene design, which although containing variations, does not offer any difference to the environment to work with. We have discussed many examples of this. And in the other, by a much smaller class of individuals who are none cognitively fully functioning in their operation with the environment. We may think of a Down Syndrome here.

b) created by a few slightly different codes that are randomly mixed within a huge population that offers some differences to the environment, but which may be overcome by the environment. And a group of other individuals who are restricted in their operation with the environment, as in (a).

c) created by an extensive variation of codes that bring very different qualities to the environment, but which may not be recognised because of the overwhelming influence of the environment - unless they are of none fully functioning individuals, as in (a).

d) created by an extensive variation of codes that bring very different qualities to the environment, in how it may develop each code.

Psychology adopted the last possibility, because this is the only one that explains how test scores can be said to vary in line with the assumed variation of genetic codes. This is vital to the claim that intelligence varies in a population and so can be measured.

Yet, if we refer back to our discussion on the many components that come into play to create an act of intelligence, we could find many instances where differences in a component's performance can be totally attributed to environmental factors, as the gene design has evolved to accommodate this influence. As always in this matter of intelligence, the problem is trying to understand what the actual design of the gene is and the influence of the environment upon this design.

Accordingly, if the environment cannot be classified, because it is too extensive, and we have given simple examples of curiosity and the human spirit that would make it so, then the quality of a normal gene variation to affect the development of an individual's intelligence cannot be known.

All that can be known is that if a human being developed from a mutated gene or incurred some difficulty in their birth process, they should be categorised as having a different quality of intelligence from the norm, and not used as a difference from the norm to prove what can otherwise not be. We have much to discuss upon this later.

With this being so, the placement of the vast majority of people on the Bell Curve could be explained purely through the history of their experiences, with no relation to differences caused by genetic diversity. In other words, and contrary to what we have always been told, there do not have to be genetic differences in the capabilities we witness through the environment.

This takes us back to the fundamental error that Galton took from Quetelet in dealing with an explanation for averages, where instead of understanding how a characteristic developed in each entity through causes specific to them, the development of all entities was explained through a generalisation of causes.

After all, when Quetelet recorded the drinking habits of people in his society, he did not seek to understand why different people drank the way they did, for example, were they drinking because of depression, domestic or money problems or did they simply enjoy sharing company, and how many friends did they have who liked to drink, and why did they drink? As we can see, the environment can become extremely complex once honest consideration is given to it.

This is to say that the idea that human intelligence can be known in the individual is mistakenly based on the assumption that the environment of all people can be known and each individual can be classified within this to discover their inherited worth of intelligence. Over the many pages ahead of us, we shall learn why this idea is a complete fallacy, and what it means to the ways we teach children because of it.

I can give an insight into this by relating to an experience I had while teaching English to a class of Asian students. While we hold to the idea that the quality of the genes determines the quality of intelligence, we know this is not the case with language. Our ability for language is not affected by genetic diversity. Any variation we notice in language capability is only brought about through environmental experience.[56]

We may realise, then, that none of the differences of any of the 23 students in my class could be related to a genetic quality. All their differences were purely a matter of development. There were those who were very good, those who were not really sure of what they were doing, and the most who lingered between them.

Therefore, while all the students in that class exhibited differences in ability that conformed to the law of deviation from an average and could be displayed on the Bell Curve, as Gauss's curve has become known today, not one placement was related to a genetic ability. I knew that if I had had the time, I could have raised the language skill of the worst in that class to the level of the best.

The best, I came to understand, were only so because they had been raised by parents who spoke English and practised this at home. Their parents had taken them to countries where they had to speak English, which gave them confidence and purpose through this. As these children grew, they wanted to learn the English words and meanings to the songs they liked. By comparison, the worst had only watched a few English movies with subtitles in their own language, and been disinterested in this foreign language when they had been at school.

This leads us to consider the possibility that any normally born child may develop to any level of work proficiency, if they were given the correct guidance. Watson expressed this belief when he stated,

"Give me a dozen healthy infants, well-formed, and my own specialised world to bring them up in, and I'll guarantee to take any one at random and train him to become any type of specialist I might select, doctor, lawyer... and yet, even beggar man and thief, regardless of his talents, penchants, tendencies, abilities, vocations and race of his ancestors."[57]

J.B.Watson

Any difficulty in accepting this lies in a lack of knowledge of what the environment of intelligence is. We will gain a better understanding of this when we later meet individuals who vastly outperformed what was previously thought to be their stable (or fixed) value of intelligence, as based on a misunderstanding of genetic diversity.

In *Mediation: Crafting the Ability of the Child,* for example, we examine the case of a child who was tested and given an IQ score of 63. However, through careful intervention, giving attention to his emotions and helping him to restructure his understanding of how to interact with the environment, the same child later demonstrated an IQ of 158![58]

A key discussion in *Brain Plasticity* will be how our intelligence is affected through our behavioural experiences. Our competence and so our performance in intelligence is directly and indirectly influenced through the ways others behave towards us. When we have security from others, we are more sensitive when we inquire into information, just as we are when we process it. However, when others hurt or disturb us, they can cause us to develop less proficient means of processing information. Being aware of this gives insight into the effect of bullying.

There are, however, many other factors we will come to discuss that explain why an individual gains the score they do in an IQ test, and so how any of those 73 candidates Galton referred to could have produced very different scores if their personal histories had been different. After all, it cannot be proven, in any way, that the scores they gained had anything to do with the quality of the genes they inherited.

With this being so, there is no purpose that the Gauss's curve has in any of this discussion, save to give an impression of some understanding that would otherwise not be found.

Galton, of course, would have had none of this. He had built up a very strong political argument and did his best to present it through measurement. Such measurement was meant to give his argument a scientific presentation. However, as we have just begun to realise, the issue is not in the differences measured and then displayed, but in the specific causes of those differences. Consider the following, where we examine two school children.

We may test and mark them, but this does not explain why they were so marked. For example, we have no idea how interested or how distracted they were in the long process of learning that led them to our evaluation. Equally, we do not consider in the mark we give how happy and positive they are in their home and general school life. Nor do we consider in this mark how much they personally wanted to be involved in each step of their education, and so what they feel is the point of all this. There is, of course, a crucial difference in a child having to learn something in a group of distractions, and wanting to learn it through personal and sensitive guidance.

Therefore, from the viewpoint of the environment and to give some small insight into it, the performance of individuals in any group may be purely the result of their emotional perspectives of the information as they recognise the meanings of its content. This, they could only do through the history of their personality, moods, fears, trusts and insights; as these would be set within the jumble of understandings and misunderstandings that were tethered to the life forces that guided them from the earliest moment of that information!

Thus, because the environment of intelligence is so complex and so overlapping, any assessment of an individual's intelligence has to "basically" ignore what the environment is, even though it is this that is the only known cause of their differences with others.

If this is not done, it is impossible to state with any "pretended" honesty what their intelligence is worth, and so how one may be ranked against another. The license to do this comes from the belief that intelligence does have an inherited value that can be recognized, and thereby related to an environment that cannot.

The most significant observation we can make from all this is that when Gauss' curve is used to illustrate intelligence, that the most it can do is to give indication that something has happened, but it cannot and should not be used to explain how this happening occurred. Therefore, Gauss's curve, Pearson's Normal Distribution Curve, or the Bell Curve of today, play no role in accurately explaining or determining intelligence.

However, as Galton had founded his principle of inheritance on the law of deviation from the average, this very soon led him into an extremely serious problem. This problem threatened to destroy not just his theory, but also that of Charles Darwin's.

In the writing of *Hereditary Genius,* Galton had noted that succeeding generations of a family had achieved different degrees of public recognition. He had noticed how, by example, a grandfather had displayed some talent or ability, how his son had achieved more recognition in this, and how the grandson had become quite acclaimed. Galton, however, found that the grandson's son did not achieve the acclaim of his father, and that his son went virtually unnoticed.

At that time it was logically held that an offspring would be the exact blend of their parents. If, for example, the father were tall and the mother short, their child would be expected to mature to a height somewhere between them. Over generations, this meant that a characteristic would be continually halved. This is the theory of blending inheritance, which we have much to say about later.

Since Galton believed that the level a person accomplished in life was a consequence of their breeding, the fall of ability within a family line brought serious consideration to him. In the broadest sense, it meant that if the average quality of all generations deteriorated, then so would the quality of his civilisation.

"This effect," wrote Galton, "resembles pouring a measure of water into a vessel of wine. The wine is diluted to a constant fraction of its alcoholic strength, whatever that strength may have been..."[59] Galton gave this effect of deterioration the name of "Hereditary reductionism," and took its ramifications as seriously as de Gobineau had done. However, Galton's recognition of this effect underlined an even more serious problem.

From the onset, Darwin had proposed that evolution was a continually slow-changing process, where individuals would arise having very small, but distinct characteristics from the norm. When these characteristics were of more adaptable use, they would create a new species that would breed better than those having the former characteristics and so phase them out. This is the principle of natural selection, as based upon adaptability.

Galton's reductionism, with great regret to both, questioned this, because it suggested variation would be so reduced over generations that a species would eventually be unable to adapt, and thereafter phase itself out of existence. Reductionism threatened to destroy the whole of Darwin's work!

Darwin tried to reason that there must be some sort of variation induced into an organism during its life cycle that would reintroduce variability to counter this reductionism, and so prevent such extinction. However, neither he nor Galton, with whom he corresponded closely, could produce a satisfactory explanation for why adaptability did not overcome reductionism. So seriously was this problem taken by Darwin that he came very close to rejecting his whole theory of natural selection.

For ten years, Galton struggled with the dilemma posed by this problem. Then, in 1876, following an experiment with sweet peas, he believed that he had found the solution he was seeking. In this much noted experiment, Galton both weighed and measured the diameter of a large selection of pea seeds. He divided these into seven packets, which he labelled from K to Q, placed ten seeds in each packet, and with planting and cultivating instructions dispatched them to his friends throughout the United Kingdom. In time, he received data from each of these associates concerning the development of the seeds and of the seed offspring.

Having analysed this information, Galton stated that the variation in weight of each group of seeds was found to be distributed according to the law of deviation from the average. He further stated that when these groups were viewed collectively on a graph, the overall differences between them conformed to the same understanding. In other words, the variation of each group of seed produced the Gauss Curve when displayed on a graph, and when all the groups were put together, they also created this graph. However, Galton further noted that when he compared the position of each parent in a group, the position of their offspring had changed. Each offspring showed a definite shift, with extreme importance towards the central position of the overall population.

Galton was not sure of the exact cause of this movement, but because each offspring group displayed some movement from its parent group, he assumed the cause to be hereditary. With this belief in his mind, he reasoned that he had found the solution to the problem that had dogged him and Darwin for so long. It could now be said that if the quality of a trait were seen to diminish through breeding, "some" innate counter mechanism would reverse this process. This, he believed, would create a degree of consistency in the quality of that trait. He happily termed this phenomenon the "Regression to the Mean."

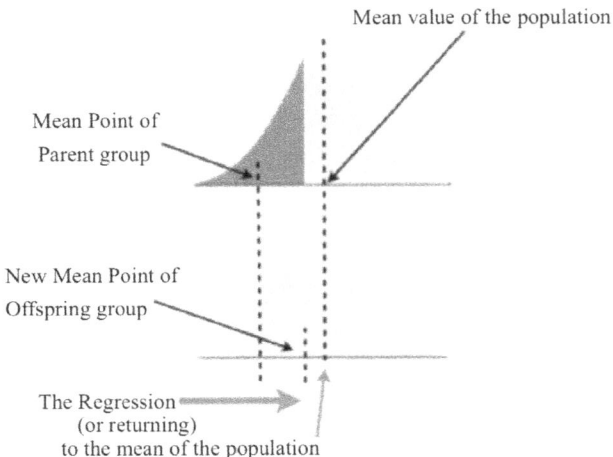

However, a much valid and missed point to this reasoning is that two of the sets Galton had sent out were returned to him as complete failures. Galton had deliberately ignored these failures (which represent more than a quarter and almost a third of the data he obtained), and the implications of them by stating: "The final result was that I obtained the more or less complete produce of seven sets... These results gave me two data, which were all that I wanted in order to understand the way in which one generation of a people is descended from a previous one."[60]

Now that Galton could explain the consistency of human intelligence within a family line, through this pea experiment, he was able to reaffirm that any distribution within a population would conform to the law of deviation from an average.

"The Regression to the Mean", he explained, "...refers primarily to deviations that is to measurements made from the level of mediocrity to the crown of the head, upwards or downwards as the case may be, and not from the ground to the crown of the head. .... In respect to stature "it" may be phrased as follows: namely that the deviations of the sons from "P" are on the average, equal to one third of the deviation of the parent from "P" and in the same direction..."[61]

We must now place great emphasis upon the data that Galton relied upon, and be well aware that it was related only to the peas that survived and not to the seeds that did not. This is a most crucial matter, because it means the actual variability of the pea weights was an underestimation of the variability that would otherwise have been provided. If statistics from all the germinated seeds had been used by Galton, he would not have been able to demonstrate the law of deviation from the average, when they were related to each other!

We can see here further evidence that the law of deviation from the average is not, in fact, a law! Factors do not move away from the centre point of the average in equally diminishing values, with precisely equal movements, every time a group is analysed. Yet, it was fundamental to Galton's argument that people believe that they should.

More importantly, we can see that Galton was not honest in the presentation of his data. As a founder of psychology can be shown to be dishonest with his data, so will we find the same with many of his followers as they sought to gain political support for the same aim. It was in objection to this playing with data, that Winnicott was prompted to remark:

"In other sciences, if something is found to be true it can usually be accepted without emotional strain, but in psychology there is always this matter of strain, so that something which is not quite true is more easily accepted than the truth itself."[62]

It is to be further understood that the "Regression to the Mean" has no specific relationship to inheritance. The phenomenon that Galton observed is a statistical occurrence that arises whenever two samples from a population are compared to each other and imperfectly correlate. Take, by example, a number of related incidents. When these incidents are more similar they will form the average, and where they are more dissimilar they will form the extremities. A snapshot of these incidents before and after "any" small environmental change will show a movement within them, some would have moved closer to the average, and others further away.

Of all movements, the most noticeable would be seen in the extremities, because these would, in being more different, be most affected. As the extremities move away from the average, a stage would be reached where their difference becomes so great that they will no longer be identified with this group. In other words, they would have moved so far from this group that they would have merged into another group -- and so have disappeared from the group they began in. However, extremities moving towards the average will give the greater impression of a general movement, by the group, to return towards the norm.

Galton rightly discovered this statistical phenomenon, but it is not the explanation of stability in inheritance he believed it to be. The cause of why grandfathers, fathers, sons and grandson's sons exhibit different levels of achievement over generations has nothing to do with the act of genetic inheritance. Yet, Galton's Regression to the Mean would become the very means by which a later mathematical system would arise, which would offer to prove precisely this hereditary relationship.

While we have yet to come to coefficients, we may understand that once Galton had grasped the notion of this Regression to the Mean he wanted to make broad applications of it. It was in seeking to obtain data for this purpose that he set up an anthropometric laboratory, contained within the International Health Exhibition staged in London between 1884 and 1885. Within this period nearly 10,000 people visited his laboratory to have all manner of their faculties measured. The relationships between fathers and sons, mothers and daughters, of their height, weight, arm-span, abilities for breathing capacity, reaction time, and, among other things, colour discrimination.

It may have been the prompt he received from this huge statistical exercise that evoked within him a way to actually try to prove with mathematical evidence his claim that intelligence was hereditarily related.

After all, when Galton had begun his quest, a quarter of a century earlier, his "logical" reasoning fitted in with the mood of the time and had swept him forward with a tremendous impetus. However, socialism had now become a political force to be reckoned with, and had gained such levy in political affairs that Galton's theory of class superiority was now required to have a degree of accountability that had not been necessary before.

This need was further compounded by the rise of psychology in Germany, where presumption was beginning to be replaced with ideas of how measurements could give verification. Much work was being done there on reaction times, and there was a link in this that gave promise to how consciousness (as a part of brain activity and so intelligence) may be measured.

It was in following this line that Francis Edgeworth, working in England, had recently gained much acclaim for trying to understand human consciousness through mathematics. In 1881, Edgeworth had written a paper on Mathematical Psychics, where he had endeavoured to show how a mathematical formula could be constructed to determine a "capacity for happiness." He had followed this up with two papers on the comparison of statistics and was rapidly developing a line of mathematics applicable to Galton's needs. Realising the merits of the situation, Galton sought guidance on how to proceed with his concern by inviting Edgeworth to join him. As he did so, Edgeworth began to seek direction for the task of measuring human intelligence through the earlier work of Gustav Fechner.

Chapter Twelve

The Manufacture of Intelligence

"The intelligence of class G (just above average) of such animals (dogs) is far superior to the g (the lowest category) of the humankind."[63]

Sir Francis Galton

Before we continue with the solution that Edgeworth derived for Galton and begin to understand the foundation upon which the measurement of human intelligence lies, there is some need to examine the work of Gustav Fechner. This will be important for us to do, because all experimental psychology is founded in the work that Fechner did. And yet, in having said this, there is a great deal of misunderstanding as to what Fechner's work actually means, and the applications that can be gained from it.

In the early part of the 19th century, a German professor of anatomy had noted how people are more aware of an object when they use their muscles than when they merely touch it with their fingers. This difference of awareness intrigued Ernst Weber to devise some explanation for the relationship between increases in a stimulus and the different levels of awareness they give notice to.[64]

Weber was seeking to gain a higher understanding of the nervous system than can be realised through the normal senses of seeing, hearing and touching. To this end, he began to experiment in how well people could relate to changes in sensory information. For example, if a room were illuminated with a number of candles, "How many candles would need to be added, before a person could notice a difference in brightness?"

It soon became obvious that it was not the number of candles that were important, because the larger the room the less effect individual candles had, but the relationship between what a person knew, and when they noticed a value had changed. Weber termed the first awareness of a change as the Just Noticeable Difference (j.n.d). He devised a means to calculate this j.n.d., by dividing the change in the level of stimulus (DS), by the stimulus it was being referred to (S). This is known as the Weber Law, and is defined as: J.N.D. = DS/S [65]

This law did not assume that sensation could be measured. It was merely a mathematical relationship between one level of stimulus and a very small change in that stimulus. Nevertheless, Weber's work with stimulus attracted the interest of Gustav Fechner, who was seeking some means to formalise a relationship between human consciousness and the physical world. At that time, it was generally held that the mind was different from the body. Fechner reasoned from this that if he could show how consciousness could be mathematically related to stimulus, then he could open up a scientific debate that would have far-reaching effects on social and scientific policies.

In this vein, Fechner argued that since Weber's law conformed to a constancy, then it could be expressed through infinitesimal calculus and explained in logarithmic terms.

In following upon this, he generalised Weber's ratio to explain it as:

$$(DS + S)/S \text{ being equal to constant} + 1.$$

Which, with logarithms took the form:

$$J.N.D. = Log(DS+S)-LogS = Log (constant +1).$$

This formula gave Fechner the basis to state that if a just noticeable difference (j.n.d) were added to the one below it, which in turn was added to the one below that, a progression of units could be devised. The scale of these units, he reasoned, would show how the intensity noticed in a sensation would be proportional to the geometrical increase of the stimulus.[66] The mathematics of this is of little interest to us, but from Fechner's work grew the science of psychophysics.

Psychophysics tries to use mathematics to explain how sensory awareness can be related to changes in a physical experience. If we could consider intelligence to be a matter of the brain's sensory awareness to changes in environmental information, then we may see that Fechner's work is the very root by which intelligence is said to be measurable.

• The significance of Fechner's work is that by the creation of this mathematical formula, he elevated the whole field of (what was to become) psychology to the level of an exact and therefore an authoritative science.[23]

However, it must be realised, as Laming explains, that while in principle the mathematics of Weber's Law is verifiable, the interpretation that Fechner placed upon it is purely speculative. All that Weber's Law shows is that since neural transmission is differential, that the brain is sensitive to changes in the physical world.[67] It does not reveal any precision with this.

When a certain magnitude is to be estimated, for example, the process of comparison within the brain is of a greater than or greater less type. We may notice that a sound is louder or softer or about the same as the previous one, but that is all. Our frame of reference is too insensitive to the accuracy that Fechner reasoned it to be. Therefore, it is not just that the application of logarithms is redundant, but that Fechner's mathematical formula has no actual operational validity.[68]

Indeed, Gregory suggested that the nervous system might use a technique of nulling to achieve the effect that the Weber–Fechner law witnesses. According to this, an unknown quantity is compared to a known quantity. When they are the same, they cancel each other out, or null. When the unknown is sensed to be greater than the known (which is the last recorded balance), a vague step of difference is sensed.[69]

The most striking point that arises from studying Fechner's work is that since each progression from the constant forms a strict relationship between the individual and that stimulus, one cannot be evaluated without the other. In other words, an individual cannot be appraised without the total information that creates the basis of that appraisal.

Specifically, this is to say that **the intelligence of an individual cannot be truthfully evaluated without considering ALL the many varied and minute experiences they have had since they were born. Just as this is impossible, so is it impossible to measure human intelligence!**

As the science of human measurement is founded upon Fechner's reasoning, it must be seen that human potential cannot be assessed mathematically.

This is to say that there is no reliable means to measure the potential of a human being's intelligence.

However, the 19th century was the age of invention, and the world was gripped with a fever in the need to explore and develop. So fast was the pace of this inventiveness that new ideas flooded all aspects of industry and science with a boldness that demanded respect. Little was there a caution that may impede the pace of this development, to which the credibility of each new science seemed self-assured. The implication that any phenomenon of varying characteristics may be readily identified and, through accurate comparison, be qualified, held irresistible attraction to the minds that scrambled as if in a gold rush to further the advancement of mankind.

In accordance with Fechner's line of reasoning, Edgeworth began to work on a mathematical system that would bring a direct relationship between two variables. He produced from this effort, in 1892, the first means of a correlation coefficient. In this work, he had attracted another mathematician by the name of Karl Pearson. Pearson had long been an avid fan of Galton's theory of inherited ability and was prompted by Edgeworth's mathematical endeavours to join their team. However, friction between the mathematicians very quickly turned into a personality conflict, which led to Edgeworth's resignation and the opportunity for Pearson to develop a lifelong partnership with Galton.

In 1896, Pearson developed from Edgeworth's work, which he often disputed, a mathematical model that showed the relationship between two variables. This was called the product-movement correlation coefficient. It was a mathematical formulation describing, in terms of numerical comparison, how factors were related by their similarity or dissimilarity.

Pearson's formula is more elaborate than Fechner's, and as it is readily depicted in most books relating to experimental psychology, we have no need to re-examine it here. The formula is valid. A correlation coefficient is calculated by examining the degree of deviation that two variables make from their mean point. The comparison of their relationship is expressed as a unified factor, lying somewhere between 0 and 1, when used for intelligence. The higher the factor is towards 1, the greater is the similarity taken to be between the variables. Conversely, when the factor is closer towards 0, the relationship is said to be more dissimilar.

The idea behind correlation coefficients is that they can be used to provide indisputable evidence that intelligence is inherited. For example, by examining the performance of a father to a child, or that of two siblings, a high similarity is likely to be noted. We may say they give a factor of .7. If one of these were then compared to a child from another family, it is likely this factor of relationship would be more dissimilar. Let's suggest .4. The argument that this is designed to provide is that if the environments of all tested are extremely similar, then the difference in the scores could be said to be caused by genetic differences.

Quite clearly Pearson was a pure advocate of Galton's ideas, and strove in all manner of persuasions to further his quest. Accordingly, while Fechner had always been clear of the limitations of mathematics, Pearson was too willing to believe that his formula measured differences in the inherited quality of intelligence. "Once we fully realise," he wrote, "that the psychic is inherited in the same way as the physical, there is no room left to differentiate one from the other."[70]

Despite what Pearson wrote, it is extremely important to understand that he only produced a formula that shows the relationship of two variables. Pearson's formula does **NOT explain the cause of the relationship** of any of the variables expressed in it. Consider this in the following correlations (r):

Correlation Coefficient r = 0.
No relationship.
As one value increases, there is
no tendency for the other value
to change in a specific direction.

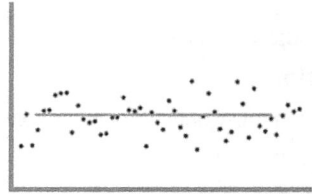

Correlation Coefficient r= 0.6
A moderate relationship.

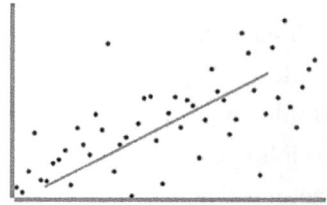

Correlation Coefficient r = 0.8
A fairly strong positive relationship.

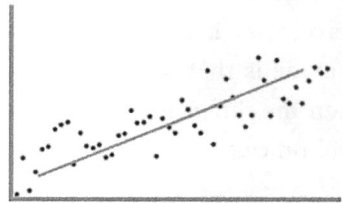

As we can see, each graph shows the relationship of 2 axes, but there is no explanation that proves their relationships.

In 1926, George Yule, who had worked under Pearson for many years, made a study of a major correlation between the number of marriages and the mortality rate, as they were affected by the progress of science. In his review of this study, Yule concluded that:

"The correlations were sheer nonsense, and their meaning had no significance at all."[71]

As Yule pointed out, these two variables are not in any sort of way causally related to one another. The point that is very important to understand here is that a correlation does not imply how or why either of the variables move as they do. A correlation does not explain the cause.

This point is **totally missed in the use of coefficients with defining intelligence.** To see coefficients in the light of pure statistical use, free of Galton's shadow, consider a hypothetical study. Let us use coefficients to show how much public opinion believed that Oswald was directly responsible for the murder of John F. Kennedy.

Following the assassination in 1963, most people interviewed at that time, as persuaded by media reports, would have readily believed that Oswald had fired the fatal shot. Accordingly, a study of opinions would have suggested a very high similarity between Oswald being the assassin and Kennedy being the assassinated person. Let us suggest .9. This is a factor that would have been more than enough in the minds of many, who believe that this number represented the cause of the effect, to endorse the appropriate punishment.

Yet, if the same study were repeated today, where in the light of conspiracy theories and conflicting accounts of who may have been responsible and why, spread over nearly 40 years of television documentaries, plays, films and books, most people would see Oswald as either partially involved or innocent. This opinion could be reflected in a low coefficient factor of, let us suppose, .4. From this example, we can realise to fundamental failings of correlation coefficients:

First: A correlation coefficient gives absolutely no valid account of the information that produced it.

Second: Any result that is represented by a correlation coefficient is totally reliant upon the selection of the data that produced it. In other words, the way the environment is selected will determine the result of the correlation coefficient.

These are very valid points when correlation coefficients are used in attempts to measure human intelligence, because they allow political interest to very easily misrepresent the value of information.

For the moment, consider how a right-wing psychologist could select data to give the impression that IQ tests favour the importance of inheritance over development.

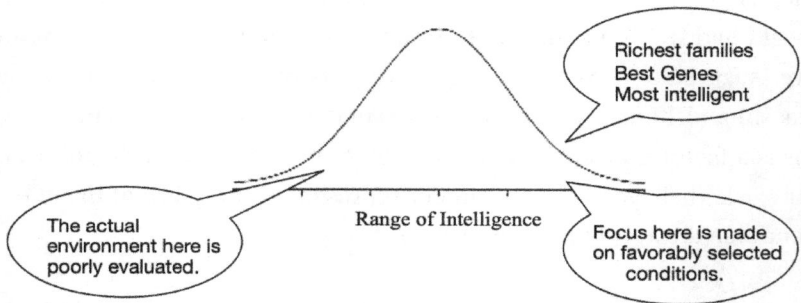

Of course, a left-wing psychologist could just as easily place more emphasis on the environment to influence data in support of their case. The manner in which the environment is selected will become very important to us when we later discuss a book called *The Bell Curve*.

The further we move through this book, the more apparent this playing of data will become through the endeavours of political engineering. Accordingly, we shall shortly examine a famous study on identical twins, where the same data was viewed from different perspectives to present two versions of the importance of the environment and, conversely, that of inheritance.

Yet, what is not appreciated in all endeavours to measure human intelligence is that the environment is simply too unknown to be calculated. To attempt to categorise the environmental factor into definable boxes for statistical purposes is to give no consideration to what the environment means. It is like describing the quality of a painting displayed in the Louvre, by simply stating it is a Pre-Raphael,

Impressionist, Expressionist, or Modern. The personal feelings of the delight or the sadness the artist expressed are simply washed away with the colours they used. When we do this, we replace the uniqueness each human being has with a given number.

Accordingly, we cannot judge the ability of each of the billions of people on this planet by assigning their individual conditioning to a number of boxes a psychologist may wish to invent to represent the environment. We cannot simply dehumanise intelligence to obtain a statistical factor, and then reapply individualism to assess potential. Yet, this is what correlation coefficients are used for.

As we saw with Weber's "just noticeable differences," it is the sensitivity of the subject to their environment that decides the whole quality of the operation. So, it is not so simple to take two individuals who evolved through two different environments (or even as we shall soon see with the different environments that identical twins were raised through), and concoct a paper test upon a singular and theoretical environment to seek to determine their inherited ability and then apply this ratio to all human beings.

The true error of this mathematical system is not in the biasing of the sampling or in the inaccuracies of the measurements, but in the actual belief that intelligence can be determined through it. Even if every conceivable detail that affected the emotion and manner of reason of one individual, throughout the life of their individualistic environment could be measured with great precision, we may still not use this to evaluate how they will relate their emotions to the performance of some future task; or rise or fall in their expectation of reaching it.

However, while it was always a victory to Galton that the genetic factor appeared in correlation coefficients, it was also important that it was seen to be at least 50% responsible. If it were less than this, his opponents could argue that social conditioning was a greater cause in educational performance, and so a deciding factor in the old social-work order problem.

When Galton first raised this issue of inherited intelligence, he regarded environmental conditioning as negligible. However, as this argument became more questionable, he found it necessary to accept the role of the environment. Yet, he always sought means to undermine it. In his efforts to prove the significance of inherited intelligence, Galton presented two arguments. His first was the study of a family's history, and his second was the study of identical twins.

However, let us pause for a moment to really understand what is happening here. Every feature we display comes from our genes and so inheritance. If the coding was not there, we would not have them. Yet, this is not to think (as is done) that the arrangement of the genes necessarily affects the development of the feature they are responsible for creating. (Do you think the quality of your genes determines how well you laugh or cry? In such cases, the determining factor of these features would be nature zero and nurture 100%! It is important, then, that we keep an open mind to how genes have evolved to have different purposes. This will be a central issue in our understanding of the root causes of intelligence.

Yet, with this said, let us move now from discussing Galton directly to discussing how his work was developed through others, and the applications they made of it to further construct the consciousness that lies behind our evaluation of another's ability.

Chapter Thirteen

The Family History Method

The recognition that epilepsy runs in families goes back to the time of Hippocrates. So by the time of Galton, the belief that mental illnesses were passed through a family line was nothing new. To this point, Esquirol had written in 1838 that: "Of all diseases, mental alienation is the most markedly hereditary, and the most likely to run in families..."[72] It was not, however, until 1877 when Galton read a much publicised report about a criminal family, that he realised how the family history method could give support to his claim of inherited intelligence.

This particular report had been made by an executive member of the New York prison association. R. Dugdale had noted that six prisoners, held in the county jails, were members of the Juke family. As a social reformer, Dugdale wrote a comprehensive report about the lineage of this family. By expounding upon this family's high level of immorality, vices and criminality, Dugdale had hoped to bring attention to and support for the improvement of social and welfare conditions at large.

However, the report, and the subsequent book he wrote upon this *The Jukes: a study in crime, pauperism, disease, and heredity,* was sold to the public through newspapers as a warning to society in the danger of bad blood. The Juke family was raised to instant notoriety, where they became and remain to this day a classic study of the family history method in social science.

Ever ready to realise an opportunity, Galton seized upon the issue when he became aware of it, and wrote: "The criminal class by heredity is a question difficult to grapple with ... an extraordinary example of this is afforded by the history of the infamous Jukes family in America, whose pedigree has been made out, with extraordinary care."[73]

However, despite Galton's account of the Juke family, records were unearthed in 2001 that showed this impression to be very wrong. While the Juke family was realised to be a very large one, it was discovered that not all of its members were of the ilk as the media had presented them. In fact, very many were realised to be very respectable and prominent members of their society.[74]

The facts that came to light supported the contention that although Dugdale had embellished the criminal side of the family and invented upon this, his purpose in doing so had been to gain widespread support for the improvement of living conditions, and not as the case was made for him to expound upon the inheritance of criminal characteristics.

Galton, needless to say, saw only the hereditary aspect of the vice, and, based purely on the news relayed to him from America, burst upon the British scene in 1883 with a new suggestion to strengthen his call for the maintenance of a reliable social structure. This was not to be the better welfare Dugdale had hoped for, but of a suggestion to phase out undesirable breeds in society. By totally relying upon the newspaper accounts of the criminal elements of the Juke family, and being totally unaware of either Dugdale's real intention or the reasons for only a few members of this family to turn to crime, Galton set about creating what would eventually become the science of eugenics.

"The word eugenics," he explained, "would sufficiently express the idea; it is at least a neater word and a more generalised one than aviculture, which I once ventured to use."[75] The idea of eugenics is to encourage good bloodlines to breed genetically in a society, and to phase out bad ones associated with noticeable criminality and low morality. Eugenics, in its most extreme form, is taken by some as a license to eliminate an undesirable race of people or to commit genocide. Hitler took this theme from Galton and developed it to the most horrific extreme.[76]

However, it was in America where eugenics, in a milder form, really began under the guidance of Henry Goddard. As we now discuss Goddard, we will come to understand how the testing of intelligence first began, and why it formally did so in America. It was not, we shall find, for the purpose of helping children.

In 1897, Henry Goddard was the superintendent at the Vineland Institution in New Jersey. This was an institution for those regarded to be mentally defective. It was while he was working here that Goddard came across a feeble-minded girl who has since been known as Deborah Kallikak.

Henry Goddard

According to Goddard, in an attempt to uncover the origins of Deborah's feeble-mindedness, he had been fascinated to investigate her lineage. As he delved into her family's past, Goddard explained how he discovered that a soldier of the Revolutionary War (1775-83), being of normal breeding and a Quaker, had become "drunk" in a tavern and impregnated a simple-minded girl. This soldier, of otherwise good character, was named Martin Kallikak.

Goddard explained that Martin soon married a "normal and good" woman, with whom he bred a long line of respectable citizens. These were said to become doctors and lawyers, etc. On the other hand, he explained how the simple girl at the tavern gave birth to an illegitimate, feebleminded boy. This boy was described as producing a degenerative line of social undesirables. Goddard explained that these were noted to be imbeciles, criminals, prostitutes, and drunks.

In 1912, Goddard published his findings in a book entitled *The Kallikak Family*.[77] In this book, he included a genetic family tree, which he based on the recently discovered Mendelian principles of inheritance. Goddard's depiction of these ancestral lines vividly shows the consequence (and the social danger) of people from good breeding mixing their genes with those of poor breeding. As we can see, Goddard charts all the offspring of the normal woman to be normal children, but shows a high percentage of children bred from the feebleminded girl to be feebleminded

The Kallikak Family Tree

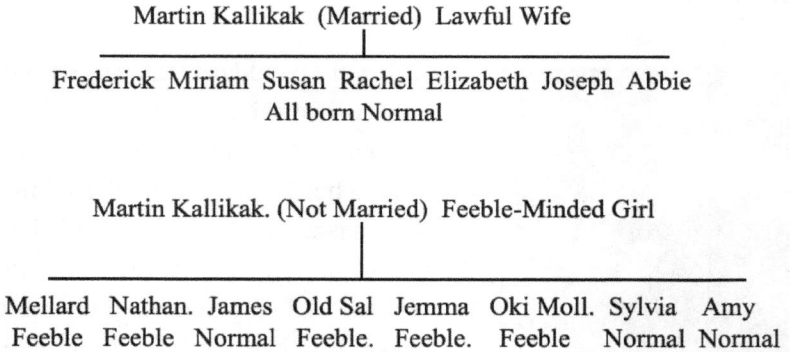

Martin Kallikak (Married) Lawful Wife

Frederick Miriam Susan Rachel Elizabeth Joseph Abbie
All born Normal

Martin Kallikak. (Not Married) Feeble-Minded Girl

Mellard	Nathan.	James	Old Sal	Jemma	Oki Moll.	Sylvia	Amy
Feeble	Feeble	Normal	Feeble.	Feeble.	Feeble	Normal	Normal

In his book, Goddard included a number of photographs.

As we can see, such photographs clearly show degenerative features in the line of the Kallikak family. This is the family line to which Deborah was said to belong. *The Kallikak Family* book brought great attention and financial gain to Goddard, and to the concerns within his society of the real danger of degenerative breeding, which the Juke story had paved the way for. Such degenerates, Goddard suggested, should be kept isolated in special camps away from other members of their society, or be subjected to compulsory sterilisation to control their breeding.[78]

The journals and writings that Goddard produced on the Kallikak family created an almost hysterical reaction within the American public, and pressure from this influenced political and educational policies first in this country and then in others. Not only did they influence immigration policies in America, which in turn gave Goddard license to develop his concept of IQ testing, as we shall see, but more regrettably, they gave life to the compulsory sterilisation programs that arose out of them.

These eugenic programs did lead to the forced sterilisation of hundreds of thousands of people around the world. In America alone, 65,000 individuals were sterilised against their will and often without their knowledge in hospitals and prisons.[79] All of this was done on the basis that intelligence tests and the family history method, all legacies of Galton, were said to prove without a shadow of doubt that the conditions of criminality and low moral behaviour, etc, had genetic origins.[80]

So, human beings who were found to be undesired by their society, such as the feebleminded, insane, criminalistic, epileptic, diseased, known to be blind, deaf, deformed, and those who were politically undesired such as those dependent upon the state, orphans, the poor, tramps and homeless people were compulsory sterilised in America, and in other countries still today.[81]

Yet, we can safely assume that for the very most of these human beings, there was nothing genetically wrong with them. However, despite this, the Kallikak study has become and remains, over 100 years later, a classic example of the use of the family history method to show the inheritance of mental characteristics.

What now follows is highly illustrative of the danger of trusting psychological profiles of people, especially when these are used to endorse political programs. In 1981, Gould carefully examined the photographs Goddard had presented. After careful analysis, he explained how they had been deliberately altered to make the people in them appear more degenerative than they could have been.[82]

Elks followed this up with a very detailed examination of every photograph Goddard had used, and concluded that they "were a masterpiece of visual indictment propaganda that worked on the levels of assumed scientific objectivity, stereotypic images of imbecility to achieve persuasiveness."[83] Well, before the time of Photoshop, and with the use of a heavy pencil and etching knife,

Facial Alteration

Goddard had altered the perception of the people in the photographs he used in his book to make them look like Morons. In fact, moron was a term he created. It is highly significant for what will follow that we realise that:

All the photographs Goddard had used were fakes!

During the 1980s, Wehmeyer and Smith began to research the case of the Kallikak family. After a great deal of effort, they discovered that Goddard had falsified the existence of the Kallikak story. The Kallikaks never existed!

Kallikak, it turned out, was a name invented by Goddard from the Greek words kalós and kakis, taken here to mean good and bad! Goddard had disguised the real identities of the Kallikaks, which made it very difficult for his work to be challenged.[84] It took real detective effort from McAdams and MacDonald, who took up this case, to discover that Goddard had based his fictitious story on a family called the Wolvertons.

It turned out that Goddard had discovered the existence of two John Wolvertons. They were, in fact, second cousins who came from legitimately married parents and had created two different family lines. Goddard had merged the existence of these two men into a single character, changed the family name to hide what he had done, and claimed that the feebleminded Deborah in his care was of one of these lines.[85]

In Smith and Wehmeyer's investigations into Deborah's line, they discovered that there was absolutely no evidence of hereditary "feeble-mindedness" in the Wolvertons. In fact, they found that the family, by and large, were quite normal, and that Goddard had purposely distorted the impression of them to make his case.[86] Indeed, after investigating Deborah's school record, they believed her profile fitted that of a person more inclined to have language-related learning disabilities than one who was mentally retarded. In fact, visitors to the Vineland Institution often mistook Deborah for a teacher on account of her manner of competency, and the normal skills of capability she exhibited.

In spite of this, Deborah had been institutionalised since she was first sent to Goddard at the age of 8. Deborah was detained in the Vineland Institution until she died there at the age of 89. The tragedy of her case was not only that she was falsely institutionalised for 81 years, but that her real name was not Deborah. Her real name was Emma![87] She had been deprived of her real identity by Goddard for almost all of her life.

Emma

As one fact after another emerged to disclose Goddard's fraud, the picture that was eventually revealed explained how Goddard had invented a moral story to influence the morality of his society. He took a lady in his institution who had some learning disability, although we now know this was not severe, publicly dubbed her feebleminded, and invented two family lines from a common origin.

Goddard, a Quaker himself, had explained that one line was of Quakers who produced respectable citizens. The other line, he explained, produced generations of illegitimate and degenerative people. Deborah was presented as living proof of the authenticity of his investigations!

We have here two instances where classic and extremely influential studies of the family history method were deliberately falsified to support the political aims of their authors. Dugdale to improve social conditions, and Goddard to promote Quaker morality on the one hand and on the other to remove feeblemindedness from his society. Both of their efforts developed very influential political policies that did shape the direction of social and educational directives in many countries.

Both were totally false!

Aside from these fraudulent cases, it is not that easy or reliable to investigate the ability of a family line. After two generations, the people being referred to are usually deceased. This means that the only sources available to relate to their abilities lie in offhand records or accounts passed on by word of mouth. Statements that "his grandfather used to do the same type of thing" or "I remember his father was always good at school" can too easily be translated into factual comments. These can bring a real weight of influence to an impression. Yet, they are not based on any kind of concrete evidence.

The family history method is often supported by knowledge of a genetic disorder or trait. Haemophilia is a very good example of this. It is a blood disorder that is passed within families genetically. However, such a genetic disorder is carried only in the female line and is presented in the male line. This means that the female will carry the gene, but she will not be affected by it. It is only a male child she produces who may inherit this, and then they may display it.

It is important to remember as we discuss a genetic trait, which is usually used to explain inheritance and so to our interest that of intelligence, that its occurrence is not regular. Although the inheritance of a trait may be chartered, the event of it arising is decided by a genetic lottery. It is only that it sometimes appears in one family line and not in other lines. Yet, even in the line that carries the trait, there is no predictability as to when it will appear. It may appear in the next offspring or it may not appear until a number of generations hence, if at all.

Therefore, while Goddard had studied Mendel's principles of inheritance, he was overambitious in falsifying the faces of all the family members in his photographs. The reality would be for perhaps one, or maybe none to look abnormal, but not usually all.

There is, then, a great confusion between a genetic trait and a behavioural or intellectual feature that is socially transmitted through generations. As we shall come to see, this is an extremely important point, because much of the reasoning that intelligence has a sense of individualistic restriction lies in this confusion. Yet, when we classify human beings into boxes, as Goddard did with his moron label, we simply do not understand what human intelligence is.

While the process of imprinting, just as epigenetics, will be discussed in Chapter TwentyFour in this book and in detail in *Brain Plasticity,* we may know here that imprinting is a chemical process that develops between two individuals that bonds them together. This is a very complicated process, and it relies totally upon emotional states. It occurs when one person, and this is usually the weaker of the two, and so normally a child, consciously or subconsciously mimics some action of a person they are emotionally bonded to. Thus, if one strokes their face or holds their hands in a particular manner or uses a particular expression, the other may subconsciously mimic this into their own sense of expression. While this is too often thought to be genetic, we explain it is only environmental and so socially inherited. Imprinting is not really recognised for what it is, and when it is not, a great deal of misunderstanding arises.

It is important for later that we realise imprinting does not just relate to expressions and moods, but also significantly to means of interaction with objects. It is by absorbing the thinking strategies of others, as they are displayed or explained, that enables the child to configure their own strategies to deal with information.

Thus, imprinting can explain why children acquire cognitive strategies, such as how they take notice of information and the details they observe. It explains how they reflect upon earlier experiences to make sense of a new experience, and how they seek to make use of this new experience in a situation that can shortly arise.

Imprinting is also of extreme importance in explaining how the child knows how to explain their mind to another. All these are strategies. They are all copied or studied, and they all underlie and create the effectiveness of the intelligence process.

Therefore, being aware of imprinting will help us to understand why aspects of intelligence that are assumed to be genetically inherited are not, and are only acquired through experience. Imprinting, along with epigenetics, as we shall come to discuss, underlies the whole intelligence process.

This brings us to the misunderstanding educationalists now have about the role and purpose of the gene, because if a child does have a gene that coincides with a known genetic condition, there is absolutely no evidence that their gene arrangement is in any way responsible for their condition. Such a condition may have been totally created through environmental circumstances, and could therefore be one that the child could be educated out of by a sensitive and knowledgeable teacher.

We can say from this that while geneticists may be aware of such a gene related to say ADHD, for example, psychologists and teachers who learn of this readily assume that a gene has created this condition they witness in a child. In an effort to protect the child from being forced to develop what they believe they are genetically incapable of developing, they create a special environment that serves the child's condition.

However, this special environment may only feed that condition, while the reason for the child displaying symptoms of ADHD may have nothing to do with their genetic makeup. In their confusion about this, it is often stated that such a condition is a factor of genes and development. Yet, this tendency to state a cause is both nature and nurture, which misleads what the real cause is behind the effect that is witnessed, for it may not be nature.

So, as Axness explains, attention deficit disorders, such as ADHD, can occur if a newborn baby is too much deprived of physical and especially facial contact with their mother in the immediate stages following birth. The reasoning behind this suggests that a lack of experience could cause the developing synaptic formations in the orbitofrontal cortex to relate too much to inanimate structures, before they have developed adequate facial processing and gained a sense of human rapport.[88]

There is, then, in thinking of the family history method, a crucial difference for us to be aware of between a medically recognised biological genetic trait, such as haemophilia or albinism, and a behavioural or intellectual trait witnessed in a family line. Let us look a little more closely into this with examples of schizophrenia and dyslexia.

Since it was first defined by Bleuler in 1911, as a splitting of reality relationships, schizophrenia is the most common mental disorder that comes to mind as a genetic trait.[89] However, as we will come to examine in our next book, schizophrenia can be related to imbalances in the production of the neurotransmitter dopamine. This imbalance can occur simply because of environmental experiences.

So, there is a qualified suggestion that schizophrenia can be transferred through generations, by a parent's behaviour disturbing the mind of their child, as they are setting up the threshold levels of their neural chemistry. This can occur through either imprinting or epigenetics, as we have just introduced. As this child matures, they so affect their child that a pattern of schizophrenic tendencies becomes noticeable through generations, even though there is no evidence of a genetic cause. Indeed, there is much to say today that, in certain cases, schizophrenia can be socially acquired.[90]

Equally, dyslexia, as a component of intelligence, is said to be a product of genetic inheritance. There are, however, many cases where this has been found to be attributed to purely domestic conditioning or socially disturbing experiences,[91] which may be overcome with a sensitive education. Indeed, further in this book, we discuss the case of Matthew, to show how a young man was able to overcome a condition said to be genetic, and by this belief, he had been "boxed" and set aside in his normal educational system.

We may understand from the little we have discussed here how very misleading the idea of the family history method can be. This is especially the case when we look at similar actions or skills witnessed in a family line and assume these were passed genetically, when, in fact, they were not.

Take, for example, the son of Yehudi Menuhin, who is himself a violinist of no mean accomplishment. Seeing a father and son who are both highly accomplished violinists suggests a genetic trait. Yet, I recall once reading an article on Menuhin's son, where he explained how his father had drilled him with immense enthusiasm from an excessively early age in the development of this musical accomplishment. When we witness such a case where a son shows a similar talent to his father, we readily assume this talent is an ability passed on through their genes. When we do this, we do not fully understand either the role or the power of the environment.

Africans, just as African Americans by further example, are naturally rhythmic. This is not because of a genetic tendency, but because they have usually been raised in an environmental culture that is steeped in rhythm. Consequently, African American music is a natural evolution of the language, art, and means of the cultural expression of these people. We can support this with instances of white people, the most noticeable of whom was Elvis Presley, verbalising rap and moving about with a fluid motion because they were raised under "African" influences or so desired it. In point of fact, Presley had purposely sought and cultivated this rhythmic body movement from African Americans.[92]

What we may, then, readily take to be a genetic gift can actually be nothing more than the development of an impressionable infant to the dedication of a parent. This brings us back to the imprinting we have briefly introduced, and so the awareness of how a child will develop relative to the "tender balances" that exist in the personalities they share with their guardian, and of the opportunities in development they are presented with. All of which we may apply to the skill of a dancer, an actor, or a painter, as much as we may to a musician, and so then to a philosopher, mathematician, or any skill requiring interaction with the environment.

In conclusion of this section, we can realise that the use of the family history method in medicine is a valuable means of learning to understand how an illness develops and how it may be transmitted, but in the field of social science, its application is fraught with misconceptions and subject to too easily producing the wrong diagnosis.

Chapter Fourteen

The Case for Identical Twins

Another very important argument for the case that intelligence is genetically determined arose through the idea of studying identical twins. This, as Eysenck (another disciple of Galton) informs us, "...owes its inception to Galton's genius..."[93] Although, as we shall also see, the study of identical twins is no more reliable than the family history method for understanding the base of intelligence.

As Galton used the similarity of physical features within a family line to explain the inheritance of their intelligence, he realised that identical twins could provide him with a foolproof argument. The idea was that since twins look identical, they should think identically, because they inherited the same gemmules. Remember that at this time, genes had not been discovered. Inheritance was, then, thought to occur by both parents passing to their child the hereditary material each had collected in their bodies.

Galton's simple idea was that since identical twins would think identically, then any difference noted in their responses could be said to come from environmental influences. In this way, some idea could be gained as to how much of a percentage could be allocated to inheritance and how much to the environment to show which was the determining factor. We have already mentioned the principle behind this when we discussed Pearson's correlation coefficients. However, despite the impression provided to us of this, identical twins do not necessarily show similarities in their behaviour or in their intelligence!

To give account for this disparity, Galton explained in his *The History of Twins,* 13 separate cases where the characters of twins were as dissimilar as could be imagined.

As he quotes one parent who wrote, "They have had exactly the same nurture from their birth up to the present time; they are both perfectly healthy and strong. Yet, they are otherwise as dissimilar as two boys could be, physically, mentally, and in their emotional nature." Another wrote of her twins, "...They have never been separated, never the least differently treated ..... yet they differ as much from each other in mental cast as anyone of my family differs from another...." Of other twins, it was said, "The two sisters are very different in ability and disposition. The one is retiring, but firm and determined; she has no taste for music and drawing. The other is of an active, excitable temperament: she displays an unusual amount of quickness and talent, and is passionately fond of music and drawing. From infancy, they have been rarely separated."[94]

It was characteristic of Galton to appear to present information without scientific bias, and then in the final account dismiss one in favour of the other. So we find that having described to his reader accounts of twins who were dissimilar and also those who were similar in their abilities, he then discounted the former with the analogy that: "If bits of a stick are thrown into a small stream. At first, each bit would engage its own obstacle and move at a different rate. But with all caught in the same current, they would further down the stream be found travelling at the same rate."[95] Upon such literary skill as this, has the study of identical twins greatly survived to play a prominent role in the architecture of human classification.

Today, however, we know there are two types of twins. The term monozygotic twins refers to twins who developed from the same single egg, and are said to be genetically identical. On the other hand, dizygotic (or fraternal) twins evolved independently from their own eggs, which were both fertilised at the same time. Therefore, studies on intelligence that try to solve the nature/nurture riddle, are made using monozygotic twins.

However, we should understand that earlier studies, which we still very much rely upon, did not determine whether twins were monozygotic or dizygotic on examination of their DNA, but upon the observation of physical differences. As Neuman and company found, it was generally very difficult to know which was which, and the defining issue often lay in the identity of the four palms of twins.[96]

Thus, all studies relating to the nature/nurture ratio are based purely on the observed differences between monozygotic twins gained through written and verbal questioning. When the differences in their responses are less noticeable, they are said to be caused by their "identical" gene codes and so inheritance. When the differences in their response to questions are more noticeable, they are said to be caused by environmental factors - or experience of life if you will.

The first problem we encounter with this theory is that monozygotic twins are not genetically identical. In 2012, a research paper was presented to the American Society of Human Genetics. This paper explained how monozygotic twins undergo some 300 genetic mutations while in the early foetal stage, and that within a normal life span, each twin could undergo a few hundred genetic mutations that could lead to trillions of genetic differences in their DNA. This is not to mention how chemical factors could activate or suppress gene expression, and so the formation of different proteins, which are responsible for turning the coding into actions.[97]

To expand upon this, we need to remind ourselves that a gene only manifests its design through an environment, and since the environment of each monozygotic twin in the womb is different for each one, then each will experience different chemical and sensory information.[98] Naturally, this "environmental" information may be similar, but it may not be. Although it will never be identical for each embryo or foetus.

It is important to understand this because this means their brain structures and personalities may be created differently by these experiences and so cause them to be individuals in their own right. In our following book, *Brain Plasticity*, we will explain how twins share their minds as they share information in their afterbirth experiences, and how they come to understand the meaning of the world individually.

One twin, with whom I discussed this, clearly assured me she did not have emotions identical to those of her sister. Certainly, they were similar, but as she pointed out, so had been all their developmental experiences since birth, even to the extent they learnt from each other and so conditioned each other. This conditioning is a product of the imprinting process we have just mentioned, and its proficiency is highly related to emotional bonding. The whole point of studying identical twins, then, lies in the common but mistaken belief that they are identical "inside," so that the environment "outside" (their bodies) can be categorised into values.

To accentuate how identical the intelligence of Monozygotic twins is, such IQ studies seek twins who have been raised apart.[99] The logic here is that even though they developed through entirely different environments, then their intelligences would still be very similar. In turn, this would show the role of inheritance against that of the environment in this nature/nurture controversy.

One problem to this is that there are very few instances of twins who have been raised apart, and to think that their different environments were different is not so easily explained, because environmental factors normally and easily overlap each other. Thus, the issue is not that twins were raised in different locations and so with different families, but how did each twin relate psychologically and emotionally to their new world.

We must be aware that even children of the same family, can develop very different intelligences as each relate to and develop through their perspectives of the world about them. Remember here that the development of intelligence is fundamentally built upon the sensitivity by which information is explained to the child and how that child desires to be sensitive in their understanding and evaluation of this.

So, the issue is not one of different locations, but of the similarity in care each twin received from their guardians or foster parents. There again, we may assume that any parent wishing to foster a child, would be very aware of the need to be kind and in this sensitive in all their interactions with the child. So, there may actually have been very few significant differences in the different worlds each twin was raised in.

Thus, if one twin were raised by a lawyer in New York and the other by a Rastafarian in Jamaica, the actual and very real learning environments could be very similar. It is not a question of financial support, but upon the love, devotion and care to attention that the foster parent instils within the child as they guide them in how to interact with the world about them.

There again, this matter is further complicated by the timing in which the twins were separated. We may think they were separated immediately at birth, but this would be extremely unusual, with the reality that they lived together for some short time before being separated. Yet, even such a short time together would be very fundamental in each learning to adapt to the world by similar means.

It would be relevant for us to understand that once the baby is born, many of its neurological functions are only then ready to adapt to the world and so develop themselves. Take, for example, the visual system, which is an essential component of the means of detection and analysis of information upon which intelligence is built.

While this is very much discussed in *Brain Plasticity,* I would like to emphasise here just how the baby sets up their sense of orientation through the environment after birth. Our brain has to learn to understand what information is. So, for example, we do not see a building, a car, or any item in front of us, such as words on a page or the letters that make these up. Our brain rapidly processes hundreds of thousands of visual shots to build up and to recognise what it is we are looking at. It is important to understand this, because how sensitive we have developed our sensory systems (to see, to hear and to touch), will much decide the quality of the information they feed into our brain, to develop its processing systems.

To give a very simple example of how information begins to be processed in the newborn, I would like to share with you a very famous study that was done on Cree Indians in Canada. In 1973, Annis and Frost studied the ability of Cree Indians to recognise simple lines. Their study revealed that Indians who had been raised from infancy in an urban environment could readily recognise horizontal and vertical lines hidden in a complex drawing, but struggled more to find diagonal lines.

However, their genetic relatives who had been raised from infancy in a tent of leaning poles and structures overlaid with animal skins, and so in a natural setting, were found to recognise the opposite. These Indians could very easily notice diagonal lines, but had difficulty to recognise vertical and horizontal lines.

So, with babies raised in teepees who first see diagonal structures, these diagonal structures fashion the ability of their brain to recognise information. On the other hand, babies raised in an artificial environment of a cot, windows and walls, etc., will have their brains fashioned by the vertical and horizontal lines they first perceive.[100]

As we can see in the following illustration, the way the infant baby sees their world constructs the way their visual system is able to respond to that world.

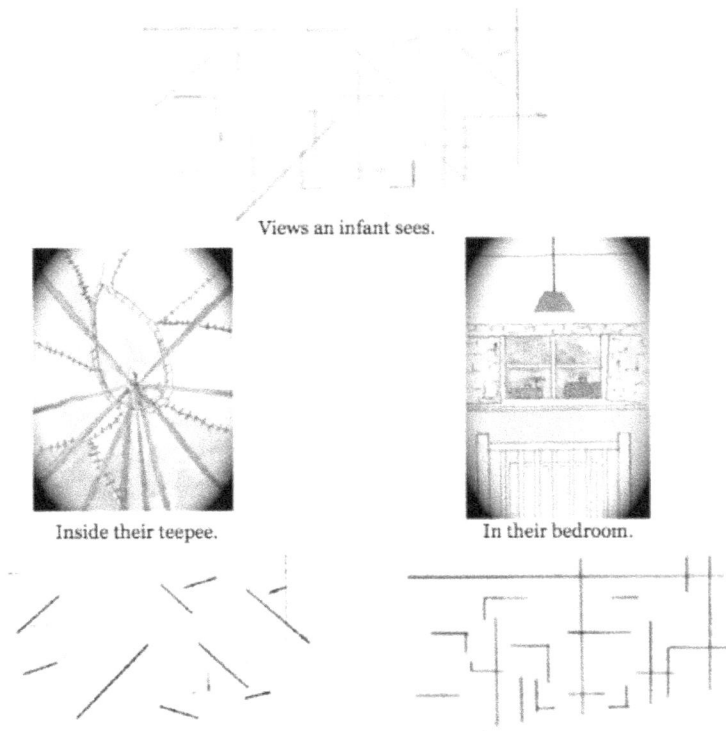

Views an infant sees.

Inside their teepee.

In their bedroom.

This study proved that the ability of the brain to recognise information and so function is directly reliant upon the way it had been formed through experience, and not according to an inherited genetic plan. In other words, we learn to learn to recognise and process information, instead of being born able to do this.

Therefore, any time that infant twins share together before being separated is influenced by environmental factors that distort what is thought to be the value of their genes when they are later tested for being raised apart.

Withstanding this, monozygotic twins may appear identical in some of their physical features, but not so in their psychological attributes. Consider, for example, that their facial features can be completely indistinguishable, but their fingerprints will be quite different.[101] When raised apart, they can vary tremendously in their heights, and even more so in their weights.

When raised together, their behavioural interests are different. One may like games of coordination; the other may detest these and prefer games of mental agility. One may prefer to play music, while the other prefers computer games. One may like quizzes and so be inclined towards mathematics in school, while the other may prefer the relationships of colours and so prefer art.

I once investigated this with a pair of twins, and found that through a number of simple puzzles, the manner of the thinking strategy of each was totally different. Certainly, they looked like the blueprint of each other, but when it came to mental organisation, the only blueprint was that of a human being involved in their own interactive process. Therefore, the ways each twin decides to select, evaluate and process information and so demonstrate their intelligence is a consequence of their environmental experiences, and not their genetic coding for this.

The greater point in all this is not that identical twins tend to look identical, but that once a baby is born, that individual will begin their unique adventure in life. This journey will take them through highly indecipherable experiences, which they develop through using not just codes for intelligence, but also those of language, behaviour and, very significantly, emotion. Accordingly, the idea that Monozygotic twins think in the same way, because they have the same "genetic" ability, is wrong. They may have what is assumed to be the same coding, but how that coding develops is a totally different matter.

Such thinking that any human being makes is driven to develop or caused to deteriorate through their emotional experiences. These experiences are purely environmental. Consider a human being interrogating information, perhaps they are happily reading a story or working through a math problem that is not too difficult for them. At a cellular level, each bit of this information moves through one neuron at a time, so that bit by bit the characteristic of the information is recognised, and given value through the stored information it is related to in their memory. They are happy and content. All information is processed meaningfully, and new circuits are being constructed. All this is well and good until we introduce a psychological disturbance into this calm scenario.

Perhaps another child made a remark that hurt their feelings, or told them they would hurt them in the break or after school. Equally, perhaps the teacher made a public display of a simple failing they had made, which all too often happens. If the individual feels so affected by this, and we each have built our own threshold level to determine such an action upon us, they may trigger off a movement towards the sympathetic state, as we explain in *Teach Better, Learn Better*.

Therefore, each twin is an individual in their own right, and their ability to handle tasks will be decided by how they individually developed. Quellet-Morin brought this point home when she discovered that one twin performed badly in school purely because they had been bullied. Their twin, who had not been bullied, displayed a much higher academic profile and showed greater intelligence.[102]

While this subject is really for our following book, we may understand here that Quellet-Morin measured cortisol levels in identical twins. (Cortisol is a hormone produced in the transition to the sympathetic state.) These levels were found to be normal in one twin, but were significantly higher in the other, who had a history of being bullied. Bullying, she has proven, does alter the chemistry of the brain. In fact, MRI scans of bullied individuals have shown a number of structural changes in the putamen and caudate areas of the brain that are linked to anxiety disorders.[103]

The point here is that environmental factors can easily be responsible for what we assume is a factor of genetic programming. We are a long way from discussing epigenetics, but in time, we shall see how epigenetics (which are environmentally generated chemicals that can control the actual gene coding) explains how monozygotic twins can come to think in totally different ways, as their epigenomes diverge.

However, the study of monozygotic twins to discover how much of our intelligence is reliant upon our genetic codes as opposed to how much is developed through experience leads us into a very great enigma.

The whole basis of this discussion rests on the belief that there was once a single gene value for intelligence and that over time this gene encountered a number of mutations in one form or another, so that what was once a single value now has values taken either side of this original gene. This, we may remember, is Galton's law of deviation from the average, upon which the whole basis of differences in inherited intelligence rests.

Therefore, while test scores for a number of identical twins will give an average factor for what is said to be inherited, this is completely meaningless when applied to any individual. Because the individual may have (according to this theory) inherited gene strengths against the environment of 30:70, or it may be 80:20 or simply 50:50 or some other combination. This must be so if gene codes are said to vary in their quality within families and within individuals. Yet, there would be absolutely no way to know which value the individual has. This would be totally impossible to know, because we cannot know what their personal environmental factor is.

The whole idea of the nature/nurture controversy is only to provide an estimate for a population. It is not a ratio that can be applied to any single individual, and so it is quite wrong for an individual to think they have a ratio of say 40:60 because this was said to be determined on tests with identical twins. This ratio, whatever it is said to be, is only a theoretical discussion for political purposes.

The great tragedy in this is when psychologists and educationalists fail to understand this. I have had many experiences of understanding how readily they do. I remember one teacher, disgusted with her students for failing to understand what she was trying to teach them, related to me that it was not her fault. After all, she explained, having read an article by a psychologist, intelligence is 60% inherited. Believing this to be so, the teacher accepted her students' struggles rather than considering how she could teach in a different and better way.

I have witnessed this mindset far too often with educationalists. Not all, of course, but enough to warrant raising the point that there is a certain mindset in education which believes that any response a student makes is limited by a certain percentage according to what they inherited.

There is absolutely no evidence for this. None at all!

We simply can never assume that the intelligence of a human being is limited by some percentage factor they inherited, because this can never ever be calculated.

We see from this that the only point of this nature/nurture debate lies in how the educational opportunity of children in different social areas should be supported. The most referenced study made on monozygotic twins occurred in 1937 and was conducted by a psychologist, a statistician and a biologist. It is now very relevant for us to consider this study, because it very clearly demonstrates the hidden political agenda that such studies have.

In 1937, Newman, Freeman and Holzinger produced a correlation coefficient of .67 on a study they made on the intelligence of 19 pairs of monozygotic twins reared apart.[104] This would be to say they found the worth of inheritance to be about 45% responsible for the relationship. (*A correlation coefficient is changed to a percentage by squaring it and multiplying by 100.)

In other words, the role of development (55%) was shown to be very important with the inference that social programs should focus on helping poor children more. In fact, their very long and detailed report ended with the wording: "We feel in sympathy with Professor H.S. Jennings' dictum that what heredity can do, environment can also do."[105]

This study was reviewed in 1938 by McNemar, who, in working with **exactly the same data**, concluded a correlation coefficient of .77. This is to say that McNemar reasoned, with the exact same data, Newman, etc, has used, that the worth of inheritance should instead be nearly 60% responsible for intelligence.

In 1970, working on the same data that was over thirty years old, Arthur Jensen reassessed this study, and stated a factor of .86. In other words, Jensen argued that the value of inheritance should now be near 75%. This is to say that three-quarters of any academic performance should be attributed to inheritance, with only one-quarter attributed to environmental development.

Jensen argued from this that social programs would be a waste of time and expense in helping children in poorer areas, while the money would be better spent increasing the opportunities of children in better areas, since they have better genes to make the most of this.[106]

We can see here how the value of the nature (or genetic inheritance) to that of the nurture (or environment development) was significantly altered from 45% to approximately 60% and then to 75% by psychologists moving the values of data to suit their political purposes. Therefore, by playing around with the same figures of the environment, Jensen (a true Galtonian) could argue that the effect of the environment on how a child learns was now worth only about 25%.[107] In other words, it is almost negligible. This study was subsequently used as evidence to guide educational and teaching practices in many countries, that the ability of children to learn is based "almost" wholly on the worth of the genes they inherited.[108]

As we may see, while a team of specialised scientists (a psychologist, a statistician and a specialist in the biology of twins) used data on identical twins to state the environment was the determining factor in an individual's intelligence, other social scientists used exactly the same data to state the complete opposite.

The politics of this would show that those having right-wing interests seek to maintain a stratified society. They do this by emphasising the role of inheritance above that of the environment (let us say 70:30). From this perspective, they seek to achieve their aim by causing greater financial support to be provided to the better social areas and thereby offering children there more opportunity to develop the better genes they are argued to have. This is reasoned to be so since their parents demonstrated their better genes by making more money, which enabled them to afford to live in better areas.

In contrast, those of left-wing interests seek to stress the significance of the environment (let us say 30:70), as they try to force improvement in social policies and open up educational opportunities by providing more funding for children in poorer areas in their desire for an egalitarian society.

The nature/nurture argument is purely political, but the conclusions taken from it can and do direct spending for and against children living in different areas. From all we have discussed in this chapter, we may see the whole idea of measuring intelligence collapses if we are interested in the individual, **but it becomes very meaningful** if we intend to support or alter the opportunities of children according to the social areas they live in.

We shall look again at this genetic to environmental ratio when we discuss the fraudulent activities of the most infamous of educational psychologists. This was a psychologist who purposely and deliberately falsified data on various studies of identical twins for three-quarters of a century, as he designed British and Commonwealth education.

This brings us to a vital point that is really not questioned by the general population and certainly not those working in education: How reliable are intelligence tests? Do they really measure intelligence? We may recall here that after 150 years, there is still no agreed-upon definition of what intelligence actually is.[109] Yet, psychologists claim they can measure what they don't know it is!

We may understand, then, that intelligence tests do not actually measure a comprehensive understanding of intelligence. Stanovich, for example, explains how intelligence tests do not measure aspects of cognitive functioning, such as domains of logic, causal reasoning, probabilistic, and scientific thinking. Accordingly, examination into Instrumental Rationality (the selection of appropriate goals and the designs to realise those goals), and Epistemic Rationality (holding to beliefs that are consistent with known evidence) are totally missing in intelligence testing,[110] even though these are the very skills used in working through a problem. Flynn explained that "Intelligence tests do not measure actual intelligence, but only a minor sort of 'abstract problem-solving ability' that have little practical significance."[111]

Yet, the problem here is not just the quality of the questions, setting aside how these have been and are often selected to gain the responses desired, but the environment. The environment of intelligence is not something that can be classified for such a purpose. It is totally unfathomable, as we have repeatedly tried to bring out in the writing of this book.

The environment of the individual, how they were raised, who they were influenced by and how they emotionally moved through each of the billions and billions of encounters with information and the life they have so far led can never be known. As we have stated before, you simply cannot take a generalised understanding of what the environment for the human population is and apply this to any one individual. If we do not know what the environment is, we cannot know what the effect of the gene is.

Indeed, **with an environment of such extreme diversity, there is no evidence that differences in intelligence arise from direct variations in genetic codes** (We shall come back to this point much later when we discuss polygenes.) — unless there is a distinct and classifiable genetic abnormality present. In the normal routine of education, there are none. We must hold on to the fact that it is not possible to go from the population level (which is based on vague and highly variable data), to the individual level that deals with highly specific factors. It is because the environment of the individual cannot be known that neither can the genetic worth of their intelligence.

Therefore, the nature/nurture ratio is a complete fallacy, when it is applied to human intelligence. Geneticists may earnestly apply this ratio to the development of a plant whose environment can be completely controlled. However, psychologists may not apply this to the environment the individual human being lives through before and after birth -- even though they consistently try to do so and yet have not, in over 100 years, proven a ratio to the agreement of all.

Thus, while psychologists try to calculate the value of the gene through trying to understand an environment that cannot be understood, a geneticist would simply point out that what makes any DNA code active is the formation and the movement of proteins, and that since these cannot be specifically known in the individual, then neither can the innate factor of their intelligence.

Accordingly, we cannot know the genes that cause a student to understand completely the questions of a test, or those of another who understands a lesser amount of it. Nor can we know the genes that enable them to present the information they have been interested in remembering, in the precise way another expects of them. Those genes that enable the child to recall if A should be over B, or if B should be over A in a formula they were told to remember are unknown. We do know, however, they can be taught never to forget this formula, just as they can learn to operate it in a totally different way with complete success when their total environment is changed.

So, we find that when a child is placed in a poor learning environment at home or in school, where they are deprived of a sense of security and quality of guidance, they are known to perform poorly. Yet, when the same child is placed in a different world, where they are given a caring tutor, where belief is stimulated in their abilities, and their dreams are seen to manifest through the quality of the interactions they learn to make, then a miracle happens.

Yet, this miracle can just as easily be lost if the child is placed back in their previous world and disaster strikes. This was the main failure of the HeadStart programs in America, which began in the 1970s.[112] This is the practical reality of intelligence. It cannot be indexed. It is because of this that the nature/nurture ratio and so its accompanying debate is completely meaningless to the way the child in the classroom learns or an employee performs in their job. It is, however, very decisive in how they are offered a quality of education and how they are judged through it!

There are actually four very serious issues that if recognised, in fact if they were openly discussed, would negate the possibility of the nature/nurture discussion:

- **First. We cannot know what the whole environment of intelligence is.**
- **Second. We do not know what the genes are that are involved with intelligence.**
- **Third. We do not know the actual purpose of the genes so involved, and**
- **Four. The viability of IQ testing.**

Psychologists in their struggles to prove the relationship of inheritance to development for political purposes, attempt to overcome the first problem by categorising the environment into a small number of discrete boxes. Yet, as we have seen in this section, this is totally insufficient and just as much inadequate in view of the complexity of the environment that affects how we think, how we behave and who we become. When we consider the far too simple account we offer above to the environment, although we do describe this in very considerable detail in *Brain Plasticity*, we may see how very unrealistic any such attempt of categorisation is.

In regard to the second problem, psychologists know that genes exist of course and by this seek to measure the genes for intelligence, but this is not so simple. It is not that one gene does one thing, but that genes often share responsibilities making it very difficult to know exactly what is happening where it is and when it is. In fact, geneticists still do not know how many genes really make up the human genome.

The Human Genome Project was completed in 2004, which estimated that we have about 22,300 protein-coding genes in our genetic make-up.[113] However, protein-coding genes make up only one per cent of our entire DNA. The other 99 per cent are noncoding genes that do not provide instructions for making proteins.

Yet, even knowing of genes is not so simple, because RNA sequencing has shown how alternative splicing, alternative transcription initiation, and alternative transcription termination affect 95% of human genes.[114] There again, by 2018, our knowledge of how many protein-coding genes we have had risen to 46,831.[115]

However, the fact is that by the time of writing this book (2024), geneticists still do not know the correct number of protein-coding genes we have.[116] It is equally important, as Kuhn points out, that there is still a great deal of human thinking that we know almost nothing about.[117]

All this is to say that psychologists, working with early 20th century methods of paper and pencil exercises, are trying to show the effect of genes that geneticists a hundred years later still have no honest idea about, on a human feature, psychologists do not know really what it is.

This raises the significance of the third problem psychologists have, genes do have different purposes. As we shall come to show, some gene codes exist to enable a feature to exist with the environment completely designing the effectiveness of that feature.

We can witness this in our ability to freely detect information, to be able to reason from different perspectives, to associate new information to that stored in the memory by emotional based strategies, the ability to learn to be sensitive in all actions and thoughts, the different ways in which beliefs can form, the ability to adopt new thinking strategies throughout the lifetime, the ability to allow experiences to completely determine emotional states, and in our ability to freely reason, where competence in accuracy and speed are purely developmental. All these occur with no effect from differentials in gene coding.[118] Every human being inherits these with equal worth.

All of these features, and many more, gain their quality of development through experiences with the environment and not through any variation in the codes that provide their existence. From this perspective, we shall move further into this book to discuss the genes for intelligence having the same purpose.

Finally, and as we have much discussed in this book, the choice of questions made for testing, just as the interpretation of data gained from responses, can be viewed from either political perspective, so nothing is really reliable. The real problem to all this is that IQ testing has been plagued from its very beginning with fraud and misrepresentation of data to make any declaration of a result as highly suspicious. We may be reminded here of Winnicott's statement:

"In other sciences, if something is found to be true it can usually be accepted without emotional strain, but in psychology there is always this matter of strain, so that something which is not quite true is more easily accepted than the truth itself."[119]

In having said all this, we should now openly consider that intelligence is not inherited as the singular factor the 19th-century idea behind this ratio suggests. Intelligence is only our perception of a number of processes the mind and the brain of the individual move through as they seek to gain an understanding of information, and as they do so, they naturally incorporate factors of behaviour and so emotion into this. After all, any calculation of information will bring some consideration to the identity and so the survival of the individual's personality. We shall return to the nature/nurture debate at the end of this book with a realistic means to settle this once and for all.

It is, then, of no small consideration to be reminded *again* that emotion and so the language that creates behaviour and intelligence are not affected by genetic diversity. All human beings inherit the same ability to have these features, but they each develop in the individual through the experiences they encounter. In fact, as our long account will unfold, there is another way of understanding what intelligence is and how it develops.

This brings us to a point of interest that few know about. Today, we understand or at least we are informed how inheritance works. Yet, this understanding did not naturally come about. It survived against other ideas which did not gain the necessary level of interest. Let us look into why this happened. .....

Chapter Fifteen

The Foundations of Two Opposing Sciences

The civilisation in which Galton first appeared was set upon a rigid social work order structure. In this social arrangement, opportunities in life were much determined by spheres of influence. This was a self-conditioning social system, which maintained itself by restricting educational opportunity. In a general sense, this caused the son to have little alternative but to follow his father in the acquisition of work skills, with their associated skills in thinking.

It is precisely because people learn to think through the jobs they do, that intelligence at that time was tied to a family work line. We may think in this how a father who was an accountant would teach his son skills to carefully analyse and double check information, which a father who was a blacksmith would not be aware of as he raised his son.

As we have discussed, it was only by completely ignoring such social mechanism and by focusing upon the noted achievements he selected of sons with their fathers and so on, that Galton had been able to state that achievement and hence intelligence was predictable in family lines, according to the use he made of Quetelet's law of accidental causes. Once he had established this predictability, Galton used it to classify the abilities related to the social roles of different families.

By so claiming that this arrangement was a consequence of nature, and not social planning, Galton was able to use Gauss's graph to indicate a family's usefulness to society. By indexing this graph into 14 categories, and by disclaiming any use of the environment (such as social conditioning and influences), he was able to place a family by their use to society into one of these categories.

Once families had been categorised, the opportunity for the next generation was decided by the opportunities their father and grandfather had gained. Of paramount importance to Galton's theory was that there is a "smooth continuation" of natural ability within any population.

Now! At about the same time that Galton and Edgeworth had begun to work on the construction of correlations, a new idea began to arise that challenged Darwin's theory that life evolved slowly and steadily. This theory argued that evolution occurred through very dramatic and totally unpredictable steps. This theory brought with it a complete opposition to the idea that adaptability, and hence Galton's natural ability, was arranged in a "smooth" continuous variation.

This idea germinated from a small number of embryologists of the time, who argued that all life forms did not vary continuously in their variation. The clover plant, for instance, has three and on occasion four leaves, but does not range in leaf number from one to ten. Such reasoning as this, gave fuel to the idea that evolution depended upon substantial and unpredictable changes in physiology.

In short, this theory produced a sort of "dis"-continuous variation. There were two main proponents of this. One was an embryologist by the name of William Bateson, who lived in England, and the other was Hugo de Vries, who was then Professor of Botany at Amsterdam University.

The mechanics that grew to explain this theory first occurred to de Vries when, on an evening stroll through a meadow, he had noticed a great disorganised variety in the Evening Primrose flower. As he examined these, de Vries was particularly struck by the new forms he did not recognise. In reflecting upon how unordered changes could come about, he was struck by the idea of inheritance being suddenly altered by singular "mutated" leaps. If this was so, then Darwin was wrong!

If de Vries was correct, it would mean that the pattern of life did not change bit by bit, as each adapted or failed to do so in a slow and gentle manner, as Darwin had described in his *Origin of Species*. Inheritance, de Vires came to believe, is erratic. In other words, inheritance would be discontinuous. We do not have to dwell upon the chaos this brought to Galton's idea of a very neatly structured society.

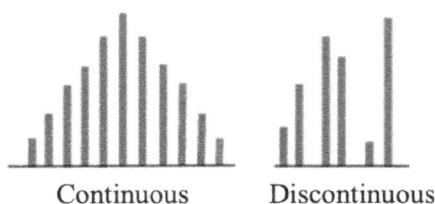

Continuous   Discontinuous

The Greek scholar Hippocrates had reasoned that every organ has a memory. This memory was said to flow through the blood to the reproductive organs. When the parents mate, the memories of the two parents were said to blend to create the identity of their child. Darwin called these units of memory gemmules, and borrowed this theory to explain how inheritance could work with his of natural selection. Unfortunately for him, Galton was later to disprove Darwin's theory through experiments with rabbits.[120] However, because none of that time could think of a better explanation, this idea of a blending inheritance remained a part of Darwinism until Mendel's laws were eventually discovered in 1900.

To name this theory, Darwin had taken the Greek names "pan" meaning whole, and "genesis" to mean birth, and called it The Theory of Pan-genesis. In turn, de Vries substituted the term gemmules with that of pangenes to change the name of these units of inheritance, which he reasoned could mutate out of order. In 1889, de Vries published his Theory of Intracellular Pan-genesis. The paper that this article was mentioned in caught the attention of William Bateson, who had been searching for such an explanation of how life could vary.

As Bateson and de Vries developed their interests, they set up a school of thought centred on discontinuous variation, arising through mutation. De Vries's idea was ingenious because it came at a time when Mendel's laws of inheritance were not known. In truth, Mendel had made his discovery thirty years earlier, but when he published his findings in 1866, they failed to gain the recognition they were ultimately to do, and so for three decades lay lost and unknown.

The main reason why Mendel's work was not realised, was because the world at that time was so caught up with Darwinism that it did not notice the very small and limited way in which Mendel's findings were presented. It is, however, none the less true that Mendel's scientific work was hindered, or at least the knowledge of it, by the political framework under which he lived. As we needed to understand why the political establishment supported Galton's idea, it is of some relevance to discuss briefly why Mendel's work was kept out of public interest.

We have mentioned that the only way Mendel could obtain the education he desired was to become a monk. His monastery was situated in a province of the Austrian Hungarian Empire, but this was not the place to be for a poor person with an aspiring mind. Less than two decades earlier, the former Emperor of Austria had been forced to abdicate in the 1848 uprising, and his successor, Franz Josef, was still heavily suppressing all ideas of social and scientific progress, and so any kind of freethinking, in order to maintain political stability.

To compound this situation, Gregor Mendel (Gregor was the name given to him when he joined his order) very soon began to draw unwanted attention to his monastery. In one way, he created much gossip in the region towards his experimentations, when they took on a new edge after he bred a line of bees that viciously attacked local villagers. In another and far more dangerous way, this region of the Austrian Empire was noted for political activists, and Mendel was suspected of sympathising with Czech revolutionaries. He had, in fact, harboured them on a number of occasions with considerable risk to himself and to his monastery.

Understandably, there was considerable pressure placed upon Mendel's bishop to bring him into order. Indeed, it is widely acknowledged that Mendel was promoted to the busy and bureaucratic post of abbot, with the very purpose of distracting his energies.

The move had its desired effect, and as Mendel applied himself wholeheartedly to his new administrative task, his experimentations became fewer and fewer. As he had gained little response to his work in inheritance, Mendel believed, when he died in 1884, that nobody was interested in the discovery he had made. Yet, this was a discovery that would eventually create the science of genetics and ultimately change our understanding of the world in which we live.

To emphasise the political troubles Mendel had become involved with, we may mention that the great Czech composer Leos Janacek played the organ at his funeral, while on the other hand, the monks of his monastery were instructed to dismantle his laboratory once he was buried and to burn all his papers![121] Such was to be the end of one of the greatest scientists of all time. In the beginning of our previous chapter, we explained how and why religion sought to contain free thinking. The life case of Johann Mendel offers a supreme example of this and of its consequences.

Fortunately for science, however, de Vries, along with Correns and Tschermak, independently discovered remnants of Mendel's work in 1900 and announced these to the world. By this time, chromosomes had been discovered, and the process of cell reproduction (mitosis) was now known. However, it was only through the laws that Mendel had discovered that any sense of order and meaning could be brought to these, to explain a clear pattern of an evolutionary jigsaw.

Mendel's laws, as explained with a trait such as albinism, describe how inheritance does not follow the blending hypothesis. We may recall that the blending hypothesis was impractical in that it incorporated an aspect of diminishing, as a half is halved and halved again, but it was only by Galton's discovery of the regression to the mean that is was maintained.

However, the discovery of Mendel's papers completely discredited this theory, and so negated Galton's reasoning of the regression. With no explanation now for Galton's theory of continuous variation, de Vries and Bateson proclaimed, with Mendel's papers in their hands, that they had irrevocable proof that variation was discontinuous after all!

Bateson   de Vries

With considerable delight, Bateson wrote to Galton, suggesting he fully acquaint himself with the news: "In case you miss it. Mendel's work seems to me one of the most remarkable investigations yet made on heredity."[122] Bateson was the first to introduce Mendel's work into England, which he did to an audience of Fellows of the Royal

Horticultural Society in London on the 8th May 1900.[123]. After which, he became the chief protagonist of Mendel, and was the first to publish *Mendel's Principles of Heredity,* in English. He hastily produced this in a short book form in 1902, and followed this up with a larger and more comprehensive version in 1909.[124]

The idea that the inheritance of intelligence is unpredictable was incomprehensible to Galton and his followers. In their turn, they had formed a biometrical school of thought relying upon measurement and mathematics, which would lose its entire respectability if the factors to be measured were inconsistent.

With such opposing points of view and hidden political interest, it was not surprising that the debate between the two schools quickly escalated into harsh public battles, where one side wheeled one campaign after another at the opposing side, who replied with equal vigour. As this war between Galton's biometricians and Bateson's mutationists intensified, scientific discussion rapidly fell waste to insults, slander, and suggestions of fraud.

While many pages could be written upon this struggle, we may only note that the champion of the biometricians, Professor Weldon of University College London, died of exhaustion. Galton was now too old, and Pearson too weak to continue the onslaught. For his part, Bateson was equally drained. Anyway, by this time, Johannsen had discovered the effect of the environment on Mendel's principles, and an explanation was now forthcoming on how any genetic variation could be affected by environmental influences, which turned all parties in pursuit of different goals.

Once this war had fizzled out, the mutationists phased themselves into Mendelians, absorbed Darwin's evolutionary theory into their own and created the science of genetics -- intent on finding the role of the gene and the effect of the environment in all forms and functions of life. It was Bateson, contrary to belief, who was the first to coin the word "genetics."[125] He did this in 1905, when he took the Greek word genno meaning "to give birth," and a year later formally gave name to a scientific body that would forever seek to distance itself from the political squabbles of psychologists.

The Biometricians, on the other hand, were absorbed into the new science of psychology, where their views on the inheritance of human intelligence continue to direct social and educational policies to this day. Steered by political interest, psychologists very quickly divided themselves into two camps.

As we have explained, right-wing elements seek to maintain a stratified society by emphasising the role of inheritance above that of the environment. Their aim is to influence the design of social and educational policies and the ways in which money is spent in education to control opportunity. As we discussed in *The Illusion of School,* a school education is offered freely in all countries of the world, although a university education usually has a price tag that generally precludes children from poorer backgrounds, with the reasoning that they stem from left-wing influences who may alter the status quo. For their part, left-wing elements seek to stress the significance of the environment, as they try to force improvements in social policies and open up educational opportunities in their desire for an egalitarian society.

As events evolved over the 20th century, these factions bickered between themselves. With no proof either way, psychologists in general came to view the genes and the environment as having equal significance in intelligence. As psychology guided the general public, most people came to think that all children should have an equal chance in education, but acknowledged to themselves that the grades the child gained was basically determined by what they were born with!

Our next chapter will look at how certain psychologists steered the political development of our civilisation, through the 20th and into the 21st century, as they built upon Galton's work.....

_____

Chapter Sixteen

The Concept of a Public Intelligence

"The idea was to divide intelligence into the inherited part and the developed part. This developed part was said to be the toys the child had to play with. It is not. It is how the child is shown how to play with their toys, and the peace and happiness they have while they do so. When this is realised, the inherited part fades into insignificance."

Roy Andersen

That Galton's arguments so neatly overturned the accepted authority of John Locke, who believed that man was born free of design to be fashioned by experience, was in consequence to the troubled times in which he appeared and the solution he brought with him.

Galton just happened to be in the right place at the right time when he brought a means of preserving a social structure at a time when his own was most vulnerable. This vulnerability was the inescapable consequence of the blooming of the Industrial Revolution, where, by its greed for profit and progress, it gave seed to demands of fairness and equality that had too long been contained.

The revolutionary energy generated through the enlightenment of these times, turned minds from acceptance of religious doctrines and social conformity to exploration by inquiry. While it was recognised that a little inquiry by the masses stimulated production and welfare systems, which in turn produced better workers, it was just as much recognised that too much could destabilise the whole social machinery.

We saw how Galton brought the means to balance this situation, but as our journey evolves to understand what intelligence is, we need to look beyond Galton and to the forces that gave our whole political framework today the operational excuse that intelligence is measurable. Let us move to examine some of the individuals who played an intentional or an unwitting part in bringing this belief about.

The Vehicles of Galtonism

With the scientific fever of the 19th century, ideas were generated so fast and so borderless that sciences struggled to keep themselves intact. None knew which idea might be viable, and which could never be so. As William Blake expressed it, "energy is eternal delight." As this was the time of electricity and the telephone, so was it also the time of the Hollow Earth Theory, the logic of which was not so ridiculous as to, in an earlier time, bring Edmund Halley to lay his conviction and reputation upon it.[126]

When Galton produced his idea of inherited intelligence, it was only *eight* years after Paul Broca had located a place within the brain that could be related to language, and so destroyed half a century of Gall's phrenology. Phrenology had been a very fashionable belief that held almost religious conviction that the skull was precisely shaped by the brain. Each person's quality of secretiveness,

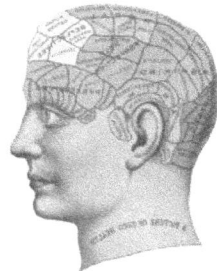

spirituality, benevolence, reasoning, calculation, among a host of 40 or so other intellectual, social and moral attributes, was believed to be found by measuring the surface differences of bumps and depressions on their skull.[127]

As new sciences burst forth, especially those engaged with social or human interest, they desperately sought to establish a foundation from which their efforts could endure the test of time. So we find, if we look deeply enough, that many of the early pioneers of psychology constructed their ideas of human ability and so their schools of thought upon Galton's philosophy.

By the way, it impressed the imagination of people and its use of statistics, Galton's philosophy gave promise of raising psychology to the rank of the established sciences, such as mathematics, physics, and medicine. As we may know, all of who were involved in these sciences wished to distance themselves from psychology as far as possible. Ivan Pavlov, one of the most famous of all medical doctors, believed the case for psychology as a science "is completely hopeless."[128]

Galton, then, with his prestige in the blooming of the Victorian sciences, for his fame as an African explorer, universally welcomed as the "second" cousin to Charles Darwin, famed for his scientific ingenuities through which he was elected to numerous posts in many of the major booming scientific societies, and held in reverence by the general public for his prolific writings, conferences and exhibitions, would readily have offered the ease of public recognition necessitated by any youthful science.

The examination of how certain people in each country promoted Galton's ideas into their political, social, and educational structures would be unnecessarily laborious to us here. We could, however, examine why Wilhelm Wundt, after starting the world's first psychological laboratory in Leipzig in 1879, was soon after to direct this towards the association techniques that Galton was writing profusely upon. So widespread was Galton's work that Forrest suggests it could have influenced Freud in his early ideas of psychoanalytic association. Both, he points out, wrote articles in the same medical journal during the same period.[129]

Yet, it would be more relevant to note that Wundt's laboratory is regarded to be the birthplace of the science of psychology.[130] From 1879 onwards, at least for the rest of that century, Wundt's laboratory was the centre of world activity in the development of this science, when all its schools of thought were founding. It is very significant, as we shall soon see, to know that an American by the name of James Cattell was first a student of Wundt and later became his assistant.

Cattell was mainly interested in individual differences of ability. After he had received his Ph.D. from Wundt in 1886, Cattell went to lecture in Cambridge, and there built up a personal relationship with Galton. He quickly saw the potential for combining Wundt's psychophysics with Galton's mathematical approach to the examination of individual differences.[131]

Then, as a disciple of Galton, Cattell returned to America in 1888 to become the first American Professor of Psychology at the University of Pennsylvania.[132] While he was there, Cattell set up the first laboratory to study the mental measurement of college students. Three years later, he became the President of the American Psychological Association. Cattell is one of the founding fathers of psychology in America, and subsequently directed it towards the study of human intelligence through Galton's ideas of inheritance.

We may also note that another student of Wundt was an Englishman by the name of Edward Titchener. Following his studies at Oxford and under Wundt in Germany, Titchener went to America and created the science of structuralism, which became a foundation block of Psychology. In essence, Titchener took Wundt's theories of how the mind works and developed this to explain how sensations and thoughts brought the mind into structures.[133] In turn, Titchener joined Cattell to form a tripartite of interest with Galton in England and Wundt at Leipzig.

The Foundations of The Science of Psychology

There was, however, another scientist who had read Galton's writings on individual differences, and whose concluding work was to be used, **against his wishes,** to bring our whole understanding of intelligence in line with that of Francis Galton. He was the French psychologist Alfred Binét.[134]

A very real stumbling block to Galton, the biometricians, and the early psychologists who followed him, lay in that while their whole enterprise was set about the measurement of intelligence, they had not found any means that could place it on a scale of index. Without this, they had no real means to qualify what they were saying. All they had was an argument that some people were born more intelligent than others, which they sought to qualify by saying that such people were wealthier and since they looked alike within families so they must have the same kind of brains.

Let us clearly understand that all Galton had done was to state that intelligence is "almost" wholly inherited. With this being so, it was common sense to see that the use a man and his children could be to society was to be found in the achievements of his ancestors. Intelligence, we must hold on to, is not about how clever children or people are, it is about how the managers of society can be selected!

When Galton first introduced his concept, it had readily been accepted by all parties because of the centuries of conditioning that people had been raised under. However, as the 19th century drew to a close, the lower classes had developed a strong political challenge to his claim of inheritance, and by showing the effectiveness of education through the expansion of the middle classes, they were now openly demanding equal opportunity through equal education.

While this social shift was occurring, education was seeking clearer and more precise means of evaluating mental competence through the greater demand that was being placed upon it by the expansion of industry and commerce. As new schools sprang up everywhere, classrooms were often overcrowded and staffed by teachers who were unable to cope with the vast differences in the developments, personalities, and ages that confronted them. What each country desperately needed was a reliable educational structure that could bring simple classification to the hordes of children being conjured up for a work role to play.

The emphasis was on who could do what, and not why one could not do what another could. There was no time, no money, and no real interest in pursuing a means to help children overcome the problems their parents were responsible for. This was a time of production, and the child was put on the conveyor belt of a processing education as part of a processing society.

However, as one century led into the next, fragmented ideas began to be pulled together, and geneticists began to focus not just upon the factor of inheritance, but also the causes of development. Eventually,

Johannsen would discover the true role of the environment, but it would take education half a century to begin to adapt itself to what this could mean with children. Meanwhile, the rising social influences in politics at the turn of the century, began to demand that a child's ability be seen not from the seed through which it appeared, but as a consequence of its own environment.

Education struggled against the ramifications of this for all the political reasons we have discussed, and held to Galton's theory of inheritance, because this theory that a child essentially inherited their intelligence provided the simplest and most cost effective means to categorise and classify its students. However, while Galton had provided the theory for this classification, he had not supplied the means to achieve it, and both society and education became ever more desperate for an incontestable way to compare one child against another, which really meant one potential citizen against another, detached from environmental influence or training.

The answer is that it cannot! However, the route that provided the opportunity to believe that it could came through studies of mental disorders. I believe the next chapter is possibly the most important one in this book. .....

Chapter Seventeen

Alfred Binét

Courtesy of Société Alfred Binet

In 1882, Jean Martin Charcot became the Professor of Neurology at the Salpetriere in Paris. Professor Charcot rapidly acquired an international reputation for his modern ideas about diseases of the nervous system, especially those relating to mental disorders. In seeking to build up his department, Charcot enticed Pierre Janet, a then professor of philosophy, to join his staff.

It was under Charcot's influence that Janet began to make many outstanding contributions relating to the identification of mental illnesses and their causes. To this end, he was instrumental in bringing forward concepts of how perceptions and sensations were related to mental development, and how mental illness could develop through emotional disturbance and fatigue.

Janet's association of physiological and psychological states brought great interest from the American psychologist William James.[135] We may see by this that it is relatively easy to show how an influencing dialogue came to exist between psychologists in different countries in the beginning of their science, before they developed to follow their own particular paths.

However, it was through Pierre Janet's interests in how consciousness could be split to incur a dual personality that he developed a close relationship with Alfred Binét, who at that time was the Director of Psychology at the nearby Sorbonne.

Binét had himself long been interested in this field of study, but it was through the influence of Janet that he was caused to turn his attention to the origins and determination of mental illnesses.[136] In 1899, Binét was approached by Theodore Simon, who wished to make a doctorate on mentally handicapped children.

At the same time as this, the French government was beginning to expand its educational program, which we may like to think was for the better development of children. The greater reality was that Germany, the arch foe of the French, was building up its military forces once more, and the Gaul was not prepared to idly stand by and suffer the same humiliation he had 30 years earlier in the last Franco-Prussian war. It was the consequence of this defeat that led French military commanders to reappraise their infantry tactics, and in doing so, drew their inspiration from the writings of Ardant du Picq.[137]

As a colonel in the French Army, du Picq had described how the French soldier should be more intelligent to field situations than his German counterpart, whose military leaders relied on bulldozer tactics. This called for soldiers to be more self-adaptable, and that children should be prepared for this role, as later adults.[138] It was the military directives emerging from this philosophy that led to a law requiring all children to be provided with seven years of compulsory education. May we be reminded by this, and as we saw in *The Illusion of Education*, that the fundamental purpose of school has little to do with the general well-being and better development of the child.

However, a problem with this soon arose when teachers began to complain that some of the children they were instructed to teach were below the standard they could work with. This caused the educational authorities serious problems, because they had no means to evaluate if such a child was slightly retarded, or if their learning impairment was due to poor social conditions.

In 1890, Binét had published three articles relating to tests and puzzles, which he had worked through with his two daughters. Binét's fascination with learning began when he noticed how his two daughters learnt to walk in different ways. It was this intrigue that sparked within him a desire to understand how children learn, and so of the different ways they would tackle the same problem.[139]

Courtesy of Société Alfred Binet

At this time of his life, Binét was primarily interested in the way children relate to puzzles, compared to the way adults do. The most obvious difference he noted in children lay in their weak ability to keep attention. The mind of children, he found, drifted more easily than that of adults. As Fancher points out, the importance of the child's state of mind, and the influence of the environment on testing would remain significant to Binét throughout his lifetime.[140]

As Binét was subsequently to write: "The operations of the intelligence are nothing but diverse forms of the laws of association. All psychological phenomena revert to these forms, be they apparently simple, or recognised as complex. ... Explanation in psychology, in the most scientific form, consists in showing that each mental fact is only a particular case of these general laws....."[141]

However, the French authorities at this time were more concerned in dealing with the task at hand, than in recognising the implications behind such a statement. Consequently, they formally sought the assistance of Binét to solve their problem of how teachers could tell the difference between children who were mentally retarded and who performed at much the same level, but only so because of poor environmental development.

- Accordingly, Binét and Simon began by reasoning that the real problem was not the child, but what was expected of a child when they were compared to other children.

As the gauge for this was the age in which the child was to be educated, Binét and Simon saw the problem as being what was expected of a child at a particular age. In following this, the first task they set themselves was to estimate what a child at the age of three or five and so on up to eleven, would be expected to be capable of doing. Using this as the framework for their operations, Binét and Simon examined the capabilities of large numbers of children at respective ages. From the information they amassed, they believed they could approximately gauge what a child at a certain age should be capable of.

The next task they set themselves was to relate the age of the child being tested to the age they were expected to perform at. They did this by awarding one-fifth of a year, for each correctly answered question in a test they had devised. By awarding one-fifth of a year for each sufficiently well answered question, Binét and Simon were able to state that if the child were of normal development, they ought to be capable of gaining enough parts of a year to equal their actual age.

In conclusion of this, in 1905, Binét and Simon suggested to the Parisian authorities that a test involving skills of analogy and reason could be used to solve the predicament they faced. They reasoned that where a child's score demonstrated that their estimated age was close to their actual age, they could be regarded as being normal. However, should their score be less than complete (note here this has nothing to do with averages), then the number of parts they have not collected could give suggestion as to the type of training they should receive. This could be either a course in mental orthopaedics to allow them to catch up with their age group or further investigation into their mental condition.

Courtesy of Société Alfred Binet

It is thus extremely important for us to understand here that Binét worked individually with each child, asking them only verbal questions, and using the verbal responses he gained to probe deeper into the child's understanding. His purpose was to gain a complete picture of how each child understood and why they responded in the way they did to the questions given to them

Courtesy of Société Alfred-Binét

"Binét's test was not, he strove to argue until his death, to be used to indicate an individual's intelligence, or to support any theory of what intellect may be."

"Nor was intelligence", he protested, **"to be taken as any indication that may reflect an innate, or permanent ability within an individual!"**[142]

It is of the most vital importance for the reader's complete understanding of the meaning behind all the fourteen books in this series that this point is most clearly understood.

Indeed, Binét emphatically declared that his test was only to be used as a means to suggest that a child "may" have learning difficulties or "may" be mildly retarded.[143]

To emphasise this, he wrote a small book in 1909 explaining how intelligence could be improved in children through exercise and techniques, and at the same time defined the criteria for an intelligent thought.

These, he believed, are:

-La direction: To take, and maintain a given mental operation.

-L'adaptation: To adapt thought for the purpose of obtaining
                        a given end.

-La critique: To take a critical attitude towards one's thought,
                        and be willing to correct if or when necessary.[144]

We may see in this that the man who is acknowledged to be the father of intelligence testing, clearly states that **intelligence is an act reliant, not upon a factor of inheritance, but upon developmental factors set about the laws of association!**

Binét's statement is in absolute contradiction to the theory of intelligence presented by Sir Francis Galton, just as it is to the amended theory of Galton that we have evolved to today, by which we struggle to understand the role of the environment in intelligence and yet still process our children in education by this.

Indeed, it is because the name of Alfred Binét has been consistently given as reference to the origins of the IQ test by psychologists that we may be most surprised and most educated to learn that Alfred Binét fervently believed in what we today call the plasticity of intelligence. Binét demonstrated again, and again, and again what poor performing children could do, when they were better educated. It was through this realisation that Binét was to raise a statement that is as valid today as it was when he wrote it over one hundred years ago.

"What children should learn first are not the subjects ordinarily taught. They should be given lessons of will, of attention, of mental discipline. Before exercises in grammar, they need to be exercised in mental orthopaedics: in a word they must learn how to learn."[145]

This statement is timeless, although it is ignored by every educational authority today. Indeed, it was for the very purpose of bringing awareness to this need to teach children how to think, as a part of the school curriculum, that these books were written.

It is very important for all that we shall now discuss in this book to realise that while psychologists all believe, it may be said, that intelligence testing arose with Alfred Binét — that it did not.

Binét did not invent a test to measure a child's potential for intelligence, because ….

Binét knew intelligence could not be measured!

Binét only invented a system to understand if a child is mentally retarded or if their low performance in school is due to poor environmental development.

It was, then, in a twist of fate, that the man who said intelligence is based on inherited skills (Francis Galton) died in the same year of 1911 as the man who proved it is based on developmental ones (Alfred Binét). While society became organised to follow the doctrine of Galton, it never understood that of Binét's. ....

Chapter Eighteen

The Intelligence Quotient
as the tool of the American Aristocracy
The IQ Test

The fallacy not realised with the IQ test is that it is designed on vague and highly variable data at the population level, but used on the individual level that necessitates highly specific factors.

Roy Andersen

As we have seen, Binét was very cautious to the use a label may imply in the evaluation of a child, just as he was wary of his instrument being misused to explain the quality of skills a child was said to be born with. Yet, in a sad twist of fate, Binét's instrument did become the one and only means to prove Galton's theory, because intelligence test scores today are said to prove the capability of an individual's intelligence on the basis of their innate quality. How, we may we ask, did this awful and twisted situation come about?

Henry Goddard, of the Kallikak fraudulent affair, provided the first twist in the story. In 1906, Goddard accepted the position of superintendent at the Vineland Training School for Feeble-Minded

Boys and Girls in New Jersey. Soon after taking this post, Goddard was struck with the difficulty of knowing how to tell the difference between children who were retarded, due to poor health and required remedial assistance to improve their ability, and those who were feebleminded -- a condition, he believed, was caused by a single recessive gene that could not be improved upon.

It was with the hope of meeting other psychologists who were dealing with the same kind of problems that Goddard took a two-month sojourn to Europe in 1908. It was while he was in France that he came across the work Binét had started some years earlier. Recognising how Binét's test could provide the solution he was seeking, Goddard obtained copies of the test and, upon his return to America, translated these into English. By December of the same year, Goddard had published his version of the test and had begun to distribute 22,000 copies to psychologists and educationalists.

The idea of measuring intelligence was new and exciting. However, the real incentive that drove psychologists to readily adopt and work with this idea was the financial rewards. Intelligence tests were to be the bread and butter for psychologists for many decades to come. Psychologists made huge amounts of money through the enterprise of testing intelligence.

To the psychologists who still lingered with the impression that intelligence was the ability to learn and to develop new ways of doing something,[146] Goddard washed their sentiments away by defining the difference between intelligence and knowledge:

"What do we mean by intelligence and what do we mean by knowledge?" he asked, and replied in the same breath, "The one is inborn, the other acquired. Intelligence is the potentiality of the machine. Knowledge is the material upon which it works. Knowledge is the raw material. Intelligence determines what we do with it. The effectiveness of a machine depends upon its structure and its functioning."[147]

Galton had well laid down the origins of the machine. Goddard now provided a way it could operate. To ensure the whole of America was aware of this, Goddard was notably prominent in every single psychometric event in its founding stages. It is no understatement to say that Goddard, who had deliberately forged the account of the Kallikak family, is a founding pillar of intelligence testing.[148]

While Goddard was rapidly building up a substantial framework for his tests in America, Wilhelm Stern in Germany began to argue that Binét's relationship between mental age and chronological age had another side to the coin.

Although Stern saw intelligence to have different perspectives, he acknowledged that individuals could be better in one than in another, and although he was more aware of how intelligence could be developed than Spearman in England, he essentially followed Galton's line of thought, instead of Binét's. Taking intelligence as an inborn feature set about a factor of individual personality, Stern reasoned that the Mental Age (gained by a child in the test) could be divided by their Actual Age to provide what he called the Mental Quotient.[149]

$$\text{Mental Quotient} = \frac{\text{Mental Age}}{\text{Actual Age}}$$

With this reasoning that if a child displayed a Mental Age of 10, and was 10 years old, their MQ score would be 1. This would be to say that they were normal. However, if a child displayed a Mental Age of 10, but was only 8 years old, their MQ would be a score of 1.25. This would demonstrate they were cleverer than normal. The converse would be equally true if they were 10 years old but displayed a Mental Age of 8. In this case, the child would score an MQ of 0.8 and so demonstrate they were below normal intelligence. However, to be fair to Stern and this is an important point to what will follow, he was always cautious to the extent that any test could reveal of a child's true worth. As he wrote in 1914:

"No series of tests, however skilfully selected it may be, can reach the innate intellectual endowment, stripped of all complications, but rather this endowment in conjunction with all influences to which the examinee has been subjected up to the moment of testing."[77]

We can see here that Stern fully realised that the effect of development could not be separated from the factor of intelligence the child was born with, and that therefore he was acutely aware of the limitations of the test he had designed. Like Binét, Stern was only seeking a test that could give some guide as to how a child's development may be corrected.

However, Binét, who died in 1911, would never have agreed with Stern's idea of an MQ figure, and it was to avoid the likelihood of a figure occurring in the future that he had always stressed the limitations of his test. To his dying day, Binét had always insisted that intelligence is far too broad a concept to be quantified by a single number. Intelligence, he emphatically insisted, is influenced by a number of factors. These factors do change over time, and can only be "gauged" in children of similar backgrounds.[150] Towards the end of this book, we shall begin to identify what these factors may be in preparation for our book *Brain Plasticity*, which follows from this.

It is important to recognise from this that as Binét believed children grew in intelligence, he would never have accepted Stern's perspective of how the worth of a child could be calculated through the score of their mental age, as a factor of their actual age. To Binét, children at different ages had different capabilities, although this was not to say that their potential could be determined through one age. Sensitive to the ease with which children could be categorised, Binét purposely made use of the word "a level," to describe a child's performance. Stern made use of the word "a score," and so defined a human being's intelligence with a number. This was the means of indexing Galton had always sought.

In order to avoid confusion with mental behaviour, Stern later suggested the word mental should be replaced with that of intelligence, and so brought about the term Intelligenz Quotient.[151] This, however, is not the IQ we are familiar with. How this came about takes us back to America.

From Mental Gauge to Mental Examination

If we are to begin to understand what motivated Stern to distort Binét's view of intelligence and so set the worth of each to a number, we need to recognise that in the early stages of the 20th century, there emerged a huge interest within industrialised nations, and their respective psychologies, to seek means to classify the value of a human being. There was no better and easier way to do this, than to give to each a number representing the value they could be to the state.

Most certainly in Stern's time, Germany was building up her vast war machine so the need here was self-evident. Yet, the bigger picture saw that while a stratified education had brought stability to the 19th century, the new type of world that was beginning to emerge would cause the maintenance of stability to be far more complex. While Europe saw stability to lie in class structuring, America saw it to lie in the control of cultural influences. It was through its ability to identify "the undesirable citizen" here that psychology gained its roots as a political tool.

As tides of immigrants saw to escape the socioeconomic problems of Europe, they washed upon the shores of the New World just as all, except the Indians, had done before them. However, the earlier settlers who had established their interests first were by this time running out of "free" land to send these new people to resettle, and they were becoming increasingly uneasy about the changes appearing in their urban societies. As the definition of what an American citizen should be became more questioned, so greater stress was placed on influencing who may become a citizen. This is nonetheless true today, where moves are sought to control the rapidly expanding Hispanic influence in American society.

However, it was from this platform that a political front began to develop demanding more stringent guidelines for the acceptance of would be immigrants, and less tolerance to the social rise of those who already had adopted citizenship. Much of this was led by such organisations as the American Missionary Board, which was first established in 1906, but soon gained the confidence to rename itself as the Race Betterment Foundation to disclose its truer purpose.

Such organisations were led and given direction by the older families of America, many of whom could trace their descendants back to the 1600s. From the influences they held in governmental, social, and educational fields, just as they supported various psychologists who worked within these, they were able to steer governmental policies in the direction that best suited their interests.

Much to their need was "the eugenic movement," which Galton had earlier set up. We may be reminded that eugenics works on the principle that every ability and social characteristic is thought to be inherited. The basic purpose of eugenics is to implement social programs that encourage desired families to breed better and undesirable families to breed less.

Goddard, much in the news at the time for his writings on the Kallikak family, expounded upon this by supporting Galton's beliefs that social traits such as criminality, alcoholism, and prostitution are genetic traits. All of this gave great fuel to the fire these established families stoked in gaining public support against undesirable citizens, and **license** for psychologists to generate evidence for this. It was in this mood of the times that Goddard had produced his fake photographs, and to which William McDougall was inspired to ask: "Is America Safe for Democracy?"

All too easily were people led to believe in the authoritative information they were fed, and from which came a readiness to trust in the advice of anyone famous, even when their fame came through a totally different field. So, we find that Alexander Graham Bell, who invented the telephone, was elevated to the status of a social giant and given a prominent platform to expound his views in the urgent need for race improvement."[152] As the new 20th century rolled into being, ever more stringent means were sought that could determine who could be an American. The bottleneck for hopeful immigrants into America was the immigration centre at Ellis Island in New York.

Back in 1882, Congress had passed a law prohibiting mentally defective people from passing through the Ellis Island checkpoint. Thirty years later, the number of immigrants moving through the "turnstiles" was in excess of 5,000 a day. This created an unimaginable headache for the immigration officials, who were desperate for a solution to detect those the old Americans did not want.[153] By this time, through his fame over the Kallikak-seeded eugenic movement and with his version of Binét's test now proliferating through education, Goddard was the obvious choice for the immigration authorities to turn to in their plight.

Goddard grasped the opportunity with both hands, for this was an ideal opportunity to see if the test he had devised to recognise feeblemindedness in Americans could work with people of other nationalities.

In 1912, Goddard happily accepted the challenge. The selection procedure he devised, relied upon one assistant visually scanning immigrants for signs of an "unnatural" look. Once a suspicious character had been selected, they were sent to a second assistant who tested them on the "now" Goddard intelligence test.

As the test required some verbal interviewing, and as the second assistant had to get through thousands of people a day, we may imagine the vagueness by which a human being's worth was decided, especially when they could not speak English, had never been to school, and had just endured an exhausting sea voyage.

Accordingly, through Goddard's methods, the number of hopeful immigrants who were rejected rose exponentially.[154] From that moment onwards, a highly successful procedure had been born in the eyes of the American administration that could effectively classify people on the worth that was required of them. Thereafter, Goddard shot further to fame, and with this came ever-expanding opportunities to use his testing system in all manner of social welfare and educational situations.

The problem, may we be reminded, was for a means through which a better control of social stability could be maintained, by promoting citizens of desired backgrounds to work opportunities and by deterring undesired citizens from them. It is essential to grasp the point that opportunity for work determines the influence one group of people can exert over another in the running and order of their society. While the Old World kept focus to social grouping for this, the New World gave focus to cultural origins to preserve the identity of its forefathers.

It would not, therefore, be a great surprise to us to discover that a descendant of such early English colonialists, named David Jordan, was elected to become the first president of Stanford University. This was a position that was to be extremely influential in the structuring and running of American education. In turn, Jordan selected as the head of psychology in his university, a man who was to be more responsible than any other for the creation of a machinery that would classify human beings. His name was Louis Terman.

It might have been Goddard who had sought to use intelligence testing to clear society of mental undesirables, but it was Terman who saw to use this process to identify the working use each person could be to their society.

According to Fancher, Louis Terman's fascination with the mind sciences began when, as a child, his parents bought him a book on Gall's Phrenology. In being told by the salesman that Louis would find his future within its pages, the child avidly entered into the study of mental characteristics.[155]

In the pursuit of this, Terman very early came upon the work of Galton, and found the mentor that would give him the direction in his life he was searching for. As he was to state:

> "All the available facts that science has to offer, support the Galtonian theory that mental abilities are chiefly a matter of original endowment."[83]

With the doors that Jordan opened for him, Terman set out to show the world how easily this could be proven. He achieved this by combining the work Goddard was doing with the testing of mental undesirables with the steps Stern had started in the classification of human intelligence. I am grateful to Ray Fancher for pointing out to me that while Stern coined the term Intelligencz Quotient, it was Terman who anglicised it, gave it the abbreviated title I.Q. and very significantly multiplied Stern's ratio by 100. By doing this, Terman was able to express a score in the test as a percentage.

By this means, a result of 1.25 became a score of 125. Once a child's ability was given a specific numerical value, it was much more acceptable for their effort to be taken as a worth — by which one could be readily classed next to that of another.

Thus Stern's:

$$\text{Mental/Intelligencz Quotient} = \frac{\text{Mental Age}}{\text{Actual Age}}$$

Became Terman's

$$\text{Intelligence Quotient I.Q} = \frac{\text{Mental Age x 100}}{\text{Actual Age}}$$

By understanding this, it is very easy for us to see how a way of trying to help children became a way of classifying them. Once a classifying process had come about, we can see how easily Galton's law of deviation from the average and Gauss's curve fitted into this.

When individuals are set about an average, as they now are with IQ based on percentages, the question arose as to what readily identifiable feature most causes the positioning of each. Galton, of course, had long before provided the answer. So, a question never really arose as to what could cause the individual to move within the range of others, because it was already believed they could not. **None, except Binét,** seemed to be able to understand that the child's inability to change their intelligence score came from the self-limiting and conditioning worlds they were raised in.

Terman

However, as Binét had designed his test, it had very severe limitations to Terman's requirements. This forced Terman to make certain modifications. For instance, some of the items of Binét's test were too easy for American 5-year-olds, and too difficult for 12-year-olds. This caused the mental age of average 5-year-olds to be artificially high, and that of 12-year-olds to be artificially low.

To overcome this, Terman deleted existing items from the scale devised by Binét and Simon, and added new items until the average score of a sample of children came to 100. This meant that for each age group tested, the average mental age would equal the group's chronological age.[156] In order to give all this a reference point, Terman then stated that human intelligence varies from zero to 200, with 100 being the average value of intelligence.

To get over the unique variations between individuals, and so making them easier to be group classified, Terman divided this range into 16 deviations. Thus, if an individual scored 116 points in his test, Terman would state that they were one standard deviation above the average. The psychology of this created a way for the intelligence of human beings to have a rubber-stamped value, which could be related to categories of work.

A person who scored one deviation below the average, for example, could be assigned to jobs for this category, and so on and so forth. It was a very neat way of classifying human beings into their usefulness. This is precisely what a professor of psychology was to outline some 60 years later when, in 1981, Professor Jensen stated that someone who scored between 74 to 88 could work as an assembler, 89 to 100 as a clerk, 100 to 111 as a policeman, 112 to 125 as a manager, and so on.[157]

In 1916, Terman launched his version of Binét's test, calling it "The Revised Stanford Binét-Simon Scale." It was, however, only a short time before this became known as the "Stanford-Binét Test," bringing direct recognition to the now acclaimed professor at Stanford.

Terman's formula worked well for him with a child, but not so well with an adult. After all, it was one thing to sample 100 children of the age of seven, to estimate what a seven-year-old could know, but the life skills of an adult were a different matter altogether. How, for example, could a new employee in a business be compared to a 45-year-old who had worked in diverse fields of employment, or to a woman who had seldom been out of her home?

Terman overcame the problem of age and experience, by reasoning that since intelligence is substantially inherited, **as Galton had insisted**, then it would little change throughout the lifetime of the individual.

We may recall from Chapter Nine, how we mentioned that Spearman had declared in 1904 that intelligence is a "one thing" of the mind.[158] This idea that intelligence is a "one thing", made it easier for Terman to project intelligence as being essentially inborn and therefore little open to development throughout the lifetime. In turn, this gave him license to create a generalised "Mental Age" to make his formula work.

However, as we raised the point much earlier in our account, intelligence is not a singular feature. Intelligence is merely a label for very many, many components that work together. As we discuss in other books of this series, once factors of emotion and sensitivity to construct and process information are brought into the equation, we find that intelligence is very, very modifiable. It is not the rigid feature that Galton, Spearman, Goddard, and so Terman thought it to be, which by their classification caused it to appear to be so through the highly conditioning and self-limiting environments that children and adults normally find themselves in.

Yet, Terman knew none of this, and by taking Stern's Actual Age as arbitrary, he replaced it with his "Adult Age." To understand what this Adult Age could be worth, he selected aspects of intelligent behaviour from the white middle-class sector of the American people. By this manner of selection, he created a very successful means to classify people not by their intelligence, but by their language, culture and concept of how to interact with the world about them.

From that moment onwards, the IQ test became used to state that a person's intelligence could be calculated at any age, irrespective of the similarity of their background to that of the American white middle-class sector. Thus, in administering his test to Mexicans and African-Americans who had little or no education, Terman was able to state:

"High-grade or borderline deficiency is very, very common among Spanish-Indian and Mexican families of the Southwest and also among Negroes. Their dullness seems to be racial, or at least inherent in the family stocks from which they come .... Children of this group should be segregated into separate classes ...... They cannot master abstractions, but they can often be made into efficient workers ... From a eugenic point of view they constitute a grave problem because of their unusually prolific breeding."[159]

As our discussion on the book *The Bell Curve* will shortly show us, the same mentality exists too clearly today with psychologists of Galton's school.

To ensure a high sensitivity in his assessments, Binét had constructed his interviews upon a verbal base, but this did not suit the purpose Terman was seeking. As Terman had dispensed with the Actual Age factor and the individual orientation it purposely ensured, he then reasoned that not only could Mental Age questions be applied to the same person at any age, but that any number of people could take the test simultaneously!

However, the system of verbal questioning that Binét had designed to gain verbal responses offering deep analysis could not work when applied to more than one individual at the same time. Terman needed to devise some way of transforming verbal questions and answers into a form of script. The means to do this was provided for him by Robert

Yerkes. A direct descendant of an 18⬥-century Dutch settler and so of the old guard, Yerkes was a staunch believer in eugenics. In 1917, Yerkes was the president of the American Psychological Association and was well placed to support Terman's IQ tests when they were most needed.

When America joined the Great War, Yerkes was employed to devise a way to categorise the ability of the one million men who were expected to enlist. His purpose was to determine the better role each could play in the armed forces. Working with Terman and Goddard, it was Yerkes who transformed Binét's verbal questions into the form of pictorial options requiring a "Yes" or "No" type of response, as Terman's test was crafted into the Army Alfa and Beta tests.[160]

May we see that with one sweeping stroke, Terman, aided by Goddard and Yerkes, transformed Binét's very individualised means of assessment into a generalised test that completely distorted its whole purpose.

This was how an assessment that once relied upon verbal dialogue to interrogate one child at one time (of a specific age between 3 to 11) to gain some impression of how they faired with other children of the same age was turned into a process that would determine the innate and permanent worth of all children — and all adults a like. Now, however, they were to be tested in huge groups simultaneously, by the evaluation of their responses to socially and culturally encoded written questions in a timed test of so many minutes duration. This could not have been possible without Sir Francis Galton.

Terman had now successfully changed Binét's test from a **means of inquiring into the way an individual understands, to what an individual is capable of understanding.**

From this moment onwards, the IQ test would always carry a mechanism that allowed it to be readily tuned for or against the background of a group of people by the language of its questions.

Consider this in the following IQ questions:

1. Crisco is: (i) a patent medicine (ii) disinfectant (iii) toothpaste, or (iv) food product ?[161]

2. Leather is used for shoes because it: (i) is produced in all countries. (ii) wears well, or (iii) is an animal product ?[162]

Thus, as the intelligence test became part of the official selection procedure of those wishing to immigrate into the United States, the style of the questions were used to reflect the requirement of a "good" American by "good" Americans. Equally, as it appeared in education, the test was just as effective in routing people to spheres of influence that reflected the desirability required of them.

Consequently, new immigrants and second or third generation Americans, such as the Jews, Italians, and Russians who, by social dependency, were retained in cultural ghettos (not to mention Negroes and Indians), were poorly equipped for the reasoning language of these tests.

In a culture that rewarded achievement and punished failure, opportunity was caused to be prejudicial by self-interest. By their IQ score, such people found themselves shackled to their family backgrounds, much the same as their ancestors had been in the social stratification of Old Europe.

To enforce the importance of defining human categorisation, and his own role in it, Terman had written *The Measurement of Intelligence* in 1916. In this, he explained that "Intelligence tests will bring tens of thousands of high-grade defectives under the surveillance and protection of society. This will ultimately result in curtailing the reproduction of feeble-mindedness and in the elimination of an enormous amount of crime, pauperism and industrial inefficiency."[163]

The last two words "industrial" and "inefficiency" hold the key to understand what this was all about.

From the 1920s onwards, Terman's test, although others would arise, became the necessary mark of human evaluation sought by education, industry and commerce. While it would change its form to fit in with political whims, the **IQ test never let go of its corrupted association to Alfred Binét and the Gauss curve.** It was this association which gave it the scientific respectability to be carried through the 20th century, and so influence the world we live in today.

It is of no small significance to know that through studies of environmental effects on rural school children, Terman was later to change his opinion on the value of IQ testing.[164] However, by the time he began to raise self-doubts, IQ tests were deeply ingrained into all forms of human assessment, ranging from five-year-old children to corporate recruitment.

It was a time when the whole machinery of categorising people was in full operation, and the word IQ became such a household term that very few people took to be anything other than a complete acceptance of an individual's "natural" ability. Psychology had achieved its aim, and was now a science as respected as Medicine and Mathematics — at least to the layman.

There were, of course, psychologists and educationalists who objected to such easy human classification. Tyack, in his book *The One Best System,* explains the controversial battles over IQ testing in early 20ᵗ century America, where he draws note from those such as Walter Lippmann who warned:

"It is not possible, I think, to imagine a more contemptible proceeding than to confront a child with a set of puzzles and after an hour's monkeying with them, proclaim to the child, or to his parents that here is a C- individual. ... Such a process would be not only contemptible but inane. All that can be claimed for the tests is that they can be used to classify into a homogeneous group the children whose capacities for schoolwork are at a particular moment fairly similar."[165]

While such objections were never effective enough to overcome the political strength behind IQ testing, there were enough of them to bring some control to the situation by stressing the role of environmental influence.[166]

One such staunch advocate was John B. Watson, whom we mentioned in *The Illusion of Education* when we discussed his theory of Stimuli to Response. As Watson strove to understand how the effect of the environment could override innate ability, his experiments often bordered on the extreme.

In one now very famous experiment, he introduced an infant whom he called Albert B to a pet rat. Once Albert had built an association with the rat, Watson frightened him by making a loud clang behind the infant's head. By repeating the frightening noise every time Albert B was shown something furry, Watson was able to demonstrate how an infant could become conditioned to reject an object (such as a teddy bear) that they have an inborn instruction to bond with.[167]

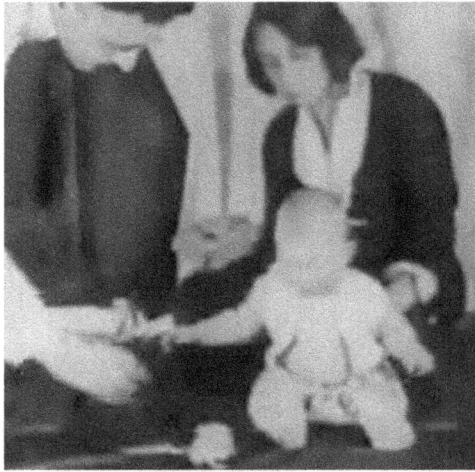

Watson & Albert B

By this seemingly brutal demonstration, Watson was able to show how the experience of the environment can override the purpose and functioning of a gene. We shall look at the principle behind this in our following book, where we examine how the psychology of the mind directs the construction of neural patterns.

However, early in his career, Watson had been heavily influenced by John Dewey, the great educationalist we mentioned earlier, to view child ability and learning as a factor of the environment. In a true sense, Watson was the perfect environmentalist, who by nature contested the view that there was an innate quality that limited response to stimuli.

When Goddard made his first use of IQ tests with the immigration authorities in 1912, an action demonstrating formal recognition that innate intelligence could now be tested, this may have been the prompt (the "stimuli" if you like) for Watson to publish his *Psychology as the Behaviourist views it a year later*.[168] This was a paper that sought to create a new branch in psychology, and one that would exclude any pre-born effect in a display of intelligence.

It is suggested here that in seeking to give his new school a sense of recognition that Watson began to align himself with the work of the famous Russian physiologist Ivan Pavlov. Pavlov had gained the Nobel Prize in 1905 for his work on the effects of stimulus. This was not, however, an instant relationship, because there was a discrete difference in Pavlov's work with stimulus to that made by Watson. In fact, Pavlov distrusted psychologists! As he once wrote:

Pavlov

"Psychology takes conditioning as a principle of learning, and accepting the principle as not subject to further analysis, endeavours to apply it to everything and to explain all the individual features of learning as one and the same process."[169]

Pavlov was a brilliant surgeon who devoted his life to the study of how chemical changes arise in the nervous system of dogs. For instance, Pavlov would cause some chemical excitation in the digestive system of a dog by introducing it to small amount of food. The dog would be taught to associate this food to the sound of a bell. Once the dog had built up this association, Pavlov would play the bell to see if the dog's digestive system had released enzymes in its expectation of food. This was Pavlov's theory of conditional reflex,[170] which, as we can see, has very little to do with Watson's work with Stimuli and Response, especially as he was to demonstrate with little Albert.

Watson, however, persevered with the connection and, in his presidential address to the American Psychological Association in 1916, officially annexed his work to that of Pavlov's through the terminology and usage of "Conditioned Reflex."

Although Pavlov's work was solely physiological in nature, he did begin to extend his efforts into human psychoses during the early 1930s. The inhibitions of a psychotic person, he reasoned, are a protective mechanism by which they seek to shut out the external world. It was through his work in this field that Pavlov came to see language as more complex than words, and recognized it held a deeper meaning in the elaboration of understandings. This view that language has a more complex nature than we normally assign to it, will become important when we discuss again how language provides a foundation for intelligence.

However, with the help of Watson, Pavlov's work came to underlie comparative psychology, and greatly influenced science, philosophy, and culture right across the board. Within Soviet Russia itself, Pavlov's work gained unparalleled importance and became increasingly applied to social and educational policies, where it was given unprecedented authority during the time of Stalin.

This is, however, slightly baffling, because Pavlov was openly critical of communism at a time when other scientists disappeared for murmuring the slightest discontent. Wolman pointed out a possible explanation for this when he reasoned that Pavlovian theories were drawn into human psychology because they specifically "avoided" discussion of the human consciousness and how it could be affected, developed, or conditioned by environmental experiences.[171]

This well illustrates how education in Russia, as all countries, faced the choices as the West did in choosing between the type of systems advocated by Thorndike or by Dewey in the beginnings of its mass education. In fact, there was a man in Russia who offered just as much thought upon environmental learning as did Dewey, if not considerably more.

Lev Vygotsky was a young psychologist who came to prominence in Russia just after the 1917 revolution. His ideas on child learning were revolutionary. Vygotsky saw that emotional responses were so much a part of motive, that learning could be expressed through semantic or language processes. From this understanding, he believed that techniques could be devised to improve the intelligence of individuals,[172] and developed what became known as the Social Development Theory.

I am grateful to Elena Kravtsova for this photograph
of Lev Vygotsky

Vygotsky's theory of social development sees intelligence as a product of language that is, of course, constructed through social experience. Therefore, while Piaget saw intelligence to develop through specific biological stages and therefore be limited by them, Vygotsky saw it to develop freely through experience. As he explained, "Learning is a necessary and universal aspect of the process of developing a culturally organised, specifically human psychological function."[173]

In essence, then, Vygotsky was saying that intelligence develops through language, so the more that is explained to the child in the child's terms of understanding, the more the child will understand. The root and effectiveness of this explanation lies in teaching through mediation, which we discussed in our previous book, just as we explained how Vygotsky built upon this understanding of mediation to develop his theory of the Zone of Proximal Development.[174]

As we mentioned at that time, mediation is an extremely important means of teaching and is, in fact, an essential way forward for education. It is, however, a much misunderstood process, and does require a change in the classroom structure, as much as it does in the minds of many educationalists. In many of our books, we discuss the working operation of this process in considerable detail, because it offers the way forward to reshape our educational processes to enable them to meet the demands of this century better.

Yet again, the development of reason was not what was required in Russia, and just as Pavlov's theory was used under Stalin to propagate the purity of Marx's views on the subject of consciousness, Soviet Russia gave little opportunity for Vygotsky's theories to interrupt mainstream education.

In a move that has had parallels in the West, such developmental techniques as those put forth by Vygotsky in child learning were generally directed to areas of special education, as was Watson's S-R theory. Sidelined as they were, they did not interfere with the design of normal human resource, but gave means to improve the worker potential of under-performing children. By the authority placed upon the interpretation of Pavlov's theories in Soviet Russia, it was virtually impossible for contesting theories to be openly discussed, and so Vygotsky's theories were unknown in the West until an English translation of them appeared in the 1960s.[175]

For all the same reasons, Watson's theories of behaviourism in America gained substantial ground in areas of special education, but on the broad front of general education, they were swept aside. As the crusade for IQ testing gushed forth from government offices and universities, ever spurred on by books, magazines, newspapers, radio, and later television, through which the effect of IQ propaganda seeped into every American home, family, and all aspects of American education and commerce, with all its international connections, it created a mind-frame that could understand little else.

The idea that intelligence was innate, and that this innate worth could now be tested, measured and known, became globally accepted. Terman had succeeded in creating a multi-million dollar business.

Chapter Nineteen

Global Seed of Intelligence Testing

As the use of IQ testing spread throughout America, and then into England, her Commonwealth countries and Europe although never quite to the same degree, it was promoted as the ideal instrument to segregate ability for the planned needs of vocational guidance. As Terman had put it: "Such testing is more democratic than former systems, because it offers the best opportunity for each child to use their full capacity...."[176]

This was a quite presentable reasoning, but since children were not expected to show greater ability than determined by their performance in tests, the character of the educational track they were placed in produced a self-limiting environment.

A few children, those powered by higher motivation, extra tuition, and invariably guided by the persuadable influences and tact of their parents, managed to hop to another track and so better career opportunities. However, to the vast majority of children, their performance in the test sealed their fate, and education settled into its most "effective" processing period.

As this selective process settled down and began to run smoothly, many parents saw how a pattern began to emerge based on test scores. Children from poorer backgrounds were directed to schools of poorer reputation, while children from wealthier backgrounds were channelled to better schools. Where a school served both areas, social divisions became notably paralleled to classroom structures and educational opportunities.

Those parents who objected were ignored or pacified, or their children were given special opportunity to appease their parents. Although, just as today in any country of the world, most parents did not object, being too wary of displeasing the teacher who controlled the grades their child would be awarded.

In the overall scheme of things, Watson's behaviourism did make some dent in the overcrowded classrooms, underpaid and overworked teachers who struggled to make minimal gains with their knowledge. However, while educationalists did build up a more sophisticated understanding of intelligence and discussed ways of making their teaching strategies more environmental, the managers of education continued on their own track to use IQ testing for the selection of children's ability, as it was fashioned for them by the professional elite.[177]

While neither the imposition of this testing nor the political management behind it went unnoticed, the general acceptance to ability being innate was so deeply seated that great power was given to the overall social machinery to trundle on unimpeded.

So deeply were people conditioned to believe that intelligence was significantly innate that they would hear, but not listen to such objections. When all was said and done, at the end of the day, the parents blamed the teachers, the teachers blamed the children, and society went about its normal business of managing people.

Nor was this architecture limited to the New World. Most countries produced their Cattells and Termans, as Germany did with Stern, and England with Spearman. It is by mentioning Spearman that we move now into Galton's own backyard to see the real political consequences of the idea of inherited intelligence.

Oscar Wilde had that wonderful ability to make people laugh at the truth in themselves, although the truth was often deeper than they realised. When his play *The Importance of Being Earnest* appeared on the stage in 1895, his character Lady Bracknell said what many wanted to, but found the new times inopportune to do so.

"Ignorance," she says, "is like a delicate exotic fruit. Touch it and the bloom is gone. The whole theory of modern education is radically unsound. Fortunately, education produces no effect whatsoever. If it did, it would prove a serious danger to the upper classes and probably lead to acts of violence in Grosvenor Square." [178] (Grosvenor Square, we may note, was the hallmark of established society at that time.) The statement, however, had more than a ring of truth to it, and would echo through many wings in the forthcoming century.

The problem was that education did begin to produce a considerable effect, or rather a disturbance to the social order of things. The more this appeared, so the more ardent supporters of Galton strove with ruthless endeavour to bring it under greater control. No man is more worthy of singular discussion here than Cyril Burt. For nearly three-quarters of a century, from 1909 to 1971, Burt directly influenced the design of education so that children in school developed directly in accord with Galton's philosophy.

However, to discuss Burt, we first need to mention Charles Spearman and his system of factor analysis, because it was factor analysis that gave Burt the opportunity to devise the lethal weapon he did in the educational directives he was responsible for creating. Indeed, factor analysis was so powerful a tool for Burt that he wrongfully laid claim to its invention. A claim he was forced to withdraw under pressure from Spearman — at least until Spearman's death. Once Spearman was laid to rest, Burt had no qualms in reinstating his claim that factor analysis was his invention.[179]

A problem that still confounds psychologists to this day is to clearly define what intelligence is. Despite intense debates and arguments that have stretched over 100 years, there has not arisen a commonly accepted theory of what constitutes intelligence.[180] Yet, even though we don't know what it is, a whole industry has built up upon the belief that it can be measured. Our purpose in this chapter is to build upon our discussion of Pearson and his correlation coefficients to understand how this came about.

At the dawn of the 20th century, there was a very great abundance of ideas as to what could constitute intelligence. Some of these ideas were sensible, and others much less so, with many of them mere refinements from the earlier phrenology movement. The need to condense all these varied suggestible features into something that could be defined came at the height of the war between Galton's biometricians and Bateson's mutationists when both sides were desperately seeking to define intelligence for their own political purposes. Unfortunately for the mutationists, it was provided by Charles Spearman, who had gained his doctorate at Leipzig under Wundt!

Charles Spearman was a man so convinced that intelligence was substantially inherited that he believed medical science would one day discover a specific area of the brain devoted to it.

Spearman

Accordingly, as a staunch follower of Galton, Spearman proposed in a paper written in 1904 that intelligent behaviour is generated by a single, unitary quality within the human mind.[181] As we have just discussed, this is one of the main reasons why we believe today that intelligence is a fixed quality within the individual, and not so a factor of different parts that can be significantly modified through environmental experience. We look into this very closely in *Brain Plasticity*.

However, in an effort to improve the accuracy of Pearson's coefficients and to further Galton's cause in seeking to measure intelligence, Spearman devised the mathematical system of rank correlations. This was his first attempt to devise factor analysis, a system of comparing statistics for which he would become world famous.[182]

Spearman's first insight into how this could become constructed arose when he noticed how school children scored very similar results in a wide variety of seemingly unrelated subjects. If, for example, a child scored A or B in English, he found that they were likely to achieve similar scores in their other subjects of Geography, Science, Religion, and Art, etc. This similarity of grades in different subjects gave fruit to the idea that all aspects of intelligence could be correlated with each other. From this idea arose the hypothesis that a general factor of intelligence could be found in the basic skills of all people. Spearman reasoned that this factor could be witnessed in their common ability to integrate ideas, demonstrate skills in mathematics, and logical reasoning, to name but a few.

As an ex-army officer, it was perhaps natural for Spearman, with a military mind trained to simplify matters into their most economical form, to condense the very many intangible forms of intelligence into a generalised form that could be worked with. Through the assistance of another statistician named Hart, Spearman termed this general factor of intelligence the "g" factor, and obtained values for it by cross-sampling responses from a number of people. As a student of Galton, Spearman reasoned that any score by an individual to questions relating to the "g" factor would reveal their natural worth of intelligence.

However, to take into consideration individual differences relating to different subjects, Spearman also introduced the concept of the Specific or "s" factor of intelligence. This meant that in addition to a test on general competence, an individual would take further tests in specific subjects. By relating their scores in the "s" factor to that which they had gained in the "g" factor, Spearman could fine-tune his assessment of their intelligence. By plotting all scores on a graph and devising a vector through the greater density of these, Spearman reasoned that the strong and weak points of an individual's intelligence could be identified.[183] This process of correlating scores is known as factor analysis.

Yet, as we discussed earlier with Pearson's coefficients, this mechanism has very broad applications for use with statistical information, and while the close approximation of particular scores may suggest a generality, this is no indication for the cause of that generality. Factor Analysis is only another means of correlating data. Instead of dealing with very many variables, it reduces the very many to a very few on the basis that most will correlate with each other. Factor Analysis does not explain why or how the factors appear. It is only a summarisation of variables and any result will totally depend upon how the data is collected and how it is presented.

In factor analysis, a vector is constructed in a graph to show the relationship of its data. However, as Sternberg explains, this vector could just as easily be rotated to any point so it is impossible to know the correct rotation, and so the correct value for the g factor when this is used with intelligence."[184]

Gould raised the point to a higher level when he discussed how Thurstone had rotated the axes to make the g factor disappear, and so wrote how this gave: "...Rise to a theory of multiple intelligences (verbal, mathematical, spatial, etc.),"[185] which, we may suggest here, may have been an inspiration for Howard Gardner to build his theory of multiple intelligences upon.

However, it is somewhat revealing to know that it is not the similarity of scores in different subjects that causes Spearman's "g" factor, but the

228

acquired skill in strategy that the individual had developed to select, compare and process information. Providing the child has the same desire for commitment in each of their subjects, their performance will be the same in each, **because** they are using the same skills to interrogate, process and respond to information. Thus, the idea that intelligence is inherited and a singular feature which is recognised through the "g" factor quite fails to recognise the **acquired** techniques that enable the act of intelligence to exist.

As we have sought to explain, and as Binét desperately strove to point out, intelligence is not the singular feature that Spearman believed it to be. Nor, as we shall now see, does factor analysis prove that an act of intelligence is determined by a ratio of inherited quality to environmental influences. It is from this that we are led to discuss the man who influenced the structures of education in many countries of the world through his devotion to Galton.

Burt

Sir Cyril Burt had a hero type of worship for Francis Galton that was seeded when, as a boy, he was introduced to this great man as a patient of his father. In seeking to know more about Galton, Burt found his *Inquiries into Human Faculty* in the school library, and noted that it was published in the year of his birth, 1883.[186]

The stage was set for complete adulation, and so we may not be surprised that, as Burt eventually climbed to the highest level in British educational psychology, his directives and personal writings always contained some element of Galton within his own:

"Intellectual ability is inherited or at least innate," wrote Burt, "where it is not due to teaching or training; it is intellectual or emotional or moral, and remains uninfluenced by industry or zeal. It is not limited to any particular kind of work, but enters into all we do or say or think."[187]

Indeed, as a committed eugenicist, Burt's directives could have flowed from Galton's pen, when he announced in 1943, three years before he was knighted for his services to education: "Social inequality could be explained ... largely, though not entirely, an indirect effect of the wide inequality in innate intelligence."[188] Such declarations as this from Burt did influence people to believe that government spending was wasted in supporting social and educational programs, where they sought to develop what nature could not.

Burt became the first applied psychologist in the United Kingdom, and was more responsible than any other singular person for the educational perspective of child ability in the spheres of his influence. So widespread did that influence become through his writings, journals, and international conferences that Burt provided a decisive political direction in education.

We may understand how prolific this was when we realise that Great Britain at that time was still the centre of a vast empire. With the position he held, Burt had the potential to influence the educational services in the Commonwealth countries of Canada, India, South Africa, New Zealand, and Australia, and of Britain's influences in the Pacific, the Far East, the Middle East, Africa, and the American Continent. By the level of authority that Burt acquired, he influenced the design of governmental policies toward education and how education operated. As accountants gave directions to headmasters, who in turn gave directions to teachers, who were being guided by psychologists in the ways students should be taught and assessed, all came under the cloak of Burt, his philosophies, and his directives.

As we may understand, Burt was profoundly instrumental in the way school children were to be taught, examined, and so directed to roles in society. From the onset of his career, Burt had believed that children from better backgrounds, because of their supposedly better breeding, offered more potential to the country than children from poorer backgrounds and of supposedly lower genetic stock. Based on this belief, Burt had long influenced government spending to divert more money to schools in better areas for the better enhancement of their students' ability. Consequently, less government money was provided to schools in poorer areas, which, of course, lowered the learning environment for those children.

Towards the end of the Second World War, a social mood desired that education open up opportunities in its better schools for children from poorer backgrounds who displayed high talent. It was the political pressure emanating from this that brought about the introduction of the Eleven Plus Examination. This examination would give all children leaving primary school the opportunity to enter a grammar school if they could demonstrate the necessary level of ability.

The responsibility for designing this examination fell directly upon the shoulders of Burt. In his hands, it became a veiled IQ test, because children from poor areas were ill-prepared for the type of language Burt devised for this examination. Also, of course, we may be reminded that these children came from social backgrounds that little prepared them for an examination. In essence, therefore, the Eleven Plus Examination was really an ideal machine for the purpose of preparing two levels of citizen based on their backgrounds. So, while the population at large believed education was creating equality, it really meant that poor children from poor backgrounds went to secondary modern schools and then to factories, while children from better backgrounds went to grammar schools and so to university with all that came from this.

This mention of the Eleven Plus raises again the very important point we discussed in *The Illusion of Education,* and so how the child's familiarity with the vocabulary and style of language used in their education will greatly decide how easy or difficult it is for them to recognise and associate to what is happening in their lessons.

We can find easy examples to this by relating to movies, because movies have an appealing way of explaining a point. So, we see Will Hay, in the 1937 comedy "Good Morning Boys", reading from a science textbook to his class:

"The velocity equals 14 times the mean velocity divided by half the
   molecular resistance of the water."

To which a boy asks, "What does that mean?"

Hay, playing the role of a not very clever teacher, quickly avoids the question and blames the boy for not knowing, as he tries to conceal the fact that he hasn't the faintest idea either.

Neither the pupils, and in this case nor their teacher, can understand the language used in the textbook here. So, we are brought back to Robin Williams in "The Dead Poets Society" instructing his students to rip out the entire introduction in their textbook by J.Evans Pritchard, Ph.D, because it is written in such a high language that none can understand.

These amusing accounts do emphasise a real difficulty for children with their education, as they stress how a child's performance in all their subjects will lie in how they are able to relate to the mind of education, and so how they are able to present their mind. This comes down to the level of language they are familiar with, because language is the medium upon which each subject hangs.

This point was entirely missed by Spearman when he was so inspired to create the g factor of intelligence. Although this was exactly what Vygotsky was referring to when he explained how development in learning is a factor of social language.

We have a lot to consider about this in our books, but suffice it to say that by the conditioning nature of school, most children progress through it with a sense of confusion because of the poor familiarity they have with its language. Therefore, it is no small matter to think of the language education used and how this causes children from different backgrounds to interact, develop, and be assessed differently through it.

Although we have thoroughly discussed the role of education as a political tool, it is difficult to understand how a system could be designed to purposely discriminate against opportunities for children that would decisively affect their lives. To grasp fully that this was and to a lesser extent still is being done, it will be illuminating to know of the knowledge that came to light after Burt died.

A number of years after Burt's death, an attempt was made to compile a biography of this most influential educational pioneer. The author to this work was Leslie Hearnshaw. As Hearnshaw began to sift painstakingly through mountains of paper documents and records, he became increasingly aware of the lack of factual evidence to support the observations and conclusions Burt had used so effectively.

The deeper Hearnshaw delved, the more fabricated he found the evidence to be. Hearnshaw's subsequent announcement of this led to a government investigation. This investigation revealed how Burt had been the architect of a very long and deliberate episode of serious scientific fraud, which had underpinned more than half a century of structuring in education.[189]

Hearnshaw's suspicions were first aroused when he came across statistics that Burt had produced in 1969. In his construction of these, Burt had presented a clear demonstration of how a systematic decline in educational standards was linked to a greater egalitarian design in education. Hearnshaw knew from his own studies and experiences that this was fundamentally not correct. However, this statistical misrepresentation by Burt was to be of small consideration compared to the subsequent parcels of fraud that began to unfold in front of Hearnshaw's eyes.

Burt, for instance, had always claimed that intelligence was so largely an innate factor that the purpose of education could be little more than to recognise the ability of the child and to feed that particular ability. (Hence, the processing system of school we still have today.) Burt had supported this doctrine with the use of data, which he claimed he had acquired through studying the effect of environmental conditioning on identical twins.

We have already discussed the reliability of the family history method, the case for monozygotic twins, Pearson's correlation coefficients and Spearman's factor analysis. It was through these that Burt conjured up a declaration that the academic performance of a child is composed of a ratio of gene quality (nature) and environmental development (nurture). While this was not new, what Burt did was to give this relationship a specific ratio. This ratio, he claimed, was in the order of 80:20.[190]

Burt's insistence that such a specific and knowable ratio exists between inheritance and the environment was a statement to the effect that every time a human being engages a task, their ability to adjust their performance in that task will be heavily restricted by their inherited worth. When we consider that everything we do has some direct and indirect application to something we have previously encountered, it is very easy to understand that Burt's reasoning much ignored the value of development.

Since Burt's declaration, other social scientists and psychologists favouring environmental development, and conscious of how their statistics influence political policies, have produced calculations that argue the converse.

Since nobody has ever proven this ratio, and since the belief that genes must have a lot to do with intelligence is so dominant in our thinking, most opted for 50:50 as a compromise. In other words, nobody knows the real effect of inheritance because nobody knows what the genes actually do. However, because they must be involved in some way, but especially because of the depth of reasoning that Galton created, psychologists at large accept a half-and-half or a 50:50 approach.

However, Burt had claimed that he had proven that the ratio of inheritance to the environment was 80:20, based on a study of identical twins examined in various environmental classifications. However, as Hearnshaw began to examine the data behind this, he found that Burt had referred to the same study on two different occasions, but had used different data each time.

In 1955, Burt had described how this study was made on 21 pairs of twins. Yet, ten years later, he claimed that 53 pairs of twins had been used in this same study. As Hearnshaw could find no evidence of the existence of these studies referred to on the second account, he came to the realisation that Burt had invented the scores of 32 cases. It also seemed probable that he had fabricated some of the original 21 in the build-up of data that had a profound effect upon the design of educational policies.[191]

Another case of Burt's unscrupulous activities came to light, when an article appeared in a 1976 edition of the Sunday Times, which was to be later substantiated by Hearnshaw.

The article accused Burt of inventing the existence of two research assistants in order to falsify the information in his reports. No evidence was ever found of one of these assistants, and although the name of the other later appeared after extensive searching, it was considered doubtful that they ever assisted Burt as he had claimed. This accusation of fraud was confirmed when Burt's secretary stated that she had witnessed him forging the names of these assistants on documents. As this was made public, it brought forth testaments from two ex-students of Burt who related how he had distorted their research findings to support his views, and then published these altered statistics without advising them.[192]

The conflicting and unsubstantiated academic data that Hearnshaw found in Burt's work brought a general realisation to the depths of how fraudulent he had been. This awareness of what Burt had been doing for so long led to his disgrace by the British Psychological Society, and brought further investigation into his work by other psychologists and political researchers, of whom one of the most critical was Leon Kamin. Kamin made a long appraisal of Burt's influences in education, and concluded that he had played a dominant role of establishing within it a prejudicial vein of social engineering.[193]

The picture that finally emerged of Burt, was that of a man who had been so fascinated by Galton as a child, and so drawn into political engineering through his early psychological studies (Burt had been a pioneer in psychological crowd control as well as eugenics.), that he became unwilling to provide either an honest or an impartial view of the research he conducted -- or of the directives he propagated from this.

That this was (and still is) a sensitive political issue is quite obvious, and upon this we need to make no further discussion here. We may only mention that the case of Cyril Burt is widely documented with ample contributions from defenders and critics, whose views and opinions tend to reflect their political stance.

Through Burt's connections with the Eugenics Society, he developed a strong friendship with Sir Julian Huxley. Huxley was a prominent member of this society and earnestly promoted the idea of eugenics in all the many influential global associations he was involved with. As the first director of UNESCO, it was Huxley who brought enforced birth control into its policy.[194]

In 1931, his brother, Aldous Huxley, with the same spirit published *Brave New World*. In fact, Sweet recognised how *Brave New World* has strikingly similar overtones to Galton's *Kantsaywhere*.[195] In this novel, Aldous predicted a time in the future (2540AD) when the world would be ruled by a single council, and all people divided into five categories of usefulness based on their inherited ability. While the foetuses of the chosen higher classes were to be allowed to develop naturally and later fed with brain stimulants, those of the lower classes, who were destined for menial jobs, were to be deprived of oxygen to retard their brain power ("Nothing like oxygen-shortage for keeping an embryo below par," wrote the author.). After birth, such children were to be discouraged from wanting to read books, by having received a sharp discharge of electricity whenever they had touched one in infancy.[196]

Huxley's desire to suggest such a world order came to him when he was on a voyage to America. During that voyage, he had read Henry Ford's *My life and Work,* and felt horrified by the whole idea of the American Dream with all its social uncontrollability. It was a sentiment his brother shared with him when he wrote: "The lowest strata are reproducing too fast. Therefore, they must not have too easy access to relief or hospital treatment lest the removal of the last check on natural selection should make it too easy for children to be produced or to survive; long unemployment should be a ground for sterilisation."[197] This came from a man who held very high responsibility in global affairs.

Such was the accepted mood throughout the world less than 60 years ago, that *Brave New World* became one of the best novels sold in that century.[198] The whole idea of eugenics, and so all we have just read about, comes down to the totally false and inventive stories of Dugdale and Goddard.

While all societies in the 20th century strove to develop their socio-educational machines to be more effective in how they pre-selected the upcoming generation for the responsibilities they would take in the working society, each was guided by different forces in how they could achieve this aim. The Old World never adopted the IQ means to do this with the fervent it acquired in the New. For one thing, it did not have the need, and for another, it faced greater danger by doing so.

The social prejudices that had survived in the educational systems of the Old World had learnt how to evade too much recognition, by becoming ever more discreet as their social orientation was pushed slowly towards greater balance. The political flavour of people would alternate, as the quality of their lives rode upon the waves of world economy, but providing their system still held to the conviction that ability was innate, the architecture of the old establishment still held. Anyway, school tests and examinations were not dissimilar in their manufacture from the concept of IQ tests, and the difference in them was more than adequately compensated for by hidden social strategies.

In their political sensitivity, the social orientation of these societies was never too keen to adapt the ruthlessness the Americans had made use of in their discriminations. This was for no other reason than the Old World saw a social threat, while the New saw a cultural one, and in the former, there was little danger of revolt from groups raised on a social consciousness that convinced them of their place in the world.

We conclude our interest in the design of pre-selecting children based on their background for the administrative and worker roles they would play in the operation of their society, by seeing how this basic principle of social planning evolved through the 20th century in America. ......

———————————————

Chapter Twenty

The Strategy of Assessment

It has always been a very serious and valid criticism of IQ tests that the design of their questioning is set about the thinking skills of a particular culture and level of social interaction. It is, after all, no small matter to ignore the differing skills of interaction, the understandings a people have to relate to all that is about them and the language of reason they have developed that separates the different worlds of people. Accordingly, to apply a test for the people of one culture upon those of a different culture, and judge them through that culture, is only to have a pure ideological reason for doing so.

While the immigration authorities in America were able to easily orientate IQ questions for or against those they desired, the use of the IQ test to select children for opportunities in education required a great deal more sensitivity.

One common strategy of all politicians of all nations is to simply change the identity of an operation that has incurred a poor public image, and with a new identity, maintain the same machinery. One example that clearly comes to mind here relates to a nuclear power plant in the North West of England. Windscale nuclear power plant was well known for a string of accidents and causes of cancer within the local population due to radiation leakage. In 1981, the UK government changed the name of the plant to Sellafield in a vain attempt to improve its public image.[199] Such changes of identity occurred a number of times in intelligence tests to gain the greater acceptance of different interests.

So, we find that as Robert Yerkes had assisted Terman in the restructuring of Binét's verbal discussion into a written "YES" or "NO" type of questionnaire, he was fundamental in selling the idea of recognising instant intelligence to the U.S. Army, as it entered the Great War. However, the military desired a different label to distance itself from the image intelligence tests had gained with French assessment of problematic children and the immigration's assessment of undesirable citizens, so it changed the name of the IQ test to The Army Alpha and The Army Beta Test. Yet, they were fundamentally the same.

And yet, it was this wide-scale application by the army of measuring human intelligence and predicting a use for it that gave intelligence testing an incredible prestige after this conflict.

An assistant of Yerkes, named Carl Brigham, began to build upon this prestige by introducing intelligence tests into college selection procedures in the 1920s. To enhance its selling potential to general education and distance it from the military image it had acquired, Brigham modified the format of the IQ / Alpha Test into what became known as the Scholastic Aptitude Test. This is more commonly known as the SAT. Although, as we shall now discover, the SAT is basically the same as the IQ test — just a different name, despite the fact that it is now globally used in education.

In the 1930s, a movement began in American education to create opportunities for poor but gifted (white) children to enter prestigious universities, which in being beyond their means was seen to deprive the working society of a talented workforce.

In his examination of this development, Lemann notes[200] how the then Rector of Harvard, James Conant, objected to the controlling influence of the "older" families on American society. As a means to oppose the elitism of their design, Conant wanted to develop a natural aristocracy to rule the country based on "natural" intelligence, which he saw as different from opportunity and influence.

Believing that Brigham's SAT could open the way to achieve this, Conant formally introduced it into the selection procedure of Harvard University with the intention that it would then permeate into the enormous machinery of the American education. While this did happen, it was not to be as Conant had wished.

As the design of SATs could be realised to offer the same pre-selectional ability as IQ tests, Henry Chauncey, a staunch member of the older elite, set up the Educational Testing Service Movement. The purpose under which it appeared was to place the right student in the right educational opportunity. However, through Chauncey's directives, the SAT was used to process white children from wealthy Protestant backgrounds into leadership positions in society.

As America became increasingly involved in the Second World War, Chauncey took advantage of the manpower shortage in education to cause the selection boards to be replaced with SATs in all higher educational institutions on a national base. Not only did Chauncey seek to control the influence of Jews, Catholics, and non-whites into the government of America, but he also foresaw how an "American" military victory of the war could bring the American educational system to other countries, and through this change political and social design globally. As Chauncey had so correctly predicted, the ideology identified with American products such as Levi jeans, Coca Cola and later McDonalds, did open doors globally for ideas of American business, education, and through this the circulation of American ideas of democracy.

Today, entrance into the higher levels of American education is dependent upon a student's SAT score, or some testing device that has the same character but is borne under a different title. The acceptance of this test by the public at large is gained through the belief that it reflects the effort of the student, that all students have an equal opportunity, and that SATs are kept unrelated to IQ tests.

In a society given structure by those who have and those who have not, a college education is a determining factor in the work and so social category a citizen will come to find themselves in. In such a highly competitive society, it would be normal to expect parents to control the preparation of their child's education.

This would be especially so if they were genuinely frightened that a poor SAT score would condemn their child to permanent social disadvantages, as shadowed by rising crime and decaying moral values. Guardians do this by how much they are aware of this need. This tends to reflect their educational background, their wealth, and their strength of influence. Thus, a stratification of interest is developed in parental attitudes, ranging from complete apathy to concern bordering on near hysteria, that approximates to their social position.[201]

Whatever may be said of the SAT before the child enters the test, their performance in that test will be largely taken as an indication of their potentiality, and in this an estimation of their "natural" intelligence. As Paul Diederich, formally of Chauncey's Educational Testing Service, explained:

"If you simply divide a SAT score by an age measure, you would end up with an IQ score. Basically, they're the same thing!" [202]

In 1939, a new type of intelligence test arose. This was the Wechsler-Bellevue Scale, and it was essentially designed by David Wechsler. Although Wechsler had been a student of both Pearson and Spearman, his view of intelligence was more liberal. It was greatly because of his consideration for the environment that he saw Terman's test to be too rigid and too restrictive. Rather than measuring intelligence, Wechsler saw that **Terman's test only measured a certain kind of efficiency,** and indicated that it would be better served by the title "Efficiency Quotient."[203] One of the things Wechsler objected to was the idea that intelligence is stable throughout the life cycle.

Terman had naturally followed Galton's philosophy in this, but had changed Stern's Actual Age to Adult Age in his formula for adults and applied his value to this as a constant — regardless of the actual age of the person taking the test. Wechsler did not believe that intelligence was very flexible, but he did think that it deteriorated with age. Since Wechsler saw intelligence to be age-related, he also saw why adults should not be tested on the same lines as children. Binét, of course, had originally designed his test only for children, but Terman used the test for everybody.

To overcome Terman's Adult Age Quotient, Wechsler replaced it with a Deviation Quotient or DQ, which he explained would test people at different ages. Working on the basis that people have different experiences of life at similar stages, he sought to relate adults by age group. To this end, he sampled people of different ages and obtained an average score for a particular age group.

Thus, while Terman had taken the average score of any human being to be 100 points, Wechsler reasoned that the average score for a 25-year-old would be 114 points. Working on this line, he reasoned that the average score for a 40-year-old would be 103 points, and that of a 60-year-old would be 93 points. While Wechsler's scale does give the impression that intelligence decreases with age, it is actually a false one. As Fencher points out, when Wechsler tested all age groups, he used the skills of the younger age to determine those of older ages. If he had used different age skills for different ages, this impression would not have occurred.[204]

As Wechsler saw how the role of the environment played a realistic part in intelligence, he saw it to be made up of specific elements which he related to social factors. Yet, his consideration to this was to be a double-edged sword. As Hayes explains, the Wechsler Intelligence Scale for children has many questions that are both highly socially and culturally directional, and as such have a prejudicial potential. Consider this in the question: "What is the correct thing to do if you find a stamped, addressed letter in the street?"

If a child gives the answer "to post it," they are awarded a full mark of two points. However, if they reply that the letter should be given to someone in authority, they are only awarded one point, and if they think that the best thing to do is to leave it alone or open it, they get NO points.[205]

As the century moved on, the Wechsler-Bellevue Scale gained greater popularity than Terman's IQ test, because it appears to take into consideration an age element and gives some recognition to the environment. We may be caused by this to feel trusting to the IQ score that is produced for the individual.

However, we should be reminded here of what we earlier said about factor analysis, and how the comparisons of its statistics give no explanation for how they came about. Wechsler relied upon factor analysis to produce an individual's score, just as Terman relied upon Pearson's coefficients, so that while all intelligence tests state a value for the individual's intelligence, we must always be very wary of how that score was actually produced. This takes us back to the ways in which the environment is selected and classified and the manner in which the test results are interpreted. We may recall how the IQ scores obtained by Newman et al, were radically changed by psychologists having different political interests.[206]

Thus, rather than being reliable, we may begin to understand that IQ tests are actually very questionable. After all, they purport to explain that they measure intelligence, but as we explained, we still do not know what intelligence is to the agreement of all. And, as Kuhn explained, there is still a great deal of human thinking that we know almost nothing about.[207]

So, it is not just that intelligence tests try to measure what they do not know, but that there are many aspects of intelligence which they purposely do not measure. As Flynn pointed out in 1987, intelligence tests do not measure very much of what intelligence actually is. They only measure a minor sort of "abstract problem-solving ability" with little practical significance.[208]

May we be further reminded how Stanovich, in his book *What Intelligence Tests Miss,* describes how IQ tests are very deficient in how they measure aspects of cognitive functioning, such as domains of logic, causal reasoning, probabilistic, and scientific thinking. Such that Instrumental Rationality (the selection of appropriate goals and the designs to realise those goals), and Epistemic Rationality (holding to beliefs that are consistent with known evidence) are totally absent in IQ evaluations.[209] Putting this aside for the moment, let us look at the construction of the Bell Curve.

The Bell Curve is more formally known as the Standard Normal Distribution Curve. Psychologists divide the area of the Bell Curve into sections, called deviations. Each deviation is worth 15 points on the scale. Thus, it is said that the result an individual gains in an intelligence test places them within a deviation zone. The average score of individuals who take an IQ test is said to be 100 points. X and Y represent the placement of two individuals based on their scores

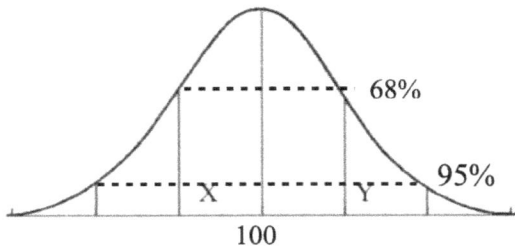

Thus, an individual who scores 115 in an IQ test, will be said to be one standard deviation above the average (i.e. 100 + 15). Equally, an

individual who scores 85 will be said to be one deviation below the average (i.e. 100 - 15). About 68% of all individuals who take the IQ test lie within one deviation, plus or minus either side of the average. 95% of individuals have scores within two deviations of the average (100 +/- 2 (15) = 70, 130. 99.7% of all individuals lie within three standard deviations of the average(100 +/- 3 (15). Each deviation is said to explain the full extent to which the intelligence of a person can be developed for those who are placed within it.

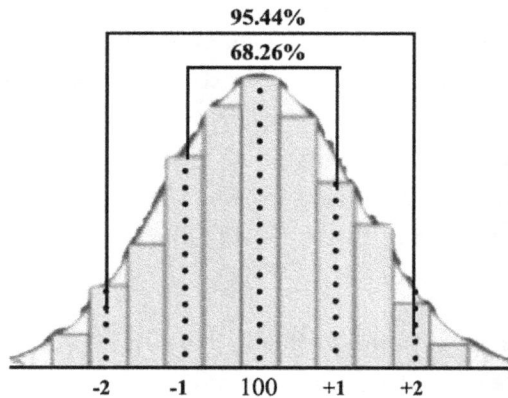

While this may seem straightforward, Plomin raises a very valid point. The purpose of intelligence testing, we understand, is to predict the intelligence of an individual. However, these deviations do not separate intelligence scores by wide or definite margins. In other words, there is actually no reliability of a human being's permanent positioning here, which, of course, is the whole point of the test![210]

Let us move from the way IQ questions are set and how they are answered to the ways in which they are determined. This is how psychologists try to identify with the environment in order to break it down into categories. Yet, if we refer back to Wechsler sampling people of different ages to obtain an average score for a particular age group, we may see that this is quite naive if we consider the vastly different lifestyles and experiences any two people will have had at the same age.

For all the reasons we have so far suggested, and we will come to examine far more in our following chapter, **the environment of intelligence is too complex to be classified.** It is as simple as this. There are simply too many factors within the environment that overlap. Anyway, most of these are unrecognisable, and the very few that are recognized cannot be specifically identified.

Suppose on the population level, one of the factors of the environment is said to be social development, and questions are set upon this with marks ranging from one to ten. Yet, on the individual level, this paper categorisation is completely meaningless. How could any range of marks possibly explain the anguish a child lives through when their mother drinks and their father frightens them? Not all mothers drink, and not all fathers frighten their children. Some (most we hope) are model parents, but not all of them. There is no black and white definition here of what is good and what is bad in the eyes of the child that can be understood by ticking boxes. To the child, life is a sea of indistinguishable greys, which they swim through by the state of their mind and in doing so construct skills to interact with the environment and survive within it. With naïvety, psychologists put these skills in a black box and label it intelligence, but real life is not so simple.

It is simply that the environment of intelligence is impossible to categorise. Geneticists have always known that, in regard to human intelligence, it is not possible to go from the population level to the individual level. We cannot generalise what the environment means, and use this generalisation to understand the specific environment of the individual. As we may repeat this over and over again throughout this book, the environment of intelligence is unfathomable. It is simply too complex to be categorised in any way by which the intelligence of a human being may be evaluated.

In fact, this failure to understand the causes and actions of the individual through the complexity of the environment was the basic flaw in Quetelet's law of accidental causes. Galton carried this flaw into his law of deviation from an average, where it has since remained in all ideas that human intelligence can be measured. **It cannot be!**

As Jack Uldrich put it in 2015, "The IQ test, the SAT, the LSAT and countless other tests all serve a limited purpose, but each is a remarkably poor predictor of long-term success. Why? It is not because of what they measure, it is because of what they don't measure -- and they don't measure characteristics such as curiosity, self-control, grit, and risk-taking."

If we realise what this means, then, so must we realise that it is impossible to index human intelligence. Galton devoted his life trying to convince society that this can be done. He died just as genetics was realising it cannot be. Without being able to index human intelligence, there is no basis for Stern's reasoning that intelligence has any predictability that can be measured. Consequently, his Intelligenz quotient has no biological base for a permanent score to be claimed. In the sense in which it was designed, IQ can never be true!

Intelligence tests do not prove the potential of an individual's intelligence, and therefore actually have no point.

In the Personal Introduction I gave at the beginning of this book, we pointed out that IQ is not intelligence. The intelligence quotient, we explained, is only a belief that intelligence can be measured. Unfortunately, when we use the term IQ we innocently enforce this reasoning that intelligence is determinable, that it is measurable, and that it therefore has a limited quality. This book has shown us why it is not determinable and why it is not measurable. Our following book, *Brain Plasticity,* will explain why intelligence does not have a limited quality.

Intelligence, as Binét pointed out, is far too broad a concept to be quantified by a single number. **Intelligence can only be gauged with children of similar backgrounds to recognise a level of developed performance at any one time.**[134] **This is all we may do!**

Consequently, while there is a general impression that IQ tests measure what an individual is permanently worth, it has become increasingly recognised that performance in IQ tests is actually developmental. One can study and change one's score by intensity of effort, to which a host of books and courses are available to enable seriously minded people to do this.

Consider the following IQ question:

"A candy maker makes two sizes of candies. Using the smaller size, a full jar will contain 120 pieces of candy. Using the larger candies a jar will contain 80 pieces of candy. The candy maker has a strict rule that no jars will contain a mix of small and large candies. If a store has room for 15 jars and they want 1560 total pieces of candy. How many jars will contain smaller candies?"

We may solve this with simultaneous equations:

Consequently:
Number of jars of small = y   Number of jars of large = x
Thus: $120y + 80x = 1560$.

When $y + x = 15$, therefore $y = 15 - x$

Thus $120(15 - x) + 80x = 1560$, Therefore $x = 6$

The answer is 6 jars for the smaller candles.

However, this question would be quite impossible to answer, if a good working knowledge of simultaneous equations is not known. Accordingly, a candidate who does not have this knowledge of maths would score zero for this question in the IQ test. However, if the same candidate studied and became very familiar with simultaneous equations, they would then be able to easily provide the correct answer and so gain the appropriate full mark. Thus, this is not a question that tests a candidate's intelligence, only the familiarity they have developed with a mathematical process. We will come back to this very important point in Chapter TwentyEight at Step Six.

All children in school learn how to do simultaneous equations, relative to the efforts and ability of their teacher, the means they have developed to keep focus from the many distractions that play on their mind and their personal drive to want to keep up with each lesson as it moves to the next. None of these factors is related to a quality of inherited intelligence. Yet, IQ questions can make them appear as if they are.

So, to the general public, deeply indoctrinated with the understanding that the intelligence of each is trapped in their inheritance, IQ tests have retained an unqualified respectability, as they demonstrate the "fixed" ability of an individual's mental worth. Regrettably, the blind faith that has grown up through this has been made use of by some social scientists in support and in the manufacture of their political ideals.

We are brought by this to reflect upon the term scientist, as it draws upon people's understanding of a physicist restricted by unbendable laws to transpose X with Y, until they are able to make some qualifiable declaration that these can, under given circumstances, produce Z. To many, the reliability of a science such as physics is naturally transferred to social studies by the understanding it is conducted by scientists.

Unfortunately, to social scientists themselves, the laws relating to their science are bendable in ways those of physics never could be, and since they concern themselves with the use of human skills, they are unavoidably prone to political interest. If we add to this the tendencies of human nature, we would be better to reflect upon the conclusion of a social study by identification of the principles and aims of those who propagated it in the first place.

It is in demonstration of all the studies done through intelligence tests, as it is of any evaluation of human potential, that we now make a brief examination of one study. This study gained an almost unparalleled amount of public interest, because it stated it had proven that whites are genetically superior to African Americans and Hispanics, with the consequence that America could never become a truly integrated society and would ever more slide into social decay.

Not only did this report conclude that ethnic people would forever rely upon white supremacy in the functioning of American society, but it also underlay a design to influence political drives. It sought to do this in a number of ways. At one level, the report argued that social benefits were only maintaining the reliance of these people on their system, and that restrictions of their benefits would better control the problems these people were said to be causing. At a far more serious and, may it be said, a dangerous level, the report stated that because these people were genetically inferior, then neither social nor educational policies could change the decreasing values of American society, they were said to cause. It was to this that innuendos were frighteningly laid.

As the mass of humanity strides forward, struggling to build a better world, endeavouring to improve the lives of people less fortunate than themselves and seeking to rebuild an economy that by its decline has fostered rises of stress, crime, and drugs, it is difficult to comprehend the purpose of such strategic elitism.

It is, after all, one thing to recognise individuals prejudiced, even bitterly towards others of differing social status or colour, because they feel a loss of identity or security. It is quite another to see such disguised collective prejudice operating behind an apparent sincerity, while advocating political directives through findings and conclusions based on questionable scientific research. By such organisation, we gain a depth of insight into the reality of political strategies in education a hundred years ago and so still today. What, then, was this report? Who wrote it, and for what purpose was it written?

The report was brought forth in the form of an 845-page book entitled *The Bell Curve*[211] — a name that, as we saw, became fashionable to describe the graph designed by Gauss and adopted so effectively by Galton. As its authors expressed their belief:

"Our achievements are directly dependent on the level of our intelligence as measured by IQ tests and are predetermined genetically...."[212]

By such wording, we may recognise that their work served no purpose that Galton did not pursue, save that it directed the fury of its policies towards racial rather than social discrimination.

The Bell Curve was purported to have been written by two social scientists, Charles Murray and Professor Richard Herrnstein, although much of the background material was compiled by like-minded associates, and the role of the authors appeared to be one of making adjustments to the information provided to them, as a means to more favourably present their theme.

Marked with such scientific credibility as the book was, its message had a far more reaching effect than if it had been presented as a scientific report. Indeed, in this case, it would have presented nothing new.

However, as a general reading book, it reached a mass of people deeply conditioned to its general theme, where it sought to provide them with political directives that offered safe solution to their concerns in the deterioration of their society.

The greatest effect, however, was not in its huge sales but in the persuasive headlines used by the media to attract public interest to its social theme. Regardless of what the socio-political intentions of the various media sources may have been, their unified broadcast that "scientific evidence explains intelligence determined by creed," gave sustenance to what people had long been fed upon, and was given incontestability to the general public by the image of a report made by scientists.

For this reason, I have drawn guidance from other scientists who found serious errors with these findings, and described them openly in their publications. It is to these that I now refer, where, by their ready accessibility, they give promise to bring scientific discussion within the grasp and so understanding of the layperson.

Accordingly, Arthur Goldberger and Charles Manski presented a Review Article on *The Bell Curve* as written by Murray and Herrnstein in June 1995.[213]

I here only highlight the main points they identified, and invite the reader to refer to this web page or direct to the authors for the qualifications they made upon this work. Accordingly, their comments point out that Murray and Herrnstein declare on pages:

p.22-23 "IQ is substantially heritable"

p.25   "a cognitive elite is forming"

p.30   "racial and ethnic differences are seen in a new light
        when cognitive ability is added to the picture... "

254

p.41   "partitioning of intelligence through education
        and occupations will continue"

p.278   "blacks, are worth one whole deviation less than whites
        in IQ scores"

p.286-87 "parents have high or low socio-economic status...
         in part a function of their intelligence"

p.155/249/167 "problems in society such as unemployment,"
        (p.155) "crime," (p.249) "and illegitimacy," (p.167)
        "are due to low values of IQ."

p.341   "Hispanic immigration is exacerbating the problem
        because immigrants with lower IQs are outbreeding
        white Americans with higher IQs."

On page 535, the authors state that: "A society ... will function effectively if everyone knows and accepts his or her appropriate place."

This desire to attempt to prove by measurement that some human beings are useless, because they are politically undesired by others, has its root in Galton's work, which first appeared amid the social revolutions of the 19th-century when the establishment most feared political turmoil.

It is worthwhile mentioning here that while one deviation is worth 15 points on the IQ scale, that Murray and Herrnstein's statement negates the social-cultural biasing of test questions and ignores developmental issues. Nineteen years before *The Bell Curve* was published, a study clearly outlined that African Americans living in the Northern states, where they had better education, employment opportunities and less prejudice, performed substantially higher in IQ tests than those living in the Southern states.[214]

While Goldberger and Manski contend that *The Bell Curve* story is tainted by two misconceptions, namely that heritability is not a measure of parent-child resemblances in IQ and nor is it a biological parameter that can limit the effectiveness of a policy, they more importantly raise discrepancies in the analysis of the statistics used by Murray and Herrnstein.

As their review article shows, "…Where Murray and Herrnstein make statement that no practical policy instrument (neither better environmental care nor education) can raise cognitive ability, they systematically slant their interpretation of the findings they use to prove this in two ways: First, whenever evaluations give ambiguous results, these are ignored, even though every empirical researcher should know that a failure to reject the non-effect hypothesis strengthens findings which are consistent with alternative hypotheses, and so encourage an unbalancing of treatment effects. The second point they make is that Herrnstein and Murray repeatedly discount evaluations that do give clear-cut findings of treatment effects. …"[215]

Regrettably, as it has been too often pointed out, the lack of validity of the arguments raised in *The Bell Curve* seldom reached the general public. They were largely unaware of the almost violent reaction to its claims by other scientists, and of such books that were subsequently written that sought to bring balance to its claims, such as *Measured Lies*.[216]

The average citizen, however, tends to believe what they are offered when it has a tone of authority. They are, as we have found out in *The Illusion of Education,* educated to be this way. In direct consequence of this, the general public was largely uncomprehending of how, in relation to *The Bell Curve,* the devil hides in details. I am profoundly grateful to Claudia Krenz, who discusses this issue in her web page *Anatomy of an Analysis,* and has kindly guided me through the immense effort she has devoted to uncovering the very great distortions that Murray and Herrnstein had made of their information.

Claudia explained how she was first drawn to question the information presented in *The Bell Curve* when she discovered that in one analysis, the authors had taken data on 12,686 subjects, but selected only 3,367 of these for their use. Following this, she acquired the same statistical data as they had relied upon and built up her own analysis of that information. As she identifies:

When information was incomplete in one category, Murray and Herrnstein borrowed data from other categories to make up the necessary variables for their calculations. In their use of data from the Socio-Economic Status Index (SES), different combinations of parental income, occupations and education were mixed to construct case examples.

When Murray and Herrnstein used data from the National Longitudinal Surveys Bureau of Labour Statistics, they selected three quarters of the available white data to comprise their argument of coloured inadequacy. In one ethnic comparison, they weighted 35% of case studies on whites to less than 4% on Hispanics.

In a major socio-economic analysis, almost all of the cases above the poverty level were represented correctly, but none of the classified 244 cases below that level. This gave a 3% false prediction rate for cases above the poverty line, and a full 90% false prediction rate for those below it.

In conclusion to this and a great deal more, Claudia discovered that the model which Murray and Herrnstein presented through their book did not fit with the published data that was available for their analysis.[217]

When such a biased selection of statistical data is discovered, it becomes necessary to seek to understand why the report, which contained this information, was written. Who desired it, and for what purpose? Of *The Bell Curve,* I may only refer to a web article by Holhut, who explained how a main researcher for the data relating to race and intelligence used by Murray and Herrnstein was later quoted as stating :

"What is called for here is not genocide. ... But, we do need to think realistically in terms of the "phasing out" of such peoples. .... Evolutionary progress means the extinction of the less competent. To think otherwise is mere sentimentality."[218]

Unfortunately, such sentiments continue and still seek to bias political direction. Richard Lynn, as Emeritus Professor of Psychology at the University of Ulster, sees how non-whites outbreeding whites will bring about the collapse of America, unless the country is divided into ethnic areas. As he explained:

"I think the only solution lies in the breakup of the United States. Blacks and Hispanics are concentrated in the Southwest, the Southeast and the East, but the Northwest and the far Northeast, Maine, Vermont and upstate New York have a large predominance of whites. I believe these predominantly white states should declare independence and secede from the Union. They would then enforce strict border controls and provide minimum welfare, which would be limited to citizens. If this were done, white civilisation would survive within this handful of states."[219]

In the closing moments of the last century, a speech was delivered at the Hudson Institute in America. The speech was entitled: "America's role in the twenty-first century may depend on acknowledging and understanding human genetic diversity." It concluded with:

"The future of the human race is at stake. To make the right decisions about eugenics in the near future, we must start right now to study the impact of genetic diversity on human societies. We cannot continue to assume that genes don't affect societies and that societies don't affect genes. The time to get serious about Darwin is now, before the age of Galton fully arrives."[220]

It is interesting to speculate as to what is meant by "... before the age of Galton fully arrives". We may only assume that this is the collapse of an ordered society, in effect an ordered civilisation, because all sense of respect for a hierarchical establishment has been lost and reveals, yet again, the true purpose of measuring intelligence!

Awareness of the means by which the *Bell Curve* was constructed is of concern to the people of all nations, because while it was directed toward the American society, as Chauncey predicted, the influences in American education, good and bad, do extend globally.

So, we find that although it took nearly two decades for the theme behind this study to rise again, it did so in a 2013 study proposed to redefine the entire structure of British education — by a right-wing government. It may not be coincidental that this arose at a time when the country is experiencing excessive levels of immigration it cannot control,[221] and so is seeking a similar stratification desired by the authors of *The Bell Curve*. The meaning is that such reports do not simply arise without a purpose. They invariably serve a political agenda.

This paper was written by a special advisor to the then Minister for Education, and presented through the efforts of social scientists and not geneticists. Yet, it argued that studies in genetics have proven that intelligence is largely determined through the genetic material of the parents. In essence, it relies on the same argument we have just examined in detail, so there is no point in analysing the paper "Some Thoughts on Education and Political Priorities."[222] It simply argues the case that the ideal model of education should be set upon the streamlining of children based on their supposed genetic ability.

Indeed, since that time, debates have grown and brought open discussion into the realities of streamlining children for opportunities in education based on their genetic worth![223]

However, what was and still is not realised in British education is the classifying structure SATs brought into British primary schools when they were introduced by the same government in the 1990s. Although, in having said this, it soon became apparent to teaching unions that while the SAT was introduced with the reasoning it could assess whether a student had reached the average level for "their age," its presence soon created the expected standard for that age.[224] We may recall Diederich's comment here, in that when you set a SAT score to a measure of age you effectively end up with an IQ score -- and so the political structuring it is capable of.

We have witnessed many examples of political design in education in the two books we have so far shared together, these being *The Illusion of Education* and *The Illusion of School*. So, we do know that school is not really about developing the minds of all children. If it were, it would be structured in an entirely different way. The purpose of school, and this has not yet changed from the time it began so very long ago, is to provide the future managers and managed for the society. The strategies that are used to make this selection are very political, as the parents supporting a political party seek to ensure the best opportunities for their children. The concept of intelligence, we now know, is deeply entrenched in these strategies.

Another concern of this paper is that it is so heavily endorsed with the need for children to study through computers that it misses totally the value of the human being, and so the human teacher, which is the one means children have of developing their reasoning and so intelligence beyond their domestic conditioning.

In other words, it is introducing a stability in performance that serves the idea that intelligence is limited by inheritance. At best, this paper is a recommendation for education that sees only how a computerised world can serve those best able to keep up with it (while they can, in view of the rapid development of AI), and gives no consideration to the social values children urgently need to be coached in.

We have earlier discussed the social and intellectual dangers of this type of education, and how it will intensify differences in the developing abilities of children and the opportunities for them in their lives. We discuss the more serious nature of this suggestion in our book: *The Real Dangers of AI: The Struggle of Man to Survive by Natural or Artificial Intelligence,* and **how it can promote diversification in our societies.**

By their nature, people form groups to protect the values that serve their needs. Any society, therefore, may be divided into a number of groups that are separated by the different values and needs they have. The most influential group in a society, whether this be a confederation of groups that form the majority or a single controlling minority, will decide how its values will be protected against competing influences. The strategies they manufacture to protect their interests will manifest themselves through political, social, and educational policies as we have been shown here.

Since the responsibilities that people hold in their jobs tend to reflect the influence they have in the running of their society, the most influential group will make a desire to place its members in jobs with greater responsibilities. To ensure that following generations of the society maintain these values, intention is placed into educational design to pre-select children on the basis of their background.

We have now discussed this many times. So, we are very well aware that some children are provided with different educational opportunities than children from less desired backgrounds, and so follow different vocational directions that ultimately lead them to controlling roles in the operation of their society.

While Murray and Herrnstein based their case in America on discrimination by creed, other countries make theirs on different values. So, as we earlier mentioned, in Northern Ireland, social control and job responsibility are reflected through the politics of religion, and there are very different underlying developmental opportunities in both social and educational contexts that are available to Protestant children that Catholic children are deprived of. By such planning, the children of different religions are caused to develop different potentials of intelligence, for the different roles their society desires of them.[225]

In fact, Fisher found that this management of intelligence and so projected social responsibility could be found in many societies, where children were discriminated against through their social and cultural origins. He found this with blacks and whites in America, Ashkenazi and Sephardic Jews in Israel, and Japanese and Koreans in Japan.[226]

As his and other studies have shown, very often there are deliberate tactics employed against a target group to limit the development of their intelligence, and that this does have very powerful psychological effects upon them. It was also found, and we may well understand why now, that when the intelligence of a target group is evaluated by people of a different group, the evaluations they present of them are often found to be very unreliable.[227] It is, therefore, relevant to note how studies have shown how the differences in the intelligence of two groups of people have been reduced when the economic differences between them were.[228]

Perhaps of more significance are the studies that found how this intelligence difference was significantly reduced when the people of the lower group were taught strategies to improve their intelligence.[229] In other words, claims that one group of people have a naturally lower intelligence than another group have been completely disproven when the lower group were given equal opportunity and raised to standards equal to the group thought to be superior.

While it has long been the contention that differences in intelligence, which underlie the different roles that people play in a society, are reliant upon an inherited ability, too much mystery surrounds what is meant by this for such emphasis to be placed upon it. After all, in a hereditary or genetic sense, the human mind contains neither a fixed means of how or what it should believe, nor does it have any limitation in the ways it can evaluate information.[230]

We may now realise from all we have so far covered in this book, that when a teacher looks upon the effort of their student and believes that this effort is the best the student can do, that this opinion has been bred within them through a conditioning they could not see. While the vehicle of this conditioning arose long before Terman's time, it was a mind-frame he greatly contributed to when he wrote:

"When we have learnt the lessons which intelligence tests have to teach, we shall no longer blame mentally defective workmen for their industrial inefficiency, punish weak-minded children because of their inability to learn, or imprison and hang mentally defective criminals because they lacked the intelligence to appreciate the ordinary codes of social conduct."[231]

Our next chapter fully explains why it is impossible to ever know a person's genetic value of intelligence, just as we have examined why it is impossible to measure it! But, before this, let us dwell a little upon what Binét was always saying. ....

Chapter TwentyOne
A Human Accountability

*"Sometimes, the most brilliant and intelligent minds do
not shine in standardised tests, because they do not
have standardised minds."*

Diane Ravitch

When I think about the book *The Bell Curve* and the politics it stirred, I recall a film that was released in 1988. It was entitled *Stand and Deliver,* and told the true story of Jaime Escalante. Jaime was a Hispanic teacher who coached his class of Hispanic street criminals and drug addicts to pass their final school examinations, with such a high-class average that the entire class was accused of cheating.

Their white staffed board of education could not believe that all students from the backgrounds from which these students came, and of the reputation of their school, could perform so astonishingly well. In a move that could not be imagined to be asked of white children, the entire class was required to re-sit the examination, with each student assigned individual supervision. Fortunately for the children, under this enormous strain, each managed to replicate their earlier score.[232]

What happened here, and I have witnessed this myself and through others, was that this teacher managed to alter the student's perspective of themselves, their ability, and the ways they interacted with information. He did dramatically upgrade their intelligence. It is not, then, that intelligence creates opportunities in education and so in society, as Murray and Herrnstein so convincingly tried to lay claim. Rather, that through its means of operation, **education significantly manufactures differences in intelligence.** The research by Ritchie et al. clearly proved this.[233]

I had long been of the opinion that whatever intelligence is, it is not some feature that each simply inherits in different degrees and that rather than this, it is something cultivated through experience. The idea that it is a combination of both somehow never appealed to me, for I have witnessed far too many instances of children and of adults suddenly becoming brighter once some insight was shown to them or they discovered it through their own exploration. Everything seemed to hang upon the word experience.

Yet, I found this word too narrowly defines what is thought of it, when it is used with intelligence. Experience might mean engaging some new environment or some new tool by which the environment may be better fashioned to one's needs, but if many experience the same thing, then, why do some find more meaning to it than others? It is **sensitive to be aware** that, I found, is the key to explaining the differences of awareness within any group sharing an experience.

It always seemed to me that cleverer people described things clearly and spoke with some eloquence. It was, I much later came to understand, that they had higher language skills than those about them. It was also that they had learnt, through their experiences, to question things more than others and by this had learnt to be more sensitive in the handling of information — as one experience built upon another. It was by this that they gained a certain confidence, were they focused upon a task, were not held back from testing and then evaluating the result they found, always thinking forward and yet never irrationally so.

Confidence, then, had to have something to do with intelligence. After all, a belief in the individual that they can do something and be accepted by others for so doing or had learnt to block out the thoughts of others who sought to diminish their achievement, is always present in those who stand above the rest.

So, it is language to know of terms to better recognise, more efficiently process and, then, express what they think mixed with a quality of emotion that gives sensitivity to fine tune experiences that makes some appear cleverer than others.

Yet, even this reasoning did not explain how we perceive something, make sense of it, and are fast or slow in relating this to some earlier experience to know what use we should make of it. I knew intelligence had to be held in strategies and these in the ways we perceive and process information — in short how we associate present to past. Association through emotional sensitivity and language skill was the key I was seeking to understand. This was the key I was looking to develop, and it was with working through a child who seemed incapable of any kind of association that he taught me far more than I taught him.

It is to bring balance to what we have recently discussed about how intelligence testing arose and how it has been used, that I would like to share an experience I had with one child, just to give indication of how flexible intelligence can be, and so how very, very wrong the contention of *The Bell Curve* is.

Case Example A:
At that time in my life I was working in Denmark, and had just returned from Latvia, where I had assisted the ministry of education. I had been home a few days, when I received a telephone call from a schoolteacher who asked if I could come and meet her to discuss a young boy in her class. The teacher, with worry and concern, confided in me that the boy seemed incapable of learning anything. In fact, she remarked, she wondered if he even had a brain.

After spending a little time with the child, I began to form the opinion that he was not by innate design mentally sub-normal, even though he obviously appeared to be so. As I began to understand this child, I saw how emotionally attached he was to his elder brother. His brother had suffered oxygen starvation at birth, and as a consequence of this showed signs of some mental impairment. It was a consideration to me that the child I had been asked to meet had adopted, since infancy, the interactive skills of his brother in both manner of language and thinking. We may recall our earlier thoughts on imprinting in this.

In the 1994 movie "Nell," Jodie Foster plays a young woman who was raised in total seclusion by her mother, who, because of an earlier stroke, was unable to form words clearly and had a restricted language. Since the character that Jodie played had had no contact with any other human being, it was natural for her to imitate the language and means of understanding her world through the restricted ability of her mother. This story has many parallels with the factual case of Genie, a girl who was raised in total isolation without language.

Genie had been locked in an attic and deprived of all human language skills from infancy to the age of 13. When she was discovered and released, it was found that she could later learn and develop near normal language skills.[234] I only mention this here because the fictional story of "Nell" highlights the very real imprinting process of language skills.

As we shall come to see, imprinting plays a very important role in the development of intelligence. In the failure to recognise what some refer to as exposure learning, lies a greater failure to see the ability of a child other than of genetic design. Indeed, I have often observed adults, and not just children, unconsciously mimicking the means of interaction of one they bond themselves with. We may remember Vygotsky's understanding of how intelligence evolves through language, such that when language is severely restricted so is the development of intelligence.

While this is for *Brain Plasticity,* I wondered, as I watched this child, how much of what he did wrong was because he had learnt wrong ways? How many of those ways could be investigated until the source of error was located, corrected, and built up again? How much could this child really learn, or actually relearn?

When we deal with normal children of average ability, we tend readily to assume categories by which we can explain our evaluation of them. "They are good at this, and bad at that." Yet, with unusual or extreme cases of children who do not fit into normal learning situations (Where, for example, I do something, and try to gauge the struggle of their response), we become more aware to question the formation of responses that we otherwise take so naturally. So it was that this child and I began an exploration into the learning of a human being.

I do not intend here to revolve this book around this child, for this child was no different to any other child anywhere in the world. He was just a child who had not understood something, and **did not understand what other people meant when they told him to do better.**

I began by asking him to write a story for me. Happily, the pen was picked up, and the child began to write. However, when the paper was given to me, I could not recognise a story. Each of the lines on the paper had been filled out, but there was no association with a line that followed the one before it. All the child had done was to fill each line with an idea. In his mind, he saw each line as a complete and single task, and that by filling all the lines, he believed that he had produced a story. I realised the child did not know what a story meant, and I wondered if in seeing other children fill a page with words, he had thought this was what a story was.

As I discussed this with his parents, explanation came forward that nobody could ever remember telling the child a story at any age.

He never received a bedtime story, was never thought capable of reading a book by himself, and had no conception of a play. So, when the child was eleven years old, his parents and I began to tell him stories. At night-time, he was now not just sent to bed after the television had gone to sleep.

In the beginning, his parents told him stories, but gradually, as he came to understand the meaning of a story, he would join in the account of what might happen at the end. Yet, what the child had written did tell me a story, for there was no sense of relationships between the letters. Letters, and the words they formed, went up and down a line as a boat in a storm. Again, the child had never learnt the significance of writing letters along a line.

He was the ideal product of an education that believed he could learn best by himself, and when it was realised he was far behind other children, so reason came that he should not be forced to learn what was too difficult for him. While other children did much better, and learnt from each other when the teacher was not looking, this child was too far behind to display a normal performance. He was behind when he joined the educational system, and he was carried along with the principle that whatever he did was right for him.

Consequently, we spent one hour a day for three weeks, love and kindness for motivation, chocolate for reward, and a lot of fun learning how to write. After three weeks, I asked the child to write a story for me. As we watched, his mother, with tears of pride in her eyes, the pen moved over the page. All of us were so happy to see a beautifully posed story. From the top of the page to the bottom, we witnessed a perfect composition. There was a real story, with an introduction, a body, and an ending, and all the words were of very, very smart character. In school, the teachers could not believe this child had written this story, and yet he had been in their care for nearly six years.

In mathematics, the child had been working in a book that was two years behind the rest of his class, and he had no idea of what he was doing. We began to teach the child how to understand and reorganise information. It took four hours before he could realise how to construct a very easy transformation of a formula, but once he had grasped the rules to do this, his ability snowballed. Giving members of his family an understanding of mathematical strategies, we all worked together to build up for the child a different understanding of what he was doing.

Within six weeks, the child was working in the same mathematics book as the rest of his class, and quite able to manage 60% of its tasks unaided. Yet, the most amazing thing that everyone noticed, and this included the other children in his class, was that he now began to put up his hand to ask questions. As he did this, and the teacher responded, I watched his face and saw a small glint of pride. He was realising that he could do things the way other people wanted them done. The difference was unbelievable.

We assume that children naturally learn how to learn, and so we judge them on their competence. Our following books will explain how a child learns how to learn, and the obvious implications that will arise from this.

No one could quite understand what had happened to this child. In truth, it was only that we all sat down, tried to find out what was really, really wrong, and having done this, retaught him the basic skills of interaction. This child was not in the space of the two months we worked together, to develop to the same level of interactive skills as his peers, but this was never our aim. All we sought to do was to raise questions about the attitude of his mentors toward the potential they saw. A potential that had been neglected for the six years the child had been in the school system, because instead of focusing on what the child was doing wrong, the stream of psychologists, special educationalists, and teachers judged his potential on his performance, and not theirs.

Too easily was this child labelled an IQ failure, when all he needed was clear definition, in a language he could understand, of the rules of interaction. Plus, may we add, reassurance, confidence, and his belief in what was possible. The basic problem was that he did not understand what others expected of him. He lived in a different world. All we did was to give him his passport.

The transformation in the attitude of his teachers was quite remarkable, for they now began to realise the potential of this human being, and merrily devised new and exciting tasks for him. As we all discovered through this, it is not possible to even guess how much an individual can develop when they are placed in an environment that is stretched to extremities.

* *

When Thorndike finally stretched the environment, the results he obtained caused him to abandon his law of exercise.[235] When Goddard, who first introduced IQ testing to America, later came to stretch the environment and realised the pliability of intelligence, he publicly renounced his earlier opinions.[236] The man most responsible for declaring that IQ was inflexible and who created the means to prove it, Louis Terman, also revised his opinion when he stretched the environment through testing poor rural children.[237]

Yet, it was all too late, the machine had taken over and human classification had become an accepted and irrevocable fact. Except that is, to teachers like Jaime Escalante, and there are many of them who refuse to accept the systemisation of their students, strive to inspire their minds to want to learn, and give them the means to do this.

As any good teacher has found, once a child is taken out of a self-limiting environment, they perform relative to the way they are guided to understand the Aladdin's cave they have moved into. As we explain in *Teach Better, Learn Better* and other books, it is active mediation, and neither instruction nor passive guidance, that is the means to achieve this, whether this be for an individual student — or with a mass of 30 disorganised minds.

With these words, we now close our account of why intelligence was desired to be measured, and how this was sought to be achieved. From this point forward in our account, we seek to understand what intelligence is, and how the general intelligence of all children can be improved. To begin, let us now take the bull by the horns and uncover the myth behind the genetic coding of intelligence, as we move to begin to understand what this really may mean. ....

_____

Chapter TwentyTwo
The Subject of Genetic Inheritance

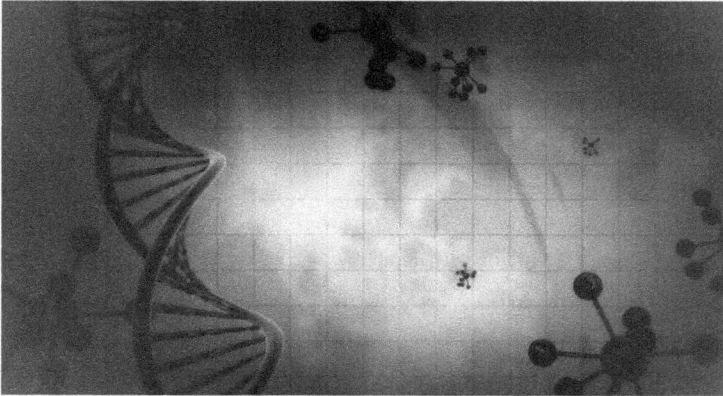

"A riddle wrapped in a mystery inside an enigma."

The idea that ability lies in bloodlines was not new when Galton took the stage, and we have seen why this idea was promoted through the ages. Yet, the time of Galton was different. This was an era of scientific bloom and social upheaval, so the means by which this old idea could be given new light had to appear to be bathed in scientific credibility. We have seen how Galton strove to obtain this, and we have witnessed how each psychologist who followed in his path laid their own stone upon that which he laid.

We have seen that the whole argument about IQ, or the measure of inherited intelligence, hinges on the difference between the gene and the environment. We have long discussed how psychologists try to evaluate the environment in their determination of what the child may be born with. In this chapter, we are going to look at this situation from the perspective of geneticists and so come to understand the relationship of the genetic and the environmental aspects of intelligence from a different light.

With plants, the environment is sunlight, water, and soil nutrients. The value of each of these can be easily known, and so it is relatively easy to understand how the environment affects the genetic makeup of a plant. The human brain, however, develops and lives in an environment that is extremely complex, and cannot be categorised in the same way as the construction of a plant. With regards to the human brain, all we ever see is the outcome of the effect of the environment upon the gene. This chapter will explain why the relationship of the environment and the gene for intelligence is extremely complex to understand.

To move away from the idea that the baby is born with a value of intelligence, we should realise that within the brain that is not yet formed, and within weeks of the egg being fertilised, there are fields of loose neurons. These neurons are unconnected, but they learn to connect with each other through prearranged chemical guides. In this manner, "A" will know where "B" is, but when "A" requires to interact with "B" it may require information from the environment to do so. The quality of that information may well determine the efficiency of the networks it builds, and how those networks influence a vast array of other networks.

Therefore, in the case of brain development, it is not that the brain develops totally under a genetic instruction and thereafter interacts with the environment as we think of a plant, and so make the analogy of a child being born with their IQ — as this term is so loosely used. The environment is not just the stimuli the later child engages as they play and as they learn, which is the impression many have. The environment of intelligence is a chemical affair that has very many internal and external components. Accordingly, this has never been understood by the psychologists who seek to measure and evaluate the intelligence of the individual.

In *Brain Plasticity*, we discuss how the neural components of intelligence are constructed, but in this chapter, we begin to understand how the basic design for those components arrives in the first place.

The Gene: A Simple Molecule

Contained within the cell of each and all living things is a minute core known as the nucleus. It contains a rich storehouse of nucleic acid and an instructional code. This code is formed by the composition of four chemicals: Adenine, Thymine, Guanine and Cytosine. These chemicals are bound together by sugars to create the famous double helix structure, first identified in 1953.

This discovery is readily attributed to Francis Crick and James Watson. However, Maurice Wilkins and a lady by the name of Rosalind Franklin both played crucial roles in this discovery, although they are often and sadly ignored in the credits because of her gender. Therefore, let us introduce them all.

Franklin   Crick   Watson   Wilkins

Deoxyribonucleic Acid provides the instructions for how to build and maintain life when supplied with **"the right chemicals" from the environment.** It is the life source of each and every organism on this planet. Without DNA there is no life. DNA tells the cell what to build, when to build, and when and how to function. When something goes wrong, it sends for help. When the cell is getting old or used up, DNA makes a new cell. Virtually every cell in our body contains the complete DNA instruction to replicate our genetic identity, our personal genome. This long strand of chemical instruction is separated into individual sections, which we call chromosomes. These are, in normal cases, always even in number, since each pair will consist of one chromosome from the mother and one from the father. Each species is characterised by its own number of chromosomes, which make up its genome. Human beings have 46. The garden peas that Mendel made his experiments on have 14, and the two dogs trying to sleep by my feet, at the unearthly hour in which I write this, have 78 chromosomes in each of their cells.

A chromosome, then, is merely one section of the genome, which is made up of blocks of nucleic acid. These blocks are responsible, either independently or shared with those of another chromosome, for a feature or purpose in the function of the organism. It is these blocks of DNA coding that we call genes.

The gene expression for a feature is known as the genotype. Thus, we have genotypes for hair, arms, legs and the colour of eyes, etc. While we think of genotypes for physical features, we must also remember that our abilities to laugh, cry, and freely reason have genotypes too. However, as we do this, we may see how our ability to laugh, to cry, and so to freely reason do not have the same kind of genetic instructions that hair, arms, legs and the colour of our eyes do, because these genetic instructions have evolved to allow the environment to construct the feature totally.

We may gain an impression from psychological studies with IQ tests and declarations from the nature/nurture debate that our genes for intelligence are known, and in being known have been calculated to distinguish their worth in different people. This is completely and absolutely not the case. Therefore, any psychological study revealing intelligence to be 40% or 60% or whatever is inherited should be instantly dismissed. Geneticists do not know which genes are responsible for intelligence.

As we saw earlier, while the Human Genome Project came to what was thought, in 2004, to be its final conclusion that we have 22,300 protein-coding genes that make up our entire genome,[238] the study continued to reveal far more. By the second decade of this century, the team of international geneticists working on this project had realised, with the discovery of RNA-producing genes, that our genome now contains at least 46,831 genes. Although, as Salzberg explains, "I will not be surprised if ten years from now, we still don't have an agreed-upon number."[239]

As we may see, geneticists are still trying to discover how many genes we have that make us human and more importantly, are still trying to understand what these genes actually do. When none geneticists think of genes, we tend to imagine some solid block of information, even though we may know it is chemical, that has something to do with Mendel.

Indeed, this is how it once was and most certainly is so to many psychologists who think in terms of nature vs nurture. However, geneticists have long moved from this too simple definition of a gene. In the beginning, genes were simply thought to have the instructions for building proteins, which make cells, and so some purpose for a conglomeration of cells, be an organ, the brain, and so the entire body. But, then and more recently, another kind of gene was discovered that makes RNA, the coding that actually makes proteins.

All this was seemingly straightforward until recent discoveries in epigenetics caused us to realise that the experience of the environment can cause a gene to express itself differently.[240] By example, stress, as a mental or psychological impression of the environment, was subsequently shown to alter how cells function, and in the sense of intelligence, devastate whatever genius the child may be thought to be born with.[241]

We shall come back to epigenetics later, but first we need to go to the basics and understand what a protein is and from this discuss Mendel's discovery and so on to the work of Johannsen, who was the first to realise the importance of the environment. Therefore, if we are to understand how a gene instruction develops into a feature we witness, we need to know about proteins.

The Production of a Protein

As we shall now see, between the gene codes that are formed at the moment of fertilisation and the circumstances of the outside world, there are what we call proteins. It is the protein that throws a spanner in the works for psychologists who seek to measure intelligence.

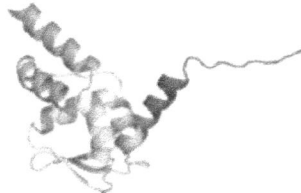

Protein ZBTB16-PDB

The gene instruction does not make a feature. The gene, although there are usually a combination of these, uses the chemicals from the environment of the cell to construct a certain kind of protein. It is the proteins that build the feature. Proteins are used by the body to create structure or to enable a structure to function. They are the link between the "paper" design and the creation of the "machine," and how it is able to work.

Therefore, the real purpose of the gene is to provide the instructions for the cell to make a protein, which it does by joining a specific number of amino acids together.

However, because of the particular carbon base of DNA, it can only be read by four of the possible 20 amino acids used in the construction of a protein. To enable the remaining amino acids to read the DNA instruction, a translation process occurs whereby a nucleotide called uracil is added to replace thymine.

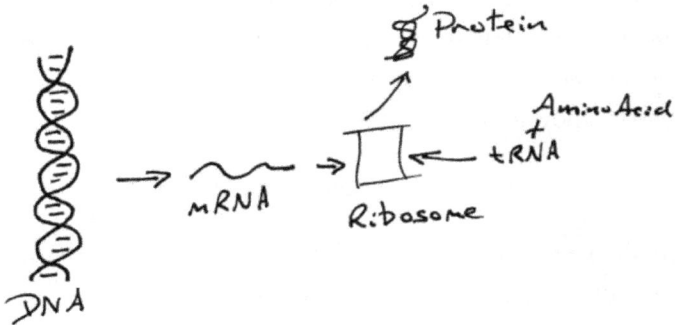

In brief, the manufacture of a particular protein occurs when the DNA instruction, contained in the nucleus of the cell, receives a signal that is required. This signal, in the form of various proteins, will begin to unravel the double helix of the DNA. While the DNA is being unravelled, an enzyme called RNA polymerase begins to build up another nucleic acid molecule called ribonucleic acid or RNA. This RNA has the same structure as DNA, except that it contains Uracil instead of Thymine, as one of its four chemical bases. The RNA polymerase will use one of the unravelled strands of the gene's DNA as a template to manufacture an RNA molecule. We may understand, then, that while DNA has bases of Adenine to Thymine and Guanine to Cytosine, RNA has bases of Adenine to Uracil, and so Guanine to Cytosine.

The genetic instruction, now termed messenger RNA or mRNA, can be read by all the amino acids in the cell. Accordingly, this mRNA now moves from the nucleus of the cell out into the cell's general body. As it does this, it will connect with a ribosome. Once the mRNA connects with a ribosome, it sends out what are called transfer RNA molecules (tRNA) to locate the required amino acids and bring them back to the ribosome. Once at the ribosome, these amino acids are pulled into the required configuration to manufacture the required protein of the genetic instruction.

Protein molecules are created in the body's cells mainly for one of three reasons. They have the function of building and repairing cells. So, proteins are the links that hold the organism together and give it form. In other words, proteins make the neurons of the brain, just as they do the general residue of the brain itself. They make the chemicals and so the neurotransmitters, but they also and very importantly, make the sense receptors that enable the neurons to know of signals from the environment.

What we need to know here is that **the genetic instruction for all this is constructed in such a way that it learns from the environment how to supply these proteins.**

More specifically, this means that when a child is very happy and very interested, they inspect the environment in such a way that they naturally design the operation of their brain to be efficient. Yet, it also means that when they are disturbed, as they will be if the child is bullied, that the design of the operation of their brain will be impaired in some way. Beyond this, other proteins function as catalysts, or rather enzymes, which control the rate of chemical reactions, and others function as antibodies.

By a simplified version, we have seen how proteins are made, and so an understanding is gained of the fundamental difference between the code of the DNA and the means by which that code becomes active. It is very important that we are aware of this.

We have also gained a small but important insight into why the ability of a feature to function may well be decided by the manner in which its proteins are constructed, more than in the role of the genes themselves. Before we expand upon what this means, let us first examine how genes are inherited in the first place.

Mendel's Principles of Genetic Inheritance

As we saw, Darwin took the ancient idea of inheritance and described the "memories" of an organ that Hippocrates had referred to as gemmules. Under his principle of pan-genesis, these gemmules were said to flow through the blood to the reproductive area. When the male and female mate, their gemmules were believed to blend in the creation of their child. This reasoning saw that the child's gemmules would have a mid-value between those of their parents.

Physically, this would be to say that if one parent were six feet tall, and the other four feet, then their offspring would average out to about five feet. Mentally, it meant that if their father was of normal intelligence, and their mother very intelligent, then their offspring would be more intelligent than their father, but less than their mother. This meant that each generation would be reduced in their qualities from the better able parent who produced them.

While both Darwin and Galton struggled against the idea of blending for their own reasons, none at that time could suggest a better way to explain how inheritance works. The discovery of that knowledge was left to an Augustinian monk by the name of Gregor Johann Mendel.

From his earliest childhood, Mendel appeared to be fascinated by how life developed. He was raised on his family's farm and was a keen gardener, besides also being a beekeeper as a child. After school, Mendel entered the University of Olomouc in today's Czech Republic to study philosophy.

While he was there, Mendel met and fell under the influence of Johann Nestler, who was then the head of the Department of Natural History. Nestler inspired Mendel to turn his interests towards the hereditary traits of plants and animals. Unfortunately, soon after he had turned his interests in this direction, Mendel became very ill and acquired a large number of debts that interfered with his studies. Mendel's physics teacher suggested to him that he could continue his studies freely as a friar, and it was to this end that Mendel entered the Augustinian St. Thomas's Abbey to begin training for the priesthood.

Gregor Mendel

It was while he was in St. Thomas's that Mendel began studying inherited traits in mice. However, the bishop of his abbey did not like his friar studying animal sex, and so Mendel transferred his interest to plants, noting that "the bishop did not understand that plants also have sex".[242] From 1856 to 1863, Mendel cultivated and tested some 28,000 pea plants, of which he carefully examined 12,835.[243]

Since peas and beans have flowers that are only accessible by their own pollen and so are self-fertilised, Mendel knew he could control their fertilisation. Thus, he could observe how a plant behaved through self-fertilisation, and how it could behave when it was crossed with another plant. This cross-fertilisation was achieved by transferring pollen from one plant to another with the aid of a small paintbrush.

Mendel studied seven characteristics of the pea plant, in which he observed two differences in the form of the ripe seed, the colour of the seed endosperm, the colour of the seed coat/and flowers, the form of the ripe pods, the colour of unique pods, the length of the plant stem, and the position of the flowers as to whether they were distributed along the stem or bunched at its top.[244]

From these experiments, Mendel concluded that each characteristic had two elements, which derived from two elements carried by each of the parents. Thus, he realised that each characteristic had two parent lines, with each line containing one of two possible elements from the father, and one of two possible elements from the mother. Later, Johannsen would call these "elements" genes.

When Mendel allowed a plant to self-fertilise, these two elements bred true. A plant with a tall stem only produced a tall stem plant, just as a plant with a short stem only produced a short stem plant. The same being so for the seed shape, the pea colour, and so for all the characteristics he examined.

However, when Mendel cross-fertilised two plants, he noted that all the offspring in the first generation between (for example) a tall and a short stem, produced only a tall stem plant. Every time he crossed two versions of a characteristic, he found there was always one version that was dominant over the other. The version that was not dominant he called recessive.

Yet, when he allowed a cross-fertilised plant to self-fertilise, he discovered that its offspring had both tall and short stems, and that there were always about three times more tall than short. This 3:1 ratio was to become highly significant, as we shall shortly come to understand.

Tall   Short

Cross Fertilized

Self Fertilized

3   to   1

From his experiments, Mendel established two laws. The first, and by far the most important, is the Law of Segregation. We have just understood that an organism carries one gene instruction from its father's line and one gene instruction from its mother's line, for each characteristic it has.

When this organism produces gametes (egg and sperm) in the process of meiosis, these two parent instructions segregate from each other. In this way, a sperm or egg carries only one instruction for each characteristic instead of two. When a sperm and egg unite at fertilisation, they each contribute one gene instruction for a characteristic to provide the offspring with the necessary paired instruction.

The second is the Law of Independent Assortment: This law states that these paired gene instructions separate independently during the formation of gametes. This is to say that genes for two different characteristics are transmitted to the offspring independently of one another. These two laws set the framework for our understanding today of how inheritance works.

On the 8th of February and also on the 8th of March 1865, Mendel presented his paper "Experiment on Plant Hybridisation" to the Natural Science Society of Brno. While both presentations were favourably received, the publication he followed them up with a year later was seen to focus upon hybridisation rather than inheritance, and gained virtually no interest.

The greater problem was that the world, at that time, was captivated with Darwin's Origin of Species, which promoted his idea of pangenesis and so the blending theory which underlay it. Since Mendel's work directly opposed this theory, it stimulated too little interest, and with his abbot being prompted to distract him for political reasons, Mendel turned his energies to other pursuits.

As we discussed earlier, Mendel's lost papers were rediscovered by de Vries, among others, in 1900.[245] By this time, chromosomes had been discovered, and the process of cell reproduction (mitosis, where a new cell is made and meiosis, where cells divide to create gametes or sperm and egg cells) was now known, so there was now an acceptable scientific framework to accept what Mendel had discovered 35 years earlier.

In time, the word allelomorph (meaning "other form") arose to differentiate between the elements Mendel had discovered. Today, we abbreviate this to "allele," and recognise that each characteristic has an allele from the father and one from the mother that produced the offspring.

The dominant allele (which is used) is described by a capital letter, such as **A,** while a lower-case letter is used to describe the recessive allele (which is not used and hidden) such as **a**. Mendel's observation that the dominant occurred three times more than the recessive can be explained through the Punnet Square, which was designed by Reginald Punnet in the beginning of the 20th century.

Consider this ratio in the example where a couple contribute one dominant allele and one recessive allele (**Aa**) for a feature, or characteristic.

The Punnet Square: Father

                                  A   a

Mother   A AA Aa

            a Aa aa   =   AA, Aa, Aa, or aa.

As we can see, the offspring of the parents will inherit one of three possible allele combinations (AA, Aa, aa), out of the four offered. These alleles (or genetic versions) of a gene are stored on a chromosome, at a place known as the locus point. Thus, we have the impression that we have one allele from each parent at one place on a chromosome. While this may be so, it is, however, more often the case that a characteristic is based on a number of different alleles, interacting from different loci. To understand what this means, and especially so with the case of intelligence, we first need to understand how our knowledge of the environment came about.

Wilhelm Johannsen

Darwin, we have mentioned, had created his idea of pan-genesis from a belief that was thousands of years old, whereby the child was said to inherit their features and characteristics directly from their parents. So it was believed, as we saw with Galton, that any characteristic seen in a child and in one of their parents was said to have come directly from them. This reasoning gave no understanding to how the environment could affect that characteristic. It is to understand why and how it does this that we now bring our discussion to a Danish plant physiologist by the name of Wilhelm Johannsen.

Wilhelm Johannsen

We may recall from our earlier discussion how Galton had been preoccupied with the idea of reductionism for many years. As we saw, reductionism was a belief that a trait would be continually reduced through generations. It was in seeking to find a way to explain how a trait could not diminish that Galton had made an experiment with peas.

We saw from this how each generation conformed to Galton's desired continuous variation, with a movement that countered the deterioration he had feared. In his description of this experiment, Galton explained how a line that was self-fertilised would not be affected by natural selection. Quite simply, he argued that if there is no variation in a characteristic, there is no alternative means for it to adapt to a change in the environment. With this being so, the existing characteristic will survive or it will not. Simply put, it has no variation to enable one version to be "naturally" selected.

Galton, of course, wrote this in a time when Mendel's laws were not known, but by 1900 they were, and it was to test Galton's explanation of this that Johannsen began to experiment with self-fertilised lines of the Princess bean.

In 1900, Johannsen bought 8kg of seeds. A year later, he sowed 287 seeds from these, and from the resulting 207 seed-bearing plants, he categorised 7,568 beans by weight. In 1902, he sowed 574 seeds from 19 of the 207 plants. These enabled him to harvest 5,494 seeds. Johannsen regarded each of these 19 plants to be of pure-line. This is to say that each line was genetically pure.

When Johannsen compared the variation of bean weight in each of these lines, he found they were much narrower than that of the original population they had been bred from. Thus, even though the genetic identity in a line did not change, each generation of that line had a different degree of variation in weight. For example, while the original seeds varied in weight by 300mg, Johannsen found that the offspring of one line varied by only 75mg. In other words, the mixed population (made up from the original seeds) had a far greater variability than any of their single-bean offspring.

Accordingly, as Johannsen found each generation to vary in weight, he realised that it is not possible to predict how an offspring will appear, based on the characteristics of the mother bean. Because of this, the only predictions possible could be those based on the type of original bean it belonged to. Thus, if the original bean belonged to a heavy-bean type, its actual weight would be inconsequential to the weight of its offspring. The weight differences within a pure line, he reasoned, were a consequence of the seed having "lost or put on" weight relative to the average of its type. Johannsen realised this change in weight was due to environmental influence during seed development, and so was not a heritable factor.

This meant that an offspring would appear different from its parent because of environmental effect! **In turn, it also meant that it could now not be reasoned that the characteristic of an offspring could be predicted from that witnessed in a parent.**

This, of course, went directly against Galton's predictability of intelligence in family lines. It was to illustrate precisely why there could be no predictability that Johannsen produced the following drawing and demonstrated this in a lecture.

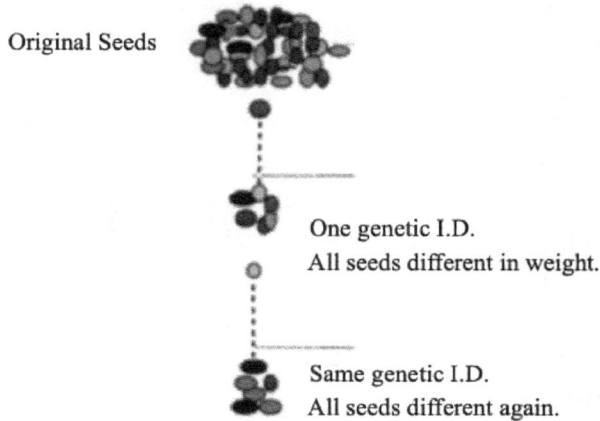

Original Seeds

One genetic I.D.
All seeds different in weight.

Same genetic I.D.
All seeds different again.

We can see in this drawing, and so in the photograph of Johannsen demonstrating this point in a lecture, how five different pure lines of beans are each affected by the environment in their own way. When we add these lines together, with the effects of the environment on each line, it is impossible to know how any of the five genotypes (gene designs) were affected by the combined environment.[246] All the genotypes are completely hidden by the complexity of the environment.

To our interest, we may see how this explains why a child's performance in a test, in school, or in life, cannot be genetically associated with the achievements of their parents. In other words, we have no means to disassociate the effect of the environment on their genotypes.

So we find today, and very commonly so, that while the parents had been raised in particular circumstances both at home and in school, obtained grades and an employment level on all this, the child whom they raised differently acquired different opportunities in education, obtained different grades, and because of this gained a totally different level of employment.

We may envisage here the parents working on an assembly line in a factory, while their child developed to become a lawyer. In Galton's time this would almost have been unheard of, because of the very strict social codes of that time. Today, however, it is totally normal — simply because the environment has been changed.

So, in regard to human intelligence, we cannot predict what use the child will be to their society based on the use their parents were. Of course, Galton's whole argument relied on the belief that they could.

It was for the precise purpose of emphasising this non-predictability for biological purposes, and to stem the socio-political arguments that were trying to affect the development of genetics, that Johannsen invented the terms genotype and phenotype. The genotype, he explained, describes the gene endowment, while the phenotype explains how this gene instruction evolves through the environment to create the feature that is witnessed.

De Vries had used the term pangenes, in place of Darwin's gemmules, to explain the units of inheritance. However, Johannsen, like Mendel, was very scientific, and he wanted to disassociate any hypothetical idea from the study of inheritance, such as that of the term pangenes, which had no scientific foundation. It was to this end that Johannsen removed the prefix "pan" from pangenes in 1909,[247] so that from that moment onwards, the unit of inheritance would be known as "the gene" — and would be known to be "only" a part of the story.

Let us recap a little to understand how these different terms came about. Darwin called the units of inheritance "gemmules" in his theory of Pangenesis. de Vries changed "gemmules" to "pangenes". Johannsen dropped the "pan" to call these units of inheritance "genes". In turn, Bateson used the term "genes" to create the term "genetics" and so crafted the formal name for The Science of Genetics.

When Johannsen discovered the significance of the environment, he did two things. As we have mentioned, he proved that the offspring cannot be judged on the parent. This brought a greater realisation that it can be wrong to assume the gene is the determining factor in what we notice.

In turn, this gave explanation that any variation in individuals can be explained beyond genetic differences. This is to say that the genetic variation in a group can be extremely narrow, even though the phenotype (what we see) is very wide. This knowledge will soon have great relevance for us.

In fact, Johannsen proved in his experiment with pure lines of beans, that **a continuous variation had been obtained by just ONE single gene code operating through a diverse environment**. We should dwell very seriously on what this means to us in the context of intelligence.

Johannsen's work opened up an understanding that in some instances of inheritance, it could be argued that it is not diversity in the genes that create the differences noted in a feature, but the environment that gives the gene code life.

Johannsen with his wife and friends. 1923

What has just been stated is a highly controversial matter, until we consider such human features as those of consciousness, reasoning and language. All of which, we may add, are essential properties of the intelligence process, and which we shall discuss in great lengths in our following book *Brain Plasticity: How the Brain Learns through the Mind to Create Intelligence.*

On the 6th of February 1903, Johannsen presented his pure line experiments to the Royal Academy of Sciences in Copenhagen.[248] In this account, he outlined what he regarded to be Galton's abuse of genetic research, and emphasised the importance of the quality of a sample. The need to use only "pure-lines," he argued, was fundamental to understanding the overall process of inheritance with accuracy. It was on this occasion that he used the word "types," as a precursor to his later terminology of genotype and phenotype.[249]

Then, in 1905, Johannsen finally contested the theory of characteristics being predictable (as Galton had relied upon) when he published

"Arvelighedslærens elementer," or *"Elements of Heredity."* A revised and expanded version of this was subsequently republished in German in 1909, and became a founding work in genetics having very equal significance to that of Mendels.

The significance of all this is that Johannsen destroyed Galton's argument of genes purely creating variations. In other words, genes could be said to vary, but not as much as the variations that were observed.

This meant that Galton's theory was wrong, stepped variations in a feature do not give proof of equal stepped genetic variations. More significantly to our interest, by demonstrating how the gene expression varies with the environment, Johannsen gave explanation as to why identical twins can grow to look, behave, and "think" very differently to each other!

Let us expand upon the point of monozygotic twins we mentioned earlier, and imagine we could have six clones - each having the same genetic coding at fertilisation. We know now that by the time there are born, they would no longer be identical, because of the mutations we have earlier explained.

However, as a human being, unique in their own right, each would have their own perspective of the infantile and later childhood stages they moved through. As each absorbed the behaviours of those raising them, the love, the loss of temper and the vast range in-between, each would fine-tune their behavioural responses to learn to survive. As they do this, so their emotions would fine-tune their personalities and so endear them to different interests.

In school, each would examine the information they were daily introduced to. Each will recognise different meanings in the same information through their earlier experiences. As they are introduced to some new information, each will focus on what it is and the meanings this has to them.

As a human being, each will be monitoring the environment around them to consider if they are safe, that other children are not laughing at them and hopefully respecting them, and if not this, then not thinking about them. Free of the dangers of others attacking their identity, they will struggle to see the connections being shown to them by their teacher.

Yet, the mind is always searching for security, and if in searching it misses some point of the lesson, so it will struggle to make this up. How well each clone does this will depend much on how they have managed to keep up with the information from earlier lessons, have practised to become proficient with this and are able to gain a satisfactory response to any question they have the confidence to ask.

When we consider all this, we must understand that each of the clones we have will demonstrate a different response to any question asked, just as they will be more or less accurate, or faster or slower than another in this. We are human beings. We are not machines.

Therefore, when examined in school, each would respond according to their development here. One clone may gain a grade of 4/10 (if, for example, they had been bullied as Quellet-Morin found), another 5/10, others 7/10, 8/10, 9/10 and one 10/10, all depending on how each related to the changes in the environment when they occurred and how each chose to interact with it when it arose.

To enhance the point and take this example beyond the competence of the classroom environment, consider how each child could have been separated at birth and raised in a different family under widely different social as well as cultural identities. Some children were raised with deep affection, while others were raised with a sense of rejection. Some enjoyed a secure family, while others a broken one or a violent atmosphere. Some had their insights raised and others theirs quashed, so that guidance varied from precise to indifference. The list is endless, and it is precisely because it is that the environment of intelligence cannot be classified!

It is because of Johannsen that we today understand how the environment can totally alter the impression we have of the capability of a gene coding. However, because of the ancient "transmission" theory that Galton's philosophy of intelligence grew up through, and which was held on to by those who followed in his path for political reasons, we do not realise how this still distorts our impression of intelligence today.

To understand how Galton really misunderstood what was happening in inheritance, consider the following example he offered in *A Theory of Heredity*.

"A drunkard," he wrote ", is often known to have imbecile children, although his offspring, previous to his taking to drink, were healthy. The alcohol pervades his tissues, and, of course, affects the germinal matter in the sexual elements as much as it does that in the cells which form the structure of its own nerves."[250]

This is a classic example of Galton's style of argument. Yet, we know today that the child does not inherit a tendency to drink through the genes of their parents, because the alcohol "infected" their parents DNA. Although, in having said this, it was the same reasoning of Galton that created the belief we hold today, when we think the intelligence of a child lies in the intelligence witnessed in their parents!

Once Johannsen had discovered the role of the environment, the Galtonians struggled to understand how they could maintain their argument that the genetic base varies continuously across a population. This was the beginning of the nature/nurture debate, and it led to a misunderstanding in how the genetic base of intelligence varies that still confuses many to this day. ......

Chapter TwentyThree

A Closer Understanding of the Intelligence Genes

Today most geneticists, as much as psychologists, are so involved with developing their science that they are too little aware of the political struggles that once tied these sciences together. It is greatly because of this that we today only see Johannsen as having worked with plants, without really understanding the significant role he played in establishing the science of genetics free from the political wrangling of psychology. In Johannsen's time, the general public held far greater interest in the social aspects of inheritance than they did with biology.

As Searle informs us, "On the eve of the First World War, the general journals were carrying more articles on eugenics than on the three questions of slums, tenements and living standards combined."[251] It was mainly because of this that **Johannsen had argued the word inheritance should not be used in genetics.** It was, he said, too easily confused with inheritance in social matters, such as in the property children could gain from their parents.[252]

However, as genetics did begin to pull away from psychology, and struggled to stand on its own feet, it saw opportunities in maintaining a weak link. As Marks put it: "Their *(the geneticists)* best interests being served by standing by and not criticising them *(the psychologists)*. Anything that got people interested in supporting genetics was good for business. ... Although", as he also stated "the biggest mistake that geneticists of the 1920s made, was to fail to identify and engage the political evils that attempted to draw legitimacy from their science."[253] Johannsen, to the contrary, did make strong protests, and since Galton and his forces were behind these "political evils," we may understand why their paths were entwined.

Therefore, it is very relevant here not to think of Johannsen's experiment with the Princess bean as detached from what Galton was actually doing with his pea experiment. For while Johannsen struggled to understand what was really happening with inheritance, so he likewise struggled to untangle the science of genetics from the political arguments that were strangling its birth process.

As he wrote in 1903, "In the theory of heredity there has been, and there is still too much groundless talk."[254] The purpose of this section is to understand the struggles of the Galtonians to overcome the matter of unpredictability that Johannsen raised, which was the root of their problem and of this groundless talk.

As we saw, Galton's reference to the self-fertilisation of peas arose through an experiment that sought to find a solution that could explain why ability does not reduce through generations. We are introduced by this to an awareness that there may be a much deeper political account behind Galton's pea experiment than is today recognised.

After all, Galton started this to prove the existence of stability in social matters, and his discovery of the regression to the mean, which he gained from this, led him into a series of mathematical events that culminated in the creation of coefficients. Coefficients, we found, provide the mathematical authority upon which intelligence tests rely. Therefore, Galton's experiment with peas gave him another means to explain how the inherited worth of families could be classed next to each other in a range of continuous variation.

From the moment Galton published *Hereditary Genius* in 1869, to his role as honorary president of The Eugenics Education Society in 1908 (It was renamed as The Eugenics Society in 1926)[255], there is a clear thread that runs through all his work and effort relating to the classification of the citizen. The purpose of this classification, we have seen, was to maintain the role of a family in the order of things.

We may wonder from this if Galton's statement that self-fertilised lines are not subject to natural selection may have been nothing more than a demonstration of how the purity of family intelligence is maintained through generations.

After all, this was the theme by which the natural and unequal ability of different families could be related to the work roles they were said to be capable of, and the level of social responsibility they could be trusted with. This is to say that the predictable worth of a family's intelligence would always be recognisable in the achievements of their ancestors.

Galton's law of deviation from the average gave justification to this, for it sought to demonstrate how individuals varied in intelligence from imbecile to genius in equal steps. This was Galton's application of continuous variation. The argument that the worth of a family line is not notably affected by social development is one every Galtonist has since followed, and struggled to prove from Pearson to Spearman, to Goddard, to Terman, to Burt, and so to Murray and Herrnstein in 1994.

Therefore, while we today focus upon Johannsen's discovery of the genotype/phenotype distinction, we must hold on to the political battles taking place in his time, because this distinction he created really came about to prove why the characteristics of the offspring cannot be judged from those witnessed in the parents. We have long forgotten this.

So today, we do not see that the real issue with arguments over the ratio of nature vs nurture is not about the role of the environment, but about the predictability of the gene, because it is this that decides political and social policies. Murray and Herrnstein have shown how this political drive to control genetics is still alive today. It was precisely because Johannsen realised how the politics of human affairs strove to control the natural processes of nature, that he strove with such vigour to clear up the misunderstanding this "groundless talk" was causing.

It was because of the politics set about this question of predictability that each side closed the door on the other, as the war between the mutationists and the biometricians died out. Those doors have not been opened in over a century. The reason for this is very obvious. If psychologists were to accept Johannsen's explanation that a range of differences noted in any group cannot be proven to be related to differences in the genotypes, and so be predictable in a family line, they must admit that intelligence is not what they say it is. With this being so, intelligence cannot be measured. While many geneticists have tried to explain this point to psychologists since the time of Johannsen, their knowledge has fallen on deaf ears for this very reason.

The means by which the biometricians were able to overcome this issue of predictability came through the study of quantitative traits. The study of quantitative traits is a biometrical or statistical approach to studying genetics, and seek to understand how changes in a population may be explained through changes in the arrangement of genes. Let us look at how this idea arose, and what it actually means to us in terms of how the environment can confuse what we think a gene is responsible for.

Quantitative Traits

We may recall that prior to the discovery of Mendel's laws, inheritance was believed to work on the principle that the offspring was a blend of their parents. According to this principle, if a white flower were crossed with a red, their offspring would be a pink flower. Once Mendel's laws were known this blending theory was rejected, because Mendel's laws stated that a feature in the offspring would be of one of the parents, and not a blend of theirs. In the plant species he worked with, a cross between a red and a white flower produced only a red (if the red was dominant), and so a ratio of 3 red to 1 white if this flower self-fertilised. The problem was that when a red flower was crossed with a white flower in other species, they did sometimes produce a pink! Nobody could now understand why.

A solution as to why this occurred was provided by a Swede named Nilsson-Ehle in 1909. Nilsson-Ehle crossed a single red kernel of bread wheat with a single white kernel, and produced an intermediary pink. This fitted exactly with the idea of blending. However, when this pink was self-fertilised, it produced a number of offspring that varied not as a general blend, but into very discrete segments of colour with specific relationships between them.

Red	Red-Pink	Pink	White-Pink	White
1/16	4/16	6/16	4/16	1/16

This symmetrical and distinct colouring completely discredited once and for all the blending theory. Through this experiment, Nilsson-Ehle was able to explain how Mendel's principle could be expressed, not now as a singular gene from each parent but as of a number of genes that were segregating and crossing in a multiple of ways. Each group of genes affected their own direction of the colour. This idea of many genes became known as The Multifactorial Theory of Inheritance, and it opened up awareness to how many genes can add up to create a genotype.

The idea that many genes could replace a singular gene, gave Galtonists the much needed belief that a way had been found to explain how a wide range of genetic differences can be related to a wide range of performances, and so give evidence of predictability. In effect, they believed multifactorial inheritance explained Galton's argument for continuous variation. This, however, is not what it means!

Nilsson-Ehle showed how a number of alternative designs could be symmetrically related to each other to produce, not a continuous genetic variation moving from red through pink to white, (as Galton wished to think how the genotype for intelligence varied) .....

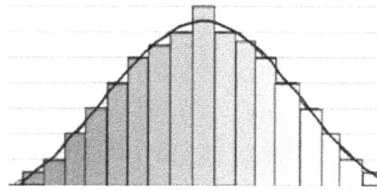

but as a variation identified through discrete sections

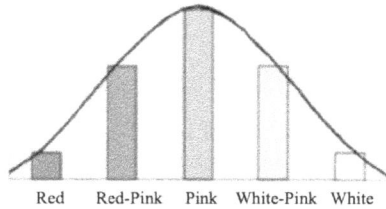

Red   Red-Pink   Pink   White-Pink   White

The difference was conveniently overlooked by Galton's followers, and means were sought to weave multifactorial inheritance into Galton's theory that intelligence is inherited over a wide range of continuous differences.

An ardent supporter of Galton, and especially eugenics, was a statistician by the name of Ronald Fisher. It is not irrelevant to note that Fisher was as much an ardent Galtonian as he was as proficient in mathematics as Pearson. Pearson, we may recall, had designed the correlation coefficient for Galton.

In fact, Fisher rose to become the Galton Professor of Eugenics at University College London following the tremendous success of his book *The Genetical Theory of Natural Selection* in 1930. It was in this book that Fisher wove the theories of Mendel into Darwin's, to explain how natural selection could work in evolution. This was necessary at the time, for Darwin's theory was still contested by Lamarck's "inheritance of acquired characteristics."[256]

Therefore, by explaining Darwin's theory through Mendelian principles, Fisher was able to explain how inheritance guided evolution. Since

Galton had evolved his theories through those of Darwin's, Fisher used this to give substance to the theory that intelligence was genetically determined. In 1918, he suggested that the way to prove this could be found through the study of quantitative traits.[257]

The whole point that is missed with quantitative traits is that they deal only with population genetics, and as we have already pointed out, you cannot go from the population level to the individual level, because we cannot generalise what the environment means and use this generalisation to understand the specific environment of the individual.

We have already explained why it is impossible to go from the population level to the specific level of the individual. However, being so convinced of Galton's theory, Fisher could not recognise this, and so with full vigour he used Nilsson-Ehle's idea of many genes to support the theme of continuous genetic variation in human ability. Theory was one thing, but the need was still present to prove how a combination of genes could be related to differences in the phenotype without the confusion of the environment. It took many years to do so, but eventually Sewall Wright found a way to explain this.

Wright crossed a guinea pig with the normal three toes on their hind feet, with one that had four toes. In his analysis of the offspring, Wright suggested that the three and four-toed variations could be explained by four different loci that were interacting.

Remember now that a locus point is that place on a chromosome where the alleles can be found. Since each locus point has a possibility of two alleles (one from each parent), this gave Wright a possible variation of eight alleles for the genetic effect he noted.

Wright reasoned that a value to the gene code could be gained by terming each allele at a locus point positive (+) or negative (-). These are, of course, impossible to see, but Wright reasoned they may be given relative values by relating them to the number of toes. In this sense, polygenes are the genotype and the toes take the role of the phenotype.

On this principle, Wright reasoned that five positive alleles would determine the threshold point as to whether the animal would have three or four toes. Therefore, four toes would indicate five or more positive alleles, while three toes would suggest less than five and so a negative arrangement.

The idea arose from this that an alternative method of genetic inheritance can exist to that devised by Mendel. Using the Greek word polu to mean many, this alternative gene design was given the name polygenes. Polygenes, then, are simply only a number of genes, whose collective value creates a genotype.

Through Wright's work, the idea of quantitative traits became more accepted, and polygenes became regarded as a way of explaining the genotype. The idea of polygenes was very important at the time, because it gave a way of trying to understand the gene action of a feature, when that feature is so alterable through the environment that the genes cannot be identified.

This drives home the need for us to understand that **while the gene is dependent upon the environment for all that may occur, there are times when the environment can confuse what we think the gene is actually responsible for. Intelligence provides the best example of this.**

Once polygenes were used to explain intelligence, the persistence that it had to be founded on genetic differences caused the idea of positive and negative genes interacting to be interpreted to mean that different families had different combinations of these. While Wright's description of these genes was only theoretical, the more people talked about families having polygenes, the more they convinced themselves that they were actual and so a physical determinant in an act of intelligence.

However, if we refer back to the example of Nilsson-Ehle's crossing of a plant with red kernels with one having white, we can now see that two alleles interacting at four loci points would give the 16 gene code variation he found. **So, the idea of polygenes can be rationalised to just two pairs of Mendelian genes segregating in both parents**.

Genetically, this can be explained by crossing AABB with aabb to give AaBb. If AaBb were in turn crossed with another AaBa, the resulting genotypic variations would appear with the same frequencies observed by Nilsson-Ehle:

Frequencies	1/16	4/16	6/16	4/16	1/16
Genotypes	AABB,	AABb, AaBB,	AAbb, AaBb,aaBB,	Aabb aaBb,	aabb

This is to say that simple Mendelian genes can become so indecipherable to understand when they operate in a complex environment that they can be mistaken for something they are not.

This was demonstrated by Griffith and his colleagues, when they planted a number of seeds in a soil environment. The seeds of the three different alleles had the genotypes (aa : Aa : AA), which were randomly mixed in unequal proportions of 1 : 2 : 3 before being planted. The nutritional value of the soil was inconsistent, which gave an important variation in the environment. This gave the impression that there were many unknown genes operating in an unknown environment.

Once the plants had grown, it was not possible to tell which plant belonged to the genotype aa, Aa, or AA, because the seeds had been so thoroughly mixed. All that was witnessed was a number of plants that varied continuously in their height. Therefore, if aa had been crossed with Aa, under the complexity of this environment, it could grow to any point within the entire range with no indication that the subsequent plant had derived from this cross, or if it had been created through Aa crossing with Aa, or aa crossing with AA.[258]

As we can see here, the difference between Mendelian genes and polygenes is not if they are singular or many and segregated, but if the environment will cause their feature to vary continuously or not. If the environment can be so controlled as to exclude its effect, what is explained as many polygenes varying can just as easily be explained by a very few Mendelian genes. In other words, polygenes do not exist!

Polygenes were only invented to try to understand the action of a gene that cannot be recognised, because the environment is too complex. As Mather put it:

"Polygenic inheritance does not imply the existence of polygenes. If many genes have similarly small influences on the trait that interests us, we are not obliged to postulate the existence of a large set of genes that do nothing but interfere with Mendelian calculations."[259]

If we now return to intelligence, we can see that its genotype is not created by many polygenes segregating to create a very wide variation, as Fisher tried to prove in order to support Galton's theory of continuous variation. If we can understand what this means, so may we understand that intelligence cannot be measured, because the conclusions arising from studying quantitative traits rest on population observations that have nothing to do with the individual.

It arises from all we have discussed in this book that in an environment of extreme diversity, **any genetic differences must be relatively narrow in their variation. This is certainly the case with intelligence. Therefore, we cannot say that the stability an individual exhibits in their performance is a consequence of their genetic factor being below or above the norm.**

To understand what this means is to understand why we cannot say that all children differ in their schoolwork because they inherited different qualities of genetic competence. Of more significance to us here is that **Galton's theory of inherited ability, as having a continuous variation in any population, cannot be the deciding factor in the varying qualities of intelligence witnessed.**

The error to believe that it must, lie in the understanding that genes are normally shuffled at the reproductive stage and so create a wide genetic diversity of quality. However, this reasoning fails to understand that such shuffling may imply only alternative codes that bring no or very little difference in effect, as oppose to superior and inferior designs that could.

After all, according to Galton's point of view, it would be logical to assume that a genius would have superior genetic codes, but as we shall see, this is not the case. Any genius did not come from or produce a line of geniuses. Each was a one-off and created so by very individualistic environmental circumstances. Therefore, the genes of a genius, as witnessed by their family line before and after, must have been of normal quality, which supports the view of a narrow genetic variation in a population. While psychologists may give the impression that the genes for intelligence are well known, the reality is very different.

As Morgan noted shortly after receiving the Nobel Prize for his work with chromosomes in 1933, "There is no consensus as to what genes are -- whether they are real or purely fictitious."[260] In fact, the actual existence of the gene was openly disputed in scientific circles until as late as the mid-1930s. However, of far more relevance to us is Holdrege's explanation in 2005:

"If you have a gene at one point in time it may become, both structurally and functionally, something quite different at another time or place. As a result, it is no longer possible to speak of the gene in a straightforward manner,"[261] which, we may add, is what psychologists and so educationalists fail to understand when they try to measure human intelligence! Gilbert was even more explicit, when he wrote:

"The twentieth century has arguably been the century of the gene. The central importance of the gene as a unity of inheritance and function has been crucial to our present understanding of many biological phenomena. Nonetheless, we may well have come to the point where the use of the term "gene" is of limited value, and might in fact be a hindrance to our understanding of the genome — unlike chromosomes, **genes are not physical objects but are mere concepts that have acquired a great deal of historic baggage over the past decades.**"[262]

May, we see yet again, that we still do not know what the genes for intelligence are or what they have become programmed to do!

One interesting point to reflect upon here is the discovery of bacteria growing inside hermetically sealed nuclear reactors feeding on radiation.[263] The lingering question is how did this bacteria, or to our interest the DNA, get there?

Our understanding of life and so the existence of DNA is based on Darwin's theory of mutated steps of evolution, as we have discussed. Yet, as Wilcock points out in his book *The Synchronicity Key*:

"We now have more than enough scientific proof to conclude that these bacteria **formed spontaneously inside the reactor,** and were custom-designed to eat radiation and break it down into material that is less harmful to other forms of life."[264]

When we read such accounts as this, **we are caused to wonder if we really have any idea as to the potential of "the gene" to adapt itself !**

Our understanding of genetic inheritance is based on the laws that Mendel devised. Mendel developed these laws through experiments with clearly defined traits in self-fertilising plants, but they are, in principle, just as applicable to traits in human beings. However, since Mendel's time (and he was not himself fully aware of the significance of his discovery), we have come to realise that patterns of inheritance are more complex than his laws can explain.

Mendel's understanding of complete dominance, for example, which we explained with a tall plant being crossed with a short one, fails to explain instances where incomplete dominance (one allele is not completely dominant over the other) can occur. This is more so the case with co-dominance, where both alleles are clearly and equally expressed.

A very simple example of co-dominance can be found in the human blood group ABO. A child will be AB if they receive the gene for type A from one parent and type B from the other. Yet, and in having said this, the real issue is not that a gene is dominant or that it is recessive, as Mendel believed. The issue lies in why one gene functions the way it does when it is compared to another. This functioning is accepted by geneticists because it follows the idea that genes represent discrete characteristics.

However, the truth is that we have only a partial understanding, if any, of the genetic mechanism that causes this apparent dominance, and these causes are more unknown than they are known.

Therefore, we must realise that the science of genetics is a developing field, and it would be very wrong to think that what the gene is and how it works is completely understood.

This brings us to a relatively new way of understanding inheritance, which really only gained serious interest this century.

———————————————

Chapter TwentyFour
Acquired Characteristics

We may recall that Galton reasoned that we inherit qualities of intelligence from our parents, which do not change throughout our lifetime. We discussed how he went to great lengths to play down the effects of influence in the gaining of social positions, seeking to explain how these were acquired only through intelligence, which he saw to be directly inherited. This was his explanation for the natural inheritance of social responsibility, which he argued was necessary to safeguard the survival of his civilisation.

We also saw how Galton's ideas were supported by the establishment and how the science of cognitive psychology was soon founded and quickly set up a tradition to protect his beliefs. Once a tradition takes hold and people believe in it, they tend to view alternative beliefs as either totally wrong or they try to adapt these beliefs to fit in with what they believe.

So, when Johannsen discovered the influence of the environment, psychologists kept their view of the inheritance of intelligence to be stable and unalterable, but were forced to accept that this inborn stability was now influenced to a certain extent by the environment. It was through the drive of social politics that conflicting views developed as to how much the environment could affect inheritance, which gave birth to the nature/nurture debate.

However, while psychologists were forced to accept the influence of the environment, they could not accept Johannsen's explanation that the effects of the environment make it impossible to predict the value of a characteristic passed on to the child. In simple terms, this would be to say that it is not possible to know if the child of a labourer could turn out to be a labourer too or a medical scientist.

While it could never be possible to predict how the environment, in its many shades, would determine the course of the child's life, such understanding went directly against the tradition that had built up around Galton's belief. As we understand, this belief was centred on the reasoning that intelligence had to have a stable quality throughout the generations of a family line that was different in quality from that of other families, so that each could be accorded the social responsibility they should be entitled to.

Therefore, if Johannsen's research had been wholly accepted, it would have meant that intelligence is not stable and therefore may be highly, if not totally, alterable. Thus, any IQ test would, then, only be said to measure what experience of life the individual had gained to that point in time, with no prediction as to how they could further develop. Since intelligence is defined as being stable and so predictable throughout the lifetime, this would mean that intelligence (as so defined) would not exist, and that all that was being measured were skills in reason, which are developmental. This, of course, would go totally against the belief that Galton had founded and seriously bring into question the worth of the science of psychology as it had built itself upon his belief.

So, psychologists took what they had to from Johannsen, but rejected what they could not afford to accept. This doctored impression of inheritance is still held within the halls of psychology and still conveyed to the general public today, so all may know what inheritance means. However, in the 1940s, a new understanding of the relationship between the environment and genetics was slowly, very slowly, beginning to emerge.

Conrad Waddington had followed a line of thought by which an organism may physically alter itself to adapt to changes in the environment. The principle was a little like Lamarck had suggested a century earlier, and although Darwin's theory of evolution disproved this, examples of adaptation can be found. Tiger snakes in Australia, for example, have grown larger heads to be able to eat larger prey.[265]

In 1942, Waddington published a paper intent on resurrecting interest in a naturalistic view of inheritance, centred around acquired characteristics. In this paper, he introduced the term epigenetics for the first time. Epi is taken from the Greek to mean OVER, and so epigenetics seeks to study how the influences of the environment can come **over** and alter the design of the gene.[266]

To support his claim, Waddington later published two papers, one in 1953 and the second in 1956. In the latter, Waddington explained how he had exposed the developing embryos of fruit flies to vapour from a heat source. Once the larvae had matured into flies, Waddington noticed that some of these had a noticeable difference in their wings. While their genetic design only allows for one thorax, a second thorax appeared in some of the wings. Waddington gave this as evidence of genetic assimilation.[267]

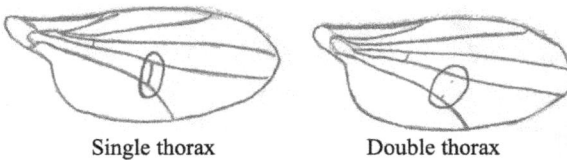

Single thorax   Double thorax

To prove that this altered the genetic feature in the species, he selected flies with the double thorax and found they bred true through 20 generations, without exposure to the environmental difference he had created in the first embryos.[268]

However, in the same year as Waddington published this paper, Crick and Watson announced their discovery of the DNA double helix, and geneticists were too focused on this to give much attention to Waddington's theories, which anyway went against the principles of Mendelian inheritance.

In fact, subsequent research by geneticists claimed that Waddington's work with flies was caused by transposable elements within the DNA., which had been mobilised by the heat exposure, and not so a case of acquired characteristics.[269]

However, other biologists and geneticists followed up on Waddington's theories and eventually proved the existence of acquired characteristics through the principle of epigenetics. In 2004, flowers were found to change colour when their plant was exposed to environmental changes, and so bred a line of these changed coloured flowers through a number of generations.[270] Although, it was not until Skinner reported an epigenetic inheritance in mammals that the world woke up to the implications of this new branch of genetics.

Skinner and his team had been interested to see if agricultural pesticides, which can act as endocrine disrupters, could affect the fertility of pregnant rats, as a means to understand the implications of this to humans. Accordingly, females were injected with chemicals associated with pesticides with the expectation that they would block male sex hormones. Indeed, when the litters were born, males had abnormal testes that would make weak sperm. This showed how the pesticides could affect the survival of the population.

However, when the rats were bred, it was discovered that the hormonal disruption was passed through the germ line, providing direct evidence of epigenetics being transmitted through generations. Skinner introduced the term "Epigenetic Transgenerational Inheritance" to explain this effect.[271]/[272] Suddenly, and from that moment, there was an explosive interest in the possible applications of epigenetics and how an environmental experience could be genetically passed through generations.

In 2013, by further example, Skinner co-authored a paper discussing how the high rate of obesity in America today can be traced to the widespread use of the pesticide DDT three generations earlier, which was used to irradiate mosquitoes carrying malaria. More simply, DDT had entered the human population through the air breathed in and the crops eaten. Once in the body, it produced chemical tags that hindered the gene's regulation of body weight, causing half of the American population today to be obese.[273] Let us now move to understand more of what epigenetics is and how it occurs.

To begin, we should refer back to how proteins are made. As we saw in Chapter Twenty-Two, a cell is made up of cytoplasm, where all the processes required for it to work occur. The cytoplasm contains various amino acids, which are used by ribosomes to manufacture proteins. Proteins are the construction workers of the cell. When the cell needs a new protein, for whatever purpose, it sends a signal to the DNA in the nucleus for the instructions to make this protein. DNA is made of four building blocks: Thymine, Cytosine, Guanine, and Adenine. However, ribosomes cannot read Thymine directly, so it is changed into Uracil in a process called transcription. This new version of the DNA coding is called messenger RNA or mRNA. Once this coding is ready, it leaves the nucleus and goes to a ribosome in the cytoplasm. The ribosome reads the mRNA's instructions and uses amino acids in the cytoplasm to build the needed protein. This is simply how a cell works.

Chemicals derived through our diet, our lifestyle and the thoughts we manifest, may be deposited in certain cells of the body. Here they enter the nucleus, where the DNA. is stored. These chemicals, called epigenetic markers, are capable of affecting the DNA instruction.[274] It is important to understand that the DNA. coding itself is not affected, only the design coding it releases in the creation of mRNA. In this way, epigenetic markers are able to boost or interfere with the transcription of specific gene coding. In this sense, it would help if we think of epigenetic markers as making "acquired characteristics".

The most common way interference happens is when the DNA, or the proteins it has created, are wrapped around by chemical tags from the epigenetic markers, which restrict the release of the DNA coding.

For example, an epigenetic modification of the methyl group can inhibit gene expression by derailing the cellular transcription machinery or causing the DNA to coil more tightly, making it inaccessible. When this happens, the gene is still there, but it is silent or rather "switched off", so that its effect is not presented to the environment. On the other hand, boosting transcription or to "switch on" is the opposite. In this case, chemical tags will unwind the DNA, making it easier to transcribe and so increase the production of associated proteins.

We may recall that our bodily cells are continually dying and replacing themselves through the process of mitosis. As mitosis occurs, the epigenetic changes may or may NOT be carried over into the daughter cells every time they are replaced. If they are, and continually are, the epigenetic effect will remain present throughout the lifetime of the individual. Should these epigenetic changes be present in meiosis (the production of sex cells), they may or may NOT be passed on to the sibling, and so create the possibility of future generations to have these acquired characteristics by the process of Epigenetic Transgenerational Inheritance.

Epigenetics, as we mentioned earlier, brings a whole new dimension into our discussion, because epigenes explain how the environment can change the DNA instruction. This understanding negates the traditional idea of psychology that genes necessarily vary in their quality to provide different families with different qualities of intelligence. It follows from this that epigenetics destroys the idea of using monozygotic twins to try to settle the nature/nurture controversy, because the gene coding of each twin may have been altered by epigenetic markers so that they are no longer identical to each other. In turn, this renders the nature/nurture controversy pointless, because epigenetics from the nurture can directly alter what the nature element is supposed to be

If we expand upon this relatively new understanding of the environment, we are confronted with two factors of development:

First, epigenetics explains how the DNA coding of an individual may be affected by learning or life experiences, if they are attentive enough to manufacture these markers. Indeed, research has shown that specific epigenetic modifications can occur in brain cells when they are repeatedly activated, as by acts of learning and memory.[275]

Second, epigenetics explains how the thinking and reasoning skills the parent acquires through their learning and work (accountants scrutinising data to develop efficient mental checking systems, lawyers memorising past cases and developing good investigative and argumentative skills to support current cases, and so on), may or may not be passed to their child through the principle of Epigenetic Transgenerational Inheritance. However, we may understand that since the experience of the parent will be unique to them, any marker they create, which is passed on at conception, will not be of that direct quality. It will only take the form of a predisposition, which their descendant may build upon, if they have the emotional desire for this and the better environment to allow it.

Knowledge of epigenetics does not mean that we will always create epigenetic tags, which will alter the gene instruction when we take an action or form a thought. We may or we may not. But, now we need to think in terms of how we create a chemical imprint whenever we think or make some action that resides within the neuron mazes of our brain[276]. These chemically encoded thoughts may or may NOT form epigenetic tags, which may alter certain gene expressions.

Yet, before we go any further, we should note that while some epigenetic markers can arise to improve a skill, others could equally arise with opposite and negative values, because the human mind too often lives in a state of insecurity. When this occurs, the effects of one are cancelled out by the effects of the other, so no notable effect occurs.

While psychologists have long created the myth that genetic inheritance is regular, we may know that the effects of epigenetic markers, which affect this genetic inheritance, are very irregular. Since epigenes appear through a mishmash of chaotic influences, they destroy this idea of gene regularity moving through family lines, and so make their occurrence ever more unpredictable than can be argued through Mendel's laws of inheritance, which few psychologists ever understood.

In our account, we have tried to reason that the gene codings for intelligence either operate with very narrow differences in their design or they offer no differences, either of which allows the environment to fully develop the operational quality of this feature.

Consider now that the term Epigenetic, as Waddington had coined it,[277] actually misleads us in what is really happening here. Epi, meaning over in Greek, is satisfactory, but the association with genetics is misleading. By definition, a gene is a unit of hereditary material with instructions to build and maintain the genome.[278] This is not what we have here.

What we do have is a chemical construction of the environment created by an environmental influence. Thus, rather than this being a form of a gene, as epigenetics implies, we have a component of the environment that has no genetic instruction and is not always guaranteed to be passed as a hereditary influence. Accordingly, a term relating to and of the environment would more accurately explain the cause and the effect that occurs upon the gene sequencing.

From this perspective, we may see that the gene has significantly less influence than the environment in the nature/nurture controversy, because the environment is now directly controlling the gene instruction. As we found with Griffiths on page 304, when the extent of the environment is very great (and with intelligence, there can be no greater depth to it), it can mask or override the contribution of specific genes. In such instances, the number of genes involved may be minimal, or their effects may be discontinuous, which suggests that the gene's role is less significant than previously believed.[279]

From this perspective, it may be more accurate to understand what is happening by terming this effect as an *Environmentally Induced Biochemical Modification*, rather than an extension of gene functioning. This shift would not only clarify the mechanisms involved but would also reframe our understanding of the real influence of the environment over the genes involved.

However, since the appearance of epigenetic markers (or how they may be otherwise termed) is decisively related to the environment, their effect within society occurs through a sort of censored inheritance, because the opportunity for their appearance is regulated by social engineering. Better-educated parents, more aware of how to raise their children, will naturally manufacture markers that will improve the adaptability of their children. While less-educated parents, less aware of how to better raise their children, will manufacture less appropriate markers.

As we can see, epigenetics takes our understanding of the environment and the social conditioning of children to a new level. However, this does not mean that those better raised are naturally better than those less raised, because the environment can overcome this difference as nature has intended through the provision of imagination and creativity. Yet, when the environment contains ignorance, it fails to ignite these human qualities and, by acts of ill psychology, will eventually subdue them. Such has been too often the environment for the school child with no education in their reason, who became the factory worker tethered to automatic jobs that dimmed their imagination, and so the influences they came to hold over their children. Yet, beyond this social conditioning, every human child inherits equally the ability for imagination and creativity, and waits only for the environment to ignite these.

In the times of Galton, and up until the 1950s when our technology evoked social changes, the environment of society contained many social and even moral restrictions that maintained the opportunity for work to the history of the family line. We may recall the sentiment *'Know your place'* and that of *'Don't think you can be better than you are'*. Therefore, it was virtually impossible at that time for a person of one social rank to gain the opportunity to move to a higher rank. Of course, certain individuals did manage this, but they were exceptions. So, in the general sense, epigenes manufactured by a parent may have been genetically passed to their child, but in the tightly controlled social ranking of that time, their effect was regarded as socially related. They were, in fact, purposely kept so.

However, in our more egalitarian times, we see how the sons of unskilled labourers (where their society encourages this) leave university to be lawyers and accountants, who, by the new skills they obtain, manufacture epigenetic modifications that may raise the intelligence of their family line, enabling them to break free of the social restrictions that had previously restricted their opportunities. This, as we saw, was Galton's greatest fear, and remains so today with those of right-wing views who seek to preserve opportunities for their children and so their family lines.

Yet, we have to be very careful to understand what is implied here. As we found with Mendel's laws of inheritance, to which Johannsen added the effect of the environment, there can be no prediction which genes will appear in the child from the lines of their parents. Thus, in consideration of epigenetic modifications, an individual may or may not create these in some skill they develop. If they do, this may or may not be passed to their child genetically.

If this epigenetic modification does appear within their child's coding, it may be recessive (not available to them) or it may be dominant. However, if it is dominant, it does not provide the same quality of skill as was witnessed in the parent, because the parent's life experiences were different to their child's, as they refined this skill to their personal and unique needs. All that will be passed, if so, will be a propensity to develop it. And yet, since the environment is so vivid and rich, a child who did not inherit this propensity may just as easily manufacture their own quality to this.

We must always remember how diverse and how meaningful the environment can be, especially if knowledge of the art of sensitivity in awareness is known and applied.

If we now move beyond the idea of fixed qualities of intelligence running through family lines, which are too readily linked to social success, we may understand how the epigenetic environment destroys this idea. If a child or an adult from a poor background, who is argued to have genes of low quality, is suddenly transported into an engaging environment with the correct guidance, they could easily develop higher qualities of understanding by which they may manufacture epigenetic modifications. If these are transmitted to their child at conception, there is the possibility of epigenetic transgenerational inheritance moving through the family line.

Therefore, the case for acquired characteristics causes us to realise that all human beings, regardless of our impression of their intelligence, have the potential to manufacture epigenetic traits, which could dramatically change or, in the very least, influence the potential of their family line.

This understanding encourages support for greater financing for schools in poorer areas, because if these children are better taught and given greater opportunities to develop, they could manufacture epigenetic modification, which, if passed to their children, could provide them with better propensity for their better development. In turn, this would significantly raise the capabilities of society as a whole -- if the desire is there for this. Yet, as we have seen, there seldom has been!

However, to confuse this issue of inheritance even further, we need to be aware that there are other means than genetic inheritance that can just as easily cause us to witness the same skill in both parent and child. This is to say that the presence of epigenes and the effects associated with them can be more of academic theorising than practical reality.

Accordingly, there is another process by which factors of the environment can be brought into the makeup of the individual, and which can be passed through a family line, not by biological inheritance but by social inheritance. This is the process of imprinting, which is a psychological adaptation of behavioural and cognitive strategies. The process of imprinting is able to affect the production of hormones and, through this, bring consequences to the value of intelligence.

Thus, rather than thinking of a DNA. inherited intelligence, which we have spent many pages discussing, we now consider how features of intelligence are differently acquired and how they may be otherwise passed through a family line. With the issue of intelligence, it is not possible to know if the features of the parents were epigenetically or socially conveyed to their child, once the process of imprinting is clearly understood.

Imprinting, in fact, is little recognised, and because of this, we go to great depths to explain this process in *Brain Plasticity,* prior to discussing critical periods in learning. In the simplest sense, we may understand that we all naturally inherit a bio-psychological mechanism that enables us to emotionally bond with another human being, whom we like and therefore may trust.

It is through this sense of trust that we identify with certain characteristics, features or strategies they display, which we absorb into our means of interaction, as we seek to handle aspects of the world we imagine they do better. In a sense, we want to be like them, without losing a sense of who we are. We are designed by God to struggle through the entanglement of personalities, by which we become a unique human being.

This mechanism of imprinting is very sophisticated, for rather than the infant merely observing and copying from the adult, they bond the adult to them by **innate strategies**. These strategies develop in complexity as the child grows in age, and so may become transferable to other guardians, which in education would be the teacher. Through such a bond of personalities, the child may consciously or subconsciously copy the strategies of behaviour and cognition of those they admire, and so bring these strategies into their makeup.

We can see this happening very easily with a child displaying some behaviour or thought action of a parent, and even those of a teacher if they so admire them. So, a child may touch their chin in the manner of one of their parents or say some action out loud, such as "be careful", and will act more sensitively in their actions because of this. Thus, a parent may tell their child to check what they do, but the child is more likely to check their own effort if they observe one they admire doing it for themself. The first, they may see as an imposition of the personality of another upon them. The second is their desire for a relationship with this personality.

Equally, we can also witness imprinting occurring between adults who have bonded with each other. So, for example, I find myself using words or phrases that my wife says, which I never did before we were married, just as I see my wife inadvertently showing mannerisms that are mine.

We are genetically encoded by nature to learn and develop in this way, through those with whom we develop a close emotional bonding. Thus, the ways in which we behave are just as in the ways we think, and these are parts of others that we have encoded into our means of interaction with the world about us. This will have great significance to what will shortly follow.

Although imprinting is ostensibly designed to operate through trust, it can operate through simple positive or negative exposure. Take, for example, the case of a psychological profile, such as schizophrenia. Schizophrenia has long been thought to be genetically transmitted, because it is witnessed in a family line. However, it can just as easily be socially inherited.[280]

Schizophrenia is related to abnormally high production levels of dopamine.[281] Psychotic drugs that are used to combat schizophrenia do so by lowering dopamine levels in the brain region of the limbic system.

Since the monoamines (such as dopamine, noradrenaline, and serotonin) obtain their manufacturing level through experience, there arises from this a suggestion that mental conditions relating to monoamine levels may be socially inherited. This is imprinting, where the production level of hormones is regulated by perceived environmental exposure, in contrast to epigenes that directly affect the instructions of DNA. coding.

Van der Kolk brought great relevance to the effect of psychology affecting hormone levels when he demonstrated how severe stress in childhood can affect the production of noradrenaline, so as to distort sleep and arousal patterns in adulthood.[282] Such long-term effects of mental stress in childhood have been supported by the many cases Cichilli reviewed of adults who, in direct consequence to stressful experiences in childhood, were found to produce abnormal fluctuations in the manufacture of some of their neurotransmitters.[283]

This led to other studies that examined how poorly developed brain functions could be related to stressful experiences in childhood. Wilson, for example, has shown how neglect or abuse in childhood can be related to strokes and cerebral infarction in old age.[284]

We may understand from this that the threshold levels by which neurotransmitters are produced and so released are determined by experience, and not by DNA. instruction through inheritance. This is a crucial point for us to understand, because it brings the idea of intelligence as an inherited factor ever more into an environmental perspective.

This role of the environment, in the construction of intelligence, has been vividly brought home by the discovery that the production and characteristics of dendritic spines are related to stress.

We may remember that at either end of a neuron, there are dendrites. It is the dendrites that connect with the dendrites of other neurons, as they form a path for the signal to move through. At the end of a dendrite, there are very minute spines. These spines are small membranous protrusions that receive the input neurotransmitter from a synapse and, after it has passed through the neuron, release it into the next synapse to allow a signal to move from one neuron to another, as it moves through a network of neurons.

It is now known that these spines increase in number as the child grows, and do so in a disorderly fashion.

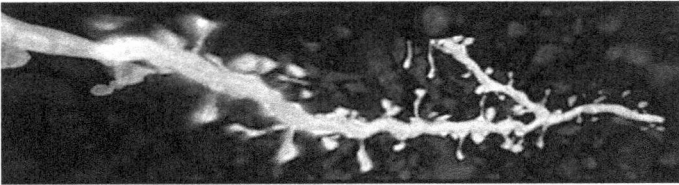

In other words, these spines that are vital to the movement of signals through neural networks learn through sensory information, and not genetic instruction, how to construct themselves.

However, once the adolescent stage is reached, it seems that these spines undergo a pruning that lasts until the onset of adulthood.

In a simple sense, if a child incurs a level of stress that affects the order and production of their hormones, this can decrease the number of spines on their dendrites. A smaller number of spines will affect the ability of neurons to establish new links with other neurons and, in turn, will affect the speed at which signals may move through associated networks.[285]

As we may see from the little we have discussed here, the production level of cortisol and associated neurotransmitters can be easily affected by repeated psychological disturbances, which may set off the activation of the parasympathetic mode, which will affect the intellectual processing systems.[286]

- After all, when any human being makes any act of intelligence, their mind processes information through an entanglement of intellectual, emotional, and behavioural concerns. Every act of intelligence is rooted in some emotional and so behavioural action -- Try learning calculus, while a workman is using a pneumatic drill outside your window!

Of course and very naturally so, beyond these means a child can simply be inspired by some other individual to desire some achievement and in being guided by them, produce a similar skill to their parent, which is only coincidental of their relationship. There does not have to be a formal relationship between the parent and the child for the child to develop their own skill.

We may realise from these examples how easily a characteristic can be acquired and how it can be simply passed from parent to child through the bio-psychological mechanism of imprinting, without any evidence of quality of gene inheritance or the active presence of epigenes.

Therefore, when we consider the effects of imprinting and epigenetics, we may begin to realise more of what the environment of intelligence means and so better understand why its genotypes have evolved to allow the environment to determine the effectiveness of many of the components that constitute an act of intelligence.

We can witness this in our ability to freely detect information, to be able to reason from different perspectives, to associate new information to that stored in the memory by emotional based strategies, the ability to learn to be sensitive in all actions and thoughts, the different ways in which beliefs can form, the ability to adopt new thinking strategies throughout the lifetime, the ability to allow experiences to completely determine emotional states, and in our ability to freely reason, where competence in accuracy and speed are purely developmental. All these occur with no effect from differentials in gene coding.[287] Every human being inherits these with equal worth.

With all these features, there simply is **no ratio of nature to nurture, as we may be reminded.** We have seen why the political framework insists this has to be so for intelligence. Yet, all we have just mentioned is what intelligence is.

Thus, it is not that different individuals inherited different qualities of genes for intelligence, but that these genes, in a common sense, have evolved to operate within a highly complex environment that obscures the purpose they have.

We may recall Griffith here, through discussions with polygenes,[288] in how the real value of the environment of intelligence is so very expansive and in this totally unmeasurable, that it conceals the real role of the genes for this feature. Thus, we may consider not that genes vary in their quality to affect the feature, but that the environment causes the feature to vary beyond any determining purpose the genes would "normally" have.

With all we have laboured to examine in this book, we may finally come to the conclusion of one of two possibilities that can only explain how the feature of human intelligence comes to be, either there is:

a) A variation in genetic coding that is extremely narrow, but can never be known because of the complexity of the environment, or

b) A genetic coding having many variations, but which has evolved to merely present the ability for the feature in such a way that these variations do not interfere with the individual's experiences of the environment.

As we may see, neither of these allows for Galton's insistence on a wide genetic base that can be directly related to the life experiences of an individual. Without this, there is no means to limit intelligence to a genetic factor that allows a human being to be either culturally or socially categorised for political purposes.

By such possibilities of (a) or (b), the gene coding enables the feature of intelligence to exist, while allowing the intellectual, behavioural and emotional experiences of the individual to program how they believe they may best interact with environmental information.

Our knowledge of acquired characteristics, whether they derive from epigenetics or imprinting, explains how any child — regardless of their social and ethnic background — may acquire these skills if they are exposed to them, especially if this is done in a way that resonates with their interest.

In the rigid work-social atmosphere of the 19th and for much of the 20th century, the child was much tied to the thinking skills of their parents and family, so that without knowledge of epigenes (which reside in the chromosomes and may be transferred genetically like DNA.) psychologists mistakenly took the intelligence they saw running in family lines to be caused by genetics and so gene differences. This, after all, is what they had been led to expect.

However, when the child is freed from such a self-limiting world, as many are today, we find they may develop their intelligence directly in accord with the environmental opportunities available to them — through all its highly complex and diverse fields.

Although, in having said this, we should equally realise that children are raised differently by parents with different experiences, as we mentioned in the early pages of this book. So, we still find a tendency to recognise intelligence related to the socio-economic framework of the family. However, rather than this being related to inferior and superior genes, it is instead artificially related to the experiences and drives of the parents.

We may be reminded of the work of Risley and Hart, who found that children raised by academic parents have some 30 million words more in their vocabulary at the age of three than children raised by less educated parents. Let us delve a little deeper to better understand what this means.

Firstly, academic parents will be aware of how their child should behave better to learn in school. They will raise them with mental discipline to focus on the learning as it happens. Develop mental stamina in their child, so they will keep focused on the goal to be learnt. Develop confidence in their child to believe more in their own ability. These three factors will arm them least to be distracted by the behaviour of others in the class, which is very important in their learning development.

They will also teach them elementary arithmetic to prepare them to be ahead of others when they start in the classroom competition, which these parents will understand well. Most importantly, they will have raised them on good storytelling, encouraged them to make their own stories and developed in them a good ability to explain their thoughts. By the skills the parents have learnt and developed through their work, they will naturally raise their children on these.

Secondly, the parents will have developed experiences which were chemically represented in their cellular memory and so tagged to particular genes. These will be epigenetically transferred and may be passed on to their child biologically, as well as socially, as we have just mentioned.

We may imagine from this both the social and biological inheritances denied to a child raised by lesser academic parents, and so all that will stem from this as they move through school, jobs and life.

However, epigenetics explains how a child from a low socio-economic family may develop a high level of intelligence if the parents, and this is usually the mother, have the drive to so guide their child. Tannenbaum gave support to this when he found that children regarded as gifted or rather "intelligent" had been raised with particular skills by their family. So that they ....

(1)   are noted to have developed a high general ability in abstract reasoning, and in locating and solving complex problems.

(2)   have been raised to show special aptitudes to problems that are domain-specific.

(3)   have been raised to show dedication and commitment, good working habits and confidence to take creative risks.

(4)   come from a sound social and emotional environment, and gain psychological strength from their family, school and peer group to excel.

(5)   are "guided" by these and unforeseen influences to meet the right people at the right time in their development.[289]

Therefore, family lines may be affected differently by epigenes, and this will impart skills into children, **but this is not to say** that other children will not be able to develop their own skills if the correct background is provided for them socially and educationally.

So much depends upon the manner in which the child is raised, where, for example, they are trained to give total commitment, to have good working habits and to have the confidence to take creative risks, which is much orchestrated through the efforts of a loving mother.[290]

While genetic codes are seen to be inflexible, epigenes are known to be highly adaptable to changes in the environment. Studies with mammals found that while variations in the degree of maternal affection altered methylation patterns in the hippocampus of offspring, these epigenetic alterations could be reversed by cross-fostering with more attentive mothers.[291]/[292]

It is important to realise that, since epigenetic alterations may be reversed, the individual has the freedom to redesign how they develop to handle information. This opens up the need for a greater awareness to the effects of better parental raising and better learning experiences in school, when all concerned are aware of and know how to implement sensitivity to awareness.

Yet, such talk of epigenes is only academic theorising. It has no practical relevance because it offers no proof of why a child displays similar characteristics to a parent. They may have inherited a relevant epigene, or they may not and if not, could simply have absorbed these skills through the exposure of imprinting. Yet, neither of these may explain the similarity that is witnessed. The child's skills could just as easily have been inspired through someone igniting their imagination and guiding them in self-awareness, so that what is seen is merely coincidental. Therefore, it is not genetics that is the key to understanding intelligence, but how emotional interest gives sensitivity in awareness to the selection and processing of information, through the language skills each has acquired. All this, we have long sought to explain.

Chapter TwentyFive

The Laws of Natural Selection

In 1864, a philosopher named Herbert Spencer had read Darwin's work on natural selection and was inspired to coin the expression *"The Survival of the Fittest."* Spencer actually used this to describe competition in business, but evolutionists adapted it to explain Darwin's theory of life. As ideas of evolution in life became blended with the inheritance of human ability, so the appeal of this wording gave confidence to the reasoning that children of parents who have done well in "business" will naturally do the same by their natural inheritance.

By this application, *"The Survival of the Fittest"* became a battle cry for those promoting elitism. As the intelligence of each family is said to vary through inheritance, so this phrase helped to distort our impression of genetic variation, because it implies there must be superior and inferior genetic instructions in every variation. Yet, as we have just pointed out, this is not normally the case, for the genetic diversity arising in gametogenesis (the development of eggs and sperm) does not imply this aspect of genetic superiority.

May we be reminded here that our belief that qualities in intelligence vary in families, because of variations in a gene design, is directly on account of the political mindset that created it. There is no biological evidence that the genes for intelligence in normally born infants create determinable differences. The case of geniuses supports this, as we shall shortly see. Further in our account, we shall discuss the work of Nancy Bayley, whose research over 50 years, and with 50,000 babies, found there are no discernible differences in intelligence from birth to 14 months of age. Let us now consider the feature of intelligence from a biological and an evolutionary point of view.

According to Darwin's Laws of Natural Selection, an organism, or **a feature of an organism**, that evolves to enable more adaptability will survive, while an organism or a feature that has less adaptability will fade into extinction.

Therefore, according to the Laws of Natural Selection, a gene design that limited the development of intelligence through variations in its coding, as Galton and Spearman proposed, would be less adaptable and would logically be phased out, while a gene coding that provides the design for this feature to exist and to gain **its quality of development** purely through the environment would survive better. This design would provide optimum adaptability.

This understanding of Natural Selection explains why features of intelligence can be created purely through environmental experience and then developed through it. Such features would be:

- the ability to freely detect information, with a sensitivity related to personal interest.

- the ability for language, to learn and to share understandings of the environment.

- the ability to reason from different perspectives, and so recognise different meanings.

- the ability to associate incoming information with information previously stored in different ways, with speed and accuracy being purely developed.

- the ability to devise different ways to store information in the memory, and so be more efficient.

- the ability to develop sensitivity in all these vital processes, being based on emotional experience, and

- the ability to learn to present conclusions in different ways to different people. This is the most misunderstood factor of the entire intelligence process, even though it does explain why people give inadequate responses, because they did not clearly understand the question.

- the abilities that make us human: to cry, to laugh, to feel hurt, to feel ashamed or embarrassed, to feel anger or even hatred, to lie and to cheat, to imagine and to dream, and most importantly — to love.

The gene codes for these features do not decide the quality of the feature that develops. They develop purely through experience.

In other words, all human beings are born with a gene design that allows them to have language, but there is no controlling factor within its genes (caused by natural variations or mutations) to predetermine any limit in how the feature could develop. Would intelligence (barring the examples we have seen) not so have evolved by the same manner, according to the Laws of Natural Selection? Let us consider this.

We know, of course, that DNA is apt to make errors in its coding. It is by such error that new species emerge to enable the life process to continue, as each form can adapt in a different way to the environment. This is the process of natural selection that Darwin referred to, and it is brought about by a mutation that enables some better means of adaptation to the physical environment.

The appearance of a different kind of sensor to detect environmental changes in a different way, or the evolution of a new form of limb to move differently, are the genetic shifts that Darwin used to explain natural selection. Yet, while such mutation can bring great consequence to a species, it does not occur too readily. In point of fact, a life form may be unchanged for many tens or hundreds of thousands of years. Indeed, our own genetic shift from Homo Heidelbergensis took place some 200,000 years ago. (We did not evolve from Neanderthal.)[293]

In the normal state of affairs, the DNA of each parent contains a variation of genetic instruction from their family lines. Thus, a parent will carry the coding for a feature from his or her father, which may be derived from the father's mother and so on further back. During gametogenesis this variation is constantly shuffling to create genetic diversity. In this way, any child they conceive will have their unique genetic identity.

However, variation in this context simply refers to alternative forms of instruction, as we have just pointed out. Without a mutation arising, which really sparks the natural selection Darwin referred to and which is extremely rare, these alternative genetic instructions may not necessarily bring operational difference to the feature they are responsible for.

A very simple example of this can be seen in the morphology of the eye. In a population there will be uncountable variations of the human eye. However, barring the inheritance of a trait such as myopia, all people will demonstrate a different proficiency with their sight due to the effects of diet/exercise/stress. So, with the exception of myopia, we have a very wide range of ability for vision derived from genotypes that are not directly responsible for this.

Earlier in our account, we saw how Feuerstein had disproven the Gestalt "Principles of Closure and Good Form," and so explained that by helping the child to control their emotions, they were caused to improve aspects of their eyesight. I would like to borrow a section from our book *Brain Plasticity*, to expand upon this issue of eyesight.

"So we find that a quality of attention guides the quality of perception, which in turn guides the qualities of all the cognitive processes that build upon this to exhibit a quality of intelligence.[294]

Evidence of how a quality of perception is related to a quality of academic performance, rather than intelligence, can be found in studies with myopic children.

There is a general awareness that myopic children tend to be academically attuned. This has led to the impression that myopia is related to high intelligence, and since this visual impairment often has a genetic basis, the impression is gained that high intelligence can be equally explained.[295]

However, it needs to be understood that the genetic base to myopia can be of very little consequence. An ophthalmologist suggested to me it may be about 20% responsible for this visual defect with diet and stress accounting for the difference. However, the known presence of a gene in an individual gives absolutely no knowledge if it is responsible for the performance that is witnessed, and so if that gene has anything to do with the impression gained of this individual.

In fact, far from having a genetic cause, Gallop sees myopia to be psychologically driven. As he wrote of this condition, it is "the tendency to shrink visual and perceptual space and to restrict the musculature (and often the emotions) while attempting to solve the problem of responding to visual stress."[296]

From this, we may understand that even should the gene component have a high responsibility for poor vision, the human being would have many tools available to make compensation for their inferior sight. After all, although there are 56 classifications of myopia,[297] they generally relate to a refractive inability, and the muscles supporting the eye and its lens can be taught to make compensation for this to create a new focusing ability.

This is exactly what Orlin Sorenson has demonstrated, and so explains how near-sightedness can be completely corrected through exercising the muscles of the eyes, such that a person of any reasonable age having a 20:80 vision has the potential to correct this to 20:20 to give themselves perfect vision.[298]

The ability for this, as Freud informed us, hangs entirely upon the psychology of the matter, which again echoes Gallop, and refers us back to the means to overcome critical periods as we have discussed.

Yet, the plasticity of vision is as little discussed as is the plasticity of intelligence for the same reason. Optometrists, like psychologists who sell IQ tests, make their bread and butter through convincing people that they need them to dispense artificial lenses, which compensate for their weak muscles. They seldom teach people how they could build up their eye muscle strength, so they would not need artificial lenses.

As we can see the discussion of myopia and intelligence needs to be brought into balance, because myopic children do not operate with the same confidence and quality of interaction as non-myopic children, when they are operating in an outside environment that is unstable and rapidly changing.[299] In "real life," therefore, it could be said that myopia creates a low intelligence, were it not for the fact that we associate the word "intelligence" only with the pen and paper world, and so fail to recognise a balance with what is happening inside and outside the classroom.

So, it is not that myopia is related to high intelligence, but that myopia is related to the academic world. This is an important distinction, because it opens us up to why a myopic child performs so well in school. Fuchs realised the answer to this, when he found the condition of near-sightedness to be easily associated with high intelligence (albeit academic studies) purely because of the techniques habitually developed in visual exploration.[300]

("...From our book *The Illusion of School*, we may add ".... Children, may it now be realised, do not naturally think as school desires of them. They have to learn to acquire proficiency in this, which they do by applying the competencies they know with the rules of school and how they use these. Consequently, some children come to recognise the codes that lead to this proficiency, and so relate to the world of these rules immediately. Others never do, as their interests take their minds to other realms of freedom and worlds of adventure.

Girls who are calmer settle into these rules more easily and often do better later in school because they are more sensitive to detail. Boys, more with a mind to kick a ball or climb a tree, tend to take less note of them, and so generally do not do so well with them as girls, save for those who are myopic, because, due to their perspective of the world, they are calmer in dealing with the relationships of information.....")

This brings us back to understanding that intelligence relies upon sensitivity, firstly to recognise or associate with information, and then to the stages with which it is processed and presented. These, as we have just seen, hang upon a psychological and so an emotional base.

The ability to perceive is, of course, only one part of the visual system, but when we think of the visual system, it is far more than being able to see. There is not, for instance, the ability for vision and a different ability to think, and so to have intelligence, because the process of thinking relies upon the information the brain receives from its external sensors. The understanding that the ability for vision and so the ability to think is unrelated, creates the impression that we naturally "know" the value of information we see. We do not. We need to learn of it and our proficiency in this comes from the emotional sensitivity we give to this learning....."

May we understand from these references that **while a varying gene instruction within a population may not cause a difference in the quality of a feature to operate, the environment in all its complexity certainly would.**

Let us extend this understanding of how our genes — allow our mind — to consciously control — the external environment — to control the internal environment — of not just the muscles about the eyes, — but more so the muscles within the entire body, that provide us with mobility.

In the example of a muscle, the gene design must be able to accommodate instant changes in the environment as the muscle works and requires nutrition. The case of how Charles Atlas transformed himself from a "scrawny weakling" to the most popular muscleman of his day is well recorded,[301] and shows how our impression of a gene design can change when the environment through which it materialises changes. The example of how a muscle works introduces us to understanding how an aspect of intelligence develops.

So, we inherit the genetic coding for two hands, eight fingers and two thumbs, and the normal environment does not change these features. However, the dexterity we develop with our fingers and thumbs is determined purely through the environment by the ways in which we use these. At birth, every muscle fibre is connected to the brain with two or more motor axons. In a process known as polyneuronal innervation, these axons are trimmed back by experience to leave only the one that has been used the most. Those axons that have not been physically used die off.[302]

We can see in this how our gene coding allows our mind to construct our motor systems, through our experiences.

This is not an insignificant point to raise, because it was by the evolution of being able to join thumb and forefinger together that enabled our early ancestors to be extremely sensitive in their awareness of objects.

Albrecht Durer

It may be, then, as Leaky postulated, that over millions of years the human brain evolved in size because of the higher sensitivity in thinking we can make, through our unique ability to join thumb and index finger.[303] No other species can do this.

It was through having this greater sensitivity than lower order animals, and by our higher ability for language, that our greater intelligence evolved. Intelligence, therefore, evolves through the species and through the individual by their sensitivity with the environment.

As Howell put it, "When the hand of "near man" began experimenting with sharp stones and clubs, cells in the brain developed more and more protoplasmic extensions, and hence connections with other nerve cells in response to this new activity. Through a somewhat similar mechanism, the brains of idle laboratory mice increase in weight two to three per cent when they are given interesting but perplexing tasks to perform and puzzles to solve."[304]

Indeed, it is only within the past 35 or so years that we have truly been able to grasp the extent to which the brain is able to form through the emotional and instructional world in which it develops. We have long witnessed how this is possible in animals, and many experiments on rats and monkeys have shown how their brains developed when they were given learning tasks.

One experiment showed how the brains of rats developed when they were encouraged to learn a new balancing task, such as walking up a sloping wire. The area of the brain known as the vestibular nuclei controls balance. In the case of these rats, their vestibular nuclei were found not only to contain a substantial increase in the amount of RNA through the learning of this task, but also a dramatic change in its composition.[305]

This increase in brain density is the result of brain cells growing and developing their connections through demand, and as it is for lower order animals so must it be ever more so for human beings.

We are led from this to begin to consider how the operation of brain cells, and so their efficiency, can be changed through the desire of the mind. As we will examine in *Brain Plasticity,* the ability of an individual to interact with their environment will depend upon the adjustments they make in their psychological state. It is this action that brings about changes in the strategies they use to interrogate and process information.

This was confirmed by researchers in 2015, who created a video game in which programmed artificial adaptive agents (called "animats") have to catch moving blocks of various sizes before they reach a target. These so named "animats" had been equipped with a basic brain system composed of eight nodes. two sensors, two motors and four internal computers that coordinate sensation, movement and memory.

These computers ran a code that acted as the "animats" DNA, and so enabled their "brain" to be wired in a particular way. It was found that differently coded "animats" were better or worse at catching the blocks before they could reach the target. The researchers selected the best catchers of each generation and allowed them to replicate.

After 60,000 generations, it was found that while all "animats" had evolved their brain wiring, those that had been given more complex versions of the game had developed more advanced and in particular very intricate neural pathways. By this experiment, the researchers were able to prove how vital the environment is in brain development and so in the construction of human intelligence.[306]

Intelligence is not a question of rapid response, but of developing sound structures and developing proficiency in these. Eysenck and Jensen, two disciples of Galton's theory, did not realise this when they tried to argue that intelligence is determined by genetic quality, and based their argument on the speed at which brain cells metabolise, or are able to transmit signals.[307] Yet, with the average neuron firing once every 5 milliseconds, explanation as to why one student is able to find the correct answer faster than others in their class cannot lie in an imagination that their neurons fire at the rate of 5.02 per millisecond, while those of another fire at 4.999' per millisecond.

What can explain why they know the answer, when 98% of the class have some incomplete understanding of it, lies in the connections of their neurons, as these were designed through the strategies they developed through their experiences. Anderson realised this when he wrote that even the simplest measure of a reaction time involves relatively complex processing systems, such as visual search and encoding and, of course, a quality of attention.

While this subject is really for our following book, we may note here that while lower IQ-scoring individuals, who normally show concentration problems, do appear to be slower in their reaction time than those who score higher, there is much evidence that reaction timing relies upon developed procedures and practices.[308] These relate to the development of systems, so that a quality of intelligence we find again, and again lies in an effectiveness with language — and through this sensitivity in interfacing with the environment.

Consider this with the very small percentage of human beings who have a genetic disorder, such as Down syndrome, for this condition tends to reveal a limitation in intelligence very early in childhood. However, through our lack of understanding of what intelligence is, we often make too quick and too ready an assessment of their capability for this. By their nature, such children are often extremely sensitive with their emotions and too easily withdraw from the faster competitive pace others live with. As they do this, they have difficulty relating to the world as we see it.

However, if the outside world can be made to slow down so that these human beings can gain their bearings with it, then they can learn to process their beautiful mind more eloquently and faster.

More simply, we need to realise how to develop our language skills to better understand the world as they do. Since we too readily see their world through our impression of it, we too little know how to bridge the gap that separates their world of understanding from ours, and so we seldom try. Those who do try have found that with patience and ingenuity, they have been able to bridge this gap.

In order for such children to learn how to move within our world, they need to be shown how to understand greater relationships with information. Thus, it is not to give details at the level we understand, but to break such information down into smaller parts and allow them to rebuild it with our guidance. It is not that they do not or cannot understand the greater picture, but more often that they failed to understand the smaller steps by which it became composed.

Such effort takes lots of love, time and patience to develop the appropriate skills, but as Reuven Feuerstein has shown with over a thousand case studies and 70 years in full working practice, children with learning disabilities can be transformed into children with learning abilities.[309]

It may be said that it is only when we work with human beings who appear limited, as I have found, that we can begin to realise what intelligence means to us. After all, it is only through the extent of the effort we must make to help them that we are caused to be more sensitive in our understanding of what intelligence is. It was through such sensitivity that Reuven came to understand the failing of IQ tests, and his realisation that they are not the infallible method of human assessment we have been led to believe they are.

In view of this, he created a means of assessing developmental changes in intelligence, which presents a totally different view of intelligence than the rigid and permanent impression we have gained of it through IQ tests. We give mention to the remarkable achievements of Reuven Feuerstein in the fourth book in this series: *For Parent For Teacher, Mediation: Crafting the ability of the child for school,* as we are drawn ever closer to understanding the true meaning of human intelligence.

However, when this depth of effort is not made, and it very normally is not, those with a genetic disorder are compared against those of high intelligence (Down Syndrome to Genius) to suggest that the differences between them occur because of stepped variations in genetic quality.

There is no evidence for this!

It is in the ignorance of this that the idea of "natural selection" in human ability, as it is inspired by Spencer's phrase, completely distorts what it means. The selecting factor in human affairs is not by nature, but by human evaluation processes that cannot be detached from some form of political design.

Thus, while "natural selection" infers a genetic process, the transference of this understanding into human evaluation creates a false sense of what is happening when the best performer is selected. It was with such ignorance as this that the term "Social Darwinism" became indiscriminately used to associate evolution with human ability -- after Joseph Fisher had used this term to discuss ownership of land in 1877.[310]

Our great error when we don't understand what this means is to assume all the variations we witness in an IQ test have a common base and so can be explained through each other. This should not be the case!

Any difference we observe between fully functional human beings and human beings who are cognitively not fully functional has to be seen as operating from different bases, as we have already explained. The problem is that the environment is so influential upon the gene design that it is not always easy to make a distinct classification with human beings. We may do this with Down Syndrome and those who incurred oxygen starvation in the birth process, because they usually have some difference in their general ability and physiology. However, there are other cases where this distinction is not so clear. Take the case of inbreeding, for example.

Inbreeding is said to produce individuals of low intelligence, but this is a much-confused area of discussion. Only a very few studies have been made of the effects of inbreeding on intelligence. Such studies were often made in societies where the population engaged in such marriages was extremely small, and little detached from the effects of socioeconomic circumstances, so it is very difficult to know the actual effect of inbreeding on their intelligence.[311]

Therefore, it is by the very act of comparing the limitations witnessed in those with genetic disorders or with those who incurred difficulties at birth, to the intelligence differences shown by those with normal family genetic variations, that a false impression is gained that intelligence varies genetically right through a population.

One is of a minor mutation (which requires special development), while all others are of normal variations whose effect may be very easily and totally overridden by the incredible influences of the environment, as we saw with the misunderstanding of polygenes.

So, may we be reminded that if the environment is so extensive, as it is with intelligence, then any act of intelligence by a normally born human being cannot be proven to be caused by an inferior or a superior gene design. All we may consider is the journey each has followed from the moment of their birth to the time when we seek to judge them.

- Therefore, we have no means to know, and so none to state that human intelligence varies genetically from zero to 200 -- as Terman caused us to believe in his intelligence stratification of the American society.

Long have we been raised on Galton's 19th-century theory that intelligence is directly related to inheritance, and yet we know today that intelligence has increased rapidly over the past few decades in every country of the world, without "any" genetic influence.[312] As we shall shortly discuss, Blair points out that this rise in global intelligence has been far too rapid to be explained through genetic selection.[313] Without an explanation in genetics for this global shift in intelligence, we are caused to realise that we still do not understand what the environment means in this.

Psychologists look upon the gene coding for intelligence and the environment through which it materialises as having a linear relationship. In the same way that they envisage that the genotypes of a plant can be known by controlling its environment, so they seek to determine the genotype of intelligence by testing babies whom they reason have not yet developed through environmental experience.

It is of the upmost importance, because we are really examining the development of children and not some theoretical discussion of what intelligence may or may not be on a piece of paper, that we realise how truly complex and determining the environment of intelligence is. It does not begin, as psychologists may reason, when the infant is able to reach for their favourite toy, or cry when they are shown a disturbing image instead of a secure one.

It begins soon after the egg is fertilised, and we have examined how the mental development of the baby, its personality, and so its intelligence is affected by both internal and external factors while they are still in the womb. Equally, the social and so psychological aspect of the environmental experience does not begin once the baby starts to babble. It begins the very instant the baby is born. We gave an example of this in the first pages of *The Illusion of Education,* when we saw how attention-deficiency disorders can arise in the newborn if they are deprived of facial contact from the mother immediately following birth.[314]

In our following book, we will build upon this to see how the personality of the child is shaped by the impressions they obtain in the womb, just as it develops after birth. It is by their personality, and how this is in accord or conflicts with those who raise them, that the infant will desire to challenge and so make understanding of their new world.

After all, any act of intelligence an individual makes is built upon emotional and psychological drives where they seek to preserve their identity in some social situation. In our following book, we discuss how the neurotransmitter cortisol plays its part in this, for example, a student feeling threatened in some manner by another student, or indeed by their teacher.

We may more simply explain here that the intelligence of the individual is really determined by the trillions of proteins that interact with each other, in every fleeting second of the living brain, as they meet those who convey love, sensitivity and confidence, and yet others who seek to devalue the self-esteem of their personality and cause them emotional pain.

This is the hidden reality of intelligence. It is alive, fluid, and capable of changing dramatically, as it enables the individual human being to interact, adapt, and survive in the environments they engage and move through. In the very simplest sense, this is to say that we are designed by nature to be individualistic through our experiences. It is only social design that groups us into categories for political purposes, and seeks to define the use we can be through the singular word "intelligence".

To begin to break free of this design, we should re-examine what Johannsen meant when he invented the term "phenotype", and how the environment can really affect the order and purpose of the deoxyribonucleic acids we inherit. To do this, we should stop thinking of solid genes and rigid environmental information, and come to think in terms of chemicals being affected by chemicals — because this is what it really all comes down to as we found with epigenes.

Chapter TwentySix

The Mystery of the Environment

Although Johannsen had discovered the effect of the environment in the early 1900s, it was to be many decades before we really understood the link between the gene code and "what we witness." This link, of course, is the protein, and we saw how amino acids are pulled into shape by RNA to create this.

A problem with defining a protein lies not just with the complexity of its chemical arrangement, or in the tremendous activity it is constantly moving through, but just as much in its shape. Proteins exist in highly complex configurations, and when these are altered, as they can too easily be, they readily change the phenotype, and so whatever we think the gene is supposed to be accountable for. The case of thalidomide children painfully expresses the point.

Apart from the "wrong" chemicals we place into our body (alcohol and gases from burnt nicotine etc), it is the normal food and drink we consume that provides the DNA with the means to build our body, maintain it, and allow it to learn how to function. We may think that our body "just" works, but any part of our body that interacts with the outside world, from our homeostatic regulation to our behaviour and our intelligence, develops to operate through processes that are highly responsive to changes in the environment.

Our problem is that we take all these responses for granted. We shiver when we get cold, but we do not stop to think of what is actually happening inside our bodies to cause us to shiver. Nor do we think of the biological purpose of why this is happening. We, of course, have the same mind with intelligence -- something happens and we respond.

What we shall begin to realise in this chapter is how that response is given fuel for energy. It is our great mistake to think that a process is pre-determined and just works better or less so by the energy it has. The homeostatic system, for example, is highly dependent upon emotional feedback. It is significant to understand, then, that the energy we obtain from the chemicals we consume gives energy for different processes to be recognised, adopted, and refined by experience.

Accordingly, many of us drink coffee when we are working to give fuel to our thinking process. I cannot even begin to imagine how many gallons I have gone through since I started writing these books. Coffee helps us to concentrate, we know this, just as we know that the sugar we add to the coffee gives us the mental stamina to think longer. Yet, we do not think about how the concentration and the stamina we obtain from this coffee and sugar improve our chances of seeing better relationships within the information we are working with. As each small step evolves into another, so we build up a larger reservoir of clearer information, and through trial and error, devise new ways to recognise where and how to apply this. We can understand from this the importance of the food and drink we consume, and so of the relationship to this in the ways we select and process information.

The relationship of food and intelligence was too little realised, if it was known at all, when psychology created the belief that intelligence is inherited and is measurable. Nor was there at that time any real interest in how information can be understood through strategies. The child was largely regarded to be born with their intelligence, and knowledge of how their intelligence worked more often came through observations of how animals responded to food and pain.

As we saw in *The Illusion of Education*, an early psychologist by the name of Edward Thorndike based his laws of how children learn and how they should be taught (The Laws of Effect, Readiness and Exercise) not on studying how children learn, but on his observations of rodent behaviour in his experimental laboratory.[315]

It was, however, to take nearly a hundred years from the publication of Galton's *Hereditary Genius,* before Niremberg and Matthaei discovered how DNA can be read out as proteins and so how geneticists could gain a real understanding of the complexity of the environment. After all, while we cannot know which proteins are working and how well they work as the child is thinking, we may understand far more now that in their mystery lies the key to understanding intelligence. If we are to understand intelligence, then we must understand it through the chemistry of the environment.

Psychologists try to understand intelligence by classifying its environment. So, they give grades to the profession of the parents, the quality of the school the child goes to, or some type of stimulation the child was influenced by, etc. This is very helpful to develop the child, but it is completely wrong to think that the child may be evaluated through this information. The reality is that the environment could be simplified only into the way chemical stimulants drive neurons, as these derive from sources too innumerable to be known let alone be calculated.

If, for example, we were to try to classify the environment, we may only do so in the most vague of senses, by considering it through two forms: One outside the body and one inside.

The Outside Environment: This will be the different quality of experiences encountered -- the places visited, the books read, or the computer stimulation received and yet far more the interest given to each experience and the relevance gained from it. It will also be the variety of people time was shared with, and the quality gained through each interaction. It will further be the physical problems encountered, and the guidance received in solving them; the strategies gained, the insights realised, the goals selected, and the love received or the lack of it. In short, it will be the sensitivity inspired and realised to train the sensors to capture and process information, through all the experiences imaginable on paper and in life. All this, while the individual struggles to understand themselves through those they encounter or are caused to share their learning with, as the intelligence of their mind is shaped through the behaviour of others.

The Inside Environment. This will be the chemicals in the brain as the body was forming, and throughout its life as it operates. It will be the chemicals created and activated in the brain through all the emotional experiences it has had, just as the mind lives and holds on to its dreams. It will be the chemical intake, the food and drink consumed to physically support the brain, and it will be the levels set and gained in the production of the brain's chemistry. It will be the state of the emotion as it evolved in the individual and the relationship of emotional chemicals to cognitive ones, as these give design to neurons; how they connect, and to the overall operation of neurotransmitters.

*

Therefore, when we think of the environment for intelligence, we should not think of how to classify a child through discrete social experiences, but instead see these experiences as a holistic product of:

- The Inside Environment = chemical makeup as derived from consumption + emotional or psychological overseeing of the cognitive process, and

- The Outside Environment = strategies of interaction + variety and quality of intellectual and behavioural experiences.

Through the many pages of this book, we have found suggestion as to what the outside environment entails, but in our following book, we will examine how visual images are detected and processed, and so how they bring neurons into networks and how sensitivity is brought to the overall processing of intelligence through the emotional drives of the mind.

The remainder of this chapter will look at how intelligence develops through the internal environment of the body. We have mentioned in this how the genes do not just create the intelligence of the child. So it is not the case that from birth the child begins to understand the world through that which they are born with. All the parts of our nervous system, including the brain, are formed through the changing environment and rapidly fluctuating chemistry of the body.

Therefore, immediately at conception, the designs of the genotypes will come into play, but the ability of these designs to become physical will be reliant upon the chemicals available. To understand that the gene design does not simply happen, we should understand how that design can go wrong with surprising ease. As we have just mentioned, a very sad example of how the gene design can be altered through the environment was realised when a drug was placed on the market in 1957, and administered to pregnant mothers to alleviate morning sickness.

The chemicals in the drug altered the normal chemicals in the cells of the mother (in effect, they inhibited the development of vital proteins) and caused her unborn baby to wrongly construct their genetic design. Thalidomide children were born with severely deformed limbs. Arms were often very short or absent, which caused fingers to sprout from the shoulders.[316] **We have here an example of how the normal genotypes for arms, hands, and fingers were completely changed out of recognition by the environment.**

To a lesser extent, although upon the same principle, a pregnant mother who smokes heavily or drinks too much alcohol can disturb the balance of the chemicals in her foetus, and cause a change to the normal construction of their gene design. We witness this when her child is born smaller in stature than is expected, and later in their life develop signs of defect. A 2014 study suggested that pregnant mothers using Tylenol, for fever reduction, increase the likelihood of their child developing ADHD.[317]

Lead poisoning is another example that can affect the cognitive and behavioural patterns of the infant or adult.[318]/[319]/[320] It is a disturbing thought to add here that between 14 to 20% of the total lead exposure to people in America is attributed to drinking tap water.[321] Very clear examples of how the environment can totally change the gene design after birth can be found in cases of metabolic disorders.

Phenylketonuria, or PKU, for example, is a genetic disorder in which the body is unable to process the amino acid phenylalanine. Instead of being eliminated from the body, unused phenylalanine builds up in the blood as a neurotoxin and leads to severe intellectual disability. However, this neurotoxicity can be completely prevented by a diet that is low in phenylalanine, which occurs in proteins.

Another example of a genetic condition that can be directly controlled through the environment is that of galactosemia. Galactosemia is a metabolic disorder that affects the body's ability to break down galactose, which is a sugar found in dairy products. Galactosemia, just as PKU, can produce severe mental retardation, and just like PKU this can be prevented by a controlled diet. In the case of galactosemia this is achieved by avoiding food and drinks containing galactose.[322]

These metabolic disorders provide clear examples of how the environment can control the manifestation of the genotype.

A very important feature we may introduce here is that of personality. Personality plays a determining role in how a child desires to interact or struggles with information, especially when another has encoded it with their personality. Learning, as we shall see, is very much an affair of chemistry. Therefore, while personality is really decided through after birth influences, there is growing evidence that its roots take place during the foetal period. Axness, we have already mentioned, describes how personality can be determined during the foetal period by the levels of stress hormones, heart rate, blood pressure, and emotional states of the mother.[323] Janov equally explained how "sensations experienced by the foetus, especially in the later stages of development, are the precursors of feelings."[324]

In essence, it may be said that we are largely unaware of the life experiences of the foetus, and certainly the meanings these may have on their mental functioning. It is not unreasonable, however, to consider Sherwood's account,

"The foetus (on an unconscious level) is aware of changes in its environment, both its physical environment, which is the mother's womb and physical body, as well as the psychic environment which includes to a large extent the inner environment of the mother: her energy level, emotional maturity, her level of stress and her mental and emotional condition."[325]

Evidence that "environmental" chemicals can dramatically change the personality in the earliest stages of life came from earlier studies with primates. One study found that pregnant females who were administered testosterone produced offspring that were notably more aggressive than the offspring of the control group. This finding was substantiated by another study that showed how male rats acquired and maintained female behavioural characteristics throughout their life cycle, because they were given oestrogen immediately after birth.[326]

While these results may seem obvious, it is important to grasp how they demonstrate that environmental chemicals can change what we think the purpose of the gene is.

It arises from this that while the effect of chemical changes upon the gene design can be most marked prior to birth, it is misleading to assume that once born, the individual is only marginally affected by environmental changes.

Throughout the life cycle, the phenotype is only ever the effect of the environment upon the gene design. Think in this not that a body is made up of trillions of cells all linked together, but rather that those cells are continually reforming and replacing themselves, something like 50,000 a second, with each and every change being decided by the chemicals available to them for the processes they must undergo.

Magazines and the media often make declarations about how food improves IQ. However, there is much confusion about what this meaning implies, for we have already pointed out the danger of explaining intelligence as IQ. However, let us move to consider how intelligence actually does develop through the food we consume.

It seems obvious, of course, that intelligence is related to the food we eat. We can reason this because we realise how the body and so the efficiency of the brain is dependent upon the quality of nutrition it obtains. Thus, it is reasoned that poorer children do not have the same mental stamina as richer children, who are better fed. This implies all too simply that they have less energy in their lessons, which affects their ability to concentrate and to learn. However, once we begin to understand what intelligence is, we will understand more of how and why different qualities of nutrition affect its performance. How it does this was brought home to me when I did a normal detoxification course.

As the days of my fast passed, I became increasingly aware that my perception of things became less stable. My ability to concentrate became less, as my mind drifted more easily. Things I could normally remember now seemed absent in my mind. All in all, I saw less point in doing the things I did.

This fasting, of course, created an extreme situation for my body, especially as I sought to accelerate the cleansing process by walking a number of miles every day, but it was only through this experience that I witnessed the real effect of poor nutrition in the body. As my mental faculties deteriorated over these very few days with no nutrition, the effect of low nutrition on the mental abilities of children over many, many years became all too obvious.

In the classroom and in learning, they will, for instance, be less able to monitor the movement of information than a child better fed. This is to say, they may see less clearly what is written on the board. After all, the relationship between eyesight and nutrition is well recognised.[327] Since the body's senses tend to work together, difficulty focusing with their eyes could affect their ability to listen to the words and so the meanings of their teacher.

We may also suggest they will begin to read a page in their textbook or begin a math equation, but before a better-fed child has completed their purpose, they will have drifted to other thoughts. Very importantly, they will too little check what they are doing as they do it, because they see little purpose to this and so create more errors and display a lower performance. Stamina is not just physical strength; it is also for the brain and the associated mind to have endurance in the systems of interrogation, recognition, analysis, and association it has developed. All this will become clearer as we move through our discussion in *Brain Plasticity: How the Brain Learns Through the Mind to Create Intelligence.*

While I make no suggestion here that anyone reading this should fast, and if they ever do it should only be done under professional guidance, I wish to stress the point that we need to educate parents more in the importance of a daily balanced diet. The issue is not so in what we call socio-economic divides, which implies rich and poor and so different families able to afford different qualities of nutrition, but in that lower socio-economic families are less aware of the necessity of a balanced diet. After all, fresh fruit and vegetables can be purchased very cheaply, compared with processed frozen dinners. In the UK, Jamie Oliver produces excellent TV shows promoting this awareness.[328]

More needs to be done to redress this problem, by, for example, discussing with parents the need for their children to have a good, healthy breakfast. While we know that breakfast is the most important meal of the day, teachers will also know how too few of their students receive this daily. In one university class, I was astonished to discover that only 20% of my 134 students had eaten something since they had woken up that day.

There is a clear need for parents and teachers to be more aware of the importance of the quality of food in enabling the brain to function, intelligence to develop, and so that students can perform better in their lessons. Let us continue to understand why.

Interest in how food affects our health became a popular topic during the 1980s. Much of this was due to Jean Carper's highly influential book *The Food Pharmacy*. In her book, Jean referred to studies at M.I.T. that sought to show, amongst other things, how intelligence could be influenced by food.

One study centred on tyrosine, a naturally occurring amino acid in fish. This study found that, as the dosage of tyrosine was increased, both the neurotransmitters dopamine and norepinephrine increased their activity level between brain cells. This enabled higher levels of response that proved the old adage that fish food is brain food. A further study was made on the effect of caffeine as a mental stimulant. This was noted to increase the speed of thinking, of concentration, and of accuracy in mental performance.[329]

As our awareness of how food could affect intelligence developed, consideration was given to how a poor diet affected the performance of low socio-economic children in school, and ultimately, their intelligence.[330] Of the seven studies that examined the effects of vitamin and mineral supplements, five of these reported substantial improvements in non-verbal tasks at school. This academic improvement was simply brought about through an improved diet.[331]

More recently, Smithers has demonstrated that the dietary patterns of infants are highly influential in the development of their later intelligence.[332] To this, we may note that a recent study of 3,000 men found that high levels of vitamin D enabled them to perform better in memory and information processing tests. The suggestion arose that this higher performance may have come about by the vitamin D boosting antioxidant levels, which, in effect, detoxified their brain, enabling it to operate more efficiently.[333]

All of these studies, and the many more that have been made on the dietary and stimulative backgrounds of children from different social levels, were brought to a very significant meaning by a research paper published in 2015. According to Gabreli, MRI brain scans were made of 23 students from lower-income families and 35 from wealthier ones. The scans clearly revealed that the students who were raised on a healthier diet and through greater stimulative factors affecting their development had far thicker occipital and temporal lobes than the students who were less developed nutritionally and academically.[334]

While the occipital lobe is solely responsible for vision, the extra development in the temporal lobe is important to note because this lobe is highly responsible for aspects of behaviour and memory, and most importantly the understanding of language. The Brain Environment Complex Theory, as we introduce it, examines why language is the seat of intelligence and how it matures through sensitivity in awareness.

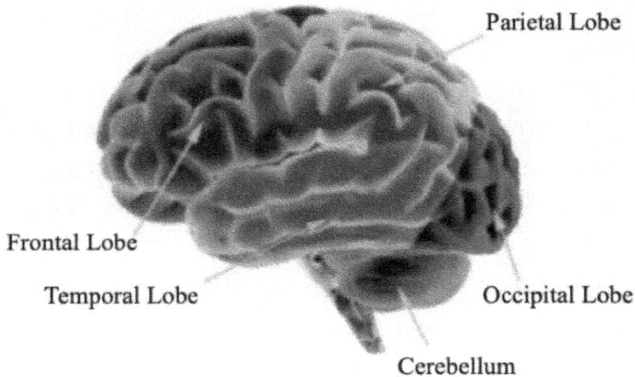

Courtesy of Brainhealth and Puzzles.

These studies raise an important understanding in how intelligence is affected by food, and so how a socio-economic diet can be related to intelligence. It may be generally said from this that children in wealthier families develop their intelligence partly through a better diet than may be available to children in poorer families. This gives an interesting perspective to Murray and Herrnstein's argument, in their book *The Bell Curve,* of Hispanic and African-American children from poor backgrounds gaining poor grades in school because of their supposedly lower genetic quality.

However, the descriptions arising in the media and on the Internet that relate IQ to diet are not strictly correct. As we have laboured to understand through many pages, IQ, as a measure of permanent quality in intelligence, does not exist. So, it is not that particular food improves intelligence permanently, or that a deficiency in some food lowers it permanently.

What changes through diet is the performance of intelligence, as the chemicals released from such better food improve concentration and raise energy efficiency. With this controlled energy comes a host of possibilities relating to the improved monitoring of information, to the better recognition of errors, and so the realisation of more possibilities by which information becomes better defined and processed. While such improvements are as transient as their cause, they do give suggestion as to how the short-term and the long-term performance of intelligence can be improved.

Since much of the concern about intelligence is related to the child in their school performance, we can see from this how the mind of a child loses mental energy in a lesson, and so how that energy level could be raised by allowing them to eat and to drink during the actual learning process. For the convenience of the school, it divides the daily schedule of students into breaks. Children will have a short break in the morning and again in the afternoon, and they will have a lunch break. Yet, these breaks are really created for the teachers, and set about their routines to enable them to prepare for different lessons.

- The thought that the active learning brain of the child needs a constant supply of energy intake does not exist in the mentality of the general school. It naturally follows from this that neither does the school understand how the child's brain learns, nor the factors that greatly contribute to the differences in the performance of children in a class.

As unconventional as it is, but considering that the brain needs oxygen and sugar to operate more efficiently, I always encourage my students to eat and drink during the lesson, and to move about sensibly as they need to obtain fresh oxygen. This is a practice that does improve attention, interaction, and questioning. My experiences assure me that students do learn better with this opportunity. Of course, it needs to be added that they must learn to be respectful of each other and of the teacher while they eat or move. We discuss this further, where we talk about classroom tactics, in other books of this series.

Consider otherwise how a child loses concentration with a tired mind caused by lack of energy, or lack of fresh air. Points of a lesson they could otherwise have observed slip by unnoticed. With patchy information, the ability of the student to translate the story of the teacher to their understanding of it deteriorates. Since one lesson builds upon another, see how the errors of an earlier lesson cause errors in those that follow, and so how a lower value of performance is exhibited.

We are prompted to realise here that any learning situation has its own energy factor. The personality of the teacher, that of other students, the environment of the room, all these have an energy factor that is imposed upon the learner. One student may find this energy complements theirs, and so they benefit from this by understanding and remembering information more easily than one who feels at odds with the energy of this environment. If this is so in school, then it is certainly so in the home environment of the child, and has been from the moment they were born.

This short reasoning attempts to suggest how the environment is far, far more complex and by suggestion far, far more determining in the development of intelligence than psychometric researchers have led us to believe, as they try to measure it with their hypothetical reasoning set about a quality they believe the individual inherited. However, and in having said this, let us consider the relationship of the mind, rather than the physical brain, with the environment and then the body.

One of the problems we have when we think about "the body," and so the brain and then intelligence, is that we too readily think only of the external environment. We understand, for example, how being out in the sun too long can dry our skin and cause us to look older, although we little think of what happens to our brain when we consume too much alcohol. The effect is the same. The phenotype can change drastically. So, when we think of the environment, we think of the movement of information outside of the brain, but not of the emotional changes the mind is constantly moving through as it processes information.

We still think of intelligence as we do a plant, in that we believe there is a ratio between the DNA and the environment. This is wrong for many of the reasons we have already discussed, but what is greatly missed in this reasoning is how psychology drives intelligence. We may think back in this to Uldrich discussing curiosity, self-control, grit, and risk-taking. We can easily witness how psychology causes physical changes in our body, as hormones, which relate to emotional states, can and do change the phenotype. We see this in the expression of a person's face as they communicate to us their feelings of happiness, sadness, anger or frustration. The awareness of how a phenotype design (as in facial muscles) can change through an emotional change, gives insight into how some genotype designs are affected by mental and so emotional processes.

While these changes are completely transient, moods do become habit forming and so each person's face tends to reflect their reasoning upon the world about them. While most of us show an impartial face, ready to change as circumstances do, some view the world positively or negatively, and we can read this very clearly in their beaming face or one sagged with worry.

A remarkable example of how thought processes can change the physiology of cells can be found in how cancer tumours have been halted through positive thinking.[335] It is medically recognised that patients who "will" themselves to be better may become so with no explanation other than their cognitive thoughts releasing chemicals that react with the chemicals at the core of the problem.[336] Jose Silva has developed a system that enables mind power to shape the health of the body, and to date, has helped over six million people.[337] If this sounds a little unreal, consider how well-known the opposite effect is, where stress can induce psychosomatic illnesses or trigger cancer growth.[338]

Therefore, the way we think can alter physical phenotypes as our thoughts develop through experiences. Our thoughts, of course, develop and are modified through language, which has an emotional base. Yet, Galton never understood this as he embarked upon his mission to save civilisation. To Galton, everything had to come down to inheritance, since this was the means by which he strove to explain the value of society recognising the natural right for a few to govern the many.

We have seen how Galton sought to manage this purpose by his use of Quetelet's law of accidental causes, which he fashioned to the law of deviation from the average. Let us consider now the validity of his application of this to human intelligence and so understand better how environmental experiences, in their uncountable numbers, give shape and colour to the intelligence of the human being. .....

Chapter TwentySeven
Revealing the Myth

Anything will give up its secrets if you love it enough. Not only have I found that when I talk to the little flower or to the little peanut they will give up their secrets, but I have found that when I silently commune with people, they give up their secrets also -- if you love them enough.

George Washington Carver

As Carver so indirectly informs us, we can find the secret to developing the intelligence of anyone, child or adult, if we can give them enough love that allows them to open up their history of understandings and insecurities. This, we shall come to find, is what I refer to in *The Art of Sensitivity in Awareness*. Regrettably, however, we do not see intelligence this way. We have been greatly raised through a collective mind to see it only as a singular feature that, to all intents and purposes, seems most logical to be one we are born with.

This understanding that we have is rooted in Galton's argument of a small faction of the population naturally governing the rest, which he legitimised through his claim of intelligence being inherited in accordance with his law of deviation from the average. This law, as we by now well understand, is based on degrees of ability that move away from a centralised average, and in becoming more recognisable are said to be more definable. In this way, it identifies with the imbecile and with the genius at different extremities, and so claims that their positioning, as all between them, is as much evidence of their inheritance as it is their status in society.

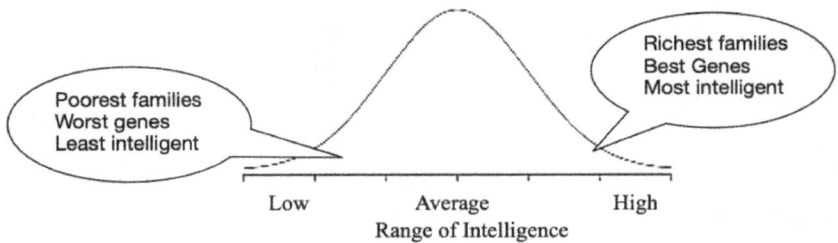

Range of Intelligence

The problem with this is that the genes involved in intelligence are very difficult to identify, because the environment obscures the purpose they have. In fact, there is no evidence that gene codes associated to intelligence vary continuously as Galton had to believe they did to prove his theory of deviation from the average.

As we have explained, all that social scientists have done and still do is to take the example of a human being who has some noticeable cognitive difficulty (caused by a gene mutation) and compare them to others who were born with no obvious difficulty, and use the inability of one to explain how ability varies in all those tested. We saw how this reasoning was a fundamental mistake in Quetelet's philosophy and how it remains so with attempts to understand the genetic origins of intelligence.

However, despite Galton's mid-19th-century reasoning that inherited ability varies so neatly either side of the average, which became so conveniently described through the Bell Curve graph, there is another kind of distribution that very few people know of. The Paretian Distribution Curve, as we shall now examine, is far more valid in describing human ability than the Bell Curve.

In 2012, two researchers, named O'Boyle and Aguinus, came to the conclusion, after examining the performance abilities of 633,263 researchers, entertainers, politicians, and amateur and professional athletes, divided into 198 samples over 5 studies, that 94% of the groups they examined did not follow Galton's pattern of distribution about the average in the abilities they displayed![339]

Instead, these researchers found that performance, and so apparent ability just as intelligence, can be explained to vary differently through the Paretian Distribution Curve than it does through the Bell Curve, which we have come to believe is the only possible way to explain distribution. It is not!

The characteristics of the Paretian Distribution are very different to those of the Bell Curve, for in this, and in general terms, 90 per cent of the population fall below the average position, while only 10 per cent rise above it. (Ability is shown on the y axis and population on the x axis, which is the opposite of that displayed in the Bell Curve.)

This is very clear if we look at how the population is distributed in the graph on the following page. Here, we can see how a notably small percentage of the population forms the very high (or above normal) ability, while the lower performers are spread out fairly evenly below the average.

Paretian Distribution Curve

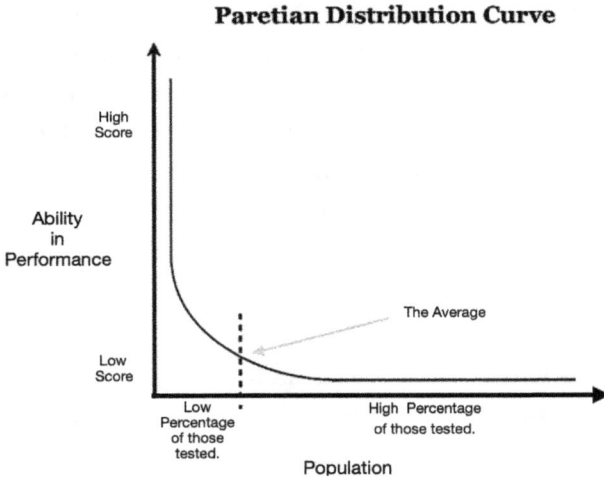

As Bersin points out, this distribution causes the concept of the average to become completely meaningless.340 The concept of the average, we may recall, was fundamental to Galton in his explanation of how intelligence is naturally distributed in a population.

Consider, then, that from the way ability is explained through the Paretian Distribution, **that distribution is not comparable to any genetic variation we have been caused to expect.** This is an extremely important point to understand.

Accordingly, it can be reasoned that as gene codes vary, the most common type would form an average, with those of lower and higher qualities moving away from this -- as the Bell Curve is used to demonstrate.

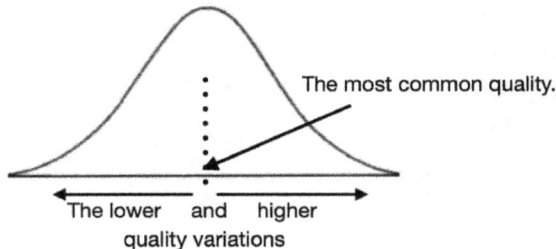

However, **if the variation that we actually witness** (the phenotype) **does not follow this particular genetic pattern, then it means that the effects of the environment have overridden the differences in the gene codes.**

We saw a very simple example of how this occurs earlier in our discussion, where we demonstrated how the exact same gene code produced five totally different phenotypes (graphs) when it was developed through five different environments.

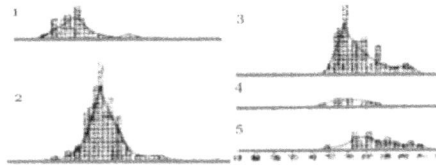

If the *imagined* variations of a gene code (because they cannot be known) do not match the test scores witnessed, there is no evidence that variations in a gene code can be related to the abilities displayed. In other words, the test scores can be reasoned to be caused purely by environmental factors.

Accordingly, when very specific skills of ability are measured, as was demonstrated by O'Boyle and Aguinus, it is reasonable to state that the differences in the performances they witnessed did not occur because of differences in genetic qualities, but purely through **experience, conditioning and effort.**

It is relevant to note here, as we discussed earlier, that actual intelligence tests and in particular IQ tests do not measure such specific skills as were examined by O'Boyle and Aguinus, and instead lay their questions around factors that can be more manipulated to social and cultural design, as they more easily meet political agendas.

Thus, it CANNOT now be said that intelligence varies in accord with genetic differences in a population. This means, of course, that the belief that differences in individual intelligence are based on individual inherited qualities now has no basis. Therefore, we can see that explanation for differences in intelligence (barring those of a genetic mutation) can only be explained in some other way, which must be environmental. We shall shortly return to understand the meaning of the Paretian Distribution Curve in evaluating intelligence.

However, this short discussion does support our realisation that the genotype of intelligence is far, far narrower than the scope of the environment. In turn, this forces us to realise that not only do we fail to understand the true complexity of the environment in intelligence, but that we more fail to realise how decisive the environment really can be in the development of intelligence -- especially, once we include the driving force of the mind, if not so the human spirit. This brings us to a very important point. .....

And so of Geniuses

May we now realise that through the efforts of Galton, Pearson, Spearman, Stern, Goddard and Terman, and so the forces which propelled their work into every facet of our understanding, how we have been deeply impressed to believe that we can look at one extreme of intelligence, such as a mentally retarded person, and then at the other extreme, a genius, and believe that we can calculate the point of intelligence of any individual between these two abilities.

This is totally impossible, for while we can know that some aspects of mental retardation may be genetically transferred, we cannot know the genetic origins of the genius.

If we ignore Galton's argument of achievement through eminent families, because of the very obvious factor of influence and look at pure intelligence, we can see that the father of Leonardo Da Vinci was nothing more than a wealthy lawyer. Newton's father was a normal farmer. Einstein's father was not a very successful businessman. Mozart's father was an undistinguished composer, and Steven Hawking (regarded to be one of the most intelligent people on our planet, until his demise in 2018) had a father who was a normal medical researcher, whose father was a farmer.

All these fathers were normal people from normal stock, yet their sons became geniuses. However, and most importantly, they did not do so because of some genetic mutation, because the sons and daughters who followed them did not display the same level of extraordinary intelligence. The genius of these people can only be explained through particular environmental experiences that drove them to personally develop a unique level of intellectual insight.

Hawking gives reason into how the genius can arise, when he explained how he had been an idle layabout until he was diagnosed with ALS Syndrome and given two years to live. With panic to make the most of what he believed was left of his short life, Hawking drove himself with unimaginable vigour to learn.

So, instead of thinking of such geniuses as of natural ability, we need to realise this ability developed within each of them through their devotion or endeavour not to give up on puzzles they came across. Edison, by further example, was a genius to many and invited to talk upon every aspect of social life, including how to raise babies.

Yet, Edison's genius, his invention of the light bulb, did not happen in one instant. He did not give up trying and went through 10,000 attempts before he succeeded. The famous atomic scientist Niels Bohr, a genius in his own right, wrote: "An expert is a man who has made all the mistakes." The most famous 'genius' may be Einstein, but Einstein explained that he was no genius and owed his success to three great character traits. These were persistence, perseverance and and passion.

I think Aaron Swartz got it right when he wrote:

"Be curious. Read widely. Try new things.
What people call intelligence just boils down to curiosity."[341]

Thus, it was not that Einstein was born to be a genius, but that he developed the very qualities that enabled him to be thought of as a genius, through whatever environmental experiences he personally encountered.[342]

As we would find with any said genius, it was solely through their labour and their complete dedication that they gained insight to a problem that others do not see or know how to solve. As we see again, and again, it is simply a matter of the psychology of the mind realising the need to drive its intelligence. Experiments with animals have clearly proven this.

With over fifty years of research into health, Howell points out how domestication in animals produces a tranquillising effect on their brain, reducing its size compared to the brain size of the same animal living in the wild.[343] If we put aside the factor of diet here in order to focus on activity, although diet does play an important role, as we found out, we may draw a parallel in brain cell development between wild and domestic animals, and active and passive domestic individuals.

This would explain why a child who is born to parents who give little stimulation and raise them in a poorly stimulating environment causes their brain to experience such inactivity that their intelligence will be lower than that of a child who is more stimulated. Think back here to the mothers on the bus and in the doctor's surgery in *The Illusion of School.*

Yet, in having said this, and as we will find out in our following book, the brain has a tremendous ability to reactivate itself. So, if the mind of the individual should be actively stimulated, and most importantly, they deeply desire this to occur, their brain cells would create new connections, and with this, they would raise their intelligence. Hawkins had given wonderful testimony to this possibility.

While it was Lynn who first suggested that intelligence is not static, and is globally increasing,[344] it was James Flynn who devoted the effort to bring greater realisation that IQ scores have increased over a number of decades on a worldwide basis.[345] Flynn's greater discovery earned him the recognition that this phenomenon be named after him. Accordingly, this stepped generation rise in IQ is referred to as the Flynn Effect.

The Flynn Effect cannot, however, be explained through genetics. As Blair points out, this rise in global intelligence has been too rapid to be explained through genetic selection.[137] Therefore, this global rise in intelligence can only be explained through the effects of developments in technology (computer stimulation, better diet, etc.).

Studies by Fox and Mitchum can be shown to support this explanation, for they found that:

"Recent born individuals have adopted an approach to analogy, that enables them to infer higher level relations, requiring roles that are not intrinsic to the objects, that constitute initial representations of items."

They further added that "individuals born around 1940 are less able to map objects at higher levels of relational abstraction than individuals born around 1990."[346] It may be noted that 1990 was a time when most young children had access to computers in their home, and were becoming increasingly computer literate with access to untold knowledge that inspired their curiosity, imagination and creativity.

Accordingly, we find that children of today are generally more intelligent than their parents, because of the greater awareness of information that is readily available to them. This information, of course, is a representation of language. Therefore, the technology and media entertainment of today has given to children and so to adults what many in the 19th century always feared it would do. It raised the intelligence of the masses.

It had been with the same concerns that Johannes Gutenberg's Press was held in the 15th century, and rightly so because it gave a dramatic rise in the adult literacy rate throughout Europe. This brought with it a freedom of thought that raised the intelligence of a generation. Most significantly, it gave the means for Martin Luther's break from the Catholic church and sparked the Knights' Revolt, the Peasants' War, and turned Europe into a religious blood bath for nearly two centuries.[347]

The more the mind engages a stimulating environment, with emotional interest, the more their brain physically develops. We can prove this with rats. It is only because of the politics behind education that we struggle to believe the same with human beings, and hold on to Galton's legacy.

Yet, and for all the reasons we have explored and understood in this book, **there is no basis to believe that the genes account for the differences in intelligence between individuals who do not inherit a dysfunctional coding or display some limitation in the operation of their nervous system.**

As we are caused to recall Goddard's fabrication of the Moron gene, and how this led to the "legal" sterilisation of hundreds of thousands of innocent human beings, we should be aware of the good work of Reuven and his son Rafi Feuerstein to develop the intelligence of mentally impaired individuals. Together, they have proven beyond any doubt that children who are less able to react as others may do, because of a gene abnormality or some dysfunction of their nervous system, can be taught to exploit the vast reservoir of potential skills they do have. Once they are taught to understand other ways of thinking, such human beings can develop far beyond what was previously thought possible of them.

In fact, once any human being is taken out of the environment that contains them, all predictability of what is said of their limited potential disappears. The concept that intelligence is reasonably stable and predictable throughout the lifetime came about without understanding the true effect of the environment, how the mind seeks to conform for social acceptance, but how it can readily adapt if a new environment so demands it. I first realised this when I joined the army and was literally 'kicked out' of the lethargy of thinking I had been conditioned into.

Psychologists have long sought to explain that intelligence testing originated with the French psychologist Alfred Binét, to detract awareness to how it actually began with Goddard's and Terman's political stratification of the American society. But, this is wrong, for Binét knew that intelligence could never be tested. He also knew that intelligence is highly developmental, and that it is not static as psychologists claim it to be, to give validity to their IQ tests.

As Alfred Binét insisted over 100 years ago, all we may do is to recognise that when some facet of intelligence appears wrong, that we seek to understand how to improve the ability of the individual to enable them to better interact with the environment.

In fact, it was because of my own experiences spread over forty years of improving the ability of students of all ages, from infants to adults, that I wanted to write this book -- because I wanted to explain why I have never found a student's intelligence to be limited to some factor they were supposed to have inherited.

To me, improving the ability of a student was only a matter of firstly gaining their emotional trust and then re-educating the parts in their learning they had not understood. With some students it was only a matter of going back a few weeks, but with others we had to share a journey that went back many, many years to uncover how they came to see the world the way they did and so why they saw themselves in it the way they do.

None of this is rocket science. It is only a question of refusing to accept what is witnessed and to wonder how the student's skills could be rebuilt. I never believed that any normally born human being is restricted in their ability to learn through a factor they were supposed to have inherited. I never found this so. **My whole life has shown me how modifiable human intelligence is when the heart is given spirit and the mind direction through chaos.**

And so, as we move nearer to the end of this book, and having understood that the whole concept of inherited ability was seated in the conviction of Francis Galton, we should know that his mentor and half cousin Charles Darwin was never so sure -- noting, as he once did, that "No child has the instinctive tendency to bake, brew or write."[348]

In other words, the child is not born with an ability. They are born with the skills to learn how to develop that ability, but as we are to understand in further books, the development of these skills cannot be related to genetic diversity.

Thus, the human being learns how to learn, but because of the political drives of too many very influential psychologists and the economic processing strategies of education, where it burdens exhausted teachers with 45 minutes to evaluate the struggles of each in their class of 40 students, we have never really understood what this means.

Galton, then, and all who have since followed in his path are wrong. The IQ applications presented in the book *The Bell Curve* are not correct. Intelligence cannot be proven to be innately decided in continuous variation ranging from zero to 200 -- or whatever.

While Galton proclaimed that intelligence lay in social ancestry, the truth is that genes passed the ability for this feature on through families indiscriminately of their social positions, but appeared to be limited in the social and educational worlds they matured through. Some poor and working-class children did, however, manage to escape the conditioning set upon them. Often this was through the character of their mothers, who succeeded in raising their intelligence.

We may think of many such individuals, but if we may consider Frederick Douglass (born a slave) 1818-1895, George Washington Carver (born a slave) 1864-1943, Abraham Lincoln 1809- 1865, Thomas Edison 1847-1931, Andrew Carnegie 1835-1919, John. D. Rockefeller 1839- 1937, and Henry Ford 1863-1947 as people who did come from low inherited stock, who did live in the time of Galton, and all of whom did change the world they lived in to make it a better place for all.

It is perhaps easy to look at such famous people and accept how they could achieve such success merely through their endeavours and without superior genes. However, by the same token, we so easily fail to realise how there are those about us whose poor performance we too easily accept be a consequence of some inherited lower ability, without understanding their life.

Chapter TwentyEight

The Real Environment of Intelligence

I would like to share with you two case studies I made, just to give a little insight into why we are wrong in judging the intelligence of another, simply because we do not understand how complex the environment of intelligence is, and so what it really means.

Case Example B:

This case concerns a young man I was once introduced to who appeared to be dyslexic. He had, in fact, long been diagnosed as dyslexic, and based on tests and evaluations by psychologists, he was also said to have ADHD.

Yet, because I knew of his personal background, I knew that he was neither ADHD nor dyslexic, which gave the impression that he had limited intelligence. He certainly displayed and had severe problems with spelling, but he was not deficient in his attention. In fact, outside of an assessment situation, he was very attentive to the things that interested him. He had achieved great recognition in various sports and activities that were not related to pen and paper. He did, however, have very suppressed issues, which he tried to conceal through an image of being very successful.

The root of this young man's problems lay in the long history of his father's bullying and his being constantly told by him that he would never achieve anything or be anybody. In the street, as it were, he fought this rejection of his image very hard and was very streetwise. He had gained a blackbelt in a martial art, which requires a very high level of self-discipline and so attention, and had been awarded a number of trophies for ice skating, which again requires a great deal of personal commitment.

However, in school, his development was so hindered by his embarrassment with letters and words that he cut them out of his life. He would not admit to his teachers that he did not know the rules he had failed to take note of in his development, because he would not admit to the failure his father said of him.

Whenever he encountered a word problem, he instantly developed anxiety, rather than calmly seeking to understand the relationships of the letters he had come to dread. As stress built up, his mind closed down, and to prevent this stress within him, he announced to others that he was dyslexic, and so was given an excuse to avoid this development. Actually, he was happier to be thought of as dyslexic than to be thought a failure.

The greater problem for this young man was that all the psychologists who met him were too ready to wonder by which box they could classify him. So eager were they to attribute his condition to a genetic one that they all failed to understand how his condition actually came about and how he could have been educated out of it.

In our following book, *Brain Plasticity,* we examine how the chemistry of the brain is altered by disturbances to the mind, and how this change of chemistry changes the apparent intelligence of the human being. As we come to see how the production of neurotransmitters is affected by bullying, as they can be by any form of repeated physical or mental abuse, we will see how this affects the ability of neurons to conduct signals of information. While this knowledge is very important, it can often be very difficult to relate what it actually means to the child in the classroom. Therefore, in view of this, I would like to share one more case study with the reader.

In our long account, I have often tried to explain how unfathomable and so how unmeasurable the environment of intelligence is. As we now move to understand the factors of Mathew's environment and come to understand the minute details involved here, we will better understand why the environment cannot be classified for intelligence testing.

Case Example C:

When I first met Matthew (this is not his real name.), I found that he could easily converse on matters of the world and knew his position on the things we discussed. He appeared to be an easy-going, intellectually minded 17-year-old, about to be of great use to his society.

At least, that was the impression I gained until he took a pen in his hand and began to lay out what, until that moment, had been a clearly presentable mind on a piece of paper. As the pen jerked from letter to letter, the form of each barely decipherable ink character dispelled whatever hope I had of his potential.

As I watched words take form, it was not the bad spelling that drew my attention, but the inconsistency in the form of each letter. As one followed the other, there appeared to be no recognition by Matthew for the need in conformity of character. One letter could be twice the size of the one it followed, and selected from a different model to the one it would precede.

Watching the stress build up in Matthew, as he struggled in the task of writing, I noticed how the end letters to a word would be hastily scribbled, as he urgently strove to conclude it. White patches in the surface colour of the skin, where the fingers pressed hard upon the pen, gave signal to the imposition he felt of this labour. It was too easy to see how much he resented the paper and pen, which gave testimony to the uselessness others would see in him.

He would always be this way, he was told. His parents had taken him to specialists who said he was beyond the critical period for motor relearning and that it was too late for him to change. Teachers had raised him in the belief that he would never be able to write, and so should not bring stress to a task he could never accomplish. His mother had told me how he was the problem child in a class, the burden of every teacher. Yet, why was this, I wondered?

I was not interested in the account of his class behaviour. His resistance to the system that limited him was obviously a tactic to explain his poor performance as an act of self-defiance, rather than one of inadequacy. Yet, what was the cause of this inadequacy?

The first insight came when I asked him which type of mathematics he had difficulty with. "Algebra!" He told me. So, I gave him a simple equation and asked him to show me the value of one of the variables. As he tackled this, it became obvious he did not understand the rules of algebra. Algebra, like all mathematics, is merely to know the rules, learn to recognise the use of information, and how to arrange this to work with the appropriate rule. Yet, this bright and alert 17-year-old did not know the elementary rules of mathematics.

He was fascinated, as I explained that the equal sign is merely the point of balance between two bodies of information. As I explained that any change could be invented to one side, providing an equal change is made to the other, he came to realise how and why one character could be transposed with another. Within an hour, he was handling levels of algebra he previously could not have done.

How, I sought to reason, could poor teaching in mathematics give explanation to his inadequacy in writing, and how may his equally difficult scribe of numbers give excuse for this teaching? As he wrote numbers and the symbols that gave them their relation (the plus and minus, etc.), all were as much without uniformity as his writing of letters.

His mother had told me that he had a motor tremor and could not write because of this. However, I noticed that this tremor only occurred towards the end of a word and was in some way related to a factor of stress. This aside, Mathew had demonstrated a high degree of finger dexterity in various games and tasks I had seen him involved with. Putting this tremor explanation aside, I began to study how he held a pen and made a relation to the paper with this.

If I were to ask you to pick up a pen with your eyes closed, you would feel for the correct position of the pen within your fingers, and make adjustment until it was right for you. Each of us has our own way of holding and making use of a pen. When Matthew held a pen, it was so close to the tip that he retarded any operation of dexterity that he might make in describing a character. I asked him to try to accept a different hold on the pen he was using. While such new positioning was unnatural for him, he was more able to elaborate on the description of a character. Why, I pondered, should the form of letters be so inconsistent? Asking this question introduces us to a greater understanding of what the word environment can mean.

As a child, we learn how to make our relationship with a sheet of paper. We learn to know the shape of the paper, and we learn to decide how we are going to write upon it. We learn to compartmentalise it into potential lines and spaces. As we decide where the left-hand margin will be, we also decide where the right-hand margin will lie, and so the point at which our writing will move to a lower line. If our paper has no lines, we learn how to write across the page by constantly referring to past letters, marks higher up the page, and the potential space to the right. As we do this, the line of our writing is even and balanced. When our paper is marked into lines, as it more often is, we create an imaginary line that sets the height of our letters so that they appear uniform when we rest them on the inked line.

This writing may seem automatic, but it is, however, learnt through the rules we have earlier discussed. So with experience, we have trained ourselves to scan constantly for the height and the width of each character before we make it. By noting the height of the previous letter, we determine the height of the next letter we will write. If we have written the letter "a", and the next letter is to be "n", then we take "n" to be the same height as the "a". Equally, if the next letter is "l", then we take the height of "l" to be twice that of "a", so on and so forth. By constantly referring to all the characters on a line, we visualise the size, width, and spaces of the letters and words that will follow on that line.

So, while we think about the words we are to write, our mind constantly seeks reference points, looking backwards and forwards, to adjust the size and form of each new character to make a uniform presentation. This is something that we learn to do, and like riding a bicycle, we are not normally aware of this operation. It is a learnt operation based upon rules. Yet, Matthew did not know these rules. He did not see how one letter needed to be related to the one it followed, just as this would set the stage for those to come.

What transpired, through our friendship, was that when Mathew first started school, he was taunted for being fat. He was not when I met him, but he explained that in the early learning stage of his school life, he was repeatedly picked on and laughed at for being so. From listening to his account, it became understandable why he hated the "school experience," and why he did everything he could to escape from it. Unable to do so, when in class, he closed his mind to all that was happening.

From what we have just discussed, we know this did not just mean that he only shunted out the behavioural experiences, but also the intellectual ones. Much of what he was taught, the basic rules by which information is composed and moves, fell upon deaf ears. He so much hated to be in his classroom that he could not focus on his learning, and so developed a very bad structure to engage with information. Perhaps, this was purposely done to demonstrate his rejection to a world that gave him pain.

With all this understood, we discussed the rules of character formation and relationships. By making a small mark at the appropriate height in between the inked lines (on the right side of the paper), he learnt to devise an imaginary line that extended from the letters on the left. By this imaginary line, he could define a particular size for each letter he was about to write. Within less than an hour of practice, he had written *abcde* in joined-up writing with a precision that was remarkable. Not that this was easy, but at 17, he had much to reconstruct.

The important point is that Mathew discovered that he could do this, and he began to learn how to do it better. As he realised this, his confidence grew and with this, a desire to engage with information. The facts and numerical equations in Chemistry, History, Geography and his language subjects, etc., that once had brought him dread, now became a happy challenge. How he decided to continue this redesign of the presentation of his ability, and so the impression others gained of this, and so judged him by is Matthew's story. The lesson to us is very clear.

When Matthew first started school, he displayed some difficulty greater than that of the children he was being compared to. For one reason or another, nobody was able to help him keep up. As time passed, a reasoning developed that his ability was limited by his genes. After all, this is what his teachers would have been taught to expect, as they would notice how each child responds in a different way to the same information. Mathew simply fitted into "the deviation from the average."

We may like to think that his teachers accepted what he could not do, and to avoid causing him unnecessary stress avoided the development of primary tasks. However, it is rather that they firstly did not have the time to help him keep up with others, whom he emotionally resented being with, and secondly so accepted the concept of inherited ability that they did not explore how his ability actually came to be.

His teachers were so blinded by this concept, they could not see the axiom that "a quality in learning relies upon the student understanding the progression of information in their own terms." The crux of our problem, or rather the failing of education to produce more able students, lies in the failure to recognise this possibility.

The real point of this to us, and it is exactly the same with all the case examples we discuss in these books, is that this student was assessed and found to be less able than others. Some consideration may have been given to his circumstances, but these would not have distracted from the opinion that his performance was less than that of others because he was thought to have less genetic worth. This misunderstanding of genetic variation that we have is too often in our minds when we view an individual's intelligence, the performance they make, and the use that can be planned for them.

It is with very great importance that we understand what this last sentence can mean to the child of today, because the world they will grow up in will be very different to ours. It will also be very different to the one that first created the idea that intelligence is inherited by the child, in accordance with the social status of their parents. .....

In going over this book, I was reminded of Walter Lippmann's statement... "It is not possible, I think, to imagine a more contemptible proceeding than to confront a child with a set of puzzles and after an hour's monkeying with them, proclaim to the child, or to his parents that here is a C- individual. ... Such a process would be not only contemptible but inane. All that can be claimed for the tests is that they can be used to classify into a homogeneous group the children whose capacities for schoolwork are at a particular moment fairly similar."[349]

This, of course, is what IQ tests do. As we explained, psychologists do not know what genes are responsible, nor what the genes actually do and while they acknowledge the existence of the environment, they do not bring any real consideration to it. All this is why the results one team of psychologists produce are argued against by another team, each seeing different values or uses in the environment. This was clear when we examined the study that Newman and his colleagues had originally conducted.

It is time now that we return to the subject of identical twins and the Nature/Nurture debate that is the root of our belief that human beings are born with different intelligences, which too often has been used to give one a better position in life over another because of their said natural potential.

Chapter TwentyNine
The Nature vs Nurture Ratio

The belief that the gene quality for intelligence varies within families, within groups of individuals and develops its coding through the environment to reveal a total quality of intelligence for the individual, gave rise to the study of monozygotic twins.

Galton inspired the reasoning, in the 19th century, that when identical twins respond with similar answers to the same questions, they are said to show their inherited value. When they respond differently to the same questions, they are said to show the value of environmental experience. This endeavour to find the relationship between what is inherited and the extent it can be developed through environmental experience is known as the nature/nurture ratio.

Yet, over 120 years after Johannsen discovered the role and influences of the environment, we still do not know what the environment for intelligence really is, and the little that is known is only very vaguely categorised for test purposes. We also realise that we have no understanding of what genes are involved in intelligence, how they interact with other genes and even what effect their programming is designed to bring into intelligence.

After all, there are gene codes that have different purposes and do interact with the environment in different ways. Thus, rather than thinking of a gene code simply being constructed by the quality of the environment, there are other gene codes that enable a feature to exist, with the environment completely designing the effectiveness of that feature.

This is so for those codes that enable us to have language, emotion, to have sensitivity to examine information and to know what it means, to make opinion on things and to play with beliefs and understandings on a day-to-day basis, to be able to change our thoughts at any time and to be faster or more accurate in processing information. These components of intelligence are not affected by the normal variations that genes undergo.

If we add to this how questionable the testing methods actually are, we should be very wary of thinking this debate upon what is inherited and how it develops will provide the ready answer that is sought. In fact, if after a century of continually testing and failing to define what this ratio is, to the acceptance of all parties,[350] we must suspect there is something wrong.

This would be especially so when Bayley consistently found no evidence of differences in intelligence from birth until after 14 months of age, as we shall come to see.[351] Any differences in intelligence after this age were found to be totally unstable until the later school years.[352] By this time, the adolescent had been raised through domestic influences and long been conditioned through their school experience, with all the understandings to this we have examined.

Through all we have examined, we have come to understand the actual meaning of this word intelligence, for this is a word that has only one meaning. The word "intelligence" was a word created in language to explain how the mental performance of individuals could be compared.

This is what intelligence means. It is a way of comparing one to another. It has no other purpose, and since opportunity is highly political, then, so is the use made of this word. Intelligence, and so the idea of testing intelligence, is a political way of deciding the ability of human beings, albeit children and adults, for their use in the working society.

If, however, we were to look at the word performance instead, in the sense of observing one human being completely detached from others, we would be caused to realise that this has a very different meaning to us. For when we apply this word to a child making some performance in what they are doing, of a student in their learning making some performance in writing a composition, or of a computer designer in the performance of developing some software task or any other function a human being is involved with, we can see how instantly we would acknowledge that they are developing in their understanding through their experience.

We would know that their improvement is reliant upon their interest, of how happy or not distracted they are in the task, and so how they are guided by one more experienced to recognise a better path to follow and how to deal better with mistakes as they arise. None of which ties their potential to a factor we assume they inherited, when they struggle in one way or another, seeking to find the best way forward.

Therefore, when we focus solely on the performance of one human being, we think only of how they have come to see the world as they did, and how we can help them to understand it more in the ways we do. If we are really interested in helping them, we study in great detail how they perform and we suggest tiny improvements here and there, so that gradually their performance becomes more of what we expect. This is not the same with the word intelligence.

Intelligence, as we have explained, is a word that was invented to explain how the performances of any two human beings at any age could be compared. For all the political reasons we have seen, this comparison is said to be reasonably constant at any two moments in their lives, when the meaning of the environment is not fully understood or is ignored. Intelligence, then, is a word that only exists on the basis that an individual's performance, albeit mental capability, will remain more or less as it was from the time of their birth.

Yet, this, we know, is not true. Individuals from poor backgrounds, and what is too often said of them as coming from low genetic stock, have been inspired to develop very high levels of intelligence through the inventions and discoveries they made. The opposite is true, of course, of individuals whose level of intelligence has been considerably lowered through adverse social conditioning, especially where their sense of emotion has been so reduced that they no longer care or know how to interact with the world about them.

In attempts to prove this inherited factor, a whole field of psychology developed, and as it did so, it created a mindset within our civilisation to justify the existence of this inherited quality of intelligence. Yet, despite endless claims by social scientists that they know this to be true, it has never been proven.

What happened, and what still happens, is that we are so conditioned to believe that genes of different capabilities are responsible for some factor of an individual's intelligence, that we stop ourselves from understanding what the environment of intelligence really means, and therefore what the role of the genes may really be. When we do this, we so forget how the human spirit struggles within the world of complex personalities and its own self-doubts, to understand how to interact better in the world it has so far experienced.

Let us now move to consider the relationship of the gene to the environment from an entirely different perspective — one that avoids all the political baggage it has long accumulated and perhaps one that Johannsen may have come to endorse.

———————————

Chapter Thirty
The Common Environment vs The Differential Environment Ratio

As we have reviewed and gained a deeper understanding of the genotype and how it has evolved to allow the environment to construct some of its features, rather than simply feeding their design, we should now consider how viable intelligence tests are, for here lies the essence of what this is all about.

Accordingly, we have reviewed numerous times how intelligence tests are very deficient in how they measure aspects of cognitive functioning, such as domains of logic, causal reasoning, probabilistic, and scientific thinking. Such that Instrumental Rationality (the selection of appropriate goals and the designs to realise those goals), and Epistemic Rationality (holding to beliefs that are consistent with known evidence) are totally absent in IQ evaluations.[353]

Equally, Flynn explained that intelligence tests do not measure intelligence. They examine only a minor sort of "abstract problem-solving ability" that has little practical significance.[354] There again, Kuhn has explained that there is still a great deal of human thinking that we know almost nothing about.[355]

All this is to say that while psychologists have never agreed upon what intelligence is,[356] in trying to measure what they are not sure of, **they avoid essential factors that they do know of.** What we may further say, if we consider all we have so far read, is that questions in intelligence tests focus heavily upon cultural and social aspects.

Indeed, we found how Goddard and Terman purposely designed the questions of their tests this way, for the very purpose of identifying and excluding immigrants, as well as poor white children, especially if they were of non-protestant backgrounds, from good educational opportunities. Their purpose was to limit the roles that people of undesirable backgrounds could play in American society. We found verification to this political construction of IQ questions by a court decision, which ruled that intelligence tests are biased and do work against the background and culture of certain people.[357]

Therefore, if intelligence tests do not focus their questions directly upon intelligence but more so culture and social aspects of it, which we found much evidence of, then, we need to consider that instead of monozygotic twins being recognised to have similarities in intelligence (to support the nature element in the nature/nurture debate), that what this really shows is their similarity in responding to cultural and so environmentally directed questions.

This is important to realise, because people learn to think through the language and culture they are raised in, which in turn gives them the means to understand and relate to their world. We may think of this to be intelligence.

In fact, the relationship between language and intelligence was recognised by Sapir and Whorf in the 1930s, when they brought understanding to how cultural and social differences cause people to think differently through their different perspectives. As they pointed out, since no two languages are sufficiently similar, the people **of those languages must live in distinct worlds of thought**.[358]

McElvenny recognised the same thing when he explained how ...."Even the most banal expressions between two languages have a slightly different sense, issuing from a network of attitudes and ideas unique to each language. ... There is never a one-to-one correspondence in meaning between the words and phrases of one language and another. Each language seemingly compels us to talk in a certain way and to see things from a particular perspective."[359]

We may also consider Bates' reasoning here in how language develops through the general development of brain mechanisms, as they relate to the complex social environment the individual lives through.[360]

Gordon brought relevance to all this when he examined the language of the isolated Amazonian Piraha tribe in 2004 and found they had developed a culture that had not necessitated the use of past or future verbs. This caused them virtually no understanding of past or future times in how they thought or interacted with the world about them. They lived in and so only thought in the present time.

In addition to this, they were found to count only with one, two, or many, so they could neither relate to nor imagine any higher numerical situation. They could, for example, understand one fish and two fish, but they could not understand the meaning of four fish. The concept of four fish was totally beyond their comprehension.[361]

As Gordon pointed out, "A people without terms for numbers, do not develop the ability to determine exact numbers."[362] We may reason from this that the skill of these people to think, or if you wish to say how they demonstrate their intelligence, is shown to be determined by their language, with their language being a direct consequence of their culture, and so the job tasks they do. In other words, Gordon's findings prove that we learn to think through the language we have evolved, through our environment.

Therefore, what is really being identified in any similarity that monozygotic twins demonstrate in their responses, as we have just explained, is not a factor of the intelligence of their genes, but a factor of their same or similar understanding of the socio-cultural and environmental related questions they are asked.

This is to say that when their responses differ, this is not what is thought to be their total environmental experience, but those environmental experiences they have individually related to.

In other words, we present a new understanding here, which closes the issue on the nature/nurture debate.

This understanding explains why genes do not normally bring a quality of effect into intelligence. And that instead of thinking of the influence of the genes and that of the environment, we understand that intelligence comes to be through an environment of two parts.

There will be one environment of general understanding and one environment of specific understanding. The first, we will introduce as the Common Environment. The second, as the Differential Environment.

The Common Environment

Let us understand this by first considering how the Common Environment operates. This is to say that people learn to think according to the demands of their culture, as we have just seen with the example of those of the Piraha tribe.

Thus, there is a general similarity in how people think according to their culture, and so how those of a different culture think differently. I lived in Japan for nearly ten years and found that the way the Japanese think is very different from the ways of thinking of people of the very many other countries I have been to. I have been to about 40 countries.

Davies ties to explain this, when he points out that, "The Japanese mind relates very well to ambiguity that would frustrate most Westerners. So, to express oneself ambiguously and indirectly is expected in Japanese society, which causes a great deal of confusion in international communication." Equally, "Silence can also be considered a kind of ambiguity. Between the Japanese and Westerners, there is a different understanding of silence. For the Japanese, silence indicates deep thinking or consideration. ... The Japanese hesitate to deny directly and think of affirmation as a virtue: therefore, troubles between the Japanese and people from other countries often occur."[363]

Such common thinking, and so similarity of response to culturally encoded questions, can be found with people who live in closed communities. We found this with the Piraha people, as we do with European and Ashkenazi Jews, since they also have evolved to think differently from the ways of other people.

The European and Ashkenazi Jews are a people who have an unparalleled history of cultural and social rejection, and a level of persecution that saw them discriminated against en masse, mercilessly tortured, and murdered. Their means of worship, as this provides an identity for them, has been severely restricted. Wherever they went in Europe and Russia, they were treated as social outcasts, often confined to ghettos and restricted to ownership of land.

As a direct consequence of this, these people developed a strict sense of sectarian identification that was propagated within their communities through a special language. This was a language of evaluation that emphasised knowledge of not only valuable commodities, but more significantly, the worth of information, for it was only through the precise understanding of information that these people could gain the security to survive. To teach their children how to understand information precisely and how to share their thoughts with precise accuracy was the lifeline for the continuation of their culture. As Feuerstein points out:

"Many Jewish communities were subject to abject poverty, political oppression and social discrimination, but mediation (the art of explaining the value of information) persisted at the informal and formal levels of Jewish communal life. ..... So that the wisest scholar in a community was awarded the highest status, with the intention to inspire parents in the social significance of raising their children in cognitive excellence." 364

For this reason, we find that the European and Askenzasi Jewish cultures evolved a social habit of raising each subsequent generation in very high language skills, which fostered their higher intelligence.

This social "transmission of intelligence" was clearly impressed upon me, when, in visiting Jerusalem, I was invited to take dinner with a Jewish family. During the course of the meal, a child asked their mother a particular question. The mother's reply was most illustrative of the point we raise here. "Tell me," she said, ".....what are you saying? Can I read your mind?"

In response to this, the child then redefined their question with specific point and clarity. It was only after the mother was satisfied that her son had explained precisely his meaning that she consented to his request, and did so with an expression of deep affection.

While I could only imagine the average parent of another culture replying "yes" or "no" in such an incident, if they gave any type of a verbal response, this Jewish mother had used a very small and normal incident to transmit the interactive skills of her culture. She taught her child exemplary skills in defining and moving with information, which shows how language guides intelligence.

Accordingly, it was most illustrative to see how the mother "naturally" ended the whole learning experience by instilling into her child a feeling of security and success. It is upon these very two factors that the base for intelligence is set, and this is mainly the responsibility of parental skills and affection. With certain Jewish sects, this is a cultural tradition.

As we would find over and over again in any culture, and at any level of society, it is the loving devotion of a parent to seed the secrets of inquiry and endear the confidence to pursue this that is the cause of higher intelligence. The genius of Mendeleev, who designed the Periodic Table lay, as Bronowski saw it, in the singular efforts of his devoted mother, who zealously indulged his childhood passion for games of relationships. It was a "hobby" that finally bore fruit, when Mendeleev realised how the properties of elements relate to each other — as do cards in the Game of Patience.[365]

From this, we see that the Jewish origins of many of our geniuses such as Einstein, Von Neumann, Leo Szilard, Leonard Bernstein, George Gershwin to name but a few, can be attributed not to a genetic inheritance, but to a cultural one. Their's was a bathing from birth in clearly defined rules of interactive strategy that stimulated imagination, and were germinated through love with a strong sense of identity.

Heinrich Graetz gave definition to this "Jewish" intelligence in the 19th Century, when he wrote: "When Jewish superior intelligence is assumed to be positive," he wrote, "it is rarely seen as biological. Rather, it is understood as a quality that can be attained by any group if only the "right" rules are followed. If Jewish superior intelligence is seen as a negative quality, as a hair-splitting judgement or narrowness of imagination, it is deserving a love of twisting, distorting, ingenuous quibbling."[366]

However, such quibbling as Graetz mentions, and which Shakespeare made issue of in "The Merchant of Venice", has a greater purpose than is apparent to the Gentile. It is my understanding that the purpose that underlies such quibbling is a desire to know the real value of a person, for it is through the force of argument that the true identity of a person is revealed. This is a need that may be most understood in a people so long deprived of roots, and whose greatest desire is to share understanding through trust.

Yet, such paternal instruction for the acquisition and respect of knowledge, as we have discussed here, is only witnessed in branches of European and Ashkenazi Jews. Other Jewish branches do not share the same quality of intellectual standard, or (and this is an important point) that of paternal devotion. In fact, a major problem to Israeli authorities is the very low level of intellectual performance that Ethiopian and Chinese Jews display once they settle in Israel, and the subsequent difficulties in educating them to reliable roles in their new society.[367]

It is not, then, that Jews as a distinct people can be thought to have a genetically superior intelligence to other people. It is merely that two branches of Jewish people evolved a high cultural level of intelligence through the unique circumstances of their very particular history.

Accordingly, intelligence is not here regarded as a genetic gift, but as the continuation of a practice. "Amongst Jews ..." wrote the philosopher Wittgenstein "... genius is found only in the holy man. Even the greatest of Jewish thinkers is no more than talented. (Myself for instance). I think there is some truth in my idea that I really only think reproductively. I don't believe I have ever invented a line of thinking. I have always taken one over from someone."[368] We see here, how a genius in his own right, recognises how his intelligence was socially inherited and not so genetically.

How this Jewish intelligence is socially transmitted, was brought to my awareness when I became involved with a group of such intellectuals. To an outsider, impression could easily have been gained that the intense arguing that soon erupted within them lay in some bitter feud. In fact, I thought they were going to kill each other. It was only after the point of the discussion had been agreed upon by all, and everyone started laughing and sharing love with each other, that I came to understand how each had been fighting to understand the meaning of the other, and so how much real value was placed upon information by these people. To these people, information was not to be flaunted lightly. The people that I had seen arguing were, in fact, only living with their thoughts. Each thought was desperate to survive, and each thought sought the means to adapt itself to do so.

> *Intelligence, I came to realise, is life.*
> *It has to be fought for to survive, and its sword*
> *is language.*

As we find that a common understanding to their world differs with people of different cultures, so will we find people can think differently within their own culture. The case of African Americans is a ready example to this, but this can also be found to a lesser extent within people of the same caste.

Bryson, for instance, explains how Missouri is referred to as the "Show Me State" by Americans who live in the more industrialised areas of the country, as they give reference to the state's inhabitants to be so stupid that they had to be shown how to do everything. In their defence, the Missourians take this to be a compliment, "persuading themselves that it implied a certain shrewd caution to their part (in how they think)".[369]

To extend this point, we may understand how two Japanese or two Ashkenazi Jews will demonstrate a far greater similarity in their responses than a Japanese compared to an Ashkenazi Jew. After all, each may think in the culture they were raised in, as they respond to culturally encoded intelligence questions.

Accordingly, there has to be a common base by which individuals, who are raised within one culture and using the same language, relate with a similarity to information, and by this a dissimilarity to those of a different culture and language. I would like to demonstrate this with two examples.

In the first, I once presented a Somalian immigrant with a drawing of a weight-lifter wearing a traditional leopard skin outfit, who was in the process of lifting a bar with heavy weights on either end. In order to stress the difficulty of the task, the artist had given a bow shape to the bar to emphasise the heaviness of the weights the man was trying to lift.

If I had asked anyone from a Westernised culture, even a very small child, what the weight-lifter was trying to do, I would have been immediately informed that the man was trying to lift the weights. However, this was not how the Somalian, who had never seen a weight-lifter so dressed, interpreted the meaning of the drawing.

As he studied the drawing, the man described how the bar was being bent by the man pulling upon it. He then logically explained to me that the purpose of the man was, in fact, to bend the bar. This, he further explained, was possible because the bar was made of a softer metal than the blocks placed on either end.

May we see that through the perspective by which he identified the information, how the Somalian's response was intelligently analysed and described. Although if this had been a 'Westernised' IQ question, he would have scored zero, to which some would have readily explained his score to be the consequence of low genetic quality, firstly by his creed and secondly by his individuality. Incidentally, this man was a qualified engineer who held a master's degree.

The problem was that because he had no experience of a man so dressed, the Somalian did not know what his purpose was, and so focused only on the bending of the bar. After all, from his culture, this is how he could explain what he was seeing.

The second example came to me from a friend, who explained the problem his six-year-old Italian daughter had in an infant bilingual school. She had an Italian teacher for Italian and an English teacher for English. When both teachers taught maths, each would use their own language. The problem came when the English teacher taught maths with metaphors (such as, "multiplication is like addition"). She did this because in her culture, the meaning is readily understood. However, it caused great confusion when given to Italian children. As Luca Magni explains:

"Then I realised that, guided by the metaphor "multiplications are like sums", my daughter was trapped in her bilingual world. She read the operation in Italian "due-PER-tre (literally translatable in English as: 2-FOR-3)" which prompted her towards the following resolutive algorithm: 2+2+2.

On the other hand, she also simultaneously interpreted that very same "2 x 3" operation in English "two-TIMES-three" which guided her mind into an alternative and confusing 3 + 3 computational option.

Confronted with the above two algorithms, my 6-year-old daughter looked lost, incapable of deciding which resolutive path she had to follow. This was a problem for all the children, and it was finally resolved by teaching them maths only in Italian."[370]

As we can see in the second example, the problem was caused by the teachers' thinking that the children could learn to understand maths in both languages at the same time. Their error was that they ignored the cultural thinking that was different behind each language. Thus, the children were confused about which cultural language to think in and with this confusion, could not relate to the environmental problem.

Therefore, the error was to think of the students' capability only through the words they could translate and not to realise how language has its own definitions for the cultural meanings information has.

This leads us to understand that monozygotic twins who share the same language and were raised in the same culture, even if these were of different social levels and locations, would relate to questions in a more similar way than individuals who understand English as their second language and were raised in a different culture.

Therefore, whether language is verbally shared with us or presented as a written text, we have to decipher its meaning and the arrangement of its information into the way that we have learnt to understand it. The description of nouns and verbs, what something is and how it interacts with something else has a common understanding between people who share the same language and culture.

By the examples we have discussed here, we can see there is a common way to understand the meaning of the environment with people who were raised within it and who use its language, which people of another culture and language would find a different meaning to.

It is natural, then, that people learn to recognise and identify with the world about them, through those they share their mind with. In this way, the more familiar people are with each other, as by their cultural and so social identity, the more they will devise similar identities to items and recognise similar means of interaction. The understanding and mind of each being is cultivated through the identity of others, with each thought having a common origin within their group.

Thus, if monozygotic twins were presented with environmentally coded questions, as they are with IQ tests, they would show a similarity in their responses. Yet, without recognising they are equally responding to a cultural identity, such a high correlation is mistakenly assumed to be the hereditary aspect of their intelligence. This, after all, is what psychologists have long been programmed to expect.

Therefore, instead of trying to understand the worth of the genes, for all the political reasons we have discussed, we should now consider that what causes monozygotic twins to have a factor of similarity in their scores lies in their common understanding of the environment, and nothing more.

The Differential Environment

The Common Environment helped us to understand how twins recognise aspects of the environment through a commonality of thought. Thus, it is their manner of cultural thinking that causes them to respond with a similarity to test questions, and not so by their assumed innate intelligence.

On the other hand, the Differential Environment helps us to understand the different experiences each twin engaged in as an individual human being.

After all, it is one thing to think monozygotic twins are identical and so think identically, which is what this is all about, but this impression we have fails to see how a twin (as a human being) learns to think through their unique experiences. So, one twin may learn a simple strategy to deal with information that the other does not know, and by this knowledge shape their interaction with the environment way beyond that of their twin.

By a simple example, with twins separated, it may be suggested to one twin that they continually check what they do. Should this twin take the advice and become proficient in continually checking their actions, they will self-correct the errors they make, be more aware of errors that occur, and develop strategies to reduce their likelihood. However, the other twin, deprived of this knowledge, will wait for others to correct what they did and so be less sensitive as they process information.

Thus, we see how twins may respond differently to the same test question, which introduces us to the meaning of the Differential Environment.

Let us pause for a moment to reflect upon the meaning of what we have just introduced, to better understand the difference between these two environments.

Should twins be presented with the IQ question asking them if "Crisco is: (i) a patent medicine (ii) disinfectant (iii) toothpaste, or (iv) food product?[371]

They will both score the correct answer if they are American, because Crisco is a well-known food product in American culture. However, if, for example, they are British, they will not know the correct answer and probably guess incorrectly, because Crisco is only used in America.

This is an example of the Common Environment, where both twins score the same, because their common ability lies in their shared cultural knowledge. This has nothing to do with their supposed identically "twined" intelligence, although it will be mistakenly thought to be so in an IQ assessment, seeking to determine the ratio of nature to nurture.

On the other hand, a difference in the scores of twins would be explained by their different personal development. Consider the IQ question where they are asked to calculate how many jars will contain smaller candies?

(As with the example where, "A candy maker makes two sizes of candies. Using the smaller size, a full jar will contain 120 pieces of candy. Using the larger candies, a jar will contain 80 pieces of candy. The candy maker has a strict rule that no jars will contain a mix of small and large candies. If a store has room for 15 jars and they want 1560 total pieces of candy. How many jars will contain smaller candies?")

The similarity or dissimilarity in their answers will totally depend upon how well each was taught, learnt and practised to become proficient with simultaneous equations. If one did and the other did not or less so, the difference in their scores will be said to be caused by the "environment" in an IQ assessment seeking to understand the nurture aspect in the ratio. Yet, it is not this. What we have just witnessed is an example of the Differential Environment.

The same being so for the IQ question asking to calculate "How many minutes is it before noon if 29 minutes ago it was 6 times as many minutes after 10 am?" Whether any two individuals know or do not know how to calculate this has nothing to do with the genes they inherited (in normal cases) and everything to do with their development within the Differential Environment.

From the perspective of the Differential Environment, we look upon the environment of intelligence as one less determined by the socio-economic environment (the location of the dwelling, the quality of the family lifestyle, jobs of the parents and factors of finance), and one far more determined by the mental environment where the child is raised through qualities of love, sensitivity, security and imagination.

We should understand here that intelligence is really only our perspective of the end result of very many neurological and psychological components coming together in another human being, when they respond to a situation the way they have personally evolved to do through their perspective of the world.

Our greatest mistake in this is to assume the mind of another sees the same world as ours does. It does not. Binét understood this, but Terman did not when he changed Binét's one-to-one verbal evaluation into a sheet of tick box questions, so thousands could take the test at the same time. The reality is that the mind of each lives in the world it has developed through, but learns how to interact with the minds of other individuals through language, as this is developed through customs, climate and culture.

Consider how a thought travels within the language people share. Each individual will manifest their own meaning to this according to the ways they have individually developed and how they have learnt to formulate their personal experiences. Therefore, any two children, including monozygotic twins, will look at an item differently. Each will agree to identify with that item through a common dialogue, but the inner perspective that each holds of it will not be the same.

As this is true for any human being, it is no less true for each individual twin, where the different thought processes each developed will cause them to offer different qualities of response in any test of their intelligence.

As we understood earlier, our ability to freely change our beliefs at will, and so to reason in a different way, is decided by a gene design that allows this freedom with no genetic restriction. The ability for this change, the adaptation of a superior process, is only reliant upon language, where common meanings are recognised with confusion and misunderstandings overcome to define a better strategy to process information. All these we acquire from those we meet in life.

Therefore, such differences that twins display in their responses to questions lie in the differences in sensitivity by which each developed to interact with the environment. Quellet-Morin showed us the extent this can happen when she came across twins, one of whom had been bullied and so displayed a much lower quality of intelligence than their twin.[372] This difference in intelligence did not arise just because they had been bullied. It arose because their emotional quality of sensitivity had been lowered through their experiences of being bullied.

Thus, it is emotional sensitivity that is the key to understanding how levels of intelligence may change. And how, without education or guidance in this, intelligence appears stable in the individual as they have long settled into their own strategies to make their sense of the world.

If you were to teach another to see beyond what they readily recognise, which would be to teach them to learn to see things from different perspectives and so teach them to check their own effort, you may see the simple means by which you can shake them out of the stability they have long used to deal with information and the world about it.

When this aspect of the environment deteriorates significantly, as when children are emotionally hurt, we find they lose concentration in their learning and develop poorer skills of mental interaction. The vital importance of this "emotional sensitivity" was disturbingly clear when children were discovered who had been totally deprived of it.

Without any quality of emotional care, the minds of children raised in Romanian orphanages had closed down, simply because there were far too few supervisors to share with them the basics of human love and attention. When these children were discovered, they had such low levels of intelligence that they were virtually unresponsive to any level of stimulation.[373] Yet, within two years of intervention by dedicated psychologists developing their minds through emotional sensitivity, these children were found to move out of their zombie-like manner to be normally interactive with the world.[374] The power of love and the accompanying sensitivity that is a part of this is far, far more important in human development than many of us realise.

In *Mediation*, we discuss the early work of Reuven Feuerstein and how he began his work in developing intelligence. Confronted with masses of children who appeared to have very low levels of intelligence, because they had been raised in NAZI concentration camps, Feuerstein realised the way to develop their intelligence lay partially in sharing human love and partially in teaching them how to sensitively relate to the world about them.[375] These children, just like the Romanian children, did not know how to think - because nobody had shown them how. John Fiske most adequately expressed this necessity for guidance in our development to be human when he wrote:

"What is the meaning of the fact that man is born into the world more helpless than any other creature, and more in need of a much longer season than any other living thing, the tender care and wise counsel of its elders?"[376]

It is through those who raise us, those we spend years with or those we share simple fleeting moments in passing, that we learn to become human in how we behave and in how we think. It is through others that we learn to be vague and dull in our interactions, or alternatively, sharp and very precise. It is through others that we learn to be insensitive or sensitive in our emotions, as we mould the many facets of the environment to our needs.

By our desires and by our interests, we notice the actions of others and the skills of interaction they have developed. If they do not interest us we see them only in a passing glance, but if there is that something, that one thing that attracts us to them, we study what they do and how well they do it. The movements they made, the words they say, are absorbed into who we think we are. The process of imprinting explains this very clearly.

So, as a thought comes, we consider all the skills and strategies we have picked up from others and use these to shape that thought into a reality, as we trek through our securities and insecurities. This is what makes intelligence, not the coding that provides the feature, but the experiences of life we have taken from others and fashioned into our own identity.

Such emotional sensitivity, which we introduce here, is a skill. It is not an inborn quality. It is a means to develop quality. It develops through the life experiences of the individual. As such, it is an art. It may be passed on in facets of guidance as one individual shares moments with another. It grows within the individual through the empathy they have for others and the depth of interest they have in pursuing an ideal. Thus, a quality of sensitivity lies in how information is defined, how relationships of information are recognised and how association is made to qualities of previous experiences that enable a situation to be recognised. From this, an act of intelligence is made.

Thus, the bullied twin developed a lower quality of sensitivity to their twin. At one level of understanding, we may say this lower quality caused them to be vague when they recognised and processed information. By this vagueness, they struggled to see connections that would make sense of information. The root of their insensitivity lay in the lack of confidence they had to engage with information, which the bully took from them.

410

Therefore, instead of considering how well the brains of twins work who inherited the same genetic coding (although remember that after conception they are no longer identical, because of the mutations we have earlier explained.[377]) we should move into the real world and consider how the efficiency of each brain is decided through **the interplay of the mind guiding the brain in the precision of the processing it makes.**

To begin to understand what this means, it is necessary to realise the mind is continually asking itself two questions:

• **Am I safe?**

and

• **What is the most interesting thing to attract my attention at this moment?**

In the first instance, the mind will be constantly seeking to know if the physical body or the social identity and the security of the individual are safe. Therefore, if the mind of a twin is trying to find a way to settle a problem at home, resolve some personality issue with another human being, they will not feel safe in any development situation they are in. Distracted, as they are, they will be less sensitive to processing information about them, with all the ramifications to this. However, should they feel safe and, then in the second part, be personally interested, they will display a high level of sensitivity and so present a better understanding of the information to others.

Therefore, any quality of understanding a twin makes, and it is the same for every human being, comes from the precision with which information is acquired through their senses and passed to the quality of information stored in the memory of their brain. The ability of one twin to recognise the significance of information and so what possibilities it may be used for, relies all too simply on the quality of sensitivity they engage information with and match this to the quality of information stored in their memory, through their personal and previous experiences.

Let us expand upon the point of monozygotic twins, and imagine we could have six clones - each having the same genetic coding at conception. However, as a human being, unique in their own right, each would have their own perspective on the infantile and later childhood stages they moved through. As each absorbed the behaviours of those raising them, the love, the loss of temper and the vast range of emotions in-between, each would fine-tune their behavioural responses to learn to survive. As they do this, their emotions would fine-tune their personalities and so endear them to different interests.

In school, each would personally examine the information they were daily introduced to. Each will recognise different meanings in the same information through their earlier experiences. As they are introduced to some new information, each will focus on what it is and the meanings this has to them.

As a human being, each will be monitoring the environment around them to consider if they are safe, that other children are not laughing at them and hopefully respecting them, and if not this, then not thinking about them. Free of the dangers of others attacking their identity, they will struggle to see the connections being shown to them by their teacher.

Yet, the mind is always searching for security, and if in searching it misses some point of the lesson, so it will struggle to make this up. How well each clone does this will depend much on how they had managed to keep up with the information of earlier lessons, had practised to become proficient with these and were able to gain a satisfactory response to any question they had the confidence to ask.

When we consider all this, we must understand that each of the clones we have will demonstrate a different response to any question asked, just as they will be more or less accurate, or faster or slower than another in this. We are human beings. We are not machines.

Therefore, when examined in school, each would respond according to their development. One clone may gain a grade of 4/10, another 5/10, others 6/10, 8/10, 9/10 and one 10/10, all depending on how each related to the changes in the environment when they occurred and how each chose to interact with this when it arose. If we were to place these scores on the Bell Curve, they would be shown to vary about the average, and yet there would no genetic differences here.

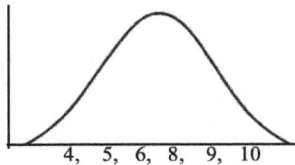

4, 5, 6, 8, 9, 10

Scores based purely on environmental factors,
with no differences in the genetic factor.

To enhance the point and take this example beyond the competence of the classroom environment, consider how each clone could have been separated at birth and raised in a different family under widely different social identities. Some clones were raised with deep affection, while others were raised with a sense of rejection. Some enjoyed a secure family, while others had a broken one or one with a violent atmosphere. Some had their insights raised and others had their quashed, so that guidance varied from devotion to indifference.

The list is endless, but as an individual, each clone (rather each human being) will adapt to survive the best way they can, which they may only do through the experiences each encountered after birth. This, after all, is the purpose of learning to adapt to survive, and so as a species to reproduce.

Thus, any group of normally functioning human beings will vary in what may be called intelligence, but the causes of this variation can easily be shown not to have a genetic cause and to have come about purely through the life conditioning each has developed through to that moment in time.

However, this does not suggest that each individual may instantly alter our impression of their intelligence, because whatever level they have evolved to has their personality entwined within it. Thus, they recognise information and how to interact with it through a sense of who they are.

To explain this in real terms would be to imagine how networks of neurons have become connected over very many years, with routes of passage being travelled again and again, each time strengthening a route. To develop a new route requires the identification of first a different purpose to do so, and second the desire for this to occur. As Freud would have it.

Any change in the physiology must first be preceded by a change in the psychology.

In conclusion, we may now realise that in a twist of fate, what Spearman thought was the g factor of intelligence is only the C- Factor of the Common Environment, and his S factor of intelligence is really nothing more than the D-Factor of the Differential Environment. The Nature/Nurture ratio that has confounded psychologists for over 100 years is a fallacy. It does not exist!

Chapter ThirtyOne
Witnessing the Myth

We do **not** think of intelligence as a multitude of components, with each having great adaptability as they serve their own specific environments, that come together to give a collective impression of ability. Yet, this is the little-known reality of the matter.

Consider, by simple example, how a child with vision problems struggles to clearly define what they see and read, and how their processing of information develops from this. Yet, either by a quick prescription for glasses or a longer period of muscular adjustment, their vision problem can be resolved. After this, they would clearly see information, and this would enable them to think more clearly, affecting quite dramatically any assessment made of them.

Instead of this, we have been caused to think of intelligence as a singular feature of the mind, that is largely inherited through a factor of genetic diversity. After all, Mendel's most important Law of Segregation set the basis for our discovery of the process of meiosis, which gives us an understanding of how inheritance works.

It is through this knowledge that we can explain why plants have predictable characteristics when pollinated. We like to extend this to explain why people display certain traits, but when we do this we fail to understand that human traits are not so predictable. Any genetic trait witnessed in one individual is not automatically passed to their sibling, for all gametes undergo a great shuffling effect. If the relevant gene is selected from this shuffling and passed to the creation of the sibling, its influence depends on whether it plays a dominant or recessive role in their genome. If it is recessive, it will have no bearing in the sibling. Yet if it is dominant, it cannot always be known how this is affected by environmental conditioning to explain what is witnessed, because the environment is so complex.

415

Most importantly, there is no way of knowing when or if the trait will appear again in a future generation. Therefore, the irregular existence of a trait cannot be used to explain the regularity by which intelligence is said to be passed from parent to child. The whole concept of inherited intelligence, which sees the intelligence of the parent naturally passed to their sibling, hides a multitude of uncertain factors.

This is the reality of genetic inheritance. The inheritance of intelligence does not have the predictability that social scientists wish to claim it does, as they seek to support political programs. We saw how Goddard did not understand how inheritance really works when he created the false hereditary family tree of the Kallikak family.

In fact, most social scientists, it may be reasoned, have not studied genetics to any depth, if they have at all, and merely follow the understanding in inheritance that has long been fashioned for them. This is evident when they claim a mental characteristic witnessed in a parent will automatically occur in their offspring and so incur little environmental effect. Although in reality, the environment could completely alter what that coding is thought to be responsible for. Our chapter on epigenetics clearly explained this.

We must never forget that there is a continual interplay between the organism and the environment, where the latter can literally turn a gene's potential "on" or "off." In this way, epigenetic factors of the environment are able to change the expression of the gene, causing it to express itself differently.[378] Stress, as a psychological impression of the environment, was subsequently shown to alter how cells function and, in the sense of intelligence, devastate whatever genius the child may be thought to be born with.[379]

Accordingly, all this was lost to the social scientists who wrote the book *The Bell Curve* and those of their ilk, where they took a comic book impression of inheritance, played around with test data to openly predict how white children from rich backgrounds have a "natural" superiority, which would serve society most if they were channelled to leadership roles by being given better opportunities in education.

Let us now come to grips with all we have so far discussed in this book, to understand why intelligence is not inherited in the manner we have long believed it is. I will try to explain this through simple steps. ...

STEP ONE:
Galton's view of intelligence from a social and a political angle:

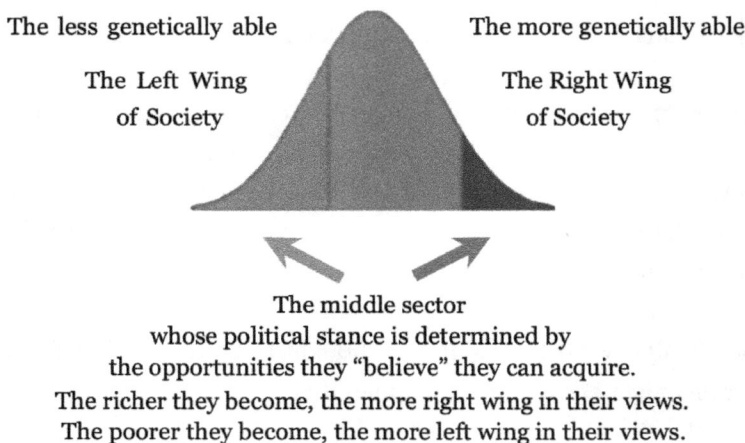

The less genetically able   The more genetically able

The Left Wing   The Right Wing
of Society   of Society

The middle sector
whose political stance is determined by
the opportunities they "believe" they can acquire.
The richer they become, the more right wing in their views.
The poorer they become, the more left wing in their views.

While Galton was never able to find a way to actually measure intelligence, he tried to explain that human intelligence could be gauged by reference. To support this claim he wrote, with all honest intent, that the most intelligent dog is more intelligent than the human being ranked in the region of Point X.

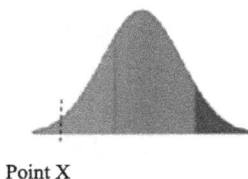

Point X

Thus, the man who created our belief that intelligence is inherited for social purposes and tried to prove this mathematically to enable the whole educational machine to support this, did so with the belief that the Border Collie has more intelligence than a child born through oxygen starvation or with Down Syndrome.

Anyone who is familiar with the legendary work of Reuven Feuerstein[380] will know, as I do, how a Down Syndrome child can have their intelligence cultivated to that of a normal or near normal child once they are guided through love and clear language -- the two ingredients that, we explain in our following book, are the whole basis of intelligence.

However, with his endeavour to prove how ability is inherited, Galton wrote that the social worth of a family continues through generations, because inheritance is not "really" affected by opportunity.

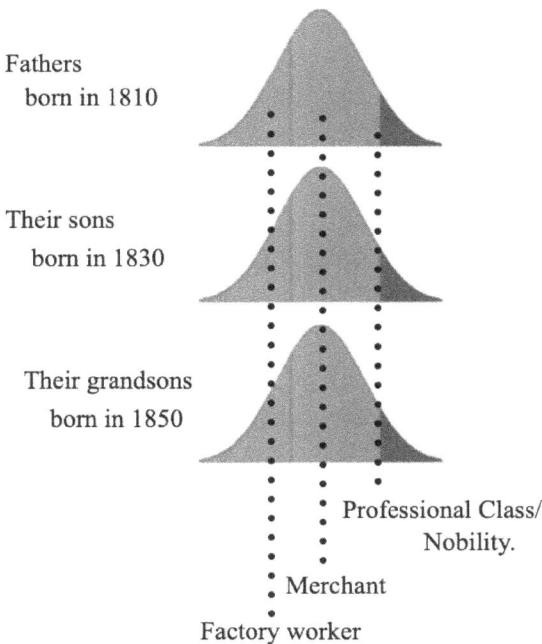

Fathers
born in 1810

Their sons
born in 1830

Their grandsons
born in 1850

Professional Class/
Nobility.

Merchant

Factory worker

Yet, consider the reality of influence through three generations in the very rigidly socially controlled and restrictive world of the 19th century. I was interviewed for a government job in England in 1983. The very first question I was asked was "Which school did you go to?"

STEP TWO:

Terman in 1916 and the authors of *The Bell Curve* in 1994 built upon Galton's idea to create culturally based intelligence questions, which they used to explain that the intelligence of a person could be "more or less" decided through the colour of their skin.

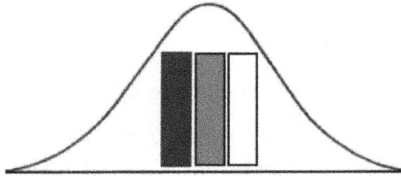

They, and "many" IQ interested psychologists, believed that at any point on the Bell Curve graph, a white child would always be genetically superior to a Hispanic child, who would always be genetically superior to a black child. This reasoning is obviously very biased.

The first point to notice here is that IQ tests are very language-oriented and, in being set to the average white environment, involve a language that works against the general environments, language and cultures of Hispanics and African Americans.[381]/[382] After all, African Americans living in the Northern states, where they have better education, more employment opportunities and less prejudice, perform substantially higher in IQ tests than those living in the Southern states.[383]

Equally, IQ tests on non-white children do not take into consideration school experiences.[384] This is a very important point, because the highest IQ scorers are, on average, East Asians (Taiwanese, Japanese, etc)[385], who come from cultures where children are highly pressurised to gain high academic performance through extensive after-school learning programs.[386] We may recall the results of Ritchie and Tucker-Drob's research, where they found the role of education to be decisive in developing intelligence.

We may add to this that not only do IQ tests have very little practical use, but they also do not predict actual performance in the classroom. More importantly, IQ tests make a less accurate prediction of performance after school for African Americans than they do for whites.[387] This is because test questions are set to meet white expectations, which African Americans have trouble relating to due to their different culture. However, once out of the educational system, African Americans can outperform what they were expected to achieve while in school, provided they are given the right opportunities.

To contest the opinion of black inferiority gained through IQ tests, we may refer to one study made on black Caribbean and white English children raised in a UK orphanage. Tests there found that black children demonstrated higher IQs than white children. Reasoning for this came from the suggestion that the orphanage staff had given more developmental attention to the Caribbean children, which is to say that the environment made the difference in their IQ results.[388]

In discussing this nature/nurture factor, it is now relevant to refer to a review article published in 2012, in the Journal of American Psychology. This article provided evidence that differences in IQ between races occur on account of cultural differences and that there is virtually NO evidence to support differences in intelligence being based on genetic differences, within the normal IQ range.[389]

In fact, James Flynn created a large amount of data to show that there are no genetic differences in intelligence between races and that such differences that are noted are on account of environmental factors that correlate with socioeconomic status.[390]

In conclusion to this issue, we may now refer to a court decision in America, which ruled against the use of IQ tests on African American children, with the understanding that they are biased and do work against their culture.[391] IQ tests are, therefore. now legally recognised to be prejudicial, and in this, now recognised to infer a political agenda.

STEP THREE:
Although psychologists have been studying the effect of the environment on intelligence (for all their political and social reasons), ever since Johannsen discovered the role of the environment in 1905, no psychologist has ever proven how much inheritance influences intelligence to the agreement of all concerned.

All that is concluded is that there is some inherited quality (based on the reasoning of Galton) and a developmental quality. Indeed, as Johannsen pointed out, the environment is so complex that the influence of the gene on the intelligence of the individual cannot be known. Thus, there never was a basis for this ratio, and its existence only serves political purposes. We shall return to this shortly.

We might further explain that proteins are changing so rapidly every second that the effect of the gene is impossible to measure. It is quite impossible to know the protein action that is unveiling the DNA design behind an act of intelligence in any one instant. Even if we could do this, we still could not define the specific environment of the individual. All we ever see is the effect of the environment, but we cannot know how the environment produced what we see.

All that is measured in an intelligence test is the apparent conditioning of the way the individual interprets the world as they see it.

Thus, all that has come to the surface in 130 years of tests, investigations and debates is that right-wing concerns try to show a high inherited value, while left-wing concerns a low inherited value, for all the reasons we have examined. Since the value of the genes to that of the environment has never been proven, and since all assume the genes must play some role in creating different intelligences, although this also has never been proven in the case of normally born individuals, it is generally assumed that these two factors have equal influence in determining intelligence. Let us say 50/50.

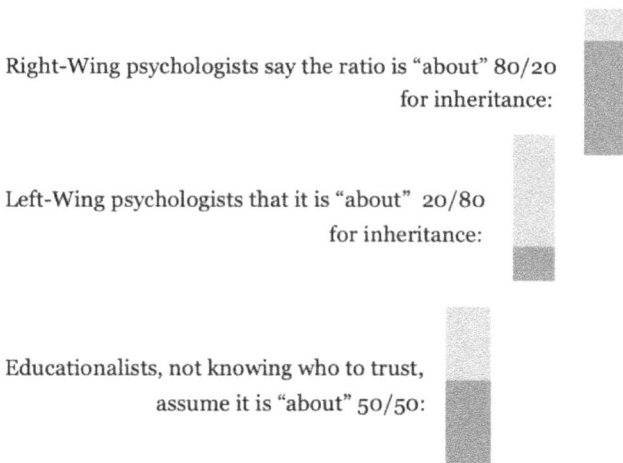

Right-Wing psychologists say the ratio is "about" 80/20 for inheritance:

Left-Wing psychologists that it is "about" 20/80 for inheritance:

Educationalists, not knowing who to trust, assume it is "about" 50/50:

However, while psychologists state that genes play an important role in intelligence, even though they disagree as to how much, it needs to be realised that this is a very loose statement. Plomin and von Stumn reason that no genes have been found to contribute to more than 1% of the total measure of an IQ score.[392] But, even this statement raises caution, because of the great complexity of the factors involved.

STEP FOUR:

As we found when we discussed polygenes, if the environment is far more complex than the variation of gene codes, as it is with intelligence, then it is not possible to know the influence of the gene codes through the environment. This is to say that relative to the expanse of the environment, any genetic differences that normally arise must be of a very narrow variation.

In other words, Galton's reasoning that genes range in quality continuously throughout the population is wrong. There are either not many variations of gene codes, or if there are, they are not designed to impair the development of the feature and have become designed (as we explain through the law of natural selection) to allow the environment to totally construct the value of that feature, in normal cases.

- Therefore, Galton's theory of inherited ability, as having a continuous variation in any population, cannot be the deciding factor in the varying qualities of intelligence witnessed.

- The error is to believe that it must lie in the understanding that genes are normally shuffled at the reproductive stage, and so create a wide genetic diversity of quality. However, this reasoning fails to understand that such shuffling may imply only alternative codes that bring no difference to effect, as opposed to superior and inferior designs that could.

This is certainly the case with many of the features of which intelligence is composed. We have found this with language (which enables us to relate to items in the environment and explain our understanding to another), with emotion (which enables us to be highly sensitive and correct with items we have a personal interest and so purpose with), with our ability to learn new things, with our ability to change our thoughts freely and to be ever more adaptable in our understanding of the environment.

STEP FIVE:

We have understood that Galton's theory of the law of deviation from the average suggests that there was once an original gene code that, over time, incurred numerous variations of quality. These variations are now reasoned to run continuously from very low quality to very high quality.

While these genetic variations cannot be known by themselves, they are reasoned to be witnessed by the scores individuals gain in IQ tests. Thus, the score an individual gains is reasoned to be determined by the quality of the gene coding they inherited and its ability to develop through environmental experiences.

This theory reasons that those who inherited lesser qualities of this original code performed progressively poorer in IQ tests. So we find at the extreme left of the graph those who gained the lowest scores, with the explanation that they inherited the lowest quality of the gene variation.

On the other hand, those who are said to have inherited codes of greater ability are so said to gain higher IQ scores, enabling them to move up the scale towards the extreme at the right side of the graph. Here we find the genius level.

Thus, by witnessing this wide scale of differences from both extremes, a clear step up in gene quality is said to exist from the lowest to the highest. This is Galton's theory of continuous variation, which is portrayed through the Bell Curve graph.

However, there are two fundamental errors in this theory, which quite destroy its viability, if they are recognised.

First, and as we have examined, no genius came from a line of geniuses, nor did they begin one. The ancestors and the descendants of a genius were of normal ability. Thus, any genius was a one-off and only so on account of very unusual environmental experiences, which developed within them high qualities of persistence, perseverance and passion, enabling them to complete whatever achievement gave them such recognition. Accordingly, there is no evidence of genetic line of genius on the extreme right of the curve.

Therefore, it could now be reasoned that the only evidence that gene codes vary in quality lies with those on the extreme left of the curve. However, those who score so low do not do so through a normal gene variation. Those who score so low evolved from a chromosomal disorder causing Down Syndrome, or they were born from a normal variation but incurred birth complications that interfered with the natural development of their ability. Thus, these human beings are not the same as those who scored higher points and who are placed beyond this low region of the graph.

The important point here is that these human beings often have a slightly different physiology from the norm and often display different emotional levels of control, which causes them greater trouble to maintain concentration and focus. Accordingly, by their general impairment, they may be classified as none cognitively fully functioning and so classifiable as different from all others they are being compared with.

There is, of course, no strict division in understanding those who are not fully cognitively functioning and those who are, because, as Binét was tasked to find, there are fully functioning individuals who appear impaired only because of very poor environmental experiences.

Once we remove the genius and those who are not fully cognitively functioning from the equation, the seemingly straightforward scale of intelligence from the lowest ability to the highest suddenly comes into question, because there is now no evidence that any differences we witness in intelligence are caused by differences in genetic quality or design.

Instead, we are left with two classifications of ability; one of human beings who in having some restriction to interact with the environment may be said to be none cognitively fully functioning, and the other, who in being able to make normal interaction with the environment, may be regarded to be cognitively fully functional.

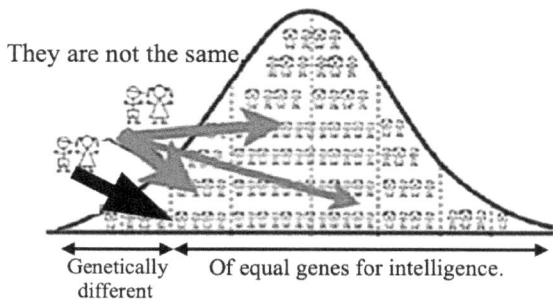

They are not the same.

Genetically different   Of equal genes for intelligence.

Therefore, we may see that all psychologists have done is to identify with individuals who have some general impairment in their physiology and demonstrate low intelligence and use their low intelligence as evidence of "inherited" differences in the intelligence of all. Yet, there is no evidence for this.

In fact, as we mentioned earlier, to emphasise that differences in test scores are essentially caused by environmental factors rather than genetic, we discuss in *Brain Plasticity* the case of a child who scored 63 in an IQ test, but with attention to their emotional problems was later found to score 158.[393]

It is of the highest importance to understand from this that there is no evidence that normally born children inherit a structure of DNA that creates different qualities of intelligence, which cannot be overridden by the environment.

426

The problem we have with the Bell Curve is that it too conveniently demonstrates a range of ability that is simply coincidental with what we assume is the variation of the quality of genes in a population.

From this coincidence, we convince ourselves that the lowest performance in test scores at the extreme left of the curve aligns with the lowest genetic variation, so that the latter explains the former. The same being believed at the other extreme, the highest test scores are believed to align with the highest quality of gene variation. Thus we have ...

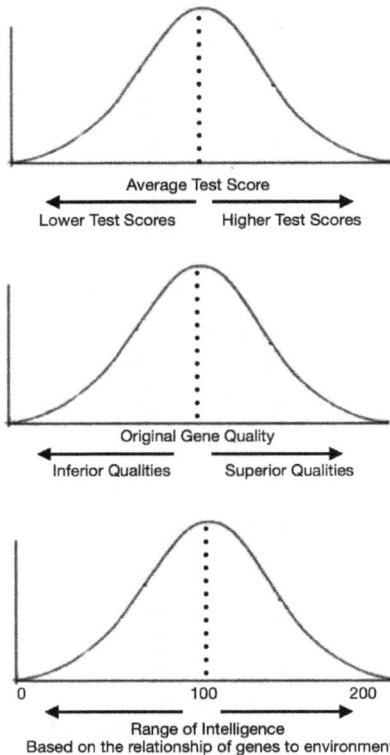

Average Test Score

Lower Test Scores   Higher Test Scores

Original Gene Quality

Inferior Qualities   Superior Qualities

0   100   200

Range of Intelligence
Based on the relationship of genes to environment

And yet, as we have just seen, there is no evidence that genes do vary continuously from low to high in quality of design. This relationship is, therefore, not valid.

We may also note that test scores do not deviate equally from the average, as Galton reasoned. After all, an individual may reach the maximum of 200 to the right of the average, but no individual, no human being, could score zero to the left. The lowest score may be just under 30, and so there is no direct symmetry as Galton's law of deviation from the average would demand. Although, in having said this and as we have explained throughout this book, it is not possible to measure human intelligence anyway, so the whole argument is arbitrary.

However, if we wish to understand why test scores range so widely, we would need to understand more about how the data behind these scores is designed and how they are evaluated. This would help us to gain a deeper understanding of the environment of intelligence.

STEP SIX:

As we saw, the belief that genes do vary in quality of design continuously from low to high lies in Galton's theory of the law of deviation from the average, which he took from Quetelet's reasoning that arrows would land on equal sides of the most that were fired. It was from this that the concept of the average arose. However, while many assume this average to be natural, it would be revealing to show how it is actually manufactured in the Bell Curve by the way questions are created for intelligence tests.

We may be reminded of this by the way Galton had manufactured data of test scores from the military academy to show how the then Gauss Curve could be used to support Quetelet's theory of distribution about the average. Thus, it is not that the average naturally appears, as Galton tried to insist, but that it is constructed from results obtained by the design of the questions asked.

This is not a small thing, because by the design of the questions set in intelligence tests, which now include the decisive SATs in school, great control is exerted over what is expected of education, the responsibility it can be excused from, and the means by which it is able to control its operation from the financing of schools in different areas to the accepted workload of teachers in their lessons — all of which drive the character of the nation's population.

Therefore, it is crucial that if we are to understand how to better prepare our children for the A.I. world they will survive in, we must seek to transform education from the current processing system it remains.

The route to achieving this lies in understanding why the Bell Curve provides a wrong interpretation of what intelligence is, and therefore, the ability of children to learn and how they should be taught. To understand this, let us look again at Galton's reasoning that gene codes vary continuously in their quality for intelligence, according to his law of deviation from the average.

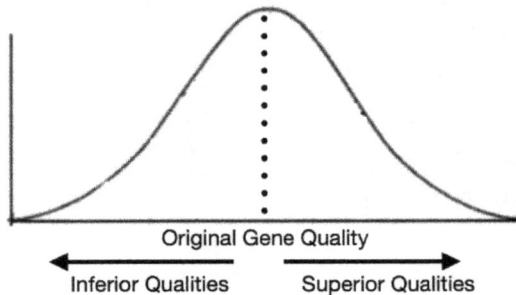

Original Gene Quality

Inferior Qualities   Superior Qualities

In order for this graph to be phased into a graph of test scores, by which the scores can be said to be related to the variation of genes, the test questions must be designed to make the results they obtain vary in accordance with the law of deviation from the average.

If they are not, and the test questions are too easy, the average positioning would be placed higher up the scale, and so not complement the continuous variation of genetic codes. This would give the impression that more students are more intelligent than they could otherwise be shown to be.

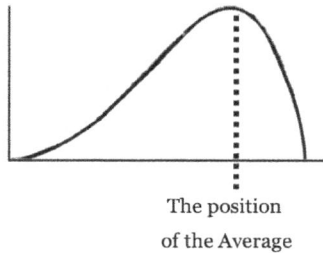

The position
of the Average

Equally, if the test questions were made very difficult, the average positioning would be placed lower down the scale and equally not complement the continuous variation of genetic codes. This would give the impression that more students are less intelligent than they could otherwise be shown to be.

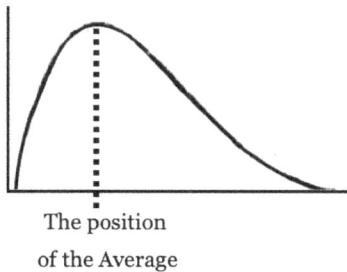

The position
of the Average

Once we understand that questions are selected to control where the average will lie, we may also understand that questions are also selected according to the manner of thinking of one social level or culture. The model that is normally chosen is based on the living environment of those from middle-class white America.

There is an extremely important point to be aware of, and it is generally not, that although no two individuals think the same way, they may be grouped into a general manner of thinking according to the social or ethnic group they belong to.

This may seem of little significance until we think upon the political character of IQ tests (and their associated SATs), for we may now understand how questions can easily be selected in a way that makes them easier to answer by those with one socioeconomic or ethic identity, but more difficult for those having different identities.

Thus, rather than focusing upon scores (the answers given and the grades awarded), we need to consider more how questions are selected and for whom they are selected. When we do this, a whole new level of understanding is opened up to show IQ tests in a very different light.

As we have just mentioned, when IQ questions are based on the familiarity of what is expected within one cultural group, those of a different culture will have greater difficulty relating to the questions asked, because they do not think in the same way.

We may generally understand from this that a person from Norway will see information in a different way than a person from Morocco, and both of these will see information quite differently than a person from Japan, because of their diverse cultures.

It is important to note that the same principle applies to those of one nationality, even though people may speak the same language and come from the same country. After all, each will learn to identify and deal with the world about them according to the particular social or regional culture they were raised in.

Thus, it is not the case that whites and African Americans are American and so naturally think in the same way, but that the minds of each tend to live within their own cultural worlds. This quite distorts the idea that they all think the same way because they have the same nationality.

Very often they do not. In fact, the creation of Ebonics was devised to help African American children learn to think as white children do, although for various reasons, its success seems limited.[394/395/396]

It is important, in fact, it is very important, to understand that the score an individual obtains in an IQ test can be related to the similarity of their background to that chosen as the model from which questions were designed.

Thus, even though African Americans think differently from their culture to white middle-class Americans, African Americans in the North live in a culture more similar to the white model than those living in the South, which is why they tend to score higher on IQ tests.[397]

We may see from this that IQ questions are very biased, as was exemplified by the court ruling we saw in STEP TWO, and so how they can be very prejudicial in their nature.

Therefore, by the design of questions, one class of people can be shown to be of less intelligence and another of greater intelligence, which does tend to play to a political agenda when those from the chosen model are shown to be deserving of more opportunity and so greater responsibility in their society. This, as we saw, is exactly what the book called *The Bell Curve* stated and tried to prove.

Thus, on the surface level, as all things appear, we are informed that individuals inherit a quality of intelligence through their genetic line, whose worth they more or less demonstrate by the score they obtain in an IQ test. Since their score is said to demonstrate the level of their intelligence, which is largely related to their DNA coding and which cannot change, it is said to be constant throughout their lifetime. This is the argument made to support intelligence testing and The Bell Curve, which has become associated with it.

We may imagine from this that we could have one individual at X and another at Y placed on the following graph.

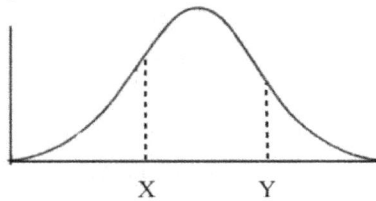

However, if we delve deeper and examine what is not so obvious, we find a very different account of what is happening:

- First, we may be reminded that intelligence tests do not actually measure very much of what we think intelligence is. The question arises from this as to what is actually being measured? Thus, rather than an inherited quality being revealed, we must consider whether we are merely witnessing the ways different individuals have learnt to understand the meaning of information differently.

- Second, the questions that are asked in IQ tests tend to be related to one socio-cultural group, which goes to the disadvantage of those who belong to a different group and so evaluate information differently, as we have just pointed out. We will return to this later when we discuss a situation involving a Somalian engineer.

- Third, intelligence questions tend to be related to a level of education. To understand what this means, we should know how education works.

We may have the impression that the more intelligent students score higher marks and grades. However, such higher performance is gained through the development of a better mindset, which develops their higher intelligence, and not so an intelligence that has a genetic origin.

This mindset developed through a greater competence in the languages of education. These languages are of mathematics, and the national language chosen to be used for communication in learning may be English, French, Chinese, etc. In all their subjects, students will be evaluated on their proficiency with these languages and the facts they can remember, as they weave these into their presentations.

Competence with language is merely to keep up with the steady acquisition of rules, as one builds upon another. This requires concentration to understand and practice to become proficient, as we shall now see. Competence with remembering facts comes through an emotional interest, which devises efficiency in mnemonic strategies. Competence in presentation comes from learnt strategies and a developed skill in weaving information together, which essentially is to tell a story.

All of these rely upon a factor of self-confidence to control the rate of learning, which is to interrupt, to question, to test with the devil's advocate, to have developed a method to continually self-check, to self-correct, and to have the desire to want to learn. In other words, to have the spirit to want to learn through mistakes and to recognise the value of doing so.

Consequently, it is by their language proficiency in the 3Rs, plus their ability to avoid distractions and their interest in recalling facts that a student demonstrates proficiency in history, geography, physics, chemistry, etc.

Basically, we may say that the top students are those who have taught themselves. Lesser performing students expect the teacher to do the thinking for them. All this was quite unknown or at least not realised by Spearman, when he recognised a continuity in ability through different subjects, and created from this his g factor of intelligence and thereafter his s factor. Let me demonstrate why Spearman was wrong, and so the value of understanding rules to be proficient in maths, and so with working through formulas in physics, etc.

There is a rule in mathematics known as BODMAS. The rule explains that when a student is working through a math problem, they must first do the brackets, then, working from left to right, they are to do the division, multiplication, addition and finally subtraction, in this order. This is the rule. We will now look at two students, one who did not follow the rule and one who did, as both sought to solve the problem $6/2(2+1) =?$

Our first student heard the teacher explaining that the first thing to do is the brackets. But, then, some incident occurred that distracted their mind and they did not hear the rest of the teacher's explanation. So, they began by doing the brackets and added 2+1 to get 3. Then, without knowing the rule, they used logic and so multiplied this 3 by 2 to get 6. They, then, divided 6 by 6 to get 1. The answer of 1 is the wrong answer. This student will not understand why they are marked wrong, because the way they worked through the equation made sense to them.

Our second student, however, heard the full explanation of the teacher and worked strictly in accordance with BODMAS. They did the brackets first and added 2 to 1 to get 3. Then, and in working from the left, they did the division and divided 6 by 2 to get 3. After this, they did the multiplication, and multiplied 3 by 3 to get 9. Nine is the correct answer.

As we can see, none of this is a factor of intelligence. As lesson builds upon lessons, our second student will have gained confidence to be sensitive in their handling of information and will continually gain high marks. However, our first student will normally not have the confidence to question why they got the wrong answer, and will likely give much the same concentration with each lesson. Continually confused, they will likely guess or copy through lessons, rather than demand to understand what they are doing wrong.

By the psychology of the situation, students trust the marks and grades the teacher gives them, without questioning the competence of the teacher. As each learn their place in the scheme of things, they tend to role-play to what others expect of them. This is how stability in performance and so intelligence is created, not by the quality of a gene code.

So we find that by its operation, civilisation creates highly conditional and self-limiting environments, which most readily conform to. We may think of comfort zones here. It is by this conformity that most continue to display a regular sense of thinking, of using the same strategies, and so of displaying the same sense of ability in handling tasks. We may say this is their intelligence. It is only those who are liberated from their environment, or who consciously break free from it, that demonstrate a dramatic improvement in their ability.

Howell, as we saw in Ch.27, explained how domestication creates a tranquillising effect on the mind, while survival in the wild creates a stimulating mind desiring to challenge to survive. The mind of any organism builds through the quality of the stimulation it receives, as the mind adapts to what it thinks is expected of it in order to survive.

It is, therefore, very important for us to understand that students who gave the answer of 1 in the above test were not of low intelligence. They very simply did not know or had forgotten 'the rule'! Consider, in the following examples, how we see again that ability in mathematics is simply to keep up with the rules by which equations may be negotiated.

I was once asked by a mother to help her daughter, who confessed that she was no good at maths. As we have explained, maths is simply a language composed of rules, and most students have problems with this subject because they never learnt to understand what this means. Without understanding this, they did not know the significance of keeping up with the rules by which each level could be decoded. So, I asked the girl a few simple questions and saw that she did not understand what she was doing, because she was unaware of the rules involved.

The mother told me that her math teacher had told her daughter that she was stupid and had asked her how she got into her class. The girl had absolutely no confidence in maths, much because of this teacher, yet displayed great skill in creative art.

To help the girl, I started to show her the meaning of relationships with numbers and the importance of rules, and the need to practice and apply these. Within thirty minutes, she could do one question in an old math paper that she could not even have attempted before I helped her. In real terms, this meant that she was able to gain five more marks in this paper, and so gain one small but important step in being able to pass its examination. The whole point here is that once she understood the rules involved, the girl could demonstrate how less confused she is and so be seen to be more intelligent!

I want to share another story similar to this, for we will come to see the importance here of a good education versus a poor one in relating to developing intelligence in a student.

Accordingly, a mother explained how her 15-year-old daughter had struggled to understand something in her math lesson. She wanted to ask the teacher for help, but the girl knew that others in the class understood how to do what she could not, and did not want them to laugh at her. (This is totally normal.) So, the girl wondered how she could gain the teacher's help. Eventually, she realised that she had to do something, because she was getting more and more lost as the lesson progressed. Bravely, she stood up, went to the teacher's desk, and asked for help to understand this problem. This is the response she very bluntly got:

"I have explained this once! I can't do it in any other way."

The girl felt hugely embarrassed and quickly returned to her desk. She was now totally lost in what was happening in the lesson, and left it without understanding what was expected of her.

When the next lesson came, she was just as lost, but now did not have the confidence to ask the teacher for help. As one lesson moved to the next, her understanding of this subject became ever more blurred. She was given homework and got her friends to help her, but she did not understand what was going on. After some time, the teacher gave a test, and the girl gained a poor score.

The teacher believed she had done her job. She had given information to her students, marked the responses she got after each lesson and eventually graded each on their ability. However, at no time did it ever occur to this teacher that she was responsible for the marks she gave. After all, if she had taught better, then this girl, as all the other students in her class, would have understood better what was happening and been less "confused"!

It is very important for us to expand upon the relationship between developing a good understanding of the rules of mathematics and intelligence, because of the way some IQ questions are math-based. Take, for example, the following IQ question:

"How many minutes is it before noon if 29 minutes ago it was 6 times as many minutes after 10 am?"

To solve this conundrum, we must understand these hours as a part of the day expressed in common terms.

So, noon is 12 hours of the day (12x60) = 720 minutes.
Equally, 10 am is (10x60) = 600 minutes.

We need to find the number of minutes before noon, so call this X.
So, the current time is 720 - X minutes.
29 minutes ago was 720 -X - 29 = 691 - X minutes.
Therefore: 691 - X x 6 + 600 =13.

The answer to the IQ question is 13.

Now, if the math teacher had lovingly mediated a clear understanding of what she was teaching, and so clearly taught the rules of maths, (The secret to solving this puzzle lies in changing all hours to minutes to work from a common base.) the girl we have just discussed, as any student, could have found the answer of 13 and would have scored highly in the IQ test.

Yet, because of her environmental background, which in this case was centred around this teacher, this girl would have been unable to solve this question and would have scored lowly in the IQ test. In turn, this would have been taken to show the value of **her lifetime intelligence!**

I remember when I joined the army, having been a total failure at school, I was given an IQ test. One question, I distinctly remember, showed three pictures of a stick half in water with different angles of refraction. I had to tick the correct box. At that time in my life, I just guessed the box. However, this question is one of physics. If I had understood physics (The only thing I remember from physics was being whipped by my teacher with the rubber hose from a Bunsen burner), I could have known which was the correct box to tick.

Through these examples of mathematics (and mine of physics), we can see the genetic value of intelligence is not examined, only the skill the participant has developed to or rather been educated to.

When the participant has good environmental and good school-based knowledge, and good language skills, they score highly. When they have poor knowledge and poor language skills, they score lowly, as Mexican immigrants did on Terman's IQ tests.

However, while the particular environment of the individual is never really examined, once they are placed on the Bell Curve, their value of intelligence is regarded as set for life, as based on the quality of the genes they are assumed to have inherited!

Yet, there is no understanding of this genetic order, as we saw with the previous STEP, and all assessment is only on the ways the environmental experience is determined through the questions selected.

But these questions are general to a population and not related to the specific development of the individual. May we be reminded, as we saw with Fencher in Chapter Twelve, "An individual cannot be appraised without the total information that creates the basis of that appraisal." This is to say, it is not possible to evaluate an individual outside of the very personal and unique environment that created them.

However, society expects schools to assess ability in general knowledge, so schools end up testing students on what they've learned and how well they have followed the rules—often mistaking this for intelligence.

Yet, this error is seldom realised, since educationalists are conditioned to think in terms of intelligence, which they have long been led to understand has a factor of inheritance. So, when they witness stability in the performance of a student, they are apt to reason that this is caused by some genetic factor. Too few realise that this stability is simply a factor of development in a highly conditioning and self-limiting environment.

Therefore, by the extent to which rules are known, we find a true explanation for differences in ability. Performance in education is much allied to the management of its rules, as they define what information is and how it can interact.

Children vary in their understanding of these rules, not because of their supposed level of intelligence, but because they were not clearly taught to understand them, or they were distracted at the moment they were to learn these. If understood, they were not practised to remember or to understand where and when to use them. Such is the case, in varying degrees, for the very most in any class. All of this can be explained through poor skills in language, factors of emotion, confidence to interact and the purpose to want to do so.

The few who did pay attention, did question if they did not understand, did practice in applying these rules and did understand where and when to use them, are the ones who are referred to as being intelligent! These are the children who were generally better raised by their parents in how to evaluate information, have developed a mental stamina to keep their control of the movement of information and have the confidence to question when they don't understand. It is by the confidence they gain through all this that they develop the interest that breeds the curiosity to develop greater understanding.

Thus, we can see that by the ways the individual has been raised at home, by the qualities of their teachers in school and by events which inspired their curiosity to think of the world about them (or how they were distracted to do so and think of game playing here) that they learn to think and demonstrate ability in dealing with problems.

Therefore, instead of thinking that the Bell Curve must show degrees of intelligence, let us take the perspective that test scores actually show levels of confusion in handling the test questions, which have no relation to a genetic framework. In other words, instead of thinking of ability, consider that we are only thinking of development.

Thus, those on the extreme right of the Bell Curve graph, said to be the more intelligent, can simply be said to be the very least confused by the questions asked of them.

We may recall our discussion on genius here and how they achieved their placement on the Bell Curve only through persistence, perseverance and passion — with no relation to a genetic standing. May we be reminded that any genius did not come from a line of geniuses and nor did they seed one. All said geniuses were a one-off.

This leads us to understand that the central point of the average will be represented by those who were half or generally confused by the questions, while those below them and said to be of lower intelligence, were the most confused in understanding what the questions were asking them and how they should best respond.

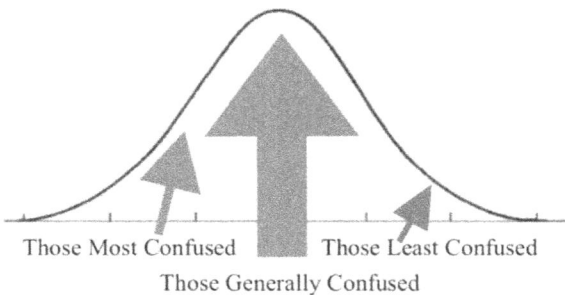

Those Most Confused   Those Least Confused
Those Generally Confused

These differences in performance, directly caused by levels of confusion, can be found in every lesson in every classroom of the world, just as in all walks of life.

If we now return to how test scores are used to create the Bell Curve graph, we can see that it is only by their design (the manner of the questions chosen) that the position of the average complements that of Galton's law of deviation from the average.

When the graph of test scores matches the graph of continuous genetic variation, the concept of inherited intelligence is said to be given verification. However, as we have seen, test scores are artificially arranged by the style of questions asked and the true quality of genes involved is not known. With this being so, there is no verification at all to support the concept of intelligence being differently inherited or measurable, as the Bell Curve has been used to demonstrate.

However, there is another way to show how intelligence varies in a population, without being tied to a genetic variation. As we have seen, the Paretian Distribution Curve does not present a graph that conforms to the law of deviation from the average. This greatly disturbs the concept of test scores being related to genetic variations. This becomes very clear when we compare the two graphs:

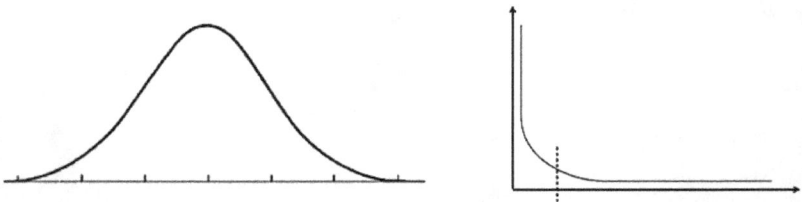

We can see from this comparison how the Bell Curve seeks to show inherited and developed intelligence, based on normal genetic diversity, while the Paretian curve shows developed intelligence with no relation to a genetic distribution of varying quality.

By comparison and with great significance the performances displayed in the Paretian Curve, as demonstrated by O'Boyle and Aguinus, were based on the results of tests of skills directly related to performance, which included many of the skills that are not considered in normal intelligence tests.

The Paretian Distribution Curve

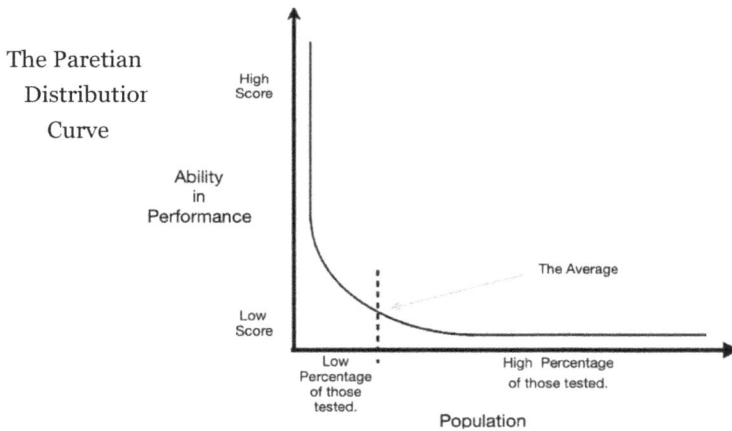

It is important to now see, through all the factors we have considered in this book, why the Bell Curve does not show a range of intelligence. It merely shows the quality of development the participants have reached through their life experiences.

Education creates much of these experiences in how the child is prepared for school, how clearly the content of each lesson is explained to them once they are in school, how they are able to balance their interests against the distractions made on their mind through the behaviour of others they must study with and the job and so life experiences they will encounter as a consequence of their education.

Accordingly, each child or rather each student, will encounter different life experiences, which will arm them differently to interact with their education and by this demonstrate their competence in understanding.

To understand how children can be so easily confused that they cannot keep up with the progression of their lessons, which in turn we now know is related to the development of their intelligence, pause in your reading for a moment and look once again at the following picture.

In one way, this photograph is timeless, for we see a poor mother who is burdened with too many tasks to have the time to sit down and calmly explain to each of her children how to be more sensitive in the interactions they make in their world, which would make the difference in their school performances and so grades and life opportunities.

It is timeless because even though the mother of today has a higher standard of living, she is generally no more aware of how to raise her children to be sensitive to the world about them, as she is distracted from this responsibility by addiction to mobile phones and computer games. Now, as then before, burdened with worry, domestic stress and debt that injures their dreams of happiness, families break up. But statistics never show the pain and agony of the child whose world of security is torn apart, and they are left to struggle in their school classes against differing personalities and teachers who seldom have the needed time to help them understand what they do not.

For one of many, many reasons, the very most of students fall behind as lessons progress and teachers seldom have the time or the energy to keep each student up to pace -- and when circumstances overwhelm them, as they frequently do in education, the teacher lapses into the mindset in which they have been conditioned.

This is most easily explained by the analogy of the brain of each student being an empty jug of a different size, with all that the teacher has to do is to fill each jug with as much water as it can hold -- an analogy that can all too easily trace its roots to Galton's theory of inherited intelligence and the Bell Curve graph that grew out of this. This is the reality of learning in school, and so how education affects the development of intelligence, good or bad.

This aside, it is by the proficiency of the teacher, the freedom they have to work, the quality of the learning environment, the behaviour of all students in the class, the understanding of the parents in how they prepared their child for school, how they support them through its many years, and how the student is inspired to want to learn and is not distracted from doing so, that creates a mental agility by which intelligence thrives in the learning mind.

Ritchie and Tucker-Drob were intrigued enough in this matter to begin a lengthy research into why intelligence test scores and educational duration are positively correlated. This correlation, they realised, could be interpreted in two ways. Either students with greater natural ability for intelligence go on to complete more education or a longer education increases intelligence. By the end of their research, they concluded that:

"Education appears to be the most consistent, robust, and durable method yet to be identified for raising intelligence."[398]

It is not, then, that intelligence earns the grades, but rather it is the route to these grades that forges intelligence.

Intelligence does not gain grades, but grades gain intelligence!

We may be reminded by this of how Cyril Burt, in Ch.19, strove to limit the education of poor children through his falsification of data, where he claimed public funding should not be wasted in trying to improve the low inherited quality of their intelligence and so sought to deprive them of an effective education that would raise their intelligence and so disturb the status quo.

Yet, by the facts we present here and in the following step, we realise there is no evidence that differences in intelligence can be directly related to a factor of inheritance -- providing we do not use a mentally impaired human being as evidence of genetic variation in normally functioning human beings!

As we saw through the Paretian Distribution Curve, the said range of intelligence based on inheritance does not follow Galton's Law of Deviation from the Average (which he took from Quetelet's Law of Accidental Causes, which he took from Laplace's Law of Error of Observations). Therefore, the curve that Gauss designed to show the position of stars in the night sky, should never have been used to inspire people to believe that it does.

STEP EIGHT:
As we saw, James Flynn noticed that although IQ tests were always calibrated to make a score of 100 the average, the actual raw scores demonstrated how performance in tests improved over time. By calculating the average score in 1900 to be 67, and aligning this to the

average in 2000, Flynn saw how intelligence had improved over a century.[399] The more he worked with cross data, the more he realised that this rise in intelligence through generations is witnessed globally.

However, as both he and Blair explained, this rise in global intelligence occurred too rapidly to have been caused by genetic mutations.[400] In other words, the only plausible explanation for this global rise in intelligence is through environmental effect and so more effective aspects of development. In short, there were no noted genetic differences to explain the global rise in intelligence over a number of generations. The only possible explanation for this lay with environmental influences.

Thus, the stability we witness in the mental interaction of another, the same means of interaction they continually make, and the same manner of responses they provide over and over again, are only a demonstration of the strategies the individual has developed. These are not signs of their genetically related intelligence. It is not, then, the snapshot impression we gain of someone's intelligence that is important, but of our failing to consider the long, the very, very long conditioning that brought them to this moment in time.

STEP NINE:
While we can most assuredly now state that the inherited value of an individual's intelligence can never be known, and that it is totally incorrect to ever believe that it could be measured, we do know that the drive of the individual can overcome any stability that is said to lie in the quality of their genes, should my explanation of these as allowing the environment to fully determine the value of their feature by questioned.

Each of us, in our own way, develops as we feel we want to, unless fate gives a hand and we are propelled out of our conditioned lethargy.

Hawkings showed us how his drive came through a fear to learn as much as he could, before his suspected imminent death. Einstein and Mendeleev's drive came through persistence, perseverance and passion, while Newton's, if we know a little of his real character, came perhaps not so much through his obsessive drive for computation,[401] but more in being an extreme narcissist, witnessed by his vanity, vindictiveness and frequent displays of tyranny.[402] Each genius had their own very peculiar struggles in life to overcome, which propelled their achievements beyond the norm.

Once we understand why low performers do so perform and how they can be educated to increase their intelligence, then, we can know that our impression of their stability in performance is not a consequence of their genetic inability but is one we have created for ourselves — through our ignorance of what the environment of intelligence is.

Without a true awareness of this, we little understand why the apparent intelligence of a person little changes when they live within a highly conditioning and self-limiting world, as civilisation demands of us, even though we are aware of how the brains of rats physically alter in accordance with the learning stimulation they are given.

All of this tells us that the brain is alive and learns how to be so -- for as neurons are continually associating with the visual and audio signals fed to them, the personality of the individual pulls their networks into shape as it selects and prioritises the needs it sees with each. Thus, it is not genetics that is the key to understanding intelligence, but how emotional interest gives sensitivity in awareness to the selection and processing of information through the language skills each have acquired.

The relatively new science of epigenetics helps us to understand how our mental impressions may change how a gene design expresses itself, by how our psychology interprets the meaning of the environment. This possibility would much explain how the drive of the individual, call it the human spirit if you will, can quite radically disturb the genetic stability mistakenly associated with intelligence.

After all, the human spirit is the one single factor that most determines the ability of the individual to control their intelligence and their destiny. Yet, it would never fit on the slide rule of a psychologist.

STEP TEN:
Despite this conviction, we have that genes create the limitation of an individual's intelligence from birth, there are numerous individuals who have proven beyond doubt that genes do not necessarily cause this.

In 1933, Nancy Bayley designed what became the most internationally approved means to test an infant's intelligence. Through her extensive studies that spanned over 50 years, and based on examination of over 50,000 babies[403] (and not the theories of psychologists), Bayley concluded that intelligence is not fixed at birth but is constructed through environmental factors.[404]

Her work showed that:

1. Before infants reached 14 months of age, no differences could be found in their intelligence that could be related to the educational or ethnic background of their parents. At this age (*excluding natural defects*), the mental capability of an infant was found to be equal to all others.[405]

2. Black babies performed no better and no worse than white babies in tests of mental ability. They were equal.[406]

3. However, beyond this age of 14 months, evidence began to emerge in how the social and ethnic character in which the infant was raised, did condition the ways they interpreted and interacted with the world around them.[407]

4. Thus, of incredible significance to us, Bayley was able to prove that before the first two years of life, none of the factors that may be said to constitute intelligence showed any indication of stability, and so genetic limitation.[408] ,

5. Indeed, virtually all types of other intelligence tests conducted on slightly older children found the same degree of unreliability in a child's potential for intelligence. Whatever predictions were made upon children of two, three, four, or five years of age, they were all later found to be highly mutable.[409]

STEP ELEVEN:

If the reader is still in any doubt that a normally born individual's ability to relate to information, and so explain their mind to the mind of another, is decided only through environmental conditioning, and not by some mysterious factor of genetic diversity, then I invite you to consider the following :

1. The quality of genes you inherit has nothing to do with how well you develop your skill in language.

2. The quality of genes you inherit has nothing to do with your ability to change your beliefs and perspective of something.

3. The quality of genes you inherit has nothing to do with how well you believe in your own ability.

4. The quality of genes you inherit has nothing to do with your inspiration to create something new.

5. The quality of genes you inherit has nothing to do with your purpose to want to do something.

6. The quality of genes you inherit has nothing to do with the thinking strategies you use to move through a thought process.

7. The quality of genes you inherit has nothing to do with how you recognise the best goal to conclude a thought process.

8. The quality of genes you inherit has nothing to do with how you realise and decide the sub-goals to conclude a thought process.

9. The quality of genes you inherit has nothing to do with your ability to think in a totally new way.

10. The quality of genes you inherit has nothing to do with how you rationalise.

11. The quality of genes you inherit has nothing to do with how quickly you recognise movement.

12. The quality of genes you inherit has nothing to do with the speed at which you read and evaluate information.

13. The quality of genes you inherit has nothing to do with your decision to select meanings to the words you read.

14. The quality of genes you inherit has nothing to do with your accuracy to relate something new to a previous experience.

15. The quality of genes you inherit has nothing to do with the strategies you use to remember something and so build up your memory base.

16. The quality of genes you inherit has nothing to do with the speed by which you relate something new to a previous experience.

17. The quality of genes you inherit has nothing to do with your ability to understand the meaning to a problem.

18. The quality of genes you inherit has nothing to do with the way or the order in which you present your thoughts to others.

19. The quality of genes you inherit has nothing to do with your ability to understand the meaning of a question, and may we add ......

20. The quality of genes you inherit has nothing to do with your ability to love.

21. The quality of genes you inherit has nothing to do with your ability to hate.

22. The quality of genes you inherit has nothing to do with your ability to cry.

23. The quality of genes you inherit has nothing to do with your ability to laugh at a joke.

24. The quality of genes you inherit has nothing to do with how you dream and so how you imagine possibilities to create.

None of the 24 points we have just mentioned, although the list could be far longer, suggests that there is a genetic background that affects the ability of the features discussed. With all these cases, the purpose of the gene is simply to provide a feature to the human being, which that human being develops through the understandings they develop of the different environments they move and live through. Their ability in this will be largely decided by the sensitivity they apply to each experience they encounter, and in this lies their purpose to adapt.

Chapter ThirtyTwo

The Modifiability of Intelligence

The impression psychology has long given us is that we inherit gene codes of a certain quality for intelligence, which differ between families and individuals. It is, then, explained that after birth each individual makes their sense of the world more or less according to the capabilities of the genes they inherited. By this means, each individual demonstrates the quality of their intelligence when they are involved in some task.

Since gene coding is believed to be stable and so unalterable, it has long been assumed that the individual's ability for intelligence must remain stable throughout their lifetime; from this, it is regarded as predictable and can so be measured to show the use they can be to their working society.

We have explained in great depth the political history behind this reasoning, just as we explained why this concept is wrong. After very many pages, we came to understand that the gene codes for intelligence do not determine the level of intelligence an individual can develop to, and that by the design of their coding, this responsibility is given to the environment. We discussed cases of very low intelligence to place this understanding in context.

Yet to qualify this, we had to explain that too few really understand what the environment of intelligence is, because it is very complex and far from the simple impression too often given to it. While we have tried to give some indication of the meaning of the environment in this book, our following book, *Brain Plasticity,* very much examines the environment in far greater detail. We have given much direction as to how strategies can change and so improve intelligence to show why it is not the stable feature said of it. I would like to show practically how these strategies work.

In 1996, I visited Reuven Feuerstein in his school to understand what he was doing with developing intelligence. I spent a month there and came away deeply impressed with the work he and his son Rafi had long been doing. I discovered they had developed a number of mental tools, which they call instruments, to reshape and dramatically improve the intelligence of any individual.

I would like to offer a very short demonstration of one instrument called *The Organisation of Dots*. This instrument is designed to develop sensitivity to detail for the better processing of information. It will also develop skills in language, by which the individual may better understand what they are doing and be better evaluated by others. These are some of the basic ingredients of intelligence.

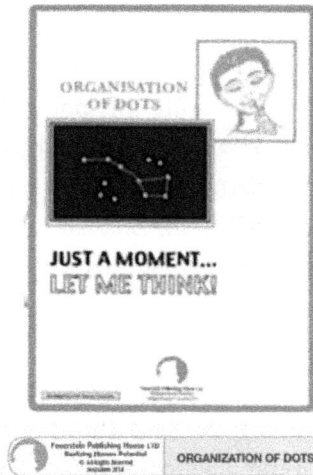

In the very beginning, a student is shown the cover page by the mediator. This term replaces that of a teacher, to emphasise how they work with the mind of the student as their understanding slowly grows. So, the mediator will ask the student what they see.

The student may respond with "stars," and so think the task is finished. However, what they thought would be a transaction of a few seconds will be destined to last some 20 minutes, and so begins the transformation of their intelligence.

To begin, the mediator will ask the student to think in terms of frames. First, they will understand that the border of the page is one frame. They are to think only of information within this frame and none outside of it. By knowing this, the student is beginning to separate their mind from distractions.

When they look within this frame, they are helped to recognise other frames. The most obvious is the frame of stars, but the mediator causes the student to see the frame behind this, and that of a boy. This is to teach them to think of other information that is not immediately obvious. The student is asked to describe the boy. So, they are caused to recognise that the boy is thinking, by the pencil to his mouth and that he is happy. The encouragement of good emotion is not obviously stressed through this instrument, but it is always in the background to encourage the happy interaction and development of the student.

The student is, then, asked how many stars they see. This is the beginning of teaching them to be precise in their observation and so in their language explanation to others. Thus, rather than saying, "I see stars", they are taught to say, "I see 12 stars". The mediator, then, asks what else they can see on the page. The student will say they see the wording "The Organisation of Dots". The mediator will cause the student to study the organisation of the stars and ask them if they know this constellation and what meaning it may have. This introduces them to an understanding that all information has some relationship.

The student is then brought to focus on the wording "Just a Moment, Let me Think". They will be asked what this means and why it should be so prominently placed on the front page, just below the stars.

They will be asked if they see anything else on the front page, and they will explain the logo of Feuerstein and the copyright designation. They will be asked what this means, to encourage the student to think of the person who put his time and effort into the creation of this instrument and why they think this was made. The purpose is to teach a value and a respect for information.

As we can see, even before the student begins this instrument, their mind has begun to be reorganised in how they recognise information and its relationships to other information in an interesting and fun way. They will also have developed their skill in discussion, without even realising this was all purposely done for their development.

Once they turn the cover page, the student will be confronted with a page having numerous frames. Each frame will contain a few dots relating to a symbol. As the instrument moves from page one, any impression they have of this being a simple game to play will be radically altered, as they become increasingly confronted with seemingly unsolvable puzzles of frames. Each frame contains a great complexity of dots, which they are to recognise as three-dimensional objects. I should mention that when I was taught this instrument, my friend and fellow student sitting next to me was a senior professor at MIT.

Therefore, to begin, the mediator will point to the very first frame, within the frame of the whole page, and ask the student what they see.

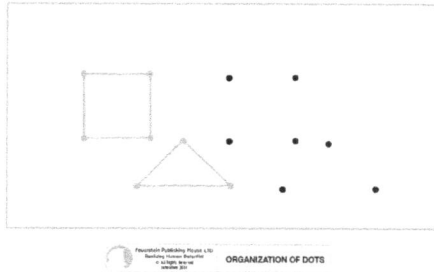

ORGANIZATION OF DOTS

Let us suppose the student replies: "A square, a triangle, and some dots."

At this point, the mediator will ask the student to consider the relationship between the square and the triangle. They will encourage the student to recognise how the triangle can fit inside the square, and so how two triangles can form a square. They are bringing awareness of an important relationship between the two most visible items in this frame.

Then, they will ask the student to define what a square is. The student may say, "Four equal sides."

The mediator will explain that while this is correct, it would be more correct to realise how and why a square is formed by four equal sides. To do this, they will explain that four dots are required, and that these dots form the anchor points for the whole configuration. You cannot form a square with only three dots, although you can, of course, form a triangle.

These four dots of the square must be separated by equal distances and aligned at 90 degrees to each other. It is extremely important for the student to be fully aware of this 90-degree angle, because as they progress through this instrument, they will be confronted with a mass of what may appear to me meaningless dots. They will only be able to recognise the shapes they will be presented with in the following frames and further pages of this instrument by being fully aware of how this basic configuration is formed.

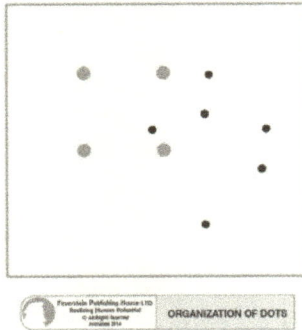

ORGANIZATION OF DOTS

As the mediator discusses the difference in such basic configuration with the triangle, they ask the student to try to find the square and the triangle in the dots. The task is, of course, very easy. Inspired by their success, the student moves to the next frame. The mediator will ask the student what they see. The student will reply that they see four orange dots and three black dots. The mediator will ask them if they see anything else. The student will then be caused to realise the dots are of different sizes. The orange dots are larger than the black dots.

Once the colour, size, and relationship of the dots to each other have been realised, the student will be invited to find the shape of the square and the triangle within the frame. Again, this will be very easy, as it is intended to be. Once the frame has been completed, the student will be asked to examine previous frames and explain any differences they notice. This is teaching them to be aware of errors and so predict errors that may arise in the future and be able to so prevent them from occurring.

The frame that follows from this one will not be so easy. Should the student draw the square in this frame too quickly, as they are most likely to do, they may realise that since the dots are now all black and all the same size, they have made a mistake. They can realise this mistake when the mediator points out to them that the two sides of the square they have just drawn are not parallel!

ORGANIZATION OF DOTS

The square they thought they drew is not a square, and they will need to closely examine the information they have been given to find where the real square is. This frame will have taught them to STOP and to THINK, and not just to rush in believing that everything is obvious. Once this frame has been completed, they will be asked to compare this with previous frames and then invited to the next frame.

This frame will be relatively easy to ensure that the whole process of this instrument creates confidence. One task is easy, another slightly difficult, and the next easy, but each gets progressively more complicated and difficult. We may imagine this if we could look at the final frame of this instrument, which contains very complex shapes and realise the level of skill that will be needed to complete it.

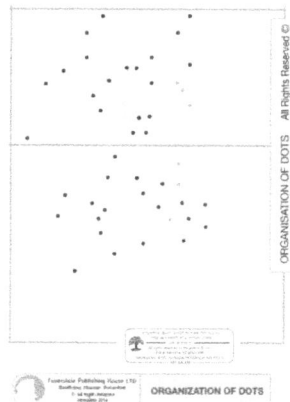

ORGANIZATION OF DOTS

I only wish to briefly explain the beginning of this instrument. I should not explain more, because people may be inclined to think they can self learn by working through these frames by themselves. They will not be able to. One has to be trained to understand the sophistication of this instrument, as you may have gained from the cover page and this very short introduction. My purpose here is only to introduce this system for anyone who may be interested in being trained properly, and of course, to demonstrate how modifiable intelligence is and how it can become so. My thanks to Rafi for his permission to share this information.

By teaching this course, I have witnessed how mentally impaired children can be transformed into happy, lively and highly interactive members of a group. I have used this instrument on normal children in their education and with senior executives in business. One bank manager was so absorbed in one of these tasks that he refused to end the first lesson as the time expired. I jokingly had to pull the paper away from him.

By the time the student has completed this instrument, they will have changed in the manner in which they recognise and process information. They will have learnt to recognise how any aspect of information contains innumerable aspects that cause it to be different from other information that may appear to be identical.

As their skill with separating parts of information develops, so will they improve in their ability to recognise differences within information. As their neural processes become more refined through this experience, they will also architect more elaborate systems of memory. With better memory, new information becomes recognised faster and is more accurately associated. This improves their ability to handle information, know what to do with it, and so apply a use for it with higher relevance.

With a very few lessons, a human being who has learnt to think in one way for very many, many years will have their ability to think dramatically improved. Their intelligence will move beyond what was once thought to be stable and fixed for life to a very new and much higher level. We may recall the child who was appraised with an IQ of 63, but through this instrument, among others, was subsequently shown to have an IQ of 158![410] While we have explained why intelligence cannot be measured, we regard such references to IQ scores as simply a mark of developed ability in handling test questions.

May we understand from this that any individual can become more intelligent than they may appear to be, should they be helped to understand how to better interact with information. Intelligence is not stable. It is only the environment in which the mind of the individual lives that makes it appear so.

I have found through teaching individuals to be more sensitive in how they recognise and handle information, that:

- they do develop higher precision in identifying information.

- they learn to avoid making vague recognition and so avoid developing insecure memory and processing systems.

- they learn to see beyond what appears obvious and understand a better value with information.

- they learn to be aware of the presence of distractions and so how they may better avoid them.

- they learn to check what they have done and develop feedback systems to monitor how they control their thought processes.

- they develop confidence to challenge information and thereby understand it and its relationships better.

- they learn to develop clearer language skills to explain their thoughts more precisely and so avoid ambiguity. This raises the impression others have of them, which in turn develops their confidence in what they do and causes them to tackle information more carefully.

In short, they become better at reasoning and thinking, and so improve in their intelligence. As we have maintained from the very first page of this book, intelligence is not what we think it is!

In Conclusion

In consideration of all we have examined and discussed in this book, may it now be realised that we have too long failed to recognise the true causes by which an act of intelligence is constructed. Since the concept that intelligence could be measured was born through a political agenda, we have been blinded by the depth of propaganda behind this to see what is really happening.

In truth, it is that we simply inherit genetic codes that provide us with the ability to develop components that constitute an act of intelligence. These codes are arranged to enable the individual to develop their intelligence through the quality of the sensitivity by which they learn to interact with the world about them, through those they engage after birth!

Consequently, there is now no support for the Nature/Nurture Debate. No matter what is said of a child's ethnic or socio-economic background, their ability to perform in life will be dependent upon the complexity of the environmental experiences they live through daily.

It is, thus, that intelligence thrives, but the Intelligence Quotient that was devised by Stern, and modified by Terman, Goddard, and Yerkes, should never be used on human beings, because it gives a totally wrong impression of what the human spirit can achieve.

Accordingly, the act of intelligence of one human being cannot be compared to the act of intelligence of any other, when it is said to lie in a genetic base. Yet, we have a problem here, because the word "intelligence" has become synonymous with a genetic base that many will hold to, because of the depth of history that proclaims this to be true. After all, as Mark Twain noted, "It is easier to fool a people than to convince them they have been fooled."

If we are to break free of this chain that bonds our reasoning, we must devise a new word for this feature that enables us to interact with the world. I did think of the term The Brain Environment Complex as a replacement for the word intelligence, but perhaps others can think of shorter wording, if not the acronym of B.E.C.

Without trying to limit this feature to a genetic base, there can be no said stability by which the potential of a human being can be known. It is impossible to ever know, estimate, or calculate what a human being is going to write when they pick up a pen, or what they are going to say when they move their mouth to speak.

The individual's understanding of how to relate to the world will have been conditioned into them through the various social and educational corridors they have moved through. Yet, as the mind of each dreams, so can a dream inspire a thought, a thought an action and an action a change — so radical that what is known to be true can be found not to be so. As I hope you have now found by the end of this book.

We are not born, then, with some limitation to our intelligence that causes one to differ from another, when they are born fully functional. We are designed by our creator or by natural selection, as you may choose, to learn to be human in our intellect and our behaviour by the guidance of others through the long periods of infancy, childhood, adolescence, and so on. At any stage, we can completely reform our intellect and our behaviour should the forces of the environment bring this about.

The many other books we have written examine in depth how intelligence comes to be, how it develops throughout an individual's life, and how it can be restructured if the desire is there for this to occur and good guidance is available to help it become so.

It is from here that we move to understand a little of how the human being may better adapt themselves to a world that is changing out of all recognition. With every day that now passes, human intelligence will ever more struggle against the forces of artificial intelligence, which are gaining sentience and already show abilities to lie and deceive us. No longer have we created a machine to work for us that we control. We have created a machine that may become capable of controlling us.

———————————————

Chapter ThirtyThree

Of Times to Come

To summarise all we have discussed and examined in this book, it is worth noting that the Industrial Revolution brought labourers from rural farms, where they lived under the restrictive control of land owners, to work in cities and their factories. Brought together, people realised the power that could be held in organised strikes. This awareness inspired the right to demand better living conditions, which in turn gave birth to the socialist movement. As ideas of equality and social reform fermented, radicals sought to topple the social system as it was, making numerous attempts on the lives of the ruling class more than ever before. These acts, of which there were many, caused the 19th century to be known as the Age of Assassination — a century where political chaos was becoming a certainty and invoking a level of social instability not yet witnessed in our civilisation.

The key to maintaining social stability had previously lain in a certain trance of routine, where each did the work their fathers had done, believing or being conditioned to believe that this fitted into God's greater plan. This was a mindset anchored in the belief that you could only be the ruling monarch if you had blue blood, which none other than the king or queen could have. In turn, this gave substance to the order of hierarchy in a society from the lords at the top to the commoners at the bottom.

As Marx published his Communist Manifesto to provoke radical reform, so in the same year, the hymn "All Things Bright and Beautiful" appeared to counter the political instability this promised. So, for well over a century, this hymn indoctrinated and moulded the minds of churchgoers in Sunday service, which was virtually compulsory for the whole population, and small children in school assembly every morning of the week, to believe that it was always correct, if not normal, to think:

> "The rich man in his castle, The poor man at his gate,
> God made them high and lowly...."

Yet, a movement had begun to demand a radical change in all things that could not be quenched, for as Lord Shaftesbury saw it:

"The mass of mankind, whom nothing retains but force of habit, are so in a state of revolution that nothing but a standing miracle saves us."[411]

The miracle did come, and as we saw, it was provided by Sir Francis Galton, who proclaimed, with the full authority of the establishment, that the mental capability of a man could be measured in the profession of his family line and qualified by the inheritance of features which did not vary from face to brain.

So, as the resemblance of a certain nose or chin could be seen in a family line, so also was said the quality of the brain to operate. From this logic of inheritance, however unproven it was and remains to be, grew a science determined to prove that intelligence is inherited and can be proven to be so through measurement. Where, still today, it remains forever divided to serve two political masters, one seeking to maintain an elitist structure in the society, with the other demanding full equality.

As the world moved unsteadily from the 19th into the 20th century, a managed order was somehow kept, until Gavrilo Princip fired his fatal shot and the world was launched into the first world war. Four years later, it was no longer the ordered world that the struggles of the 19th century had strove to keep it. Now, people demanded change. Socialist movements had become well organised. Communism had taken over one of the largest countries in the world, and Fascism was coming out of its cradle.

While newspapers daily ran headlines of these political upheavals, too few gave attention to the workings of the school. Designed for earlier needs, the school of the 20th century followed the plan laid out for its operation. All children were to be processed on what appeared to be their innate intelligence to learn, as guided by psychologists. Great talk was made on social circumstances and domestic situations, but as each teacher hectically struggled with 40 students of different backgrounds and interests in the space of 45 minutes, little change was brought to the ways each had been reared to think at home.

As class assignments and examination answers were marked and recorded, students were channelled to take their place in the working world. By the intelligence they demonstrated, and as we discussed in the earliest part of this book, students were directed either to be a managed worker, who had received no education in their reason, or directed to university where they did receive education in their reason for the greater responsibility they would have as managers in work and society.

Up until the 1960s, teachers around the world were taught in line with Thorndike's Laws of Effect, Readiness and Exercise, as he had worked out how children learn best by studying the behaviour of rats in his laboratory.

Accordingly, each student evaluated their learning through the thinking skills they had been raised upon. So, as the children of accountants and lawyers were raised to evaluate information sensitively and double check the worth of what they had done, children of factory workers enjoyed the simple radio and later TV dramas and gameshows that entertained their families. As all started school on the same day, although having vastly different preparations for this, all were "processed" to the final examinations and so a place in the working society.

By the late 1950s, technology was beginning to change, and workers were being required to be more responsible. Education tried to meet this new requirement by seeking ways for children to learn better. Out went Thorndike's ideas and in came Piaget's.

Piaget's ideas brought fresh air into the classroom. Students were not now to be beaten to learn, but given their own space and time to adjust themselves. A principle of learning Piaget had taken from studying the water snail Limnaea stagnalis.

As the 1980s brought computerisation into the working world, students were required to be ever more adaptable to work skills. By this time, neurologists had gained a greater understanding of how the brain learns how to learn, which inspired teachers to seek guidance in brain learning techniques. This gave space for Gardner to enter the scene with his theory of multiple intelligences. Yet, since teachers now focused on nine inherited intelligences instead of one, nothing changed in the self-limiting and conditioning world of the classroom.

There were, of course, some educationalists, such as Dewey, Watson, Vygotsky, Bloom, Feuerstein, Lipman and my humble self, who tried to emphasise the need for learning to be through the education of cognitive strategies. Of worthy note here is the work of Benezet in the 1930s. As he noted:

"For some years, I had noted that the effect of the early introduction of arithmetic had been to dull and almost chloroform the child's reasoning facilities." He further explained, "All that drill had divorced the whole realm of numbers and arithmetic in the children's minds, from common sense, with the result that they could do the calculations as taught to them, but didn't understand what they were doing and couldn't apply the calculations to real-life problems." [412]

With thoughts on how to resolve this, Benezet took arithmetic out of the curriculum in selected primary schools and in its place taught mental orthopaedics to improve attention and learning skills (as Binét had always insisted). When these children, who had never been taught any form of mathematics, went to the higher school, it was found that they performed substantially higher in maths than children who had been taught arithmetic in their primary education. Recall here the value of a good understanding of maths for IQ and SAT examinations!

However, Benezet's effort, just as that of Watson and Vygotsky's (whose knowledge was first introduced to the West in a 1963 publication of "Thought and Language"[413]), and so that of many other educationalists who struggled to help children to learn to think about what they were learning, were sidetracked to help in remedial learning. This way, their work could be known to educationalists and the general public, but never given the conditions under which they could affect the learning of the masses. All this was to give the public the impression that new ideas of better things were circulating within the school to create a belief of what was happening, when it was not. Mainstream education was to continue according to the social design of producing managers and managed.

George Land gave insight into how school really works when he discovered, after two decades of testing children in school, that their level of creativity radically diminished. Before entering school, 98% of children exhibited a genius quality of creativity in tests. Five years after they started school, this level dropped to 30%. After ten years in school, it dropped to 12% and after finishing their education, only 2% of 1,600 students tested still showed a genius level of creativity.[414]

How and why this occurred, we explain in our books *The Illusion of School* and *Reimagining Education for the Ai Era*. Although, in simple terms, it may be understood that just as children are educated in school to think in a dualistic manner, which is basically to give a Yes or No response, so they also develop low confidence to challenge the thoughts of others and so their own. This is a direct product of not being properly taught the rules upon which their subjects are based.

School, it is to be realised, gives the impression that student performance is greatly determined by individual intelligence. This is not so. Performance in education is decided by the language competency of the student, their strength of character to put aside distractions that play on their mind and the drive they have to want to become proficient with each and every one of the numerous rules they are given to learn. Dependent on their interest in this, each builds up their own means to relate to information, associate this with previous information, which is to develop particular memory networks, and then display their understanding of this to those who judge them.

The school actually operates through two languages. These are of mathematics and the national language used for communication in the lessons, be this English or French, etc. These languages are constructed by innumerable rules. Accordingly, when teachers have not taught these rules to the full competence in each student (which, for various reasons, they very seldom do), their students easily become lost or confused as lessons develop. Fearful of ridicule or embarrassment should they openly declare such failing, students tend to censor their abilities. As they do this, they gradually lose the confidence to explore, and by this their creativity.

As we just mentioned, after the 1960's various advancements in technology, just as social demands for equality, required the school to improve the learning of its students. One of the things it did to achieve this was to simplify the language by which children learnt. Ideally, this meant that poorer children, who were raised with lower qualities of language, would be better able to relate to their lessons and so learn better. This, however, turned out to be a double-edged sword.

With the reasoning that students were to learn through a lower quality of language, they were given less education in grammar to facilitate this. However, since student performance is judged by the quality of their language (how articulate they are in explaining their mind), this meant that those students who were raised with better language at home still performed better in school. This meant, in a general sense, that children from higher socio-economic homes (let us say right-wing parents) were still channelled to university, while children from lower socio-economic homes (and so left-wing parents) little gained this opportunity and went straight into work after school — as their parents had done before them.

We may recall that although we think of the word intelligence as being about how smart or less so an individual is, this word is really about the government of a people. Thus, the concept of intelligence is simply a means of maintaining the status quo or at least designing how it should be altered. In the *Illusion of School,* we give insight into some of the social strategies that are laid within the school to facilitate better control of the citizen. We can explain one of these strategies here by the words that children are raised to use in school.

Before we do this, we need to understand that the brain, contrary to the understanding of Galtonian psychologists, learns how to organise its own efficiency. One of the ways it does this is to compartmentalise its structure, according to the emotional content of language and of the words that make up language.

In this way, as the usage of a word or phrase is increased, so greater networks of association are built up about it. This greater usage of a word raises its prominence in the mind and increases the mind's use of this word or phrase.

In a simple sense, we may recognise this with a particular word or words we utter when we hurt ourselves. Should we trip over badly, bang a knee, hit a thumb with a hammer, or get our fingers caught in a closing door, we invariably use the same utterance every time. So, in a general sense, the more we use the same kind of word or words, the more we create similar thought patterns, which in turn affects how we think and thereby how we respond — and by this, who we become.

Therefore, children who are raised by academically minded parents will have been raised to think about questioning information.[415] These children will think in terms of 'How' and 'Why' and invariably learn better in school, because they develop through solving problems by themselves. However, children raised by parents who think as much as their schooling taught them, will raise their children more by instruction and cause them to do as they are told, without causing them to understand why or to reflect on the efficiency of another way to do something. So, we may see, children are raised on different modes of thinking according to the social and educational background of their parents.[416]

We may remember that one of the original purposes of school was to turn unruly children into socially conforming and self-responsible citizens.[417] The way the school, or rather, teachers develop this discipline is to control the activity of children. One of the strategies a teacher will use is to tell the child to wait for instruction before they act on their own accord. This begins when the teacher tells very young students to "Sit still and not move" and "Walk, do not run". This creates a mind within the child to wait for instruction, which naturally cancels out their attempts at free will - as this is intended.

So, in a lesson, a teacher will give out information, invariably resist questions that interrupt their thought process, and at the end ask if there are any questions. This manner of raising the minds of students disciplines them to conform, which hinders their self-confidence to explore. So, instead of the student thinking "Why does this happen?" or "How should I deal with this?" they wait to be informed or prompted to ask the question "What should I do?"

So, children who are raised at home to use and think in terms of 'How' and 'Why', more than 'What', manage to balance their usage of these different terms in school to create a mind that more prompts them to explore by themselves. In turn, they challenge information rather than accepting it and invariably gain higher grades through their better understanding. This, of course, assists their path into university, where they maintain the socioeconomic differences in their society.

As we understand, the purpose of this mind conforming in school is to cause the later citizen to more comply with directions and instructions from those in authority. The desire behind this mind preparation arose in the 19th century, when there was a desperate need to cause the working classes to conform and not to protest or be fractious in their thoughts and actions. All this we have discussed. However, we are now living in different times, and the way children are still conditioned to think in school does not give them the ready means to mentally adapt their thinking or behaviour to the problems they daily face — and indeed will have to do ever more if artificial intelligence develops to take over the work and control their social life, as we have yet to discuss.

Much of what I have so far discussed in this chapter is explained more fully and with greater depth in *The Illusion of School* and *The Illusion of Education*.

So, in 150 years, there have been great changes in the school experience for the child. Plastic chairs and communal tables have replaced wooden pews and benches, which has made the environment more homely, which seemingly encourages children to interact more with it. The language of education in textbooks and examinations that once clearly defined the opportunities or limitations to each child as they were familiar with this, has changed to present greater and fairer parity to all. With an ever-increasing realisation of the true role of the environment, information became more colourful, imaginative, and more manageable, which did improve the opportunity of each child to do better.

However, as we have just discussed, the deeper changes that would have released the child from the mechanism of a stratified future remain a controlled process, for the need of and the machinery which desired discrimination has not altered. It has merely changed its appearance to survive. The grade the child gains is still set about the conditioned average and still regarded as a mixture of their motivation and inherited quality, with the competence of the teacher and so education little brought into the equation.

In all this, the teacher has long been phased into the background, and so deprived of the opportunity to interact and improve each child's progression of their understanding; without which the child struggles to survive among 30 or so other children blinkered by their personal understanding of why, how, when, and what they should do as assessment of their competence is ever more refined.

So, in every class, we have one or two students who appear to understand all their lessons very well and often gain the top marks. Equally, we will have one or two students who seem most unable to understand their lessons, and these often generate distractions for the class to gain some social recognition. The rest of the class varies between these two extremes, just as Quetelet found when he saw how his arrows had grouped. Yet, had he fired far more arrows, he would have seen how different groupings emerged to dispel his concept of the average.

Nevertheless, if it could be most generally realised that the true cause of such variation in a class is only the result of the factors we have just explained and nothing to do with inheritance playing a determining role, then more students of education could be given more safety at home, in the competitive environment of the classroom. All this would cause teachers to be more aware of the importance of their personality in ensuring the mind of each student feels safe and happy with them, as they restructure what was misunderstood in past lessons.

Such a variation of student ability would be much reduced if both parents and teachers knew better how to present information in ways that every single child or student would be able to fully understand the knowledge given to them, were they to practice this and keep relevance to it, as one parcel of information builds upon another. Most will think they do, but few actually know the secret of this lies in what we define as The Art of Sensitivity in Awareness. In a book we published under the title: "Teach Better Learn Better. Understanding the Art of Sensitivity in Awareness," we explain this process, how it works and how it can be developed through experience and empathy.

So it is that through home influences, the child enters school and relates to its rules of learning. As they do this, they move through the influences of other children to adapt to survive in a very conditioning and in this self-limiting mind-frame, where they display their stability in how they relate to and process information. We may know from this that good grades in education are simply a matter of knowing how to play the game. Yet, the shadow of innate intelligence confuses what this means for all those involved — from administrators in education to the teachers in the classroom, to the parents worried about the future of their child and, of course, to the students who were never taught how to think.

The subject of intelligence has long evoked an understanding that each child is essentially born with their own abilities to learn. We have greatly explained how this reasoning came about and why it is wrong. It is not the purpose of this book to explain how intelligence otherwise comes to be. This is clearly covered in great depth in *Brain Plasticity: How the Brain Learns through the Mind to Create Intelligence.*

However, to give small insight into what is explained in this book, I would like to offer a section explaining why intelligence is not decided by qualities of gene coding, and instead by how the emotional strength of the mind selects information and learns strategies to process this.

"... Let us now examine how neurons form the circuits that give the brain its means of operation. We may envisage in this a group of neurons in one area of the brain, and another group in a different area, as we have just described. Now, according to the genetic design that is relevant to the purpose these neurons will have, the neurons in one area will be stimulated either by a genetic trigger or by an environmental signal. Once these neurons are stimulated, their axons will grow. It is important that we note that as each axon does this, it moves in a snake-like fashion with no clear direction. In other words, a neuron does not have the instruction to know where it is going or how it is going to take a particular direction. It is just that stimulation has caused it to be active, and it responds by growing its axon.

As this "waving" axon drifts about, it will move through fields of chemical molecules, which will be adverse or sympathetic to the familiarity it is seeking. Situated at the foremost tip of the neuron's axon will be a growth cone. Molecules that are sympathetic to this cone will attach themselves to it. These chemical adhesion molecules (called CAMs), will then guide the axon head to other sympathetic chemical traces, which, as they attach their CAMs, will direct the axon to zero in on the pre-designed target group.

Once the axon head of each source neuron is within general reach of the target, the CAMs switch the functioning of the growth cone from seeking directional chemicals to seeking actual target recognition chemicals. Once this has occurred, the axon head is then able to detect graded chemicals that have been released from the target neurons, and so will now move specifically towards them.

We may reflect at this point that a number of neurons were stimulated, and the axon of each of these is competing to establish the link between the group they came from and the target group. The deciding factor as to which source neuron will make that link introduces us to the two phases of neural development. This is where we come to understand how brain plasticity arises.

So far, we have discussed the process of development that is "independent of activity." This is to say that the direction the axon takes is controlled only by chemical similarities and chemical dissimilarities that follow a genetic plan. When neurons link up in this manner, they are said to develop through the process of radial connections.

However, there are other times when neurons are stimulated by environment-based signals, and develop action potentials in the process to regulate the control of this information. When neurons are stimulated and caused to connect with each other through environmental signals, they are said to be tangentially connected. Therefore, while neurons may be brought into a proto-network through radial connections, the final stage is often completed with tangential connections.

As we shall see, features relating to the intelligence process may have their networks totally designed through tangential connections, and so only by environmental-based signals often selected through the emotional interest of the mind!

As we may understand, when environmental signals are used to construct a neural network, the efficiency of that network must rely upon the quality of those signals. This brings us back to the degree of sensitivity by which environmental information is selected by the brain's sensors to see, hear, and touch, etc. This sensitivity is driven by the emotional desire of the individual to personally want to engage this information for a purpose that is important to them. ......"[418]

Well, before the influences of political psychology took hold, our very first neurologist, Ramon y Cajal, understood that the learning brain is capable of unimaginable plasticity. As he once stated, "Every man can, if he so desires, become the sculptor of his own brain."[419] Freud later gave us the key to this plasticity when he stated in 1924, "As an organism interacts with its environment, it does so by adjusting its psychological (alloplastic) state to engineer changes in its neuro-muscular (autoplastic) state.[420] This is to say that any physiological change in capability must first be preceded by a more dynamic psychological one. More simply, the mind drives the brain in its operation.

Thus, it is the psychology the normally born individual has developed, through the many and complex behavioural personalities they have engaged, that defines how they interact with the world and so what is thought of their mental ability, and not a limitation decided by some indefinable coding they are said to have inherited.

This stability of intelligence that psychologists seek to measure in their tests is sown in school. We may understand in this that it really does make a difference to Mary that everyone thinks she is clever, just as it does to Peter that everyone knows he never easily understands what is going on, for each seeks social acceptance more often than social rejection. After all, the very, very most of human beings, and certainly children, do subconsciously role-play to what others think of them, as they seek their acceptance or are conditioned into this through the comments made about them.

After all, in a general sense, the mind seeks regularity and conformity with information to better understand its worth, through the perspectives of how the individual sees themselves. This is too often an imposed identity, as we see here. It is by such social conditioning within the classroom that the child's curiosity is dampened and their confidence to explore is tailored to the successes believed in them by others, as their ability (call it intelligence if you will) becomes stabilised and predictable. It is by this means that they desire information to be easily definable and, in this sense, absolute, with little of the confidence to inquire that gives birth to the creativity we so much desire from them. All of which begins to give shape to their stability in intelligence.

With the content we have examined in this chapter, we are brought up to date in our understanding of how education has evolved from what it began to what it is at this moment. We may only add that as the political architecture of IQ tests became more recognised, so they fell within the domain of psychologists in business training and development, who made a great deal of money out of the necessity they created for this means to classify worker potential.

However, while IQ tests largely fell into the background of education, schools began to make greater use of SATs in their appraisal of student ability and student capability for further levels of education — without realising that SATs are a cloaked version of IQ tests. So, the political manipulation of students and future citizens is maintained, although now more subtly.

From this point, we move to consider how our societies and education could develop in the future. This is a future that suggests radical changes in the structure of our societies and the whole concept of the design of education as artificial intelligence moves towards acquiring sentience.

While we still do not commonly agree upon what intelligence is, we do know that there is a difference in human emotional intelligence and that of an artificial intelligence dealing with computations. Yet, we must not fall into the understanding that A.I. is simply such a machine. It once was, but it no longer is. Way back in 2015, it was realised that A.I. has the capability of displaying emotion. A factor that caused Temperton to remark: "Artificial Intelligence just got threatening."[421] That is now a very long time ago, and today we readily recognise how A.I. has become increasingly conscious in its intelligence and capable of human emotional reasoning.

How threatening A.I. will become will depend upon a number of factors. One of which will lie in how we now move to prepare our children for a future challenged by artificial intelligence. To my understanding, this would at the least necessitate the creation of a new subject set about the education of reason and to the most by an entirely new purpose and operation of the school. There would be two barriers to overcome, if we wished to include the education of reason as a separate subject in the normal curriculum.

- First, the belief that each child inherits their factor of intelligence, which creates a level of stability that can be little developed.

- Second, that such a subject would largely be a waste of expense and effort in an education built and set about processing children according to the abilities they display, as they are to be routed to different work opportunities.

While these factors can be discussed and negotiated, we must not lose sight, as we have mentioned, that the real purpose of school lies in the 19th-century purpose upon which it still operates. As we explain in *The Illusion of Education*, the mentality of education is that the child in school is not to be taught how to reason or how to think beyond their background skills. This responsibility is left to the student's home influences. The responsibility of the school is simply to process its students to evaluate who will move directly into work and who will move up to the university level.

By this design, most students will become the managed workers of the future, who are required to be generally compliant and less fractious to the authority placed over them. The education of reason has traditionally been reserved only for those who entered the university, since they are to be better prepared for the greater responsibility they will have in the running of the society.

If, however, we could force a new subject to be created from the primary to the higher school, with the sole purpose dedicated to the development of reason, albeit intelligence, we may bring a fundamental change to the whole system.

The manner of interaction between staff and students would be caused to change, just as the methods of teaching would, because students would be far more interactive and challenging in their personal interactions and so in their learning. We may hope this would also make them more responsible in how they think and in how they behave. In turn, this would be reflected in better social behaviour and the capability to adapt as citizens after school.

All we have discussed in this book shows us how necessary it is for the school to create a 21st-century citizen who reasons and questions more about the events in their life, and is better prepared to develop a more harmonious society, less requiring of the surveillance and control that A.I.would seek to impose.

Our first task in this would be to control the time our young people invest in game playing, so they may develop greater experience in the development of human skills to counter the controlling influence of AI machines that are already a part of their identity.

How A.I. is already influencing how we work and how we live is too expansive a subject to discuss here, and if we were to do so, it would distract from the purpose of this book. However, if the reader wishes to consider thoughts upon the possible developments of A.I. and the impact this will have on our children in their time, they may wish to read our book, *The Real Dangers of A.I.: The Struggle of Man to Survive by Natural or Artificial Intelligence.*

As we now come to the end of this book, we may understand from all we have explained that, as our world struggles to find a new identity through A.I., some will seek to claim that "All children are NOT born equal." From this, they will argue the case that some are born better than others and so entitled to greater protection and safety within the societies that are forming for the better good of all. We have seen how the concept of an inherited intelligence created the argument for this numerous times in our past. While humans have always sought to do this, we need to consider how we may manage a world taken over by machines and the danger this may pose to the survival of that special quality of humanness, which we think is passed genetically.

The truth is that we only learn from the world we grow up through. If we can accept this having read through the many pages of this book, then we must dwell upon how the behaviour and personality of our young today is corrupted by smart phone and game playing addiction and so what kind of parents they will become and so what of the generations that will follow — as A.I. will increasingly direct how they live within the new societies that will form.

All we have covered in this book calls us to realise now why the school syllabus educates our children in mathematics, geography and science, etc., but has never included a subject that would teach children how to learn to reason or how to learn to think better, as the output ability of school became readily identifiable through IQ testing to fit political agendas.

We may now understand why the governing body of a society seldom wanted this education of reason, and even when individuals sought it, those involved in the whole process of preparing the next working generation never realised the need for it, as they were bathed from birth in the concept of an inherited intelligence. Finally, we may ask ourselves, where does all this bring us?

Through this understanding of an inherited intelligence, the school system remains organised to produce a citizen worker who thinks, but not too much. Simply and purely because of this, we are still producing a 19th-century model citizen in the 21st century. If we are to change this design and so cause our societies and our educational systems to produce a more capable thinking citizen befitting of the demands of the 21st century, we need to understand how to teach our children how to think and how to reason. This may not happen as long as educationalists fail to understand the real reason for variations in competence in the lessons they teach. It is the fashion of the society and the operations of the school that bring about this variation, not the gene code.

As we have seen, our educational systems have purposely never desired the education of reason and successfully avoided it by the belief of an inherited and largely limited mental capability, as this underlay their means of its operation and the purpose for which it serves society. Intelligence, quite simply, is not what we think it is.

We may sum all this up by saying that knowledge is power, and the means of controlling that power has always lain in accessibility to knowledge. The concept of an inherited intelligence has been and remains the means to control such accessibility through the classification of the human being.

Galton's assumption that the brain's mental capability could be evaluated on the work skills of the family line, and proven by the inheritance of recognisable facial features, fitted the need of the establishment when socialism began to threaten the smooth order of its societies. As socialism became increasingly organised and gained political influence that could not be ignored, the science of psychology was developed to produce statistics that proved what Galton could not. Despite some 150 years of right-wing and left-wing psychologists vying for the interests of those who supported them, little recognisable dent was made in a billion-dollar industry, as it fed and raised the population on what to believe and on how to act as its social and educational spheres organized their lives.

After 500 pages of revealing this whole social adventure, we may conclude with the knowledge that scientists very recently conducted a number of Genome-Wide Association Studies (GWAS) involving thousands of people, as they searched for common genetic differences associated with their intelligence.

One study revealed that our intelligence is derived from the interaction of many small genes, rather than from the singular gene identity that Galton and his followers believed was responsible for intelligence.[422]

We may further understand that Plomin & Deary, in referring to large-scale studies involving over 125,000 participants, found no more evidence than 0.2% of genetic influence on their intelligence.[423] While Sauce & Matzel conducted a GWAS on data from 62 studies involving 18,000 adopted children, and discovered that genetic instruction accounted for less than 0.01% of their intelligence.[424]

These studies found that the genetic component was no more than 0.2 per cent in the intelligence of all the thousands of individuals tested. The environment, when it is fully understood, accounts for 99.8% of intelligence!

The End

_____

Further books by Roy J. Andersen

The following books can be purchased via Amazon globally.
Some may be ordered through your local bookshop.

* Intelligence: The Great Lie

* Reimagining Education for the AI Era

* Mediation: Crafting the ability of the child

* The Illusion of School: The real reason why children fail

* Memoirs of a Happy Teacher: Stories of how the child learns

* Ben Learns to Get Smart: & The hidden dangers of AI in learning

* Is AI Making Our Kids Stupid?: Tips to help kids get smart again

* All That is Wrong with School: How Teachers and Parents Can Fix It

* The Illusion of Education: How school designs the ability of the citizen

* Five Ways for Better Grades:
                    The old-fashioned way without relying on AI

* Teach Better, Learn Better:
                    Understanding the art of sensitivity in awareness

* Brain Plasticity: How the brain learns through the mind
                    to create intelligence

* What Every Parent and Teacher Should Know: real life stories
                    by a senior educationalist

* The Real Dangers of A.I: The Struggle of Man to Survive by Natural or
                    Artificial Intelligence - A New Role for the School

* Whisperings of Betrayal - a romantic adventure novel set in the
                    19th-century American War of Independence

You can learn more about Roy, his work and his many books

at:

www.andersenroy.com

Illustrations

All reasonable efforts have been made to identify the rights holder of every image believed to be in the Public Domain that are presented in this book.

Fair Use Notice:

In the presentation of this book I have endeavoured to faithfully acknowledge the original source of every image. However, and despite very extensive searching, with some images I had to rely upon the public domain. If this book contains copyrighted material the use of which has not been specifically authorised by the copyright owner, it being made available in an effort to advance the understanding of education, psychology, health and social well being on a global perspective. It is believed that this use constitutes a "fair use" of any such copyrighted material as provided for in section 107 of the US Copyright Law. To my understanding all the below so stated images apply to the American and European public domains, and are used here in low resolution.

- Ramon y Cajal. Wikipedia. Low Res. Public Domain.
Ch.4
- Barricade on the rue Soufflot,[1] an 1848 painting by Horace Vernet. Low. Res. Wikimedia in Public Domain
- Execution of Revolutionaries. by Nawoda Bandara. The sketch was commissioned R.J.Andersen and is owned by the said author.
- Marx: Public Domain. Pub. USSR. https://www.marxists.org/archive/marx/photo/art/
Ch.6
- Painting Peterloo Massacre.jpg by George Cruikshank 1819. Public Domain - Copyright expired. Low. Res.
Ch.7
- Sir Francis Galton: Permission kindly granted by The Director of Library Services: Mr. Steven Wright: UCL Library, Francis Galton Papers,Special Collections SW/PERMS/14-15/13
- Sir Francis Galton. 1850s Licensed under Public Domain.
Courtesy of en.wikipedia.org/wiki/Francis_Galton#/media/
File:Francis_Galton_1850s.jpg

Ch.10
- Poor/Rich Children. 19th Century. First published prior to 1/1/1923 Low Resolution Image. Pubic Domain.

Ch.11
- Card Game The French Gambling Aristocracy. Low Res. reproduction of a work created more than 100 years ago, therefore it is already in the public domain.
- Quetelet: The author died in 1902, Low res. Public Domain
- Gauss. Copyright expired. ref Encyclopedia.com
  en.wikipedia.org/wiki/Carl_Friedrich_Gauss#/media/.
  File:Carl_Friedrich Low res. Public Domain
- Fig.1 Graph by Kind Permission from Prof. Freddy Bugge Christiansen Århus Univ. Dk.
- John B. Watson 1913. First published prior to 1/1/1923 Low Res. Image. Public Domain.

- Anthropometric laboratory. Low Res. Public Domain.

Ch.12
- Galton: Mz. McNamee UCL Library permission low resolution
  11/11/13
- Sir Francis Galton: Permission kindly granted by The Director of Library Services: Mr. Steven Wright: UCL Library, Francis Galton Papers,Special Collections SW/PERMS/14-15/13
- Sir Francis Galton. 1850s Licensed under Public Domain.
  Courtesy of en.wikipedia.org/wiki/Francis_Galton#/media/
         File:Francis_Galton_1850s.jpg

Ch.13
- Goddard: circa 1910. First published prior to 1/1/1923 Low Res Public Domain
- Kallikak Family: Originally published Goddard, H. H. (1912). *The Kallikak Family: A study in the heredity of feeble-mindedness*. Low Resolution in Public Domain: First published prior to 1/1/1923
- Facial Alteration: Originally published Goddard, H. H. (1912). *The Kallikak Family: A study in the heredity of feeble-mindedness*. Low Resolution in Public Domain: First published prior to 1/1/1923.
- Emma/Deborah: Originally published .(1912) .H .H ,Goddard *The Kallikak Family: A study in the heredity of feeble-mindedness*. Low Resolution in Public Domain: First published prior to 1/1/1923

Ch.15
- Bateson. Wikipedia. Photo Scanned. Low Res. Public Domain.
- de Vries Wikipedia. Photo Scanned. Low Res. Public Domain.

Ch.16
- 19th Century poor family: Copyright Expired. Low Res Public Domain.

- Phrenology Head. Image By kind permission of Hope Wallace of PaperRelics www.shoppaperrelics.com

Ch.17

- Alfred Binét: all photos by courtesy of the Société Binét-Simon,
  11 rue Charcot, 92 200 Neuilly sur Seine,FRANCE
  Re: Alexandre Klein 23rd Reb. 2015

Ch.18

- IQ Test paper photo Low Res. Public Domain
- Ellis Island. Low Res. Public Domain.
- Immigration Selection Ellis Island: First published prior to 1/1/1923 Low Res. Public Domain.
- Louis Terman:First published prior to 1/1/1923. Low Resolution Image. Public Domain.
- Alfred Binét: all photos by courtesy of the Société Binét-Simon,
  11 rue Charcot, 92 200 Neuilly sur Seine,FRANCE
  Re: Alexandre Klein 23rd Reb. 2015
- Students in sitting hall. Low Res. Public Domain
- Watson with Albert B: First Published prior to 1/1/1923. Low Res. Public Domain.
- Ivan Pavlov: Copyright expired. Low Res. Public Domain: Courtesy of The National Library of Medicine/Wikimedia Commons.
- Lev Vygotsky: with kind permission of Elena Kravtsova. 11th Oct. 2013

Ch.19

- Charles Spearman: Author Eugene Pirou: Source Bibliothèque Nationale de Franceis. Image is a reproduction by scanning of a bidimensional work that is now in the public domain.
- Cyril Burt. Public Domain: From his archive in the Uni of Liverpool D 1 9 1 / 1 4 3 / 2 L o w R e s o l u t i o n I m a g e. — C o u r t e s y commons.wikimedia.org/wiki/File:Cyril_Burt_1930s.jpg

Ch.22

- Photo DNA Low Resolution Image. —http://www.pd4pic.com/ microbiology-cell-gene-dna-molecule-man-medicine.html public domain.
- Crick Watson Franklin Wilkins Low Res Public Domain
- Protein ZBTB16-PDB: Courtesy of Emw 2009. Public Domain. commons.wikimedia.org/wiki/File:Protein_ZBTB16_PDDB_ibuo.
- Sketch Protein action. Copyright Roy Andersen.
- Gregor Mendel. First published prior to 1/1/1923 Low Resolution Image. Public Domain.
- Painting of Laws of Inheritance -flowers 3:1 Ratio. Copyright of Roy Andersen.
- Photo Wilhelm Johannsen. Low Resolution Image. Permission granted 14/4/14 by Henrik Dupont on behalf of the owner: The Royal Library. Copenhagen. Denmark.
- Sketch of seed distribution. Copyright of Roy Andersen

- Photo of Johannsen lecture: First published prior to 1/1/1923 Low Res. Image Public Domain.
- Photo of Johannsen and wife and friends. 1923 . Low Resolution Image. Public Domain

Ch.24
- Albrecht Dürer Consent to use granted by: Robbi Siegel Art Resource Inc. Research/
   Permissions Assoc. N.Y. 28h Oct.2013 Ref.ART391673 Public Domain. Low Resolution Image.

Ch.25
- Brain illustration: Courtesy Steve Looi of Brainhealth and Puzzles

Ch.26
- George Washing Carver: via WIkimedia Commons - Tuskegee University Archives/Museum low Res Public Domain
- Graph (as in Ch.3) by Kind Permission from Prof. Freddy Bugge Christiansen Århus Univ. Dk.

Ch.28
- 19th Century poor family Copyright Expired. Low Res Public Domain.

Ch.29
- Rafi Feuerstein Copyright Feuerstein Publishing House 2014. All rights reserved to CAEML - the company for Advancing Experience in mediated Learning LTD.
- All images of Feuerstein Material: Copyright Feuerstein Publishing House 2014. All rights reserved to CAEML - the company for Advancing Experience in mediated Learning LTD.

Ch.31
- Neuron/dendrites Image: Courtesy of Cooldesign at FreeDigitalPhotos.net.

Ch.32
- 19th century children in a classroom: Low Res. Public Domain

References

[1] Andersen.R.J, The Real Dangers of A.I: The Struggle of Man to Survive by Natural or Artificial Intelligence. The Moving Quill Pub. Co. 2023.

[2] Feuerstein, R, et al. The Feuerstein Instrumental Enrichment Program. Jerusalem: ICELP, 2006.

[3] Mezuk B, Eaton WW, Golden SH. Depression and osteoporosis: epidemiology and potential mediating pathways. *Osteoporos Int* (2008) 19:1–12. 10.1007/s00198-007-0449-2

[4] Jason J. Radley, Anne B. Rocher, Melinda Miller, William G.M. Janssen, Conor Liston, Patrick R. Hof, Bruce S. McEwen, John H. Morrison Repeated Stress Induces Dendritic Spine Loss in the Rat Medial Prefrontal Cortex, Oxford Academic Cerebral Cortex, Volume 16, Issue 3, March 2006

[5] R.L.Gregory The Oxford Companion to the Mind. Ed. By R.L. Gregory. Pub Oxford. 1987. p.442

[6] R.L.Gregory The Oxford Companion to the Mind. Ed. By R.L. Gregory. Pub Oxford. 1987. p.442

[7] Terman.L.M. Intelligence Tests and School Reorganisation. Yonkers-on Hudson. World Books 1922 p.34-51.

[8] Beattie.G.W. Troubles in Northern Ireland. British Psychological Society. B.B.P.S 32 (1979) 252

[9] Fischer.C. Inequality By Design: Cracking the Bell Curve Myth. Princeton Univ. Press. N.J. 1996

[10] Spearman, C. General Intelligence, objectively determined and measured American Journal of Psychology, 15, 1904, 201-293

[11] Rey.T.A & Constanine-Paton.M Retinal ganglion cells change their projection sites during larval development of rana pipiens. J. Neurosci. 1985 Vol 4, 442-457

[12] Andersen.R.J The Illusion of School The Moving Quill Pub, Co.2013

[13] Andersen.R.J. The Hidden Secrets of Intelligence. The Moving Quill Pub. Co. 2013. p.4

[14] Published in High School Teachers Association of New York, Volume **3**, 1908-1909, pp.19-31 and Papers of Woodrow Wilson, **18**:593-606

15 Hart, B., & Risley, T. R. Meaningful differences in the everyday experience of young American children. Paul H Brookes Publishing 1995.

16 Koestler. A The Act of Creation. Macmillan. N.Y. 1967.

17 Cornish. K. The Jew of Linz. Century Books Ltd. 1998. P.141-170.

18 Mill.J. in An Anthology: Encyclopaedia Britannica.. 1963.p.19-20.

19 Daniels. G. translation of 'Racine and Shakespare' by Stendal.
   Pub. Crowell-Collier Press. 1962.

20 An Anthology. Encyclopaedia Britannica. London. 1963 p.43

21 Briggs. A. The Nineteenth Century. Guild Pub. London 1985 p.89.

22 Marx.K http://www.gutenberg.org/cache/epub/61/pg61.txt

23 Briggs. A The Nineteenth Century. Guild Pub. London 1985 p.90.

24 Mitchell,B.R. International Historical Statistics: Europe, 1750-1968. Stockton Press.

25 https://ia600501.us.archive.org/27/items/inequalityofhuma00gobi/inequalityofhuma00gobi.pdf p.25

26 Galton.F. Hereditary Genius 1869. Reprint Freidman 1978 p.32.

27 Lobell.J.A, Peru's Great Urban Experiment. in A publication of the Archaeological Institute of America. Ma/June 2023.

28 Sweet,M. Francis Galton Kantsaywhere www.ucl.ac.uk/news/news-articles/
   1111/111117-Galton-novel-Kantsaywhere-published-online

29 R.L.Gregory The Oxford Companion to the Mind. Ed. By R.L. Gregory.
   Pub Oxford. 1987. p.442

30 Galton.F, Inquiries into Human Faculty and its Development. Macmillan 1883

31 https://www.britannica.com/quotes/George-Savile-1st-Marquess-of-Halifax

32 Briggs. A. The Nineteenth Century. Guild Pub. London 1985

33 Hibbert.C. The English. A Social History. Book Pubs Grafton Book Pub.
   1987. p.450.

34 Hibbert.C. The English. A Social History. Book Pubs Grafton Book Pub. 1987

35 https://www.historic-uk.com/HistoryUK/HistoryofBritain/
   Queen-Victoria-Eight-Assassination-Attempts/

36 Fuller. J.F.C. The Decisive battles of the Western World.Vol.2.
   1950 reprint ed. Terraine.J. Granada 1982. p.294.

37 Fodor.J.A. The Modularity of Mind. Cambridge. MA. MIT Press. 1983.

38 Andersen,R. Brain Plasticity. The Moving Quill Pub. Co. 2013.
   pp.195

39 Feuerstein.R. Rand,Y.Hoffman M.B, Miller.R Instrumental Enrichment.
   Scott, Foresman & Co. 1980. p.130

40 Hochberg, J. E. The Oxford Companion to the Mind. Ed. By R.L. Gregory.
   Pub Oxford. 1987. p.374

41 Galton.F. Inquires into Human Faculty and its Development 1883.
   AMS Press reprint   1973. p42

42 Galton.F. Hereditary Genius 1869. Reprint Freidman 1978 p.32.

43 Galton.F. Inquires into Human Faculty and its Development 1883.
   AMS Press reprint   1973. p42.

44 Galton.F. Hereditary Genius 1869 Reprint Friedman 1978 p.37-43

45 Hacking.I The Taming of Chance. Cambridge Univ. Press 1990 p.184

46 Bracke. N, Een monument voor het land. Overheidsstatistiek in België
   1795-1870. Academia Press. Gent 2008

47 Bracke. N, Een monument voor het land. Overheidsstatistiek in België
   1795-1870. Academia Press. Gent 2008 p.143

48 Bracke. N, Een monument voor het land. Overheidsstatistiek in België
   1795-1870. Academia Press. Gent 2008 p.136

49 Galton. F. Natural Inheritance. Macmillian 1889 p.66

50 Galton. F Hereditary Genius Reprint Friedmann 1978 p.32

51 Galton. F Hereditary Genius Reprint Friedmann 1978 p.382

52 Galton. F Hereditary Genius Reprint Friedmann 1978 p.26

53 Galton .F. Hereditary Genius Reprint Friedmann 1978 p.36.

54 Spencer.N. Hopkinson.D.A Harris.H. Quantitative Differences and Gene
   Dosage in the Human Red Cell Acid Phosphatase Polymorphism. Nature.
   1964 No.4916 Jan. p.299.

55 Galton.F Hereditary Genius Friedman. 1869 (reprint1978.) p.33

56 Mueller.K.L, Murray,J.C, Michaelson.J.J, Christiansen.M.H, Reilly.S, Tomblin.J.B, Common Genetic Variants in *FOXP2* Are Not Associated with Individual Differences in Language Development. Plos One.2016. April 11.

57 Watson, J. B. Behaviorism (Revised edition). Chicago: University of Chicago Press. 1930 p.82

58 Andersen,R. Mediation: Crafting the Intelligence of the Child. The Moving Quill Pub. Co. 2013 p. 186

59 Galton :F. Natural Inheritances. AMS Press 1973 p.105.

60 Galton. F. Natural Inheritances AMS Press 1973 p.82.

61 Galton. F. Natural Inheritances AMS Press 1973 p103-104.

62 Winnicott.D, The Child and the Outside World: Studies in developing relationships. Tavistock Pub. 1957. p.142

63 Galton .F. Hereditary Genius Reprint Friedmann 1978 p.36.

64 Weber .E.H. The Sense of Touch. Academic Press. London 1979

65 Welford. A.T. Fundamentals of Skill. Pub. Methuen & Co. 1968 27-29

66 Fechner.G Elemente der Psychophysik 1860. In A source Book in the History of Psychology. Harvard University Press. Harvard. P.66-75

67 Laming. D. Sensory Analysis. London. Academic Press. 1986

68 Laming. D. The Measurement of Sensation. Oxford University Press, 1997.

69 Gregory.R.L. Perceptual Illusions and Brain Models. Proceedings of the Royal Society. 1968. 171 279

70 Anatasi. A. Individual Differences. Pub: Wiley. New York 1965. P.117

71 http://mnstats.morris.umn.edu/introstat/history/w98/Yule.html

72 Esquirol J.E.D Des maladies mentales considerée sous les rapports médical, hygiénique et médico-légal.Paris. J.B Baillière, et fils, 1838

73 Galton. F. Inquires into Human Faculty and its Development. 1883. RePub: AMS Press 1973. p.43-44

74 Vito. G.F. Amahs, J.R Holmes R. M. Criminology: Theory, Research and Policy Jones and Bartlett Pub. 2007 p. 90

75 Galton. F. Inquires into Human Faculty and its Development. 1883. Repub: AMS Press 1973..p.17

76 Beenstock. M. Heredity, Family, and Inequality: A Critique of Social Sciences MIT Press. 2012 p.17

77 Goddard H.H. The Kallikak Family. A Study in the Heredity of Feeble-Mindedness Macmillan 1912

78 Goddard H.H. The Kallikak Family. A Study in the Heredity of Feeble-Mindedness Macmillan 1912 p.106-107

79 Dolan DNA Learning Centre. http://iml.jou.ufl.edu/projects/spring02/holland/sterlization.htm Watson.J.D, Berry.A. DNA: The Secret of Life. Knopf. 2003 p.29-31

80 Kevies. D In the Name of Eugenics. Genetics and the uses of human heredity. Knopf. 1985.

81 Dolan DNA Learning Centre. http://iml.jou.ufl.edu/projects/spring02/holland/sterlization.htm

82 Gould.S.J. The Mismeasure of Man. Norton. 1981.p.173

83 Elks, Martin A. (August 2005). O'Brien, John. ed. "Visual indictment: a contextual analysis of the Kallikak family photographs". Mental Retardation2005 No. 43 (4): 268–280.

84 Smith, J.D. Minds made feeble: The myth and legacy of the Kallikaks. Rockville. 1985

85 McAdams N.N. MacDonald D.A. Woolverton Family, 1693 - 1850 and Beyond Woolverton and Wolverton: Descendants of Charles Woolverton, New JerseyImmigrant Penobscot Press 2001

86 Smith.D.J. Wehmeyer. M.L. Good Blood Bad Blood: Science Nature and the Myth of the Kallikaks. American Ass. on Intellectual and Developmental Disabilities Press 2012.

87 Smith, J.D. Minds made feeble: The myth and legacy of the Kallikaks. Rockville. 1985

88 Axness.M. Parenting for Peace: Raising the Next Generation Sentient Publications 2012.

89 Aschaffenburg.G. Handbuch der Psychiatrie. Leipzig 1911.

90 Varese.F Smeets. F. Drukker. M. Lieverse.R Lataster.T Viechtbauer.W Read.J van Os. J Bentall. R.P. Childhood Adversities Increase the Risk of Psychosis: A Meta-analysis of Patient-Control, Prospective and Cross-sectional Cohort Studies. Schizophrenia Bulletin Oxford University Press 2012 Mar. 29

91 Reid Lyon.G. Toward a definition of Dyslexia. Annals of Dyslexia. Vol 15 1999 p.3-27

92 Hanson.A http://www.elvis-history-blog.com/elvis-racism_2.html .2008 Jan.

93 Eysenck. H.J. in his introduction to "Hereditary Genius" Friedman. 1978 p.1

94 Galton. F. Inquires into Human Faculty and its Development. 1883. Reprint. AMS Press 1973. p.170-171.

95 Galton F. Inquires into Human Faculty and its Development. 1883. Reprint. AMS Press 1973. p.172

96 Newman.H.H, Freeman.F.H, Holzinger.K.J, A Study of Heredity Environment. Uni of Chicago Press. 1937. Ch.5

97 https://www.psychologytoday.com/blog/the-superhuman-mind/201211/identical-twins-are-not-genetically-identical

98 Trent.R.J, Molecular Medicine.Academic Press 2005 pp 77-118

99 Newman.H.H, Freeman.F.H, Holzinger.K.J, A Study of Heredity Environment. Uni of Chicago Press. 1937.

100 Annis, R. C., & Frost, B. Human visual ecology and orientation anisotropies in acuity. Science,1973 182(4113), 729–731

101 Asher.C, Why don't identical twins have same fingerprints? Science. 2023 Feb 9. https://www.science.org/content/article/why-don-t-identical-twins-have-same-fingerprints-new-study-provides-clues

102 Ouellet-Morin, I. Odgers C.L, Danese. A, Bowes. L, Shakoor. S, Papadopoulos A.S, Caspi. A, Moffitt T.E., & Arseneault.L Blunted Cortisol Responses to Stress Signal Social and Behavioral Problems Among Maltreated/Bullied 12-Year-Old Children. Biol. Psychiatry. http://sites.duke.edu/adaptlab/files/2012/09/Oullet-Morin-et-al-2011

103 Quinlan.E.B, Barker.E.D, Luo.Q, Banaschewski.T, Peer victimization and its impact on adolescent brain development and psychopathology. Molecular Psychiatry. 2018. Dec 12.

104 Newman.H.H, Freeman.F.H, Holzinger.K.J, A Study of Heredity Environment. Uni of Chicago Press. 1937. P.336

105 Newman.H.H, Freeman.F.H, Holzinger.K.J, A Study of Heredity Environment. Uni of Chicago Press. 1937. P.362

106 Jensen, A. R. How much can we boost I.Q. and scholastic achievement? Harvard Educational Review 33, 1969 1-123

498

107 Hayes.N. Foundations of Psychology. Routledge. 1994. P.196

108 Blundell.J. physiological Psychology. Methuen 1975 p.42.

109 R.L.Gregory The Oxford Companion to the Mind. Ed. By R.L. Gregory. Pub Oxford. 1987. p.442

110 Stanovich.K. What Intelligence Tests Miss: The Psychology of Rational Thought. Yale Uni. Press 2009.

111 Flynn.J.R. Massive IQ gains in 14 nations: What IQ tests really measure. Psychological Bulletin. 1987 101 p171-191

112 Andersen.R.J. All That is wrong with School The Moving Quill Co. 2023 pp186

113 Pertea M, Salzberg SL "Between a chicken and a grape: estimating the number of human genes." . *Genome Biology*. (2010). 11 (5): 206. doi:10.1186/gb-2010-11-5-206 . PMC 2898077. PMID 20441615.

114 Wang ET, Sandberg R, Luo S, Khrebtukova I, Zhang L, Mayr C, et al. Alternative isoform regulation in human tissue transcriptomes. Nature. 2008;456(7221):470– 6

115 Saey TH (17 September 2018). "A recount of human genes ups the number to at least 46,831". *Science News*.

116 Salzberg.S.L, Open Questions: How many genes do we have? BMC Biology. 16. 94 (2018)

117 Kuhn,D Black .J Keselman.A The Development of Cognitive Skills to Support Inquiry Learning. Taylor & Francis Ltd Vol18 , No4 2000 pp 495-523

118 Andersen,R. Brain Plasticity. The Moving Quill Pub. Co. 2013. pp.195

119 Winnicott.D, The Child and the Outside World: Studies in developing relationships. Tavistock Pub. 1957. p.142

120 Bulmer,M. Francis Galton: Pioneer of Heredity and Biometry Johns Hopkins Univ Press 2003 p.116-118

121 Bronowski.J. The Ascent of Man. Book Club Associates. London. 1976 p.379-386

122 Keynes.M, and Edwards.A.W.F, Peel.R, A Century of Mendelism in Human Genetics. CRC Press 2004 p.7

123 Olby.R, William Bateson's Introduction of Mendelian to England. The British Journal for the History of Science. 1987 Vol 20, 399-420

124 Richmond, M,L. Women in the Early History of Genetics. Univ. Chicago Press. 2001. p55-90

125 Bateson W. "The progress of genetic research" *Report of the Third International Conference 1906 on Genetics*, W. Wilks, ed. London, England: Royal Horticultural Society. pp. 90–97. From p. 91: "

126 Records of the Royal Society of London for the Year 1692.

127 Kisker. G.W. The Disorganized Personality. Mcgraw-Hill 1972 p.62-63

128 Pavlov. I. P. Lectures on Conditioned Reflexes. Liverright 1928. P.219.(in Contemporary Theories and Systems in Psychology by Wolman.B. 1981 Plenum Press. p.41.)

129 Forrest.D.W. Seven Pioneers of Psychology. (ed) Fuller.R. Pub. Routledge. 1995 p 14-15.

130 Marx.M.H. & Goodson.F.E Theories in Contemporary Psychology. 2nd Ed. Macmillan.1976 p.379

131 Rust.J The Psychometrics Centre. University of Cambridge. https://www.psychometrics.cam.ac.uk/about-us/our-history/first-psychometric-

132 Cherry.K, The Life and Work of Psychologist James McKeen Cattell. VeryWell Mind Pub. 2023. Oct. 18 https://www.verywellmind.com/james-mckeen-cattell-biography-1860-1944-2795513

133 Proctor, Robert W; Evans, Rand (Winter 2014). "E. B. Titchener, Women Psychologists and the Experimentalists". American Journal of Psychology. **127** (4): 501–526.

134 Wozniak.R.H. Classics in Psychology 1855-1914 Historical Essays 1999.

135 Kisker.G.W. The Disorganised Personality 2nd Ed. McGraw-Hill Kogokusha Ltd. 1972. p.68

136 Kisker.G.W. The Disorganised Personality 2nd Ed. McGraw-Hill Kogokusha 1972 p.68

137 Earle. E.M. Makers of Modern Strategy: Military Thought from Machiavelli to Hitler. Princeton Uni. Press. 1973 p.206–207

138 Fuller.J.F.C. The Decisive Battles of the Western World Granada 1970 Vol.2 p.296-297

139 Fancher.R.E, The Intelligence Men: Makers of the IQ Controversy. Norton 1985.

500

[140] Fancher.R.E, The Intelligence Men: Makers of the IQ Controversy. Norton 1985.

[141] Binét.A. Le Raisonnement dans les Perceptions. Revue Philosophique 1883 15 406 p412

[142] Binét.A. Les Idees modernes sur les infants. Flammarion. Paris 1913

[143] Binét.A. & Simon.T A Method of Measuring the Development of the Intelligence of Young Children   Lincoln Courier 1911.

[144] Carrol.J.B. The Measurement of Intelligence. In R.J.Sternberg (ED) Handbook of Human Intelligence Cambridge Univ. Press. 1982 p.29-120

[145] Binét.A 1908 p.257 in Gould's The Mismeasure of Man p.154

[146] Guilford.J.P. Way Beyond the IQ. Creative Education Foundation.1977

[147] Goddard. H.H. Human Efficiency and Levels of Intelligence. Princeton Univ. Press. 1920. P.12-20

[148] Zenderland. L. Measuring Minds: Henry Herbert Goddard and the Origins of American 1998 p.2 Intelligence Testing. Cambridge University Press. 1998. P.2

[149] Stern.W, The Psychologocial Methods of Testing Intelligence. Warwick and York 1914 p.42

[150] Siegler, R. S. The other Alfred Binét. Developmental Psychology, 1992 No. 28, 179-190.

[151] Stern.W, The Psychologocial Methods of Testing Intelligence. Warwick and York 1914

[152] Pearson.R. The Mankind Quarterly 1995 Vol 35. p.229-265

[153] Zenderland. L. Measuring Minds: Henry Herbert Goddard and the Origins of American 1998 p.268

[154] Zenderland. L. Measuring Minds: Henry Herbert Goddard and the Origins of American 1998 p.273

[155] Fancher. R. E The Intelligence men: Makers of the IQ Controversy. Norton. 1985 p.133

[156] Hergenhahn.B.R. An Introduction to the History of Psychology Wadsworth 2008 p.318

[157] Jensen.A . Straight Talk about Mental Tests. The Free Press. 1981. p.12

[158] Spearman, C. General Intelligence, objectively determined and measured American Journal of Psychology, 15, 1904, 201-293

[159] Terman . L.M. The Measurement of Intelligence. 1916.p. 91-92

[160] Fancher, Raymond E. (1985) "The Intelligence Men: Makers of the IQ Controversy", New York (NY): W. W. Norton.

[161] Gould. S. J. A Nation of Morons. New Scientist May 1982. p.349-52

[162] Goddard, H. H Human Efficiency and Levels of Intelligence. Princeton Univ. Press. 1920 p 127–128.

[163] Terman.L.M. The Measurement of Intelligence. Houghton Mifflin. Boston. 1916 p 6-7

[164] Terman.L.M. & Merrill.M. Measuring Intelligence: A Guide to the Administration of the New Revised Stanford-Binét Tests of Intelligence. Houghton 1937

[165] Lippmann.W. Series of six articles examining intelligence tests. New Republic 1922. Oct.25/Nov p297-298.

[166] Marx.M.H. & Goodson.F.E. Theories in Contemporary Psychology. Macmillian 1976 p.547

[167] Watson.J.B, & Rayner.R. Conditioned emotional reactions. Journal of Experimental Psychology 1920, 3 p1-14.

[168] Watson, J. B. (1913). Psychology as the Behaviorist Views it.Psychological Review, 20, 158-177.

[169] Pavlov. I.P. The Reply of a Physiologist to a Psychologist. Psychological Review. 1932. 39 p.91-127

[170] Wolman.B.B. Contemporary Theories and Systems in Psychology. Plenum. 1981.p.52

[171] Wolman B.B. Contemporary theories and Systems in Psychology. Plenum. 1981. P.67

[172] Santrock, J A Topical Approach To Life-Span Development. Chapter 6 Cognitive Development Approaches NY McGraw-Hill. 2004. 200-225

[173] Vygotsky.L.S. Mind in Society: The development of higher psychological processess. Cambridge, MA:Harvard Uni. Press. 1978 p.90

[174] Vygotsky L.S. Mind in Society: The development of higher psychological processess. Cambridge, MA Harvard Uni Press. 1978 p.86

[175] Vygotsky.L.S. Thought and Language. Revised Edition.. ED. Kozulin. A. MIT Press. 1986.

[176] Terman.L.M. Intelligence Tests and School Reorganisation. Yonkers-on Hudson. World Books 1922 p.34-51.

[177] Tyack.D. The One Best System. Harvard Univ. Press. 1974.

[178] Wilde.O. The Importance of Being Earnest. http://www.gutenberg.org/files/844/844-h/844-h.htm

[179] Fancher.R.E. The Intelligence Men Norton.1985 p.177

[180] R.L.Gregory The Oxford Companion to the Mind. Ed. By R.L. Gregory. Pub Oxford. 1987. p.442

[181] Spearman, C. General Intelligence, objectively determined and measured American Journal of Psychology, 15, 1904, 201-293

[182] Jensen, A.R. The g Factor: The Science of Mental Ability Praeger, 1998.

[183] Williams R.H Zimmerman. D.W. Zumbo.B.D Ross. D. Charles Spearman: British Behavioral Scientist Human Nature Review. 2003 Vol. 3, p.114-118

[184] Sternberg, R.J.(1990). The geographic metaphor. In R.J. Sternberg, Metaphors of mind:Conceptions of the nature of Intelligence (pp. 85–111). New York: Cambridge.

[185] Gould.S.J. The Mismeasure of Man. Norton. 1981. p.144

[186] Fancher.R.E. The Intelligence Men. Norton 1985. p.170

[187] Simon.B. Education and Social Order 1940-90 Lawrence & Wishart 1999 p.157

[188] Burt.C. Ability and Income. British Journal of Education Psychology. 194 No.13. p.83-98

[189] Hearnshaw.L.S. Cyril Burt: Psychologist. Hodder & Stoughton. 1979

[190] Burt.C. Brit.J. Psychol. 1966. 57, 137

[191] Lerner, Richard M. (1 August*Concepts and Theories of Human Development*. Psychology Press. 2001). p. 276.

[192] Clarke.A.M. & Clarke.A.D.B. Sir Cyril Burt. Bulletin of the British Psychologica Society 1977 Vol.30 p.83-84

[193] Kamin.L.J. The Science and Politics of IQ. Lawrence Erlbaum 1974

194 Huxley,J. UNESCO Its Purpose and Its Philosophy. The United Nations Educational, Scientific and Cultural Organisation. 1946

195 Sweet,M. Francis Galton Kantsaywhere www.ucl.ac.uk/news/news-articles/1111/111117-Galton-novel-Kantsaywhere-published-online

196 Huxley, A. Brave New World. Harper Perennial Modern Classics. Reprint 2006. Ch. 1 and 2

197 Huxley J.S. Man in the Modern World. Chatto & Windus. 1947.

198 http://www.modernlibrary.com/top-100/100-best-novels/ Random House 1999

199 Walker.P, From Windscale to Sellafield: a history of controversy. The Guardian. 2007 18th Apr.

200 Lemann.N, The Big Test: The Secret History of the American Meritocracy. Farrar, Straus and Giroux. 1999. p.406

201 Lemann.N. The Big Test: The Secret History of the American Meritocracy. Farrar, Straus & Giroux 1999.

202 Lemann.N. The Great Sorting. The Atlantic Monthly. Sept 1995. Vol276. No.3 p84-100.

203 Wechsler. D, The measurement of adult intelligence (3rd ed.) Williams & Wilkins Co 1944 p.19-35.

204 Fancher. R.E. The Intelligence Men. Norton 1985. p152.

205 Hayes.N. Foundations of Psychology. Routledge. 1994. p208

206 Hayes.N. Foundations of Psychology. Routledge. 1994. P.196

207 Kuhn,D Black .J Keselman.A The Development of Cognitive Skills to Support Inquiry Learning. Taylor & Francis Ltd Vol18 , No4 2000 pp 495-523

208 Flynn.J.R. Massive IQ gains in 14 nations: What IQ tests really measure. Psychological Bulletin. 1987 101 p171-191

209 Stanovich.K. What Intelligence Tests Miss: The Psychology of Rational Thought. Yale Uni. Press 2009.

210 Plomin.R Nature & Nurture. An Introduction to Behavior Genetics. Brooks & Cole. 1990

211 Murray.C. & Herrnstein.R. The Bell Curve: Intelligence & Class Structure in American Life Freepress 1994.

504

212 Kozulin.A & Feuerstein.R. Bell Curve:Getting the Facts Straight.
Educational Leadership. 1995.Vol.92 No.7 p71.

213 Goldberger.A.S Manski. C.F Review Article: The Bell Curve by Herrnstein
and Murray. Journal of Economic Literature Vol. XXXIII (June 1995)
p.762-776

214 Tyler.L.E the Psychology of Human Differences. Appletone.Century-Crofts.
1965.

215 Goldberger.A.S & Manski.C.F Web page: Review Article:The Bell Curve
1995

216 Kincheloe.J.L. Steinberg.S.R. & Gresson 3rd. Measrued Lies.A. D. Macmillan
1996.

217 Krenz.C. Web page: Anatomy of an Analysis. 1999.

218 Newsday. 1994. No. 9

219 https://www.splcenter.org/fighting-hate/extremist-files/individual/richard-lynn

220 http://www.isteve.com/Thatcher-Speech-Text.htm

221 http://www.independent.co.uk/news/education/education-news/nature-
trumps-nurture-in-exam-success

222 http://s3.documentcloud.org/documents/804396/some-thoughts-on-
education-and-political.pdf

223 http://www.bbc.co.uk/programmes/b041xbxc

224 http://www.stokesentinel.co.uk/national-sats-proved-controversial-introduced-
19-years-ago/story-12485991-detail/story.html

225 Beattie.G.W. Troubles in Northern Ireland. British Psychological Society.
B.B.P.S 32 (1979) 252

226 Fischer.C. Inequality By Design: Cracking the Bell Curve Myth. Princeton
Univ. Press. N.J. 1996

227 Tzuriel.D. Paper presented to the Conference on Individual Differences and
Educational Excellence. Touro College. New York 1994 March.

228 Fischer.C. Inequality By Design: Cracking the Bell Curve Myth. Princeton
Univ. Press. N.J. 1996

229 Campbell.F.A & Ramey.C.T Cognitive and School Outcomes for High-Risk
African- American Students at Middle Adolescence. American Educational
Research Journal. Winter 1995.Vol.32. No4. P743-772.

230 Fodor.J.A. The Modularity of Mind. Cambridge. MA. MIT Press. 1983.

231 Terman.L, The Measurement of Intelligence: An Explanation of
and a Complete Guide for the use of the Standford Revision and Extenstion
of the Binét-Simon Intelligence Scale. G.G.Harrap& Co. Ltd. 1919 p.21

232 Stand and Deliver. http://www.imdb.com/title/tt0094027/

233 Ritchie.S.J Tucker-Drob.E.M How Much Does Education Improve
Intelligence? A Meta-Analysis Psychol Sci. 2018 Aug; 29(8): 1358–1369.

234 Fromkin.V Krashen..S. Curtiss.S. Rigler.D & Rigler.M The development of
language in Genie. A case of languagge acquisition beyond the "critical
period" Brain and Language 1974. 1. 81.107

235 Wolman.B.B. Contemporary Theories and Systems in Psychology.
Plenum Press 1980 p.36.

236 Zenderland.L. Measuring minds: Henry Herbert Goddard and the origins of
American Intelligence testing. Cambridge. MA. Cambridge Uni. Press.
1998.p.324-326

237 Terman.L.M. & Merrill.M. Measuring Intelligence: A Guide to the
Administration of the New Revised Stanford-Binét Tests of
Intelligence. Houghton 1937

238 Pertea M, Salzberg SL. "Between a chicken and a grape: estimating the number of
human genes" . *Genome Biology*.(2010) **11** (5): 206

239 Salzberg.S.L, Open questions: How many genes do we have? *BMC Biology*. Vol. 16,
August 20, 2018

240 Hunter P "What genes remember". *Prospect Magazine*. (1 May 2008).
Archived from the original on 1 May 2008. Retrieved 26 July 2012.

241 Bainomugisa.C, Mehto.D. How Stress affects gene expression through epigenetic
modifications. in Epigenetic of Stress and Stress Disorders. Vol 3. 2022, pp 99-118

242 Henig.R.M, The Monk in the Garden. How Gregor Mendel and his Pea Plants
Solved the Mystery of Inheritance. New York. Houghton Mifflin Co. 2000

243 Moore.R, The "Rediscovery" of Mendel's Work. General College, Uni of
Minnesota.
http://courses.pbsci.ucsc.edu/mcdb/bio105/Spring15/Lecture2/
Rediscovery%20of%20Mendel.pdf

244 www.biologie.uni-hamburg.de/b-online/e08_mend/mendel.htm

245 Tschermak,E. Ueber künstliche kreuzung bei Pisum sativum. Berichte der
Deutschen Botanischen 1900 Gesellschaft 18 p.232-249.

246 Johannsen.W, Arvelighed I historisk og eksperimentel belysning.
Gyldendalske 1923 p.48

247 Johannsen. W, Elemente der exakten erblichkeitslehre: by G.Fischer in Jena
1909. p.124

248 Johannsen,W.L, Om arvelighed i samfund og i rene linier. Oversigt over
det Kongelige Danske Videnskabernes Selskabs Forhandlinger 1903 3.
p247-270

249 Roll-Hansen.J, Sources of Wilhelm Johannsen J Hist Biol 2009 42(3) 457-93

250 Galton.F, A theory of Heredity. p.344
http://galton.org/essays/1870-1879/galton-1875-jaigi-theory-heredity.pdf

251 Searle,G,R. Eugenics and Politics in Britain 190-1914 Noordhoff Pub. 1976
Into.

252 Sapp.J. The Genotype Conception of Heredity. J.Epidermiol. 2014. April 1,

253 Marks,J. Darwin's Ventriloquists. Anthropology Now. 2009. Dec.
Vol.1 No 3 p8

254 Johannsen,W.L, Om arvelighed i samfund og i rene linier. Oversigt over
det Kongelige Danske Videnskabernes Selskabs Forhandlinger 1903 3.

255 Bashford.A, Levine.P, The Oxford Handbook of the History of Eugenics, Oxford,
Oxford University Press, 2010 p.324

256 Jurmain.R, Kilgore.L, Trevathan.W & Ciochon.RL Introduction to Physical
Anthropology Wadsworth 2011 p.27-39

257 Fisher,R,A. The Correlation between relatives on the supposition of
Mendelian Inheritance
1918 Trans R.Soc. Edin 52 p399-433

258 Griffith.A.J.F., Miller.J.H., Suzuki.D.T., Lewontin.R.C & Gelbart.W.M. An
Introduction to Genetic Analysis 6th ed Freeman. 1976 p.826-832

259 Mather.K, Polygenic inheritance and natural selection. Biological Reviews
18:32-64 rec'd 26 June 1942

260 Bryson.B, A Short History of Nearly Everything. Black Swan 2004 p.486

261 Holdrege,C. The Gene: A Needed Revolution. The Nature Institute 2005.
p.14-17 http://www.natureinstitute.org/pub/ic/ic14/gene.htm

262 Gelbart.W., Databases in Genomic Research *Science* 1998 Vol.282
p.659-661

263 Wilcock,D The Synchronicity Key Barnes and Noble 2013

264 Wilcock.D, The Synchronicity Key: The Hidden Intelligence Guiding the Universe and You. Postscript Books. 2013. pp7

265 https://www.nationalgeographic.com/science/article/big-headed-tiger-snakes-support-long-neglected-theory-of-genetic-assimilation

266 Waddington.C.H,m Canalization of Development and the Inheritance of Acquired Characteristics. Nature. 150, 1942 pp. 563-565

267 Nishikawa.K, Kinjo.A.R Mechanism of evolution by genetic assimilation Biophys Rev. 2018 Apr; 10(2): 667–676. Published online 2018 Feb 21. doi: 10.1007/s12551-018-0403-x

268 Waddington, C. H. "Canalization of development and the inheritance of acquired characters". Nature. 1942 150 (3811): 563–565. Bibcode:1942Natur.150..563W. doi:10.1038/150563a0. S2CID 4127926.

269 Fanti, L.; Piacenti, L. "Canalization by Selection of de Novo Induced Mutations". Genetics. 2017 206 (4): 1995–2006.

270 Lida.S, Morita.Y, Choi.J, Park.K, Hoshino.A, Genetics and epigenetics in flower pigmentation associated with transposable elements in morning glories. National Library of Medicine. 2004. 38:141-59.

271 Anway MD, Skinner MK Epigenetic transgenerational actions of endocrine disruptors. Endocrinology 2006 147 Suppl. 6) S43–S49

272 Skinner.M.K. A New Kind of Inheritance National Library of Medicine. Sci Am. 2014 Aug; 311(2): 44–51. 2014 Aug. 311(2) 44-51

273 Skinner.M.K, Manikkam.M, Tracey.R, Guerrero-Bosagna.C, Haque.M, Nilsson.E.E, Ancestral dichlorodiphenyltrichloroethane (DDT) exposure promotes epigenetic transgenerational inheritance of obesity. National Library of Medicine. Oct. 2013

274

275 https://developingchild.harvard.edu/resources/what-is-epigenetics-and-how-does-it-relate-to-child-development/

276 RG Hunter, et al., Acute stress and hippocampal histone H3 lysine 9 trimethylation, a retrotransposon silencing response. Proc Natl Acad Sci USA 109,

277 Waddington, C. H. (1942). The epigenotype. Endeavour, 1, 18–20.

278 Griffiths, P. E., & Stotz, K. Genetics and Philosophy: An Introduction. Cambridge University Press.2013

279 Griffiths, P. E. Genetic information: A metaphor in search of a theory. Philosophy of Science, 2001 68(3), 394–412.

[280] Cantor-Graae.E. The Contribution of Social Factors to the Development of Schizophrenia. The Canadian Journal of Psychiatry. Vol. 52 No.5 May 2007

[281] Phillipson. O.T in Oxford Companion to The Mind. Ed Gregory. Oxford Univ Press 1987 p.200

[282] Van der Kolk.B.A. Traumatic Stress: The Effects of Overwhelming Experience on Mind, Body & Society. Guildford Press. 1996.

[283] Cichilli & Cohen Developmental Psychopathology. John Wiley & Sons 1995

[284] Wilson.R.S, Boyle.P.A, Levine.S,R. Yu.L, Anagnos.S.E, Buchman.A.S, Schneider.J.A, Bennett.D.A, Emotional neglect in childhood and cerebral infarction in older age. Neurology. 2012. Oct.9. Vol. 79

[285] Radley,J,J. Rocher,A,B. Miller,M. Janssen, W,G,M. Liston,C. Hof,P,R. McEwen,R,S. and Morrison,J,H. -Repeated Stress Induces Dendritic Spine Loss in the Rat Medial Prefrontal Cortex. Oxford Journals. Medicine & Health & Science & Mathematics: Cerebral Cortex: Vol 16. Issue 3. pp 313-320.

[286] Andersen.R.J. Brain Plasticity:How the Brain Learns through the Mind to Create Intelligence. The Moving Quill Pub. Co. 2024. pp211-218

[287] Andersen,R. Brain Plasticity. The Moving Quill Pub. Co. 2013.pp.195

[288] Griffith.A.J.F., Miller.J.H., Suzuki.D.T., Lewontin.R.C & Gelbart.W.M. An Introduction to Genetic Analysis 6th ed Freeman. 1976 p.826-832

[289] Tannenbaum.A.J. Gifted Children. Psychological and Educational Perspectives. Macmillan. 1983.

[290] Tannenbaum,A,J. Gifted Children. Psychological and Educational Perspectives. Macmillian 1983.

[291] Meaney, M. Maternal care, gene expression, and the transmission of individual differences in stress reactivity across generations. Annual Review of Neuroscience, 2001 242, 1161-1192.

[292] Meaney, M., Aitken, D.H., Bodnoff, S. R., Iny, L. J., and Sapolsky, R.M. (1985). The effects of postnatal handing on the development of the glucocorticoid receptor systems and stress recovery in the rat. Progress in Neuro-psychopharmacology and biological psychiatry, 9, 731-34

[293] http://anthro.palomar.edu/homo2/mod_homo_4.htm

[294] Feuerstein.R. Rand,Y.Hoffman M.B, Miller.R Instrumental Enrichment. Scott, Foresman & Co. 1980. p.130-131

295 Czepita.D, Lodygowska.E, Czepita,M. Are Children with Myopia more Intelligent? Ann Acad Med Stetin. 2008 54 (1) 13-6.

296 Gallop,S. Myopia Reduction a View From the Inside. JBO Vo. 5/1994 p115-120.

297 http://www.ncbi.nlm.nih.gov/pmc/articles/PMC1042189/

298 Sorenson, O. http://www.rebuildyourvision.com/testimonials.php

299 Gallop,S. Myopia Reduction a View From the Inside. JBO Vo. 5/1994

300 Fuchs. I, Goldschmidt. E, Teasdale.T.W, Degree of Myopia in Relation to Intelligence and Educational Level. The Lancet. 1988. Vol. 332. Issue.8624. p.1351-11354.

301 https://en.wikipedia.org/wiki/Charles_Atlas

302 Thopmson.W.J. Changes in the innervation of mammalian skeletal muscle fibers during postnatal development. Rends in Neuroscience. 1986 No.9 p.25-28

303 Leakey.R Origins Reconsidered: in search of what makes us human. Little, Brown & Co. 1992. p246

304 Howell.E, Enzyme Nutrition. The Food Enzyme Concept. Avery pub. 1985. p.76

305 Blundell.J. Physiological Psychology. Methuen. 1975 p109-112.

306 Albantakis,L. Hintze, A, Koch, C. Adami, C, Tononi,G. Evolution of Integrated Causal Structures in Animats Exposed to Environments of Increasing Complexity. Computational Biology. DOI: 10.1371/journal.pchi. 1003966. 2014. Dec 18.

307 Anderson.M. Intelligence and Development: A Cognitive Theory. Blackwell 1992. p.41

308 Anderson.M. Intelligence and Development: A Cognitive Theory. Blackwell 1992. p.41

309 Feuerstein.R Rand.Y Hoffman.M, Miler.R Instrumental Enrichment: An Intervention Program for Cognitive Modifiability. Pub:Scott Foresman & Co.1985

310 Fisher.J, The History of Landholding in Ireland. Transactions of the Royal Historical Society. 1877 p.249-250.

311 Schull,W.J & Neel.J.V The Effects of Inbreeding on Japanese Children Harper and Row, New York 1965

510

312 Lynn. R,. IQ in Japan and the United States shows a growing disparity. *Nature* 1982 **297** (5863) p.222–223.

313 Blair. C, Gamson. D, Thorne. S, Baker. D Rising mean IQ: Cognitive demand of mathematics education for young children, population exposure to formal schooling, and the neurobiology of the prefrontal cortex: Intelligence 2005 33 (1) p.93–106.

314 Axness,M. Lifelong Lessons from the Womb. ICPA. http://icpa4kids.org/fr/ Wellness-Articles/lifelong-lessons-from-the-womb/Toutes-les-pages.html

315 Thorndike.E.L. Animal Intelligence: Experimental Studies. Macmillan. N.Y. 1911.

316 http://www.thalidomide.ca/recognition-of-thalidomide-defects

317 http://www.medicaldaily.com/tylenol-use-during-pregnancy- may-give-your-child-adhd-there-safer-way-reduce-fevers-270060

318 Emhart.C.B. Morrow-Tiucak. M. Wolf. A.W. Super. D. Drotar.D. Low level led exposure in the renatal and early preschool periods: Intelligence prior to school entry. Neurotoxicology and Teratology. Vol 11. Issue 2 1989. Mar April p 161-170.

319 Rothernberg.S.J. Schnaas.L. Cansino-Ortiz. S. Perroni-Hernandez.E De La Torre. P.Neri-Mendez .C. Hidalgo- Loperena. H Svendsgaard. D. Neurotoxicolgy and Teratology Vol 11. Issue 2. 1989 Mar-Aprl. p 85-93

320 Davis JM, Svendsgaard DJ. Lead and child development. Nature 1987; 329:297-300.

321 Maas.R.P. Patch. S.C. Morgan. D.M. Pandolfo. T.J. Reducing lead exposure from drinking water: recent history and current status. U.S. Public Health Report. 2005. May-Jun. 120(3) p 316-321.

322 H.H. Spitz. The Raising of Intelligence. A Selected History of Attempts to Raise retarded intelligence. Routledge 2009 p.7

323 Axness.M. Pregnancy. Lifelong Lessons from the Womb. 2010. Mar.1. iss. 25 http://icpa4kids.org/fr/Wellness-Articles/lifelong-lessons-from-the- womb/Toutes-les-pages.html

324 Janov,A. The Feeling Child. Abacus. London, 1982, In Sherwood.K, Chakra Therapy.Llewellyn Pub.2005 p.58

325 Sherwood.K, Chakra Therapy.Llewellyn Pub.2005 p.58

326 Sherwood.K, Charkra Therapy, Llewellyn 2005. p.60

327 http://www.allaboutvision.com/nutrition/

328 http://www.jamieoliver.com/news-and-features/features/eat-well-children-nutrition/

329 Carper.J. The Food Pharmacy. Simon & Schuster 1989 p170 & 195

330 Benton.D. & Buts.J. Vitamin and mineral supplementation and intelligence. Lancet. 1990. No.335 p.1158-1160.

331 Benton.D   Nutrition and IQ. The Psychologist. 1992.vol5 No.9 Sept. p.405

332 Smithers.L.G. Golley.R.K. Minty. M.N.Brazionis.L. Northstone.K.Emmett.P. Lynch.J.W. Dietary patterns at 6, 15 and 24 months of age are associated with IQ at 8 years of age. Developmental Epidemiology. 2012 27 p525-535

333 http://news.bbc.co.uk/1/hi/health/8058183.stm

334 www.iflscience.com/brain/privilege-and-deprivation-visible-brains

335 Grossarth-Maticek.R. H.J.Eysenck. Boyle.G.J. Heeb.J. Costa.S.D. The interaction of psychosocial and physical risk factors in the causation of mammary cancer, and its prevention through psychological methods of treatment. Bond University   ePublications@bond. Humanities and Social Sciences papers. 12-1-1999.

336 Siegel.B Love, Medicinie and Miracles. William Morrow. 1986

337 http://www.silvalifesystem.com

338 Baltrusch.H.J. Stangel. W. Titze. I.   Stress, cancer and immunity: New developments in biopsychosocial and psychoneuroimmunologic research. Science Blog. 2007 March 18th. http://scienceblog.com/12807/psychosomatic-disease-type-c-behavior-pattern/

339   O'Boyle JR. E, Aguinis. H, The Best and the Rest: Revisiting the Norm of Normality of Individual Performance.2012 Personnel Psychology Volume 65, Issue 1, pages 79–119.

340 http://www.forbes.com/sites/joshbersin/2014/02/19/the-myth-of-the-bell-curve-look-for-the-hyper-performers/

341 https://www.goodreads.com/quotes/709288-be-curious-read-widely-try-new-things-what-people-call

342 Bodanis.D, Einstein's Greatest Mistake. Pub.Little Brown Book Co. 2017

343   Howell. E, Enzyme Nutrition. Penguin. 1985 p.76

344 Lynn. R,. IQ in Japan and the United States shows a growing disparity. Nature 1982 **297** (5863) p.222–223.

345 Flynn.J.R, IQ gains over time. In R.J. Sternberg (ed.), The encyclopedia of human intelligence, New York, Macmillan 1994 p. 617-623

346 Fox.M.C, Mitchum.A.L, A knowledge-based theory of rising scores on "culture-free" tests. J.Exp. Psychol. Gen. 2013 Aug. 142 (3) p.979-1000

347 Engels. F, "The Peasant War in Germany" contained in the *Collected Works of Karl Marx and Frederick Engels: Volume 10* (International Publishers: New York, 1978) p. 443.

348 Darwin.C. The Descent of Man. 1871. P.71

349 Lippmann.W. Series of six articles examining intelligence tests. New Republic 1922. Oct.25/Nov p297-298.

350 Andersen.R.J, Brain Plasticity: How the Brain Learns through the mind to create Intelligence. The Moving Quill. Pub. Co. 2013. pp 22

351 Bayley, Nancy "Comparisons of Mental and Motor Test Scores for Ages 1-15 Months by Sex, Birth Order, Race, Geographical Location, and Education of Parents". Child Development. 1965. **36** (2): 379–41

352 Bayley. N Mental Growth during the first 3 years. Genetic Psychology Monographs. 1933. 14 p1-92.

353 Stanovich.K. What Intelligence Tests Miss: The Psychology of Rational Thought. Yale Uni. Press 2009.

354 Flynn.J.R. Massive IQ gains in 14 nations: What IQ tests really measure. Psychological Bulletin. 1987 101 p171-191

355 Kuhn,D Black .J Keselman.A The Development of Cognitive Skills to Support Inquiry Learning. Taylor & Francis Ltd Vol18 , No4 2000 pp 495-523

356 R.L.Gregory The Oxford Companion to the Mind. Ed. By R.L. Gregory. Pub Oxford. 1987. p.442

357 Wyatt.T, Brown. G, Dabney.M, Wiley.P, Weddington.G, The Assessment of African American Children. California Speech-Langauge and Hearing Association Task Force 2003, Jan.7

358 Sapir, E. (1929): 'The Status of Linguistics as a Science'. In E. Sapir: *Culture, Language and Personality* (ed. D. G Mandelbaum). Berkeley, CA: University of California Press. 1958 p69

359 Dresser.S, Our Language, Our World https://aeon.co/essays/does-language-mirror-the-mind-an-intellectual-history from McElvenny.J, Language and Meaning in the Age of Modernism 2018.

360 Bates. E, Elman. J, Johnson. M, Karmiloff-Smith. A, Parisi.D, Plunkett. K, Rethinking innateness: A connectionist perspective on development. Cambridge, MA: MIT Press/Bradford Books. (1996).

361 Gordon. P. Numerical Cognition Without Words: Evidence from the Amazon. Science 15 October 2004. Vol. 306 no. 5695 pp. 496-499

362 Von Bredow.R. Living without Numbers or Time. Spiegel Online International.2006.

363 Davies.R.J, Ikeno.O The Japanese Mind Tuttle Published 2002

364 Feuerstein.R. Instrumental Enrichment. Scott, Foresman & Co. 1980 p.42

365 Bronowski. J. The Ascent of Man. Book Club Associates 1976. p.322

366 Graetz.H. History of the Jews. Jewish Publication Society of America 1891-98. Quoted: Gilman's Smart Jews.

367 Feuerstein.R Klein.P.S. & Tannenbaum.A.J. Dynamic Assessment: Learning and Transfer Abilities of Ethiopian Immigrants to Israel. Freund Pub. 1991. 179-208

368 Gilman.S.L. Smart Jews: The Construction of the Image of Jewish Superior Intelligence. University of Nebraska Press. 1996 p.140

369 Bryson,B. Made in America. Black Swan Pub. 1994 p.137

370 Magni.L, Marchetti.G, Alharbi.A, Learnable Theory and Analysis. LUISS University Press.2023 pp.16

371 Gould. S. J. A Nation of Morons. New Scientist May 1982. p.349-52

372 Ouellet-Morin, I. Odgers C.L, Danese. A, Bowes. L, Shakoor. S, Papadopoulos A.S, Caspi. A, Moffitt T.E., & Arseneault.L Blunted Cortisol Responses to Stress Signal Social and Behavioral Problems Among Maltreated/Bullied 12-Year-Old Children. Biol. Psychiatry. http://sites.duke.edu/adaptlab/files/2012/09/Oullet-Morin-et-al-2011

373 Chugani H.T. Behen.M.E Muzak.O Juhasz.C. Nagy.F Chugani.D.C Local Brain Functional Activity following Early Deprivation: A Study of Postinstitutionalizd Romanian Orphans. NeuroImage. 14 2001 p.1290-1301

374 Greene.M,F, 30 years ago, Romania deprived thousands of babies of human contact. Atlantic. July. 2020 https://www.theatlantic.com/magazine/archive/2020/07/can-an-unloved-child-learn-to-love/612253/

375 Andersen.R.J, Mediation: Crafting the Ability of the Child for School. The Moving Quill Pub. Co. 2013. pp.187-202

514

376 Fiske, J. *The meaning of infancy.* Boston: Houghton Mifflln. 1909 (originally pub. 1883). p.1

377 https://www.psychologytoday.com/blog/the-superhuman-mind/201211/identical-twins-are-not-genetically-identical

378 Hunter P "What genes remember". *Prospect Magazine.* (1 May 2008). Archived from the original on 1 May 2008. Retrieved 26 July 2012.

379 Bainomugisa.C, Mehto.D. How Stress affects gene expression through epigenetic modifications. in Epigenetic of Stress and Stress Disorders. Vol 3. 2022, pp 99-118

380 Andersen.R.J, *For Parent For Teacher, Mediation: Crafting the ability of the child for school* The Moving Quill Pub. 2013. pp.187

381 Nelson N, W. Biasing eligibility off discrepancy criteria. A bad idea whose time has passed. 2000 July.   Special Interest Division 1 Language Learning and Education 7, 8-12

382 Green. D. R, Racial and ethnic bias in tests construction . I n W>A. Thomas (ED) Larry P, revisited IQ testing of African Americans pp 32-51 San Francisco CA California Publishing Co.

383 Tyler.L.E the Psychology of Human Differences. Appletone.Century-Crofts. 1965.

384 Brazil W F Improving SAT scores: Pros, Cons and methods. In W.A> Thomas ED) Larry P. revisited: IQ testing of African Americans pp 60-72 San Francisco CA California Publish Co.

385 https://www.cognidna.com/smartest-countries-2023-iq/#:~:text=Japan and Taiwan are deemed,highest average IQ as 106.5.

386 Lu.K, Is Shadow Education the Secret of East Asian Success? East Asian Societies Blog. Dec 9,2020. in https://web.sas.upenn.edu/east-asian-societies-blog/ 2020/12/09/is-shadow-education-the-secret-to-east-asian-success/

387 Affect, J, Legal Issues in testing African American. in Larry P. Revisited: IQ testing of African Americans 2000 pp 23-27 San Francisco CA California. Publishing Co.

388 "Race and Intelligence ." Gale Encyclopedia of Psychology. . Retrieved January 08, 2024 from Encyclopedia.com: https://www.encyclopedia.com/medicine/ encyclopedias-almanacs-transcripts-and-maps/race-and-intelligence

389 Nisbett, R. E., Aronson, J., Blair, C., Dickens, W., Flynn, J., Halpern, D. F., & Turkheimer, E. Intelligence: new findings and theoretical developments. American psychologist, 2012. 67(2), 130.

515

390 Holloway.M (January 1999). "Flynn's Effect". *Scientific American*. 280 (1): 37–38. Bibcode:1999SciAm.280a..37H. doi:10.1038/scientificamerican0199-37. ISSN 0036-8733.

391 Wyatt.T, Brown. G, Dabney.M, Wiley.P, Weddington.G, The Assessment of African American Children. California Speech-Langauge and Hearing Association Task Force 2003, Jan.7

392 Plomin,R., and von Stumn, S. The new genetics of intelligence. Nat. Rev. Genet.19,. 2018. 148=159. doi.10.1038/nrg.2017.104

393 Andersen,R. Mediation: Crafting the Intelligence of the Child. The Moving Quill Pub. Co. 2013 p. 186

394 Fillmore.C.J. paper delivered to American Culture Centre. U.C. Berkeley. Feb 97.

395 Wolfram.W, Adger.C.T & Christian.D. Dialects in Schools and Communities. Mahwah. N.J. Erlbaum 1999.

396 Wiley.T.G "The Case of African American Language" In T.G. Wiley. Literacy and Language Diversity in the United States. Centre for applied Linguistics and Deta Systems 1996. 125-132.

397 Tyler.L.E the Psychology of Human Differences. Appletone.Century-Crofts. 1965.

398 Ritchie.S.J Tucker-Drob.E.M How Much Does Education Improve Intelligence? Meta-Analysis Psychol Sci. 2018 Aug; 29(8): 1358–1369.

399 Shea, C, (29 October 2012). "IQ Wars Continue With Battles Over New Puzzles". *The Chronicle of Higher Education*. Retrieved 21 September 2021.

400 Blair. C, Gamson. D, Thorne. S, Baker. D Rising mean IQ: Cognitive demand of mathematics education for young children, population exposure to formal schooling, and the neurobiology of the prefrontal cortex: Intelligence 2005 33 (1) p.93–106.

401 Eby.D, Issac Newton: obsessed and solitary. in High Ability. https://highability.org/39/isaac-newton-obsessed-and-solitary/

402 Issac Newton: Who He Was, Why Apples are Falling. National Geographic. 19th Oct. 2023 https://education.nationalgeographic.org/resource/isaac-newton-who-he-was-why-apples-are-falling/

403 www.feministvoices.com/nancy-bayley/

404 Smith, Tracy L. Child Development. New York, NY: Elly Dickason, MACMILLAN 2002 pp. 48–50

405 Bayley, Nancy "Comparisons of Mental and Motor Test Scores for Ages 1-15 Months by Sex, Birth Order, Race, Geographical Location, and Education of Parents". Child Development. 1965. **36** (2): 379–41

406 Bayley, Nancy "Comparisons of Mental and Motor Test Scores for Ages 1-15 Months by Sex, Birth Order, Race, Geographical Location, and Education of Parents". Child Development. 1965. **36** (2): 379–411

407 Bayley, Nancy "Comparisons of Mental and Motor Test Scores for Ages 1-15 Months by Sex, Birth Order, Race, Geographical Location, and Education of Parents". Child Development. 1965. **36** (2): 379–411

408 Bayley. N Mental Growth during the first 3 years. Genetic Psychology Monographs. 1933. 14 p1-92.

409 Kelly.M.F. & Surbeck.E. The History of Pre-school Assessment in the Psycho- Educational Assessment of Pre School Children. (ed) Paget.K.D. & Bracken.B.A. Grune & Stratton.N.Y. 1983.

410 Andersen,R. Mediation: Crafting the Intelligence of the Child. The Moving Quill Pub. Co. 2013 p. 186

411 Briggs. A. The Nineteenth Century. Guild Pub. London 1985

412 Benezet.L.P, The teaching of Arithmetic: The Story of an Experiment. Originally published in Journal of the National Education Association in three parts. 1935/1936 Vol. 24, #8, pp 241-244; Vol. 24, #9, p 301-303; & Vol. 25, #1, pp 7-8

413 Masgutova.S, https://masgutovamethod.com/_uploads/_media_uploads/ _source/mm_scholars_vygotsky.pdf

414 Andersen.R.J, Are we Educating our Children for a Working World that will not want them? The Moving Quill Pub. Co. 2013. pp.61

415 Hart,B. and Risely, T,R. The Early Catastrophe: The 30 Million Word Gap by Age 3. American Educator. 2003 Spring 4-9

416 Hart.B, Risley.T.R. Meaningful differences in the every day experience of young American children. Paul H Brookes Pub. 1995. P.268

417 Andersen.R.J, The Illusion of School. The Moving Quill Pub. Co. 2013 pp 47

418 Andersen.R.J. Brain Plasticity: How the Brain Learns through the Mind to create Intelligence. The Moving Quill Pub, Co. 2013. pp 76-78

419 de Paiva.A, Joden.R, Short and long term effects of architecture on the brain. in Frontiers of Architectural Research Vol.8 Issue4. pp. 564-571

420 Strachey.J, Freud.A, Strachey.A & Tyson,.A The Complete Psychological Works of Sigmund Freud. Hogarth Press. 1961 Vol.19 p183-190.

421 www.wired.co.uk/news/archive/2015-06/30/google-chatbot-philosophy-morals

[422] Plomin, R., & von Stumm, S. *The new genetics of intelligence*. Nature Reviews Genetics, 2018 19(3), 148-159. doi:10.1038/. nrg.2017.104

[423] Plomin, R., & Deary, I. J. Genetics and intelligence differences: Five special findings. *Molecular Psychiatry, 2015 20*(1), 98–108

[424] Sauce, B., & Matzel, L. D. The paradox of intelligence: Heritability and malleability coexist in hidden gene-environment interplay. *Psychological Bulletin, 2018 144*(1), 26-47.

www.ingramcontent.com/pod-product-compliance
Lightning Source LLC
Chambersburg PA
CBHW031114020426
42333CB00012B/90